Unstoppable

Norwegian Pioneers
Educate Their Daughters

GRACIA GRINDAL

Lutheran University Press
Minneapolis, Minnesota

Unstoppable
Norwegian Pioneers Educate Their Daughters
by Gracia Grindal

Photos on pages 156, 160, 176, bottom of 181, 190, 214, and 240 are from the Norwegian-American Historical Association, and are used with their permission.

The drawings on pages 61, 64, 77, 80, 83, 84, 86, 89, 91, 93, 105, 107, 122, 128, 129, 133, 135, 142, 143, 144, 146, 151, 153, 158, 159, 162, 174, 185, 194, 198, 212, 213, 236 and the cover are by Linka Preus, included in her diary. They give a rich and detailed picture of life in a Norwegian-Lutheran parsonage and especially the training of girls during the time of the Norwegian Synod. For more drawings, see *Linka's Diary: A Norwegian Immigrant Story in Word and Sketches*, Marvin G. Slind and Gracia Grindal, editors, published by Lutheran University Press.

The many letters quoted are from the Luther College Archives, Decorah, Iowa.

Library of Congress Cataloging-in-Publication-Data applied for.

ISBN: 978-1-942304-16-6

Lutheran University Press, PO Box 390759, Minneapolis, MN 55439
www.lutheranupress.org
Printed in the United States of America

Dedicated to the memory of Ruth Mostrom,
longtime Latin professor and registrar at Luther College,
and to Mary Hull Mohr, longtime mentor and colleague
in the Luther College English department.

Table of Contents

Standing (left to right): Thora Larsen, Marie Reque, Margrethe Brandt, Emma Larsen, Rosina Preus. Seated: Lulla Hjort, Caroline Koren, Henriette Koren, Mathilda Stub.

Preface

This book is the culmination of forty years of work. Corinne Nelson of the Development Office of Luther College asked me to prepare a slide-tape show on the college's Founding Congregations for its 125th anniversary. That meant digging through the Luther College Archives. There I spent some weeks ferreting out information on the congregations; this necessitated reading many primary materials carefully tended by Martha Henzler, librarian in charge of special collections, and Oyvind Hovde, the head librarian at that time. I give thanks to God for their work!

Most amazing were the many letters that the Preus family had saved, in large part the letters of the pastors' wives to Linka Preus. My Norwegian had become a bit rusty since I had first learned it some years before, but I knew enough to see what had to be done. This was a treasure that needed study: hundreds of handwritten letters in the old Dano-Norwegian of the pioneers.

Aided by a Dano-Norwegian dictionary, I began. It was a labor of love much like what Kierkegaard described on reading the Scripture in his *On Self-Examination*—like reading a love letter in a language one does not quite understand, but treasuring it none the less, struggling every day to learn the language a bit better. Every summer after that I would walk through the bright sunlight and muggy heat of Decorah and—through the generous grace of the librarians, especially Leigh Jordahl—descend to the dark and cool archives for the day. Over time I came to be able to read the letters fairly well and transcribe them on the typewriter and then the computer.

One day—a day that changed my life—I reached into one of the boxes and took out a large book of pencil sketches. When I opened it and examined it, I found that it was filled with the sketches of Linka Preus. She had recorded many scenes of the founding of the college and the Norwegian Synod. There was one on the 1865 dedication of the Main

Building, another on slavery, an old bugaboo of the Synod tradition. Each sketch, often a depiction of an event of which there is no pictorial record, revealed more as I learned more of both the language and the context. This was a treasure that needed interpretation and publication to make it available to an American audience.

Every summer since I have returned to the sketches and learned more and more about the daily lives and concerns of these families, especially the women. Elisabeth Koren's frequent letters gave the context for understanding Linka's sketches and setting them in the history of the college and church. This changed my view of that history.

Barrels of ink have been spent on interpretations of the theological debates of the pastors—debates that exhibit verve and sophistication on the prairies, rather like the brilliant divines of New England facing off with the devil in the wilds of Massachusetts. However, the lives of the women and thus the families did not always make it into those accounts. Ironically, because of the diaries of Linka Preus and Elisabeth Koren the women's accounts are still most alive. They continue to be read, and they enrich the history of Luther College and the Norwegian Synod much more than the ecclesiastical histories.

Although I have spent my life on the distaff side, the interpretive task has meant having to learn what their husbands were living through as well. This was especially challenging because the women were not to talk politics or gossip. Elisabeth Koren held to this rule rather strictly, though at times hints flash out, discreetly, but still rather keenly. It came through most clearly when I read her rather arch, but discreet, sentence about Erik Ellefsen, the man known as the "King of Big Canoe," who violently opposed the Synod pastors on slavery. Mrs. Koren wrote that she had heard from him, the "King up there, whom perhaps you have had the honor to know." ("*Kongen deroppe som kanske du har den ære å kjenne.*")[1] It took a couple reads to get the full impact of the withering sarcasm of the line. Without knowing who he was in the slavery debate, it would have gone unremarked.

This work has not been mine alone. Harris Kaasa, professor of religion at Luther, read my first attempts at telling the stories and said that if he could survive his ultimately fatal illness, he wanted to work with me on the material as well. Øyvind Gulliksen, professor emeritus from Telemark High School, has been a true companion in the arcane world we both inhabit gladly. Professor John Christianson has also been a great help, giving me hints along the way, especially on the fascinating world of the Neuberg sisters, who have entertained and moved me for years. The Preus family has also been generous in supplying me with pictures and conversation on the family, especially David Preus, who graciously read many of my takes on the story that is the backbone of this book. My colleagues at Luther College endured my constant telling of these stories during the summer, when I emerged from the archives with yet another new detail. I am most grateful to them.

There are many others to thank: the staff in the archives at Luther College who have continued to be gracious and generous in their help to me; Kari Bostrom of the Luther Seminary Archives; the St. Olaf College archivist Jeff Sauve, associate archivist for the Shaw-Olson Center; Kristin Anderson, curator of the Augsburg College Archives; the staff of the Goodhue County Historical Society who generously provided me access to its materials on the Red Wing Lutheran Ladies' Seminary; the National Archives in Norway, Sweden, and Denmark. I am especially grateful for the generosity of the Christiansfeld, Denmark, archives where I was able to find—with the crucial help of the Danish professor, Jørgen Kjærgaard, president of the International Hymn Society, in an undisturbed old room—the school records of Diderikke Brandt neé Ottesen, and Christiane Hjort neé Ottesen. Such an experience is one of the true pleasures of historical research. Thanks also to Pastor Todd Walsh of Albert Lea, whose passion for the story of Red Wing Lutheran Ladies' Seminary made my work easier, as did our conversations about my chapter on the school. He helped me understand several issues I had not quite fathomed. Wilfred Bunge, a valued colleague from my time at Luther College and a historian of the college, read the manuscript and offered invaluable comments and editorial suggestions. All of the above have been helpful and vital to this work, but the mistakes are all mine. The recent digitalization of newspapers has made it possible to find some things quickly that before would have taken more years than a human being is given. For all this I am most grateful. Finally, many thanks to Karen Walhof and Lutheran University Press for her help in editing and producing the book. She has been a true blessing to me in my vocation!

In some ways, the women of the Norwegian Synod have been my Bloomsbury group. (The thousands of books on that literary neighborhood seem only to whet the appetite for more.) The more I have come to know about these women the more I, and others, have wanted to know. It is my hope that others will see the richness here and work to elucidate it further. It is a bit sad now to write the last words of this book and in some significant ways bid adieu to "my ladies," as I have come to call them. At the same time, there will be more to say.

As a break between chapters or themes, I have included a eulogy for each of the five main women in this story, Karen Larsen, Christiane Hjort, Linka Preus, Diderikke Brandt, and Elisabeth Koren. As I was writing I realized that this had to be a book on more than the educational ideas and practices of the pastors and their wives as they sought to educate their children. It also had to put that story in its context. These five women all played their parts in the home, so their impact on the public lives of their society is not always known. All of their stories are in Norwegian, and not so many people today can access these materials. I took it as a kind of vocation to get as much of these stories into English as I could so those studying these women and their children will have as much information as possible. It was pure pleasure to do.

All of the translations are mine, unless otherwise noted. All of the letters, which I have identified by date, are in the Luther College Archives, neatly numbered and classified. Once again the ability to search newspapers and nineteenth century books online has made it possible to discover many things that even a couple of lifetimes sifting through old documents would never have afforded. In every case I have worked to make sure that my sources were clearly noted. Once again, thanks to Luther College where my career began and where this project first saw the light of day. And thanks to Luther Seminary where generous sabbaticals and support provided a chance to follow these ladies throughout my career!

As I bid these pioneer women farewell, I also want to thank my friends, especially Marilyn Preus, who gave me good advice and pictorial treasures; several colleagues at Luther College—Ruth Caldwell, Carol Gilbertson, Clara Paulson and Diane Gabrielsen Scholl—with whom I taught for many years; most especially to another pastor's daughter and my mentor, Mary Hull Mohr, a Swedish Augustana pastor's daughter taught by Augustana College (Rock Island, Illinois) Professor Henriette Naeseth, Mrs. Koren's granddaughter. To her, and to the memory of another pastor's daughter, Ruth Mostrom, I dedicate this book. Ruth's leadership at Luther College was significant for all of the women who joined the faculty over the years when she was registrar and later elegant hostess-in-chief. Our background in the parsonage had been invaluable to us as we entered into a professional career not unlike, but different from, our mothers. We shared a wonderful legacy that helped to enrich the life of the college. However, nothing is as rich as the original work of Linka Preus and Elisabeth Koren, whose work it has been my privilege to study and grow to love over these many years. They have given us all much that we would never have had without their work. *Soli Deo Gloria*!

These five women were first generation immigrants from Norway,
pastors' wives in the Norwegian Synod who were instrumental
in training the next generation of women for parsonage life.
They provided a strong foundation for women's education.
Although their husbands were the church leaders
and these women had no voice in church councils,
their insistence on education and training for the
church's daughters as they understood it kept the topic
of girls' education always in front of the church,
finally culminating in opportunities for college education
for both women and men.

They are (clockwise from top left): Christiane Ottesen Hjort,
Karen Neuberg Larsen, Elisabeth Hysing Koren,
Linka Keyser Preus, and Diderikke Ottesen Brandt.

Introduction

In 1968 when I began teaching in the English Department at Luther College in Decorah, Iowa, nestled in the scenic hills and valleys of northeastern Iowa, one of many memorable people I met was Sigrid Reishus Harrisville (1897-1999), dorm mother at the Diderikke Brandt Hall for women. She and her sister, Martha Reishus Langemo (1888-1980), had lived there after the untimely death of Sigrid's husband, Roy Harrisville, Sr. (1894-1951), after a short time as pastor at Bethlehem Lutheran Church in south Minneapolis. Mrs. Harrisville, a well-turned-out lady, was heir to the traditions of the Norwegian Synod, traditions that I came to know and love while teaching at Luther.

Diderikke Brandt, portait by Herbjørn Gausta

Mrs. Harrisville and her sister, Norwegian Synod pastor's daughters, had graduated from the Synod's Red Wing Lutheran Ladies' Seminary—Martha had taught there—and become the elegant pastors' wives the founders had intended to produce at the school. Now Sigrid was the dorm mother at the women's residence hall named for one of Luther College's most beloved founders, Diderikke Ottesen Brandt (1827-1885).

Brandt's portrait by Herbjørn Gausta, which hung in the Brandt dormitory vestibule and then in the Brandt parsonage, the oldest building on the Luther College campus, shows a woman of moment. Diderikke represented the beginning of the tradition in America; Sigrid, the ending. Their stories frame the history of the Norwegian Synod's efforts to educate its daughters to fulfill their calling as ladies, ready to take their place as pastors' wives in the Synod or other roles open to them, even as the role of women in the culture was changing.[2] While this story is unique to Luther College, a similar story could be told about many religious educational institutions during this same time. This work is set in the context of both the

Norwegian and American histories of women's struggle to achieve equality as they are pertinent and shed light on the Luther College story.

Luther began as a school to prepare men for the ministry. It used the time-honored pattern of taking boys out of their homes while still young teenagers and teaching them Latin, especially, Greek, and Hebrew to prepare them for the ministry or other professional work. This had been the pattern for boys to become men almost from the beginning of Western education. Its unstated, but implicitly understood, aim was to create men by "toughening" them through almost brutal lessons and even corporal punishment. Latin lessons became a kind of puberty rite for the boys.

Sigrid Reishus
Harrisville

In the official class of Norwegians studied here, the girls also had a process for becoming women. As they approached puberty, pastors' daughters would be sent to their aunts to learn housekeeping, something every woman needed to know, no matter what her class. While with her aunt, she could receive confirmation instruction from her uncle and be confirmed, the long-standing puberty rite of Lutheran adolescents.

The girls' time with their aunts would also give them a kind of finishing school education in modern languages, history, literature, history, geography, math, and other necessary disciplines that would make them fitting wives for educated husbands. Through the late eighteenth and early nineteenth century, educators began establishing finishing schools for girls. They were frequently called Ladies' Seminaries. These would go further in the disciplines the girls had learned from their mothers and their aunts.

While the boys and girls were together in primary school, usually in the kitchen at their mothers' knee, they were separated at puberty when the boys left for school. In Norway these were usually called Latin schools and often were connected with the cathedrals of the various cities. Most well known were the cathedral schools in Oslo, Bergen, Kristiansand, and Trondheim. These were a model that Luther College used for its practices and curriculum as it was being established in the middle of the nineteenth century. Co-education was not considered at those schools. These were schools that made gentlemen ready for leadership in society. Similarly, schools for girls were to create women—ladies—ready to marry these men and raise children worthy to take their places in society.

When these leaders came from Norway in the middle of the nineteenth century, they brought these patterns with them. Educational plans for each gender were based on deeply held beliefs about what a man was and what a woman was. Teenage boys were to be educated at a school away from home—Luther College. Girls were to be educated in the parlors of an aunt or close friends of her parents. Parents cared as much about the education of their daughters as their sons and made provisions for both. At the time they immigrated, how to educate their children had been central to the cultural debates of their day. Those arguments lived on in this country while the Norwegian Synod pastors were deciding how to build such institutions for their children. The girls' education would proceed at home for some time, but a school for boys that took them away from home and gave them a place to be educated needed to built as soon as possible. For these reasons the question of co-education at Luther College did not present itself with much urgency for some generations.

During the Civil War and after, Norwegian-Americans began to build schools. Seminaries came first, and the schools they built were like prep schools for seminary. Although some, such as St. Olaf College and not a few academies, were coed from their founding, this model did not interest the founders of Luther College. They had in mind the education of their daughters to be ladies. This education could not be coeducational, because one institution could not take the young through their appropriate puberty rites and make them into gentlemen and ladies. These understandings were implicit and hardly even understood, but such is the way tradition works.[3] That is one reason the story of the women's movement is important, one context for the ways the Synod educated its sons and daughters. The push for coeducation had behind it a slightly different understanding of what men and women were and, therefore, how they should be educated. Now we believe that boys and girls should be allowed to follow their interests, whether they cross the old gender lines or not. Then, although education was important for both sexes, what and how they were taught in school tended to be consistent with the theories of what a man should know and what a woman should know.

After they had established both a seminary and a college, the founders of Luther College realized something had to be done for the further education of their daughters. In the 1890s, a group of Synod pastors and laymen built the elegant Red Wing Ladies' Seminary in Red Wing, Minnesota, on a high promontory overlooking the Mississippi River. There, for over a quarter century, it taught girls how to be cultivated ladies and wives. After the school burned down in 1920, the newly united church, the Norwegian Lutheran Church in America, decided not to rebuild it, although the Luther College community, still strongly connected with the tradition of the Norwegian Synod, continued to debate the question of how to educate its daughters. This question was as urgent as it had ever been. But times were different. Men's schools through the country were gradually going coed. Luther's rival school, St. Olaf, and other schools of the Norwegian-American Lutherans, such as Concordia College in Moorhead or what became Augustana College in Sioux Falls, had enrolled women from the beginning. Augsburg College and Seminary, first established as a seminary, began enrolling women in 1921, when it became clear that its college was not only educating men to be future pastors but also for other work.

Luther remained the only college among Norwegians-Americans that did not admit women. Oscar Olson (1872-1955), the president during the Roaring Twenties and the beginning of the Great Depression, argued unsuccessfully for the admission of women students—mostly for reasons of increasing enrollment. It was only after the economic downturn of the Great Depression, when the college needed more students in order to survive, that coeducation became a necessity. The argument to make Luther College admit women reveals some of these deeply traditional understandings of men and women. To our eyes these arguments look sexist, but they need to be understood. There are still educational theorists, both liberal and conservative, who argue it is best to educate boys and girls separately. That being said, the next and more important question is what the young are taught. Even with coeducation, until recently there were lines of study that seemed to fall either to men or to women. Those barriers have fallen over the past fifty years.

Mrs. Brandt and Mrs. Harrisville, both pastors' daughters and wives, are emblems of a society's attempt to adapt a venerable Old World set of traditions and expectations for the role of women in the New World. Now they lived not only in a new land and culture, but also in a new era when the role of women was changing. Their epoch frames the end of the traditional story, almost a thousand years old, with glimpses of what was coming, when women could be ordained as Lutheran pastors. The Luther College story illuminates the history of Lutheran parsonage culture in this country and the education a girl needed to become a lady ready to take up the vocation of pastor's wife. To tell it well and to show how deeply the tradition ran in the blood of these people, it is necessary to review the history of the Christian parsonage in Western tradition. The Scandinavian and Norwegian Lutheran traditions are part of this larger story.

CHAPTER ONE

The Beginnings

"My husband shall be a minister!"

—Linka Preus

When the young Linka Preus (1829-1880) declared to her future father-in-law, "My husband shall be a minister," she knew exactly what that
meant.[4] Her father had been a pastor, as had her grandfather, Bishop Johan Michael Keyser (1749-1810), along with many other male relatives.
She had grown up watching what the women of the parsonage did, and
she knew the vocation in her bones. It was the family business the way
most vocations at the time were. Sons and daughters tended to follow
their parents' footsteps into the same vocations.

The clergy had been part of the leadership class in Scandinavia almost
since St. Olaf and the Christianization of the land. Soon parsonages were
built throughout the kingdoms of Denmark and Norway, and clergy lived
on land or acreages set aside for them. These came to be called a *prestegaard*, or pastor's farm, where the parson lived and farmed, in addition to
receiving tithes and sustenance from the locals, required by law. Despite
the celibacy requirements of the medieval church, the constant reprimands
of bishops urging pastors to give up their wives or concubines show that
the pastor's wife was often a part of the local congregation's life.

After the Reformation and the establishment of the parsonage family
by Katie and Martin Luther, the Lutheran parsonage followed the model
of that famous family. Katie industriously cleaned up the Black Monastery where Luther and several other monks had lived for years, and she
helped to establish a routine for the family as it grew. Out of this developed a set of understandings and routines natural to life that became the
template for Protestant parsonages around the world.

When Linka and her generation became pastors' wives, the tradition
of the Lutheran parsonage had persisted for over 300 years. This tradition continued until the middle of the twentieth century when women

entered more and more into their own professions. Eventually they could become pastors themselves—by 1970 among Lutherans in America.

When the newly ordained and just married Hermann Amberg Preus (1825 -1894) and his young wife, Carolina Dorothea Margrethe Keyser Preus, "Linka" (1829-1880), boarded the *Columbus* sailing ship in Kragerø, Norway, for their journey to America, they faced a future in an unknown world. Although both were young, they were well equipped to take up their roles as pastor and pastor's wife in the burgeoning New World. Their work in the congregations in and around DeForest, Wisconsin, and what became the Norwegian Synod would challenge much of what they had learned about their vocations and stations from their families in Norway, but they were able successfully to adapt their traditions to the new land.

Hermann and Linka Preus, 1851.

As a young theological graduate, Hermann had not been able to find a suitable call in Norway—at the time calls were at a premium—and grew intrigued with the possibility of the new work in America. After some complications with the call from the Spring Prairie congregation in Wisconsin and difficulties convincing a Norwegian bishop to ordain him, on April 30, 1851, Hermann was ordained by Bishop Jens Lauritz Arup (1793-1874). The young couple married shortly afterwards on May 5, 1851, in Halden. Two weeks later, on May 22, the Preuses set sail for America, beginning their lives together as pastor and pastor's wife. Well-schooled in their vocations, their actual practice started when they settled into life on board ship. Linka recorded their first attempts in her diary with her typical self-awareness of the comedy—and seriousness— of her calling. During a worship service at sea, one of Hermann's first, the waves were so violent she feared that she might be pitched forward on her face. This made her smile. She covered her smile, however, lest people think she was laughing at the service, inappropriate for a pastor's wife, she thought.[5]

She found herself wondering how critical she should be of Hermann's preaching and work, one of the expected roles of the pastor's wife in every parsonage. Just before they landed in New York she was asked to carry a baby, born on ship, to the baptismal font. It was one of the first things she did as pastor's wife, and it pleased her to do so. "I had the great honor of carrying the child. The minister's wife has already begun her mission."[6] That the parents expected her to carry the baby—"the little screamer"— and were pleased with her willingness to do so shows the importance of the custom. It was a significant event for Linka during a time of firsts.[7]

While he had been waiting for the call from Spring Prairie, Hermann had continued his theological and biblical studies, focusing especially on a book of pastoral care by Erik Pontoppidan, *Collegium Pastorale*, which he found to be especially effective in his own spiritual life and self-examination.[8] There is, however, nothing in that book on the role of the pastor's wife. This would change. In the nineteenth century many such books of advice began to speak of the role and vocation of the pastor's wife. Linka read these books about the parsonage which now included sections on the role of the pastor's wife. She would take exception to some ideas published there. She knew better, since she had been well tutored in the vocation and the various domestic skills and fine arts one needed to know to be a successful member of her class by her mother, grandmother and aunts.

Not only did the young couple know their chosen vocations well, everyone in their society did. The local priests, or pastors, had been, from the time of St. Olav, servant of both the state and the church. The Preuses knew what was expected of them and were well-equipped both temperamentally and spiritually for their work in a land far away from their home. The great difference was that there was no state church in America— something completely new for them and their flock.

Together they had to work out how they were to function without those established structures. They quickly took stock and, after some missteps, they adapted quickly and helped build a flourishing church in America, known as the Norwegian Synod (Synoden for den Norsk Evangelisk Lutherske Kirke i Amerika). The Synod founded Luther College in Decorah, Iowa; Luther Seminary; and Red Wing Lutheran Ladies' Seminary. Hermann eventually became president of the young church, and Linka became a church president's wife.

Fortunately for us, Linka kept a diary of her early life in Norway and her first years in America, along with a number of sketches of their lives both in Norway and America. They are some of the first pictorial records of the intimate and public lives of these pioneers. This was one of the skills she had mastered in her education, a skill she passed on to her daughters and the daughters of other pastors in the small group of clergy working together in Wisconsin, Iowa, and Minnesota.

Hermann and Linka's family became some of the most important leaders of the church and its schools. Her sons Christian Keyser and Johan Wilhelm were pastors, and Christian became president of Luther College. Her two daughters, Rosina and Anga, were also pastors' wives. Her grandsons served with distinction as pastors and leaders: Ove Jacob Hjort Preus was president of both Augustana (Sioux Falls, South Dakota) and Luther Colleges, and Jacob Aall Ottesen Preus (1921-1925) served two terms as governor of Minnesota. Two of her great-grandsons, Jacob Aall Ottesen Preus II (1920-1994) and David W. Preus (b. 1922) served as presidents of the Lutheran Church–Missouri Synod and the American Lutheran Church respectively in the 1970s and 1980s.

Christian Keyser Preus while president of Luther College

It was natural for Hermann and Linka to raise their children for service in the church; it was a family tradition that continued in America for well over a century. That the couple did so well adapting the tradition to a different culture is a tribute to their sturdy characters and strong faith. While this book focuses on the way they educated their daughters to be pastors' wives in the New Land, it is important to understand what the tradition was and how it developed.

The Parsonage in Christian Tradition

When Protestants, particularly Lutherans, think of the origins of the parsonage, they turn their thoughts almost immediately to the home of Martin Luther (1483-1546) and Katherina von Bora (1499-1552), frequently referred to as the founders of the Protestant parsonage. In the popular imagination, the clergy of the medieval church, like the clergy on the pilgrimage in *The Canterbury Tales* by Geoffrey Chaucer, were celibates who dwelt in some kind of a monastic cloister. Many assume that the celibate situation of Catholic clergy today has always been the norm for the Roman Catholic Church. The history is a bit more complex. The Christian parsonage with its clergy family has a longer history than many think.

Christianization of the North

As the church settled into the culture of the West, parish priests gradually moved north to lead local parishes. Naturally, they needed to be

trained and provided for, so they could adequately fulfill their priestly duties. In the late sixth century, Pope Gregory the Great (540-604), in his book *Liber regulæ pastoralis*, dealt with such issues, advising on the 1) establishment of the office, 2) the pastor's own life, 3) the education of the pastor, and 4) the priest's daily practice of meditation on his own weaknesses. These rules spread widely and became the norm for clergy throughout the Western church. Archbishop Hinkmar of Rheims (845-882) advised that each bishop should take

Gregory the Great

Gregory's book in his hand and swear to use it as a guide throughout his life and teaching. King Alfred (849-899), the remarkably learned king of England, translated it into Anglo-Saxon for use among his people. From there it was brought north to Scandinavia.

In the letters of Gregory we see how provisions to support the local priest naturally evolved. In a letter he wrote to an Italian duke, Anio, who wanted to build a chapel beside his castle and needed to call a priest, Gregory noted that the duke would need to provide a good place for the priest to live: a farm, a house, a team of oxen, two cows, fifteen sheep, and whatever else was necessary for a well-run farm, besides four marks of silver. This became the model for the parsonage throughout Europe and America, a model Hermann and Linka used as they and their congregation built the Spring Prairie parsonage. While they probably had no idea of Gregory's advice to Anio, the needs were the same: They had to have a home and a way to feed and clothe themselves in order to serve on the Wisconsin frontier. The Scandinavian parsonage was to be a self-supporting institution that would provide a living for clergy and their households—with additional support from the community through tithes and gifts.

Gregory also recommended where the churches and parsonages should be built. He wanted parsonages very near the church. In a letter to the Abbott Melittus (d. 624) of Canterbury he suggested that the missionaries build Christian churches in the places of the old gods and sanctify them for Christian worship. Shrewdly, he suggested that new Christian altars, filled with relics, be placed over the old altars where pagans had sacrificed their animals. He advised erecting a building where the people of the parish could enjoy what we would now call a church supper. They were to gather together at great banquets for the entire parish. Careful to avoid changing everything at once, Gregory recommended a moderate, slow alteration of the old rituals.

At the first Christian synod in England, at Hertford, in September 673, under the leadership of Bishop of Canterbury Theodore of Tarsus (602-690), England was divided into bishoprics (dioceses). These were then divided into parishes on the assumption that everyone in the parish was a Christian. Twice a year the priests were to assemble together with their bishop at the cathedral for continuing education and to enjoy fellowship with each other. This established the importance for priests of the cathedral as the mother church to which they looked for leadership and guidance. This was a practice the young Preuses as church leaders contemplated early in their work, planning such gatherings for the yearly conferences with their colleagues who were serving in the far-flung reaches of the Upper Midwest. Linka expressed concern several times that they might provide a place where they could "discuss their business there. Then they could visit each other for their own pleasure when they feel like it or there is an occasion—that would be a lot nicer and a lot more fun."[9]

While the duties of the parish pastor may seem self-evident now, the Medieval church made sure that they were clearly spelled out as it moved north. The Synod of Aachen (836) determined, for example, that the parish priest was to preach, baptize, hear confessions, comfort the sick and dying, and preside at funerals—in other words, care for the spiritual needs of all of his people in the parish from birth through death.[10] This synod also made provisions for the pastor's support. Each parish was to care for the priest by providing a parsonage that included a farm where he could raise and tend animals for food. In the kingdoms of Norway and Denmark the old pagan practice of paying the priest an honorarium for each occasional service continued, something Christian priests came to expect when they performed baptisms, burials, and weddings. This practice, called *Tidkjøb* (time purchase) caused Adam of Bremen (ca. 1050-1085), in his history of the Archbishops of Bremen and Hamburg, to remark on the probity of the Norwegian clergy, except their greed. He marveled that

> baptism and confirmation, the dedication of altars, and the
> ordination to holy orders are all dearly paid for among them

and by the Danes. This, I think, proceeds from the avarice of the priests. As the barbarians still either do not know about tithes or refuse to pay them, they are fleeced for other offices that ought to be rendered for nothing. For even the visitation of the sick and the burial of the dead—everything there has a price. Their excellent moral character, as I have learned, is therefore corrupted only by priestly avarice.[11]

Such honoraria, Adam suggests, appeared to be necessary for the priest to survive economically. These practices still obtain today among pastors who expect to receive honoraria for baptisms, weddings, and funerals.

The parsonage naturally needed buildings for certain necessities in the life of any farm at the time, as well as special rooms for the functioning of the priest's office. Because pastors lived like most of their parishioners as farmers, much of Linka's practical training had to do with managing the farm, raising animals, and knowing how to raise them for food and clothing. This meant, of course, knowing about planting and harvesting crops to feed both the animals and the family. This knowledge became vital for their survival as they built their home in Wisconsin, but it was knowledge

St. Olaf, who Christianized Norway

nearly everyone needed before the Industrial Revolution, whether urban or rural. Olaf Olafson in his history of the Norwegian parsonage notes that there was some difference between the city parsonage and the country parsonage. The city parsonage had fewer acres to farm than those in the country, with smaller provisions for the animals. However, like the rest of the parishioners in the city, they needed gardens and fields enough to feed the family and the necessary stock animals—probably some assortment of horses, oxen, sheep, goats, and chickens. Nearly everyone had to raise their own food, especially in the rural areas. Even when Linka lived with her grandmother in Majorstua, now a highly urban shopping district in Oslo, they had a garden and animals to tend.

The first farm parsonages were made up of a great room, something like the Vikings' long buildings, with an open hearth in which a fire would always be burning for both heat and cooking. Here the household would sleep, prepare the food, cook, eat, make clothes, and entertain. The wealthier the parish, the larger these buildings would be. There were usually rows of beds along the walls, somewhat sheltered from the smoke of the central fire. In the center, or to one side, would be a long table for the meals. Besides this main building, which in poor parishes probably served

A stabbur

as the only parsonage building, there was usually a storehouse (*bu* or *stabbur*),where food could be stored. Richer parsonages might have had a loft above the main room or in the *stabbur*, where people could sleep free of the ever-present smoke from the fires needed for cooking, especially in the warmer months. Until central heating was available, most homes were really one great room with a fireplace, beds, and tables.

There might be another building for guests, given the long tradition of hospitality expected in monasteries and convents. Parsonages were places one could stay while on a journey. The pastor's wife was

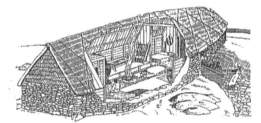

Long houses of the Viking time

expected to provide meals and beds for visitors who might happen by, usually without notice—one reason the parsonage was often the most spacious home in the village. On some farms the barn, necessary for any farm, was below the family room, so that the animals could provide some heat for the family and not be too far removed during blizzards and extreme cold.

Almost without exception, the parsonage served as the center of the local culture, since the priest was one of the most learned and important men in the community. Not only did he represent Christ and the church, he represented the king and the state. We can see from the design of these parsonages that the pastor's home and farm were not the dwellings of a single man living a monastic life undisturbed by worldly things. The old parsonages of Denmark and Norway, like most farms, housed many people—generally a large extended family, maybe several families, with enough servants to function well.

After the decrees of the first four Lateren Councils (1123, 1139, 1179, and 1215) and the proscription of married priests, northern bishops spent a great deal of time trying to persuade parsons to put away their wives. As these decrees began to take effect, the clergy no longer dared to marry, but often continued to live with their wives in secret marriages or, if they were far enough away from oversight of the bishop, openly. In some cases, these marriages were accepted by the congregations, but the toll it took on faithful priests and their wives began to tell. It was a nagging problem that bishops constantly warned against and had to deal with. It was solved only by the Reformation, well supported in Scandinavia by the illegitimate sons of priests. Embittered by the proscription of their parents' marriage and their exclusion from what they regarded as their rightful inheritance, they enthusiastically supported Luther's reformation.

As the Danish and Norwegian churches grew in their influence, they developed more laws and recommendations for the support of the clergy by the parish. In addition to a farm with meadows, fields, and woods, the priest was to receive tithes from the parish. People were to give the church a tenth of some of their produce: grain, meat, honey, fish, etc. The priest then divided the tithes to send part to the bishop, who would send, in turn, a portion to Rome. This meant that the priest and his family shared intimately both the good and hard years with the parish—and also made the priest's apparent privilege an object of resentment from people hard pressed to survive on the little they had. Every Christmas, Easter, and Pentecost, the priest received an offering, as well as the "soul gifts" (*Sjælegaver*) he received after attending the death and burial of a parishioner. A few today may remember this tradition, but it was quite strong in the country churches where I grew up in the 1940s. Every major church high holy day—Christmas, Easter, Pentecost—concluded with the congregation rising and proceeding to the front of the church around the altar, leaving money for both pastor and cantor/janitor.[12]

The sustaining of the priest was a continuing concern for the bishop and the parish. The tithe, often reluctantly given, was the life-blood of the parsonage. As noted, the people were required to give offerings at the various festivals, along with their tithes.[13] Linka herself noted in her diary about receiving the annual fish tithe on February 15, 1845, while living in her uncle's parsonage in Askevold. After Easter and the end of winter the priest followed an old custom of visitation, going around the parish with holy water to bless the food in the pantries, kitchens, and cellars of the parish; he then also received some food as a thank offering. These customs, however, could also lead to corruption, so the bishops watched them closely to see that the priests carried them out appropriately.

In sum: The place of the parish priest, his calling, and his home filled a natural role in the life of the community in Scandinavia from the beginning of the establishment of the church there. The priest expected to be supported by the parish with a home and a farm on which to raise some of his food and clothing. Like most of his people, he had to farm in order to live. He had to know about seedtime and harvest, animal husbandry, the preserving and storing of food, especially fish and meat, making cheese, churning cream to make butter, skinning animals for clothes, raising sheep and preparing their fleece for use in clothes. He and his wife, concubine, or housekeeper,

A typical Norwegian pastor's wife in the seventeenth century

were expected to be skilled in the knowledge and preparation of herbs for medical purposes—an old tradition from the monasteries and convents. He expected to be paid extra for performing certain acts of ministry in the parish—baptisms, weddings, and funerals, among others. At festivals of the church, people brought part of their tithes for an offering. His home was to be open to travelers in need of a place to stay, similar in a small way to the open hospitality of the religious houses of the medieval church.[14] He attended to the welfare of the poor in the neighborhood and taught the children the basics of the faith.

Katie and Martin Luther, when they left the convent and monastery, adapted these practices to their own married life, as they took on the natural routines of life in the parsonage. What they did became models for almost 500 years of Lutheran parsonage life. Following the example of Katie, pastors' wives made many of the tasks and duties of parsonage life their own calling or profession. In the same way they educated their children to take up their own vocations, teaching them to read and write, along with some arithmetic.

CHAPTER TWO

Katie and Martin Luther

Establishing The Lutheran Parsonage

The parsonage was a "school for young girls who needed to learn housekeeping, as a place where confirmands could come and work in return for catechism instruction, and a place for good counsel in both physical and soul care, and many other earthly problems that the parishioners trusted her [the pastor's wife] to give them."[15]

Although Martin Luther was not the first priest to marry, it was his marriage to Katherine von Bora that created the model for succeeding Lutheran parsonages. Establishing a tradition for a Lutheran parsonage was the farthest thing from his imagination when he began working out his theological discoveries in the actual lives of his followers, but marriage naturally became one of the first issues he addressed. When he wrote his tract on marriage, "The Estate of Marriage" (1522), he had no idea that he would marry Katherine von Bora three years later on June 18, 1525.

Katherina von Bora

The topic, however, had become more compelling to the reformer as he was dealing with former nuns and priests whose vows of celibacy and the issues surrounding them troubled them. Could they break their sacred vows? Did they have to honor their vows of celibacy even if they no longer believed in them? Could they marry? Already in 1519 he had given a sermon which he published, "A Sermon on the Estate of Marriage."

His great treatise of 1521, "On the Babylonian Captivity of the Churches," directly addressed these issues from the point of view of a priest or pastor. In it Luther tried to sort out whether or not marriage was a sacrament, along with the Byzantine complexity of laws that the church had laid down concerning marriage over the centuries. In this treatise he was more interested in what priests should advise concerning marriage—why it was not to be regarded as a sacrament.

He returned to Scripture to discover God's intention for marriage. Fundamentally, both men and women were the work of God. The pagan writers who had demeaned women and marriage were, according to Luther, doing the work of the devil who contrived to sully the estate of marriage.[16] Contrasting the pagan view of marriage with the biblical one, he argued that marriage was a vocation, or calling. This was one of the central tenets of his theology and a radical turning from the medieval idea that only the religious—monks and nuns—could have a vocation. Christian faith, he wrote, viewed marriage differently from those who complained about the drudgery of marriage, its work, its sorrows, and its bitterness.

> [Faith] says, "God, because I am certain that thou hast created me as a man and hast from my body begotten this child, I also know for a certainty that it meets with thy perfect pleasure. I confess to thee that I am not worthy to rock the little babe or wash its diapers, or to be entrusted with the care of the child and its mother. How is it, that I, without any merit, have come to this distinction of being certain that I am serving thy creature and thy most precious will? O how gladly will I do so, though the duties should be even more insignificant and despised. Neither frost nor heat, neither drudgery nor labor, will distress or dissuade me, for I am certain that it is thus pleasing in thy sight."[17]

This remarkable picture of a married man, written by a monk with no apparent interest in marriage, has attracted notice for its tender picture of the father rocking the baby to sleep or washing its diapers. On the other hand, the next paragraph, which advises a wife to think of her own situation in the light of her vocation, has not been commended by feminists. It states, rather starkly, the consequences for a woman of entering fully into the married life, and childbirth, with its possible dangers to the life of the woman.

Dear Grete, remember that you are a woman, and that this work of God in you is pleasing to me. Trust joyfully in his will, and let him have his way with you. Work with all your might to bring forth the child. Should it mean your death, then depart happily, for you will die in a noble deed and in subservience to God. If you were not a woman you should now wish to be one for the sake of this very work alone, that you might thus gloriously suffer and even die in the performance of God's work and will.[18]

The frank advice to the woman to "die happily" in childbirth seems grisly to moderns, as is much lore about childbirth for women. Childbirth, even today, brings every prospective mother to thoughts of her own death. The old wives' tales about the sorrows of childbirth told a truth which pregnant women needed to hear. Women's diaries, especially from the nineteenth century, are filled with devotional contemplations of the coming journey through the "valley of the shadow of death," recommended for the woman before she is brought to childbed. *Linka's Diary* records such a prayer just before she gave birth to her first child.[19]

Martin Luther about the time of his marriage

As late as November 1524, only some months before his marriage, Luther wrote Spalatin that he thought he would never marry. "It is not that I do not feel my flesh or sex, since I am neither wood nor stone, but my mind is far removed from marriage, since I daily expect death and the punishment due to a heretic."[20] Only two months before his wedding, in April 1525, Luther was assuring his correspondents that marriage was not on his mind. In a letter to Spalatin, his old friend, he joked "It is rather strange that I, who so often write about matrimony and get mixed up with women, have not yet turned into a woman, to say nothing of not having married one."[21] He then made a curious statement to the effect that he had thought seriously about at least three women. "I have had three wives simultaneously, and loved them so much that I have lost two who are taking other husbands; the third I can hardly keep with my left arm, and she, too will probably soon be snatched away from me."[22] Scholars

think he was referring to Ave von Schönfield, Ave Alemann, and Katherina von Bora.

His strange reference to the "left arm" may be an ironic hint that she
could become his concubine in the
manner of decadent priests at the
time. He then made a puzzling jest
that he could overtake Spalatin in
the finding of a wife. Katie, whom
he had vainly tried to marry off
to others whom she found unap-
pealing, had suggested to him she
would marry only him or one other.
Her proposal may have been working on him, for even though Luther
scoffed at it, he very quickly came
around for reasons that appear to
have less to do with the desirabil-
ity of Kate than with his situation.
On a visit to his parents, Luther
once again heard his father, Hans,
pressing him to marry to give him heirs.

GUSTAV KÖNIG

Martin and Katie Luther are married.

At the same time, he reacted with irritation to increasing taunts from
the church hierarchy against him, especially the marriage of priests that
his movement allowed. When Hieronymus Shurff, his good friend and
lawyer, told him that the gossip was that "If this monk were to take a wife,
then all the world and the very devil would laugh, and [Luther] himself
would ruin everything that he had created," Luther scoffed.[23] Nothing
could have spurred on Luther more. With his strong sense of the devil's
opposition, Luther heard this as a challenge that he would have to meet.

Only two weeks later, on May 4, 1525, Luther wrote to John Rühel,
"Before I die I will still marry my Katie to spite the devil."[24] This he proceeded to do with dispatch. On June 18, 1525, he married her. Some days
later, on June 27, 1525, he hosted a large banquet, in Wittenberg, complete
with his parents and many of his friends to seal the arrangement. In a letter
to Amsdorf inviting him to the feast, he gave several reasons for the marriage. Noting that he married not for passion, but to obey his father's wish
for progeny, he admitted to dutifully cherishing his new wife.[25]

After the festivities the Luthers settled down to life in the Black Cloister in Wittenberg, a monastery where Luther had lived for fourteen years

as a monk. It was in a bad state of repair, given that it had never really been finished or kept up. It had originally been intended as a dwelling place for a group of about forty monks as they went about their duties. Thus it had sleeping rooms, a dining room, sheds and barns for the livestock, a brewery, and a garden. In addition, the property included a small run-down chapel where Luther preached on occasion. The monks lived on the third floor—really an attic close to the roof. Katie and Luther took over the second floor as their dwelling place. Here they built their living room, dining room, and bedroom. Out of the old cloister study, hall, and auditorium for lectures, they made a place for schooling and family devotions. They held their large feasts and festivals in the lecture rooms, where they were able to feed a good many guests. This became more and more important as the curious from around Europe made their way to little Wittenberg to visit with the great reformer.

Katie immediately set about to make the cloister habitable for a family. It was obvious that only men had lived there. Luther's own bed of straw had not been changed in an entire year. He blamed his slovenliness on the fact that he had worked so hard that he could not be bothered with cleaning. "I worked all day and fell into my bed and did not care about anything else," he wrote. Katie vigorously took up the work of cleaning and disciplining Luther's life. Luther soon began to call her the "Morning Star of Wittenberg" because she would rise at 4:00 a.m. to begin her work and would keep at it until 9:00 p.m.

Her first task, according to the sources, was to apply whitewash to the filthy walls. With the help of a maid and others, she cleaned all the rooms, and then set about cultivating the garden which had gone to seed during Luther's time there. Soon she had whipped the entire parsonage into shape so that its acreage was fruitful and capable of making the family self-sufficient.

The skills she had learned at home on her father's farm and in the nunneries where she had lived after her mother's death stood her in good stead. She fished in the pond beside the cloister, grew vegetables, tended to the fruit trees, raised stock while learning the best ways to breed animals, brewed beer, and made wine—all on the cloister property. She managed the preservation of food as well, learning to salt down the beef and pork so it would keep. Her skills as a nurse, learned at the Nimbschen nunnery where she lived until she escaped, were useful as others in the community came to her for advice. This skill required knowledge of herbs as well as of attending the sick and dying. Soon the house was running smoothly. The cloister—now parsonage—grounds provided food for the growing family, the students who boarded with them, as well as the myriads of guests who came to visit them over the next twenty years until Luther's death.

After some altercations on budgetary matters, Luther turned over the finances of the parsonage to Katie. She guided the household to prosperity, despite Luther's annoying habit of giving to those with greater need than they seemed to have. Katie made sure that the students sitting at Luther's table understood their responsibility to pay for their instruction as well as for room and board. She soon became well known as a manager and a cook. Luther once referred to Katie in a letter to Justus Jonas as "our Lord Kate, the chief cook."[26] In later letters, after he purchased a farm for Katie in Zülsdorf, he began to address her as "my dearly beloved Kate, *Doctora Lutherin*, and the Lady of the New Pig Market."[27]

All told, the Luthers thrived. Without Katie's shrewd management this would not have happened. Her example was a precedent for clergy to marry commonsense women who could keep soul and body together. Katie also attended to Luther's health expertly. Although it may not be correct to call Luther a hypochondriac, he was certainly ill many times during his career. His troubles with constipation, kidney stones, his bouts with dizziness, depression, and many other ailments proved to be a challenge for her. However, she had learned about the treatment of these illnesses from her work with her aunt at the convent where she grew up. Luther very early on understood his Katie's skills as a nurse and midwife. He warmly recommended her to several of their friends' wives who were recovering from difficult childbirth or other troubles.

He had barely recovered from a bout of depression and "the English sweats" (1527-1529) when the Luther house and its inhabitants were faced with an outbreak of plague for which they were scarcely prepared. (It was around this time he is thought to have written "A Mighty Fortress is our God.") Nevertheless the Luthers remained in Wittenberg, against the advice of the Elector who urged them to flee. This demonstrated that the parsonage family trusted in God no matter the circumstance. The Black Cloister became a virtual hospital and poorhouse, as the Luthers and Bugenhagens ministered to the sick and dying. For Luther it was a time to demonstrate how his theology included a strong component of love for the neighbor in need of help. Only one inhabitant of the house died from the plague, although several became sick nearly unto death, a testimony to the strength of the family and Katie's good nursing.

GUSTAV KÖNIG

Luther and his household singing hymns

Teaching the Faith at Home

Few pictures of the Luther family are more deeply burned into the Protestant mind than that of Luther and his family singing together for their family devotions. Luther loved music and valued it as being next to the Gospel. Like the external word of the gospel, it changed the heart from the outside with its rhythms and tunes. His devotion to Frau Music was strong. An accomplished lutenist and a singer with a fine tenor voice, Luther was the perfect man to rethink the function of music in devotional practices and establish it as central to Lutheran teaching. Katie helped her husband establish a strict schedule for the day. It began early in the morning with devotions, at which the household would gather for a recitation of the catechism, prayer, and Scripture, along with a hymn or two.

From the very first, Luther was concerned that his theology and teaching aids become available to the Germans in their own language, so they could learn (and teach their children) the faith and become active laypeople practicing their vocations in daily life. He suggested in his letter to the German nobility that they send both boys and girls to school in order to maintain its temporal estate outwardly the world must have good and capable men and women, men able to rule well over land and people, women able to manage the household and train children and servants aright. Now such men must come from our boys, and such women from our girls.[28]

Luther expects here the traditional separation of the boys from the girls in order to create men and women ready to take their traditional parts in society.

Although he does not make it explicit, to "train children and servants aright" can hardly mean anything less than teaching the faith along with household skills. At the time he wrote this, he was not married. He had, however, just finished his first collection of hymns in 1523, compiled with his friends, especially Johann Walter, as they began preparing worship materials in German. The hymns, intended to be sung as part of the worship service, were written so that ordinary lay people could learn the faith and teach it themselves.

Luther teaching the catechism

His introduction to the German service, the *Deutsche Messe*, written one year later in the fall of 1525, shows how strongly he felt people needed religious materials in their own language. First of all, he writes, any worship service in German must have a simple and easy catechism attached to it "to train the young and to call and attract others to the faith."[29] For this reason, he wanted the service to include the regular catechization of the congregation, especially the young. That meant the people were to be taught the Ten Commandments, the Creed, and the Lord's Prayer during the worship services.

People in Luther's time gathered in church frequently, so this was not meant just for Sunday. So that children would learn these central parts of the Christian faith, Luther suggested that they be "repeated or read aloud evenings and morning in the homes for the children and servants, in order to train them as Christians."[30] While it is part of the baptismal promises to teach these golden texts to the children, Luther added that it was important that they not simply be able to repeat them by "rote," but also be questioned on them so they fully understood them. His example of how one should question a child looks like the beginning of what became his Small Catechism. "What do you believe?" Answer: "I believe that God the Father . . ." to the end.

While Luther was considering the development of a Lutheran version of the mass in German, he married Katie. Even before their children were born, Luther suggested an order for family devotions. He made this even more explicit in the Small Catechism, which came out in 1529, after he had considerable practice managing home devotions with the help of Katie. His understanding of children is clear in his advice to the pastors on how to transmit these teachings to the children. He recommended that they avoid using different versions of a text to be memorized because it would create confusion and make it difficult for the children. For this he pointed to the wisdom of the ancient church, which prepared one universal version of the three great texts included in the catechism: the Ten Commandments, Creeds, and Lord's Prayer. One can assume that the clarity and purity of the language of his Small Catechism can be credited to his having young children underfoot as he wrote it.

His morning and evening prayers and prayer at noon include the suggestion of how the ritual should begin and end. At the beginning, one is to make the sign of the cross and then pray to the Trinity: "God the Father, Son, and Holy Spirit watch over me. Amen." He then suggested reciting the Apostles' Creed and Lord's Prayer, after which his prayer should be prayed, and then a hymn sung, preferably one on the Ten Commandments in the morning. At evening, sensibly, without the boisterous singing of a hymn, one is simply "to go to sleep quickly and cheerfully." Scholars suggest that he got these prayers and the little orders from the Roman breviary, which is not surprising, given his long experience as a monk and the rituals of observing the hours throughout the day. They are, however, much reduced in length and show Luther to have been aware of the attention span of a child.

Both Katie and Luther, having experienced the daily round of prayer in the monastery and convent, had a strong sense of the need for daily prayers that were, however, not monastic, but appropriate for a family with children. The convent had a rich round of devotional activities that were not possible after she married. Things were more hectic for her, and the traditional "hours" of the convent were too onerous. However, the three services of the family altar, adapted from the monastic rituals, have endured until today, with their sensible understanding of the life of the family.

Central to these little services was the singing of a hymn or two. We know that Luther led the singing in the home. Katie, however little we know about her singing abilities, had a good bit of instruction in singing in the convent, at which traditionally a bit of time was devoted to teaching its novitiates the importance of singing well and appropriately. She did not play an instrument, as far as we know, but she must have sung along with the family. Katie did help with the education of the young, besides running the very complicated household that Luther's work demanded. Music continued to be the most important art in the Lutheran parsonage through the centuries. We will see that when we observe the pastors' wives on the frontier making sure their daughters especially were well educated in this art.

Colleague

Although Luther's mind was protean, and he had as many contradictory voices in his own head as almost any person could, Katie provided him with a kind of collegiality none of his male friends could. In addition to cleaning up his house, raising their children, providing him with a good living on the parsonage land, and showing hospitality to any and all comers, she could hold her own in conversations with him, theologically. Her training as a nun, and now close companion to the reformer, made her a valuable colleague. She had to listen to him as he preached, taught, and as they sang together. Artists have portrayed her listening attentively to Luther in the Wittenberg church where he is preaching, like many a succeeding pastor's wife has done.

Luther discovered very quickly that Katie was strong minded, and he very soon came to treasure her, writing a friend that "she was more precious to him than the kingdom of France and the republic of Venice." He noted in letters and in *Table Talk* her reactions to many of his ideas, scriptural readings that troubled her, and her reluctance to agree with him on everything. She took particular exception to the practice of biblical patriarchs of taking more than one wife. Luther was amused at her in his

Luther preaching

report of the conversation, which showed her to be worthy of his later sobriquet, Herr Katie. Once she had questions about the meaning of a passage in Psalm 18 and why David could claim before God to be righteous. Luther explained that David was not speaking to God, but to them, as though they were speaking to each other among themselves.[31] She had become part of his daily conversation. The students sitting around the table, enjoying the fruits of her labor, listened quite closely to what their great teacher was saying and the conversation between the two.

Many of the incidents between the two appear to be Luther putting Katie down. However, if one could reconstruct the actual scene, it might be possible to hear these comments, many of them rather misogynist, as Luther teasing her to see what Katie would say about some of his more outrageous comments on women. During an argument sometime between December 11, 1532, and January 1533, he noted that female governance had been a disaster from the first when Eve took over the moral governance in the household. He then blamed the fall on women: "We have women to thank for that! With tricks and cunning women deceive men, as I, too have experienced." Maybe he had lost an argument and is saying, "Go back to the kitchen!" Or he may be slyly ribbing Katie who is working about the table as he speaks. We simply can't know his tone in these exchanges, but they could be played in a theater very easily to suggest either kind of attitude.[32]

He constantly noted in *Table Talk* the difference Katie had made in his life as a theologian. He commented that it would have been good for St. Jerome, the crotchety church father, to have had a wife, because he would have thought quite differently about many things.[33] He even noted that he understood God differently now that he had watched the mother of his children dealing with the helpless innocent child at her breast. "God must be much friendlier to me and speak to me in friendlier fashion than my Katy to little Martin."[34] The pictures we see of their married life show him marveling at what she could teach him in her daily life. When she had dragged him away from his desk long enough for him to go fishing for food in the little pond in their garden, he compared her joy in getting just enough to eat to the nobleman's greed and his desire for altogether too much.[35]

She frequently chided him, he reported, on his blustery tone, and sought on occasion to soften his blows, to no avail. When Luther was commenting on the stupidity of Schwenkenfeld, Katie chided him, "Ah, dear Sir, that's much too coarse!"[36] He listened to her, but blamed it on his opponents. Katie's answer is not recorded. In making such a response, however, she kept him aware of what his opponents and friends might be thinking of him. These comments show the force of her personality on the reformer. Although he could not be called one who believed in the equality of men and women, and *Table Talk* is plentiful in comments about the inferiority of women, he obviously respected and held his wife in high esteem. He commented on how strange it was to awaken next to pigtails and saw in his marriage a wonderful means to annoy the devil.[37] In this he understood how God had given marriage as a means for supporting the structures of the world by providing parents for children, homes for the betterment of society, and the pure joy of daily life, with its incumbent sorrows. Although he knew this from his own parents, he learned it anew in his own marriage to Katherina von Bora.

Katie and Luther developed patterns that became almost universal for Protestant parsonage life. These would have arisen naturally, simply from the fact of a married couple living together in one household and raising a family. However, Luther's marriage to Katie seems to have been attractive enough to his followers that their particular way of living together was admired, and it became the norm for Lutheran parsonages down through the ages.

Legacy

Scholars looking at the parsonage tradition as it developed in Lutheran lands have noted that there are several important legacies left by the inhabitants of parsonages in the cultural life among Lutherans, both here and in Europe. Most significant is the reformation it caused in the standing of women. Although attitudes toward women did not change overnight, they changed considerably when Luther defended marriage and described women also as creations in the image of God, not as lesser beings sent into the world to distract religious men from their devotions. For Luther marriage was natural, the way God chose to keep creation going and prospering in such a way that children and the family flourished.

The work of Luther and his followers offered women a higher position than they had occupied in the minds of the medieval church, which often viewed them as temptresses ready to bring men down. It was the devil, Luther thought, who led the early Christian fathers, such as St. Jerome, to view women as obstacles to piety and to consider celibacy as the better way to be spiritual. To be sure, Luther, while coming to honor Katie as his lord in the home, could hardly be called a feminist. He lived in a time of hierarchical thinking about all of creation, so that men were over women, women over children, and all humanity over the animals, etc. These orders of creation put women somewhat below men in Luther's thinking. At the same time he came to see that she dominated him and the household in ways that helped them to flourish, as he would not have alone without marrying her.

In order to understand the parsonage family over the centuries, it is important to recognize that until the nineteenth century, and in some places even later, the home was the economic unit of the culture. In that respect, the parsonage was no different from other homes. Except for the very wealthy, everyone in the family—husband, wife, and children—all had to work to provide food, shelter and clothing for the family. Katie freed Luther from most of these duties, but she also made him take the role of husband and father.

The most important thing to see, however, is that Luther identified and lifted up domestic life as the place where men and women lived out their religious vocations in place of the cloister. This meant that Luther's theology of the family and the stolid virtues of faithfulness, civic duty, and stoic devotion to the challenges of daily life began to shape a truly Lutheran domestic piety. This was in sharp contrast to medieval spirituality represented by the great Catholic saints like the anorexic Catherine of Sienna or Francis of Assisi. Heroic rejections of the things of this world were not, by Luther's theology, pleasing to God; what God wanted was for us to enjoy his creation and take a healthy joy in the pleasures and seriousness of family life in this world. This changed nearly 1000 years of a spiritual tradition that endorsed fleeing the things of this world. Pleasure in our creation as physical beings received a rich revitalization when Luther and Katie married and began to enjoy each other's company, even as they suffered the typical vexations of close proximity and their very different, but complementary, personalities.

Luther made the faith profoundly domestic through his Small Catechism and hymns; the faith was to be passed on in the home. Sturdy burghers could teach the faith to their children at morning and evening devotions, apart from the finely nuanced theological debates the scholars were waging. Lutheranism was both for the ordinary Christian and the advanced scholar. Women and children could learn it and teach it as part of their vocations in the home.

The pastors' wives, especially on the American frontier, took this as a given. Consistent with that, Linka Preus resolved that when her husband was away on church business, which was more frequent than not, she would lead the family in devotions, reading them a *postil* (sermon) from Luther or Kierkegaard among others, using the Small Catechism to teach the doctrines of the faith.[38]

Educating a Girl

Luther's ideas made the Lutheran territorial churches realize they needed to teach girls as well as boys to read and write and master other subjects as they began their adult lives. The pastor's wife was often considered the most educated woman in the community, especially in the rural areas. Katie's example was the model for most of these wives. Over time, the vocation of pastor's wife would change and mutate as the understandings of women changed.

Some generations before Linka was born, in the mid-eighteenth century, thoughts about women and their nature—and thus what kind of education they needed—remained a hotly contested topic. Jean-Jacques Rousseau gave serious thought to who and what a woman was in his classic book *Emile: Or Treatise on Education* (1762). After four books

Jean Jacques Rousseau

on the education of the young man, Emile, Rousseau imagines the perfect mate for Emile: Sophie. For Rousseau women were no longer down one step on the hierarchy of the order of creation, as Lutherans had thought, but complementary. "In what they have in common, they are equal. Where they differ, they are not comparable. A perfect woman and a perfect man ought not to resemble each other in mind any more than in looks."[39] She was different, complementary; men were reason, she was sentiment. She was to be educated differently because she was a different being, one who existed for the man and was always dependent on her relation to a man.

A woman's education must therefore be planned in relation to man. To be pleasing in his sight, to win his respect and love, to train him in childhood, to tend him in manhood, to counsel and console, to make his life pleasant and happy, these are the duties of woman for all time and this is what she should be taught while she is young.[40]

In order to be pleasing, a woman needed to be decorative, learning very early to care for how she looked and fit into the society:

What people think of her matters as much as what she really is. Hence her education must, in this respect, be different from man's education. 'What will people think' is the grave of man's virtue and the throne of a woman's.[41]

Women by nature, Rousseau argued, are responsive to others and eager to please, especially by coquetry made effective by their appearance. Thus girls needed to learn, in their education, how to dress a doll so they could learn many arts—sewing, style, learning to intuit what people thought of them. "Little girls always dislike learning to read and write, but they are always ready to learn to sew."[42] They would in this process learn cutting out material for the dresses, embroidery, lace-making, and especially drawing so they could learn to be tasteful in dress. Their drawing however should not be landscapes, but decorative: "leaves, fruit, flowers, draperies, planting that will make an elegant trimming for the accessories of the toilet." Counting would be important, but reading and writing less so, until she became old enough to know why. Finally, gentleness and docility were most important because man, a creature often vicious and always faulty, she [the wife] should early learn to submit to injustice and to suffer the wrongs inflicted on her by her husband without complaint; she must be gentle for her own sake, not his. Bitterness and obstinacy only multiply the sufferings of the wife and the misdeeds of the husband; the man feels that these are not the weapons to be used against him.[43]

Finally, he suggested that women should learn the basics of their religion so that they could learn to love—the chief virtue of Christianity—and teach the faith to the children, and avoid making them Jesuits and casuists.

Mary Wollstonecraft violently opposed Rousseau's notions of how to educate a girl in her *Vindication of the Rights of Women*: "My main argument is built on this simple principle, that if [woman] be not prepared by education to become the companion of man, she will stop the progress of knowledge and virtue; for truth must be common to all." She agreed, however, as did most, that a woman also needed an education in order to raise her children for modern society.

Mary Wollstonecraft

This argument raged through the French Revolution and through the early twentieth century, and remnants of it can still be heard in any discussion of the education of girls. While Rousseau's anthropology of men and women is offensive to moderns, it was the common understanding of women, with permutations of the Lutheran theology of the orders of creation as well as Victorian sentimentality about men and women, during the nineteenth century.

This view was reinforced just as men began working outside the home, leaving women in charge of the home—encouraging the notion that men took care of the public sphere and women the home. The Victorians believed almost without question that "the hand that rocks the cradle rules the world." It affected how women were educated, what they thought about marriage, and how the family should live together in the parsonage.

Women at the time of Rousseau's treatise and well into the nineteenth century still had to know how to manage a household and a farm. However, as technology developed, the family was increasingly freed from the time constraints of providing for the basic needs of food, clothing, and shelter. These inventions began to change marriage from being primarily an economic agreement to something else. Perhaps it was the wealthy who first noticed this—given that women were increasingly not needed for the economic survival of the family. What they were married for was their wealth. The great epistolary novel by Richard Sheridan, *Clarissa* (1750), exposed its readers to what they already knew about the horrors of marriages in which the prospective husband, often in reduced circumstances, deceitfully courted a woman with greater means than he had, knowing that upon the conclusion of the marriage ceremony his wife's fortune would be his. This became one of the most pressing issues for the early feminists, most of whom were wealthy. They wanted to change the inheritance laws so that a woman on marrying would no longer become what Elizabeth Cady Stanton called "civilly dead," with no right to her father's fortune.

Jane Austen's novels fully explored this issue. They featured the difficulties of finding a man and woman who actually loved each other and whose means, while a part of the negotiations, were not the only reason for the marriage. Victorian novels picked up this theme and ran with it, even as the system was changing. Marriage began to be less and less an economic arrangement between families, especially fathers and future husbands, and moved more and more to what has been called companionate marriages. Men and women married for reasons of love rather than economic benefit, something Wollstonecraft recommended and had practiced, though it turned out disastrously for her. Marrying for love and companionship was especially encouraged by evangelicals in England, who tended to support women's rights. This required educating young women and men using the same curriculum so that they could be genuine companions in the home. An unintended consequence was that women came to expect they could do the same things as men.

Hermann and Linka inherited all of those understandings of women and wives, much as Hermann might have disagreed with Rousseau. The young couple seemed to have married for love. Given the penury of the clergy at the time, they did not unite for economic reasons, despite their place in the upper class. However, because the parsonage at the time of Linka's youth was still a farm, the old ways still remained. At first Linka was something of the household manager who ran both house and farm. As production moved away from the home and men left it for jobs outside of the home, women came to be the ones with the domestic virtues that ruled the home and they passed on the virtues of the heart to her children.[44]

Over time, however, the vocation of pastors' wife came to be something of a public vocation, which many women entered almost as a way to have a profession or a vocation beyond that of wife and mother. The pastor's wife became a kind of pastor to the women in the congregation, especially in the later nineteenth century. Women came to be seen as spiritual leaders in the churches and society. The distance from leading home devotions to leading the ladies' aids in the larger congregation seemed short. Young women with ambitions saw the work of the pastor's wife as a true public vocation which they prayed they could practice by marrying a minister. When the colleges associated with seminaries in this country became co-ed, they attracted numbers of women who came to find a pastor husband. Being a pastor's wife was an honorable profession, but it could only be entered if one found a willing pastor!

As Linka began to think of her future, she knew that parsonages were the center of cultural life in the community and that pastors and their wives were community leaders. She understood that the pastor's wife made the parsonage the school for young girls who needed to learn housekeeping, a place where confirmands could come and work in return for catechism instruction, and a place for good counsel in both physical and soul care as well as many other earthly problems that the parishioners trusted to her. It gave the pastors' wives a strong sense of their importance to the community and her place in it.[45]

The pastors' wives of the Norwegian Synod became such leaders: the diaries and letters of both Linka and Elisabeth Koren give testimony to their roles in continuing that tradition in the New Land. Both understood themselves in the traditional way. Mrs. Koren believed the woman's place was in the home raising children and making a good home. Linka did as well, but she chafed more at the requirements for housework than Mrs. Koren seemed to do.

Linka, as the mother and teacher, transmitted the high culture of the West to her children in the school around the kitchen table and in the parlor during evening activities. It was her calling as a pastor's wife, and she knew it well. In order to practice it, she had to be educated for it. In what follows we will see how the pastors and pastors' wives of the Norwegian Synod in America trained their daughters to be pastors' wives as they would have in the old country, and how they adapted these traditions to the New World, little knowing that 150 years later little would be the same, with their granddaughters flowering in public vocations. Part of the reason for this book is to tell the story of a tradition that now largely has vanished.

CHAPTER THREE

Learning the Vocation of Pastor's Wife in Norway

Applying It in the New World

"Surely our Lord wants us to develop our abilities, though most of all to be good housewives. After all, that is our calling, and we shall and should prepare ourselves to meet this request with good conscience, piety, order, love humility, and eagerness as our principles."[46]

—Linka's Diary

As we have seen, a pastor's wife, to be prepared for her vocation, needed to have an education similar to our liberal arts degree—literature, history, modern languages and the arts—especially music, drawing, fine handwork, plus the Bible, Luther's Small Catechism, and hymns. More vital, however, for the sake of the family's survival, she needed to know how to be a good manager of a farm, with the knowledge and skills necessary to maintaining life. Most women in her time practiced these skills: managing the farm and kitchen, raising animals or crops to provide materials for food and clothing, knowing how to turn the raw materials into usable stuff, and keeping the family and house warm and comfortable. The education of Linka and her generation of potential pastors' wives involved learning many more things about farming than any girl today could imagine. Before the Civil War even the most privileged of wives had to know how to do most of these things— not necessarily to do them, although on the

Linka Preus, 1851

frontier they did, but to oversee the work. Linka kept a diary from the age of fifteen to twenty-five, until her increasing responsibilities as a wife and mother prevented her from continuing it. The diary details all the different branches of knowledge she had to master in order to be a proficient and successful wife and mother in Norway. That knowledge was more crucial in the New Land, given how isolated people on the frontier were.

Linka (Dorothea Margrethe Caroline Keyser), born May 3, 1829, in Kristiansand, Norway, to Pastor Christian Nicolai Keyser (1798-1846) and Agnes Louise Carlsen (1799-1840) grew up in the parsonage milieu. The men in her father's family tended to be pastors and/or professors. Linka's father served the Tvedt parish some miles northwest of Kristiansand, from 1830-1837. Tveit church, still in use, was one of the oldest stone churches in Norway. It is hidden in a wooded glen near the parsonage where Linka spent her first seven and a half years.

In 1837 Keyser moved with his family to Christiania (Oslo) to begin teaching theology at the University of Christiania, Norway's first university, founded in 1811. Her grandfather, Johan Michael Keyser, had been Bishop of Christiansand. Her uncle, Rudolph Keyser (1802-1864), was a professor at the university, and another uncle, Frederik Wilhelm Keyser (1815-1901), librarian there. Her mother's father, Carl Andreas

Urianienborg, where Linka lived with her grandmother after her parents' deaths. It would later be parceled out into apartments.

Carlsen (1775-1838), an official in the army (*Overkrigscommissær*) and later chief officer of customs in Christiania, was also from a family that included pastors and professors.

Her father's half-sister, Anne Rosina Keyser (1788-1839), married Paul Arctander Preus (1779-1867), after his first wife had died. Paul Preus served as the head of the Cathedral School in Christiansand where both Hermann Preus and Peter Laurentius Larsen, later president of Luther College, were students. Paul and Anne were the parents of Hermann Amberg Preus, Linka's first half-cousin, who was to become her husband.

It is, then, not surprising that Linka said "My husband shall be a minister!"[47] It became her chosen profession, one of the few professions that a woman at the time could enter; it was also the family trade. Her family tree shows how intertwined the families in this small group of leaders in the small country had become over the generations. In many respects the clergy families of the Twin Kingdoms of Denmark and Norway were a regiment of cousins, all part of the leadership class of both the church and state, most of whom probably knew each other.

Linka's Diary gives us a vivid picture of her world, the vocational training and liberal arts education she received from the family as she prepared to become a successful pastor's wife. What she learned helped her especially in the New Land when she and her husband arrived in Wisconsin in 1851, where life was even more primitive than it had been in Norway. Because of her diary and sketches we can watch as the young woman, an eager and gifted student, grows into her vocation as pastor's wife.

Linka, whose mother had died in 1840 when Linka was ten, had been living in Christiania (Oslo) with her father and grandmother Doris (Dorothea) Carlsen (1783-1853), from Altona, Slesvig, who became a teacher for the young motherless girl as she approached puberty. For her further education, as was typical, the family decided that Linka should remove to Askevold, to live with her mother's sister, Rosalide Isabella "Rosa" (1815-1898), and her husband Pastor Johan Carl Christie (1808-1898). Aunt Rosa came to Christiania to take Linka home with her in the summer when the trip could be made overland.

Linka's first entry in her diary was on January 1, 1845, with her recollection of leaving Oslo on August 19, 1844, for Askevold, (Askevoll), a small

Doris Carlsen, Linka's grandmother

The parsonage at Askevold, where Linka lived

village on the seacoast north of Sognefjord. In her day it was no small journey, involving horse-drawn conveyances over some of the highest mountain passes in Norway, and then down to the coast. She appears to have enjoyed the long and difficult journey, probably because she was with her aunt Rosa who had taken a special interest in her since her mother's death four years before.

The time in Askevold had a purpose common to the families of this class: Linka was to learn from Aunt Rosa the skills of managing a parsonage and other domestic arts; develop further her skills in the fine arts—drawing, embroidery and other handiwork—necessary to the life of a lady at the time, (also recommended by Rousseau); and continue the study of reading and writing, literature, history, geography, some math and religion, as well as the most important languages of the day—German and English, along with some French.

At about the time of their first menstruation, a stormy time for many a young girl who is just discovering how to be a young lady and wife, the daughters of the parsonage were regularly sent off to an aunt to learn the domestic arts and skills from someone who was not their mother. She assisted her aunt with the normal chores of a household, including care for the younger children. She would also be catechized and confirmed by her pastor uncle, or his vicar, as she was learning the domestic arts from a teacher with whom she did not have such a complicated relationship as she might have had with her own mother.

As she made preparations to leave on her long journey north, Linka reported meeting with a number of aunts, uncles, and cousins who gathered to see her off with gifts of cakes, baskets of fruits, especially cherries, and other goodies. From her description, we can see that the extended family was a joyful one, happy to be together, and fully supportive of the motherless Linka. Her father, in poor health, hardly figured in the description of her departure, although she did admit that it made her feel a little sad to leave him alone with her five younger sisters. Together she and Aunt Rosa traveled the long journey from Oslo to Drammen by *calash*[48] to Hønefoss, down through the valley of Valdres, to Lærdal on the Sognefjord and then north to Askevold by boat. Unfortunately, we do not have the diary kept while on that journey. Askevold parsonage, portrayed here by the painter Anders Monson Askevold (1834-1900), lay nestled between the sea and the mountains behind it. Like all parsonages at the time, it was a center of life and culture for the fishermen and farmers of the parish as they eked out a frugal existence during the long winters and short, glorious summers of the north.

Calash

Although the parsonage and church where Linka was confirmed have since disappeared, the landscape of the little village remains as beautiful and remote as it was in Linka's time. For Linka it was a romantic refuge in the wilds of nature. There she learned to live and flourish or suffer as her people had for centuries. This stood her in good stead some few years later on the Wisconsin frontier, where life was more primitive, but not a lot different. As a future pastor's wife she had to learn to be a farmer and manager of the parsonage as well as teacher of the children, and serve as a medical and agricultural advisor to the parishioners who came to her for guidance.

There were in the neighborhood several young people her own age with whom she, still a child, could play games, skate, ride in a sleigh, and otherwise enjoy her time while learning how to be a grown up and fulfill the vocation she aspired to: becoming a successful pastor's wife and mother. The first, and most vital, study in her curriculum, were the many things she had to do to feed the family.

Preparation of Food

When Linka began her diary in Askevold on January 13, 1845, she recounted how she started learning to prepare food. While she was no stranger to the kitchen, she needed to study far more than simply cooking the food stored in the cupboards. Now she had to learn how to manage the household, to assure that there was food in the pantry to prepare for food on the table. Moderns would call it animal husbandry, from raising the stock to slaughtering and preserving it. The curriculum began with whatever presented itself in the daily needs of the parsonage kitchen. Her first job was to grind veal into hamburger (*karbonade*). "I did a really good job!" she remarked in her diary.[49] While we are not told that part of this work was the slaughter of the animal, she may have been around for that event since meat had to be preserved almost immediately after butchering, given the lack of refrigeration. Grinding the meat was almost the last on a long list of things to do to prepare for meals.

Some days later she helped her aunt with a duck she had bought. They kept it in the hen house to keep it from flying away before they could kill, pluck, and clean it. This was a daunting task for the young woman. Every animal involved a different kind of tending.

Dwellers in the parsonage, who may have been somewhat removed from the more immediate work of their congregants, could not escape these basic chores, because they too were farmers. When their parishioners flourished, the pastor and his family did; when they suffered from poor crops and meager fishing, so did the parsonage family. The tax system required parishioners to give the pastor ten percent, or a tithe, of some of the food they produced: live chickens, slabs of beef, pork, freshly caught fish, milk, butter, cream, and eggs.

In Norway this tax obligation was about to end when Linka was in Askevold. On February 11, 1845, Linka described the last of the gathering in of the "fish tithe" for the pastor, by law the duty of fishermen to give the pastor ten percent of their catch. Whether they sold the fish or preserved it, the pastor's family had to know how to store it over a long time. The herring run was pivotal for the continuance of life in the North Sea villages and everyone had to pitch in to preserve the abundance of the catch. Linka watched her aunt with a small group of women in the brew house (*ildhuset*), an outer building on the parsonage grounds, cleaning the herring and either salting them or hanging them up to dry in the smokehouse for later consumption.[50]

On October 18, 1845, she helped stuff the sausages, kneading the minced meat to go into the newly cleaned intestines of the animal. For her it was a lot of fun, but it would be unsavory to moderns unacquainted with the farm. This may have been the first time she had actively participated in butchering an animal, although she had surely seen it on her grandmother's acreage in Christiania. Getting the animals ready to be butchered by fattening them up and preparing them for slaughter was an important step in the process. She must have watched her aunt give the animal an oily mixture of food so its intestines would be easier to clean when they prepared them to be filled with the sausage mixture. At this slaughter, they had two hogs, one steer, and one cow. Over the next three days she wrote, "Wednesday was spent slaughtering the creatures and salting them, and I was there to see how all this was done."[51]

Five years later, when she returned to help her aunt and uncle again at Askevold, not long before her wedding to Hermann, she noted:

All the duties of a housewife have rested on my young shoulders. In the beginning, I thought it was very troublesome, but now the work is going smoothly and well, as if I had been keeping house for years. Food was especially troublesome for me, and the entire Monday was spent only thinking about food for that week. In my difficulties I had to slaughter a calf a few days ago, but I gave proof to the proverb, "Out of season the trolls will be killed." The slaughtering was hardly even done before Uncle was presented with a quarter of an ox's shoulder. The same day we got a load of big flounders and some lobsters. Have you ever seen such a thing? If the meat and the fish had come two and a half hours earlier, everything would have been well, but now I had to salt something, either calf or ox, and we have plenty of salted food. I wanted to get Uncle something fresh, since he likes that best. Now I deserve a scolding from Auntie because her pretty calf was no longer in the cowshed.[52]

The young woman after five years seemed to be practiced and ready for her role as housewife. Although it is not clear how much actual work she did, she had to learn how to do the work so that she could order the servants intelligently. Thus she was closely involved at least in overseeing these tasks. The management of food troubled her in this situation for she had made what turned out to be an untimely decision to slaughter the calf. This meant that the opportunity for fresh veal had been lost. They would have to eat the fish first, because it would spoil quickly without refrigeration.

Much of what they did every day had the goal of finding and keeping food for their daily sustenance. Linka loved to fish, but fishing was not merely a sport. They were gathering in food for their table—no idle amusement. They had to be ready to clean and prepare food at any time, should the occasion present itself. Once to their surprise they found in the boathouse an enormous codfish three feet long and a foot wide, a gift from someone in the parish. They had to scale it, clean it, and prepare it for eating immediately. The men carried rifles with them wherever they went so they could shoot game along the way. What they bagged needed to be dressed and cleaned for the table. Each animal required different treatments and skills, such as tanning hides, gathering goose down, and rendering fat. As old timers used to say, when we butchered the hog, we saved everything but the squeal.

Learning how to prepare the food for the table, she was also learning how to cook and bake, a major part of preparing food for the table.

Linka's Aunt Rosa Christie

Linka forthrightly recorded her failures as well as her successes. She tells a charming story of her aunt's lesson concerning the steps in preparing the Shrovetide buns. Linka rose early, at 3:30, in order to use the Shrovetide branches as whips to waken the family—traditionally cut just before Ash Wednesday to be forced for blossoms by Easter. She discovered her aunt and the maid already in the kitchen kneading dough for the buns. Aunt Rosa asked Linka to make coffee for them, even though it was now only 4:30, and continued her work. Linka noted that her efforts at coffee were a success, but then she was baffled by her aunt's request that she "turn the dough." She thought it a technical term which she did not understand and asked her aunt to show her how.

Uff, you split hairs more than anyone I've ever met, Linka. Of course you don't turn the dough, but the bowl the dough is in! When the bowl is completely warm, you can move it away from the oven.[53]

This little scene, which involved learning about the working of yeast in the raising of bread dough, is a window into the way the aunt and niece interacted as one is teaching and the other learning. We can hear the note of exasperation in the voice of the aunt, but also some amusement and shame in Linka's voice. One of the troubling parts of growing up and mastering these tasks was learning the vocabulary and when to take words literally, technically, or metaphorically. Here Linka learned how literally her aunt meant "turn," and laughed at herself, when she had understood what her aunt meant.

Linka learned about the preparation of foods not only for regular meals, but also for festivals when certain foods were particular to a celebration. The Shrovetide buns for Ash Wednesday (like hot cross buns with a cream filling) needed to be prepared early in the morning, Princess (seminola) pudding for birthdays, *eggedosis* (yolks of eggs beaten with sugar) for children's parties. Most extensive were the preparations for the Christmas holiday with its required menu. There was always a Christmas butchering in order to have fresh meat for the elaborate meals of the holidays along with the baking of the typical treats of a Norwegian Christmas: flatbread, *fattigmandsbakkels*, *sandbakkels*, and *julekake*. In addition, they made Christmas gifts for each other as they sat around the parlor at night. Linka showed her self-awareness as a novitiate when she described working on a rug they were making for a gift, and "we were also supposed to take part in the baking in order to learn. I watched how both the slaughtering and baking were done."[54] She needed these lessons in order to establish the parsonage in Wisconsin. The one thing she would lack were the maids and servants her aunt and uncle in Askevold employed. The census of 1865 notes that the Christies, her aunt and uncle, employed a governess, two hired men, and four maids. It would not be like that in America.

Clothes

Linka also had to learn how to make clothes from scratch: to spin yarn from wool, make linen from flax, and weave the material to create rugs, knit it into sweaters or socks, in addition to doing embroidery and other fine hand work. While not new to these activities, she began these sessions almost immediately after she arrived in Askevold. When she had finished her lessons, she began sewing until dark, when she took up her knitting of mittens, something that required less light, for one of her cousins, Doris.[55] (The planning of work around the availability of sunlight is something we barely understand today, but should remember when we read these accounts.) These activities continued, as she wrote on February 6, 1845, in a round of "eating, drinking, cooking, and sewing, and in the evening, playing whist."[56]

She watched with interest as Dorthea (Presteøen) started creating a web on the loom for them to weave into linsey-woolsey, a material in which the vertical threads were of linen and the horizontal ones were of wool. The making of the web involved stretching the linen yarn across the loom. Linka noted that in this case the linen yarn was poor. When the work began, Linka saw that it was fun to see it coming to fruition.[57]

Before it was done, however, her aunt returned with some linsey-woolsey from which material for a bodice was cut so that she would be able to wear it in a few days. "I started the skirt right away, and the housemaid started the bodice, since the dress was supposed to be done on Monday" for a party Linka was planning to attend at the neighbors, the Landmarks.[58]

They always kept wool in the house. While enjoying each other's company in the parlor after supper, they could card, spin, and prepare the wool for knitting or use in the loom. This was a skill that she would find most handy in the new land. She also had an eye for flax, the source of linen. She admired the blue flax fields of summer not only for their beauty, but also for their potential for linen. "I wish I had that flax when it's ready, then I would spin and weave!"[59]

By December 1850, she had become proficient with dyeing yarn.

> It's not only knitting and needlework that takes (sic) up my time; I also do dyeing, and that went really well today, I must say. But I'm not surprised, with the help I had, even though it was the first time—it has to be called first time since the yarn from Askevold was the one I tried unsuccessfully to dye a few days ago, and today we did it over.[60]

She needed daylight to see the colors accurately enough to do the work, and she worried that she was not skilled enough with the skimmer and candle she needed to ready the material and see it well enough to judge its quality. Boiling it in the pot on the fire, she described how she and her assistants got down on their hands and knees.

> Hvoslef [the vicar and English tutor for Linka] stood there, he had taken the candle from me, the cook was standing behind me holding a bundle, and finally the maid and I on all fours in the chimney, she with a long stick and I with the ladle. Now it was done—beautiful! Congratulations, dye-girl,—soon a skillful dy-er![61]

After all this preparation she then had to sew the material together into a dress or suit for someone in the family, usually done while sitting around in the parlor at night. Though she preferred drawing, her skill with the needle was sufficiently regarded that her brother Johan Keyser (Kalla) asked her to make him a black cap. He wanted one that would be smarter than the one he had because "the cockade and badge don't look good on the one he has."[62] How one looked in fine company concerned these children. They were of the official class, but because of their father's death and the genteel poverty it caused, they did not have the resources to afford all the desirable accouterments of high society.

Gardening

Besides the actual slaughter and preparation of food in the kitchen, Linka also had to also learn how to grow vegetables and herbs in the garden. She observed closely as her aunt taught her how to make a garden grow and what to plant when. On March 6, 1845, she wrote that "they spread fertilizer in Auntie's garden." Six weeks later, on April 19, she and her aunt Rosa sowed timothy, a grass for the animals to graze on. She, however, was not permitted to sow her seeds in the field, only in a small plot beside the summer house. Timothy was an important seed crop for the feeding of the cattle and horses, whether they ate it while it was growing in the pasture or later, as hay for feed during the winter. Feeding the family meant also learning how to feed the animals one would milk or later eat, or, in the case of horses, use for preparing the soil for planting, cultivating, and harvesting the crops, or as transportation.

In addition to sowing the fields, Linka also learned from her uncle how to start a hotbed and how to graft cuttings from one plant and set it into another. The short growing season in the north meant that they often needed to force some of the fruits and vegetables. They were not entirely on their own for this, however. Every year greenhouses in Bergen sent them a variety of seedlings and seeds to be planted in their garden.

When she came back to Majorstua in Christiania where her Grandmother Carlsen lived, she was skilled in the garden. Even her sickly grandmother had to join in preparing the meat for the table. She wrote her Aunt Rosa that they were "in the middle of slaughtering (a great slaughtering, not like the little affair you were going to have), as here we killed one tough old cow. For Christmas, we're going to slaughter a couple of pigs, too, I believe so then there will be a lot more to do."[63] In February 1847 she wrote Aunt Rosa to say that she would receive "early seed potatoes from Uncle Carl."[64] She told Aunt Rosa they did not need to set them (plant them) until later. Then she added a comment concerning the price of oats, that it was especially high at the time and still necessary to feed the horses, a typical concern of a farmer.

Since the mid-1700s, potatoes, brought from the New World, had become essential to the Norwegian diet, as they had in Ireland. Norway was also affected by the Irish potato blight that had contributed to Ireland's large emigration. It came to Norway from Ireland fairly quickly. Her grandmother had walked the potato fields in September 1847 to observe the harvest, which by all accounts had been good. The next year, however, in September, 1848, Linka wrote another letter to Rosa, saying that over half of the potatoes seemed diseased, something that worried her grandmother for good reason: They needed them to live.[65]

When Linka returned to Askevold again in 1850, she used the knowledge she had gained in the garden as she worked to keep the household fed. In April, she saw that the trees were budding, and realized it was time to grow greens for her soup. To do that she had to get the hotbeds ready. As she started the project with the help of two men, she regretted that she had not learned or remembered everything about the preparation of a hotbed that her aunt had tried to teach her some years before. Part of the work also involved properly instructing the servants, a new thing for the young girl.

> It has actually been quite amusing, commanding two men today, though what if it will not warm? Then I will be just as embarrassed as I was confident the first time I was here, when Auntie wanted to teach me to make a hotbed. I can recall very well how unwillingly I stood next to Auntie and watched how it was done. I do not understand what came over me then, for I usually like doing things outside a lot better than working in the house.[66]

Puberty Rites

In a letter to her uncle on December 19, 1846, Linka made the observation that the party she had just attended was what her grandmother called her "debut" party. It was her first "grown-up party, and, to use Grandmother's expression, I made my first entrance into the world."[67] Later, in a letter to her Aunt Rosa, Linka ridiculed the concept. "I care less about balls, and I would stay away with great, great delight if I were ever invited to such a party. People are so critical toward simple young ladies such as myself, that I am quite scared."[68] For these events, the young girl had to make clothes of many kinds of materials as taught by her aunts and grandmother. She had to have a good sense for patterns and the design of clothes. To be beautiful, to be well dressed in order to make a good impression was as important as having good manners.

By the time she had returned to Askevold to help her aunt and uncle in 1850, she had matured into a young woman of twenty whom the family could trust with many of the important tasks of the home. She enjoyed most of them and felt competent to do them. When her Aunt Rosa left them all alone, she remarked that she was

> again quite alone as commandant of the parsonage. I was not happy about it, but with God's help I was hopeful, and I comforted myself with the belief that everything would be all right.[69]

Now she had even more responsibilities as the teacher and governess of the children, her cousins.

Reading and Writing

Among the most basic skills a child needed was the ability to read and write. This was necessary for modern life, something women needed to know, despite Rousseau's advice to wait with it. Luther had recommended to the German nobility that both girls and boys learn how to read, so they could read the Bible and the Catechism. This is one reason the Northern European immigrants from Lutheran lands tended to be fairly well educated. Most of them could read write and do their sums when they emigrated.

The parsonage reading list, however, included more than the Bible and the Catechism. A well educated girl of the day needed to have read a number of classics from what we might call *belle lettres*. Linka read Sir Walter Scott's romantic historical novels, for example *Redgauntlet*, all the rage in Europe at the time. She also read edifying spiritual works such as Kierkegaard's *Works of Love*.

Reading novels was an evening or Sunday afternoon entertainment, along with playing music, singing, or drawing. In their letters and diaries the family is portrayed sitting together

Søren Kierkegaard

in the parlor, reading, writing, sewing, conversing, playing music, all together. Linka described this in her February 2, 1845 entry: "I spent the day partly reading *Redgauntlet*, partly eating stolen apples, partly playing the piano, and partly playing whist."[70]

Linka did not say whether or not the book had been translated into Norwegian. The chances are good that it was not, because young women her age often used the reading of novels to learn another language. This may have justified them as worthy reading materials, since the clergy, especially, looked askance at such materials, partly because of the romantic adventures of the heroines. In addition to English, Linka learned German and French. After her return in 1846 from Askevold to live with her father, who died shortly afterwards, she was once again residing with her Grandmother Carlsen. Her grandmother had grown up in Altona, in the Slesvig part of Denmark, and was as fluent in German as Danish. She insisted that they speak only German while they were embroidering. Linka explained,

> We are not to talk any language but German, but when Grandmother and all of us are in a good mood, we can speak easily. Rosa [Linka's sister Rosemette] is participating, of course but Hexa [Linka's sister Waleska] is the master of us all, as she is taking private lessons. I suppose I ought to be the most proficient, since I am now schoolmistress and am teaching both German and French, but I'm not. Grandmother wanted me to learn more languages but that is unacceptable; she could never afford such an expense.[71]

Linka also said that Hexa was instructing her in English. After she and Hermann had decided to go to America, she became more deliberate about her English, even finding a tutor, Fredrik Waldermar Hvoslef (1825-1906), to help her with the language.[72] Her study with Hvoslef intensified as the time for their departure neared. "All my thoughts have been occupied with America, Hermann, and [Pastor]Dietrichson."[73] Because she was alone, she was able to reflect fully on their coming adventure, writing that "Today I have not been disturbed in my reflections. . . . Hvoslef, my English teacher is in the city. I just remembered my lesson for tomorrow."[74]

Along with their reading the women of Linka's day kept diaries and wrote letters—very important genres in their parlor culture. The keeping of a diary became a popular way for a woman to reflect on her spiritual growth. To her diary she could confide her deepest spiritual anxieties and troubles, while also recording her daily life. Although the journal or autobiography had a long history in Christianity, ever since Augustine's *Confessions*, the practice was renewed by Lutheran pietists, especially through the work of Count Nikolai von Zinzendorf (1700-1760) at Herrnhut in Germany.[75] Under that influence Lutheran pietists had re-engaged with the notion of spiritual autobiographies. The keeping of diaries became something that women learned to do from such examples.

Mor Koren

Thus a diary was a familiar genre for the young Linka. If she did not know of the recommendations of Zinzendorf, she did know the journal of Mor Koren, Christiane Birgitte Koren (1764-1815), a pastor's wife (and Elisabeth Koren's grandmother). This journal of her trip, *Moer Koren's Dagbog*, to Copenhagen, just after the loss of Norway to Sweden, received praise for its vivid picture of travel by coach down the coast of Sweden, to Copenhagen.

Linka's diary is different from that of Mor Koren and her friend, Elisabeth Koren. Elisabeth's diary, like her many letters, contains telling details especially interesting to the historian. Linka's work is a spiritual work, a serious self-examination of her soul and her actions during the day. Linka does not seem to be writing to provide history with a record of her life. Her entries are more in the character of a letter to herself (or God) about what is going on in her life, both physically and spiritually. As she matures and goes through the various stages in the life of a woman, she turns her thoughts more and more to her spiritual condition. In those reflections she reveals the struggles of her life and faith.

Writing letters was also a kind of journal of the day's events. These were the only method of communication between distant family, friends and lovers. As she sat, of an evening, in the parlor, with others, talking, singing, reading, sewing, and also writing letters, she recorded the scene and how she was engaged with the entire family in the room.

The nineteenth century letter is one of the best windows we have into the mind of the average woman of the time. We can be thankful that Linka kept this diary and wrote and received (and saved!) letters. One of its best features was that it was also a semi-public act, since letters from one parlor were read aloud in another. The burden on the novice writer was to learn to make the reports interesting and literary, a skill

Linka mastered in her letters, diary, and sketches. It was also something of a school for women who wanted to become professional writers, like Jane Austen. Benjamin Franklin (1706-1790) suggested that letters were a way of improving composition skills. Catherine Beecher (1800-1878) who promoted the education of women in ladies' seminaries throughout America in the nineteenth century, also emphasized the importance of letter writing.

The Finer Things

Linka also recorded experiences of learning about the finer things in life, such as literature, the arts, conversation, languages, and edifying classics. All of these prepared her for her chosen vocation as a minister's wife. Shortly after Linka arrived in Askevold to help her aunt, she reported that their neighbor Johan Daniel Landmark, a theological student, came to the parsonage and told the girls that he had found a play for them to perform together. They did not like his selection and found another play, reportedly by Johann Ludvig Heiberg (1791-1860), *Power and Cunning* (*Makt og List*). Linka was given the part of a young man about twenty-four years old. Heiberg, one of the heroes of the Dano-Norwegians, was Denmark's greatest playwright at the time, although the play was considered scandalous and removed from the theater's repertoire.[76]

Linka's grandmother, Doris, loved the stage as did her grandfather, Carl Andreas Carlsen, a businessman and commissioner in the government. Both were prominent members of the Dramatic Society in Christiania (*Det Dramatiske Selskab*).[77] Carlsen was said to have done his business as something of an avocation and spent much time in the theater.[78] As the children prepared for the production, memorizing parts, building sets, and inventing costumes, they learned many explicit things as well as implicit things about life. Although it was pure fun for them, it provided an opportunity for these young people to use their imaginations. In addition to training their memories, they learned handiwork skills as set designers and seamstresses as well as acting and public

Carl Andreas Carlsen, Linka's grandfather

speaking. In playing the roles of the lives of others, they came to understand how people of every age felt, acted, and expressed themselves. The presentation of the play, a success according to Linka's account, attracted a very large audience, namely the judge and his wife, six little boys, and the attorney's wife and six children. In addition to these, there were some uninvited members of the audience standing outside the windows, but as they thought they did not see well enough from there, they tiptoed into the living room to see this beautiful and very well-performed play, ha, ha![79]

Theater was one of the many entertainments that occupied the youth in the family in an age without entertainment centers. Many novels or diaries about or by young women tell stories of such entertainments. It was not, however, the only kind of amusement these resourceful young people had. During the long evenings of the northern winter, they found escape in games, some more active, some more quiet, like cards or board games. While they played, the older people were reading, conversing, writing letters, doing fancy work, drawing, singing, and playing the piano for the entertainment of the entire group. Because they had to find a warm spot for cold winter evenings, they all tended to be in the warmest room in the home, usually the parlor.

Linka recorded the details of a party at their neighbors, the Landmarks, where there was music and singing, "Attorney Landmark on the

Moving in the piano to Linka's parlor: "Hermann, be careful, hold it steady." Farmer (in dialect): "That's for sure. She is heavy." Henriette: "Ack, du lieber Augustine." Rosina: "Gubban Noa. Gubban Noa!" Linka: "Don't scratch it, boys." Farmer: "It is hard to be careful; this is heavy!"

violin, the Doctor on the flute, and Minister—more accurately—Curate Friis on guitar."[80] When she returned from the party, she noted that she had now resumed her usual domestic activities: "cooking, reading, sewing, knitting, and in the twilight, either playing the piano myself or dancing to what Uncle Minister played."[81]

These times became dear to Linka. In a letter written to her uncle, Wilhelm Keyser, on New Year's Eve 1849, she recalled the delight of these times, especially when her father was still alive.

Rudolph Keyser,
Linka's uncle

> Do you recall when you, Uncle Rudolph Keyser, and Father came home from Messels, how we hurried to light the Christmas tree? And how you grownups seemed just as happy as we children? How you played the pianoforte and Father the flute, and all the rest of us chimed in with our voices, singing most lustily, with Uncle Rudolph and the Preuses in the lead?[82]

Memories of these evenings stayed with her for the rest of her life as she herself established such patterns for her own parlor in the new world.

Whether at concerts in the cities or in the parlors of the parsonage, these parsonage families loved music and wanted it in their homes. It was the art most practiced and beloved in the parsonage. Linka described these musical evenings showing how the musical tradition got passed on to succeeding generations. The entire family sat together in the long evenings, pursuing their various interests together, listening to music or performing it for the gathered household. Music was the one activity that drew them all together, a cherished tradition in the parsonage ever since Luther.

While it was common for the men to play the lute or guitar as they accompanied the singing of folk songs and hymns, the piano began to dominate in the nineteenth century, about the time that Linka was a teenager. It was becoming more common for the women to help lead the musical evenings because of their training on the piano. A young woman expecting to be a pastor's wife in this era was almost certainly skilled at the pianoforte. It was part of the portfolio of a desirable wife and mother. Not only was she usually trained to be an accomplished singer, but also a pianist ready to play duets with her sister or mother. Toward the end of the nineteenth century, she also played the organ for church services, as reed organs became popular for use in churches. Before, in the smaller rural churches, there had been only the cantor's voice to lead the service. However, women's command of the piano began displacing the male cantor (*klokke*r) in church, as well as the male lute and guitar players in the home. Although Linka remembered an evening when her uncle played the piano in the parlor, it was not as common as when the women in the family did.

As the century progressed these solos and duets ("four hands music") gave people in the farthest reaches of the country a chance to hear and learn the great music of the past and the latest rages of the day, not only the old chestnuts such as von Suppé's "Poet and the Peasant," or Sullivan's "The Lost Chord," but also entire operas by Wagner or Offenbach. These little concerts taught young people the art of leadership and gave them a sense of confidence performing before their family.

When the Preuses arrived in this country, the lack of pianos in the home and the distance to the concert hall were a major deprivation. The nearest concert hall was in Milwaukee, some distance from them in Madison. Linka recorded with great joy the first time the pastors and families met and a piano was available for them to play.[83] After the Preuses returned home from a long sojourn in Norway, on January 17, 1868, their neighbor, Pastor Jacob Aall Ottesen (1825-1904), wrote to Linka welcoming her home and announcing that Ole Bull, whom Linka had heard in Christiania twenty years before, was going to visit Koshkonong. She hoped that Bull would play for them there.

Drawing Life

Ladies of Linka's day learned how to draw sketches recording the life of the family. Drawing was a part of the curriculum for every young girl in Linka's class and time. They were taught genre painting—the recording of small dramatic moments in the life of the family. This resembled how cameras today record significant family events. However the drawings reveal far more about the character of the subjects than our cameras do. The young, both boys and girls, learned how to sketch these scenes of the family in much the same way that they learned to play the piano, do fine needle work, or master modern languages. They learned from their mothers and aunts, usually in the parlor as they sat around in the evenings.

One of Linka's earliest known sketches showing her in Askevold with her cousins, June 20, 1850: "On the parsonage lawn, the day of my departure." Linka is sitting in the middle of the children.

We can see from the beginning of *Linka's Diary* that she was especially dedicated to and proficient in this art. The first mention appears in her diary on March 5, 1845, when she reported that she had gotten good lead pencils in the mail from Bergen. On April 18, 1845, after sowing timothy, she worked on her drawing and reading and writing. What she was drawing we do not know. We can assume that she was looking closely at life around her and practicing the skill of getting it down on paper, both in her diary and sketchbook. In a later entry she reflected on how she learned to draw from her uncle Wilhelm Christie, whom she considered a master drawer, and her mother, who sketched only flowers. That did not appeal to Linka. Her father, though he seems to have had the gift of drawing and entertained the children with his sketches of horses, did not engage in the art as a hobby of any consequence. Linka concluded her reflections on her early years as a student of drawing with "I regard myself as the master of you all, as I draw both horses and flowers and all kinds of strange subjects—tremendously clear, am I not!" This uncharacteristic boasting reveals that she rightly thought it was her gift.[84]

Some months later, during her time at Askevold, she wrote about drawing scenes to entertain the children as she told them stories about wolves, which seemed to entrance them. Her eye for the physical details of her surroundings show her to be a keen observer of the human drama around her. In a letter to her Aunt Rosa, she painted a vivid picture in words of exactly what she was seeing from where she was sitting in her grandmother's home in Uranienborg.

> I can almost imagine sitting in my old room in your house, Auntie, as the ocean is right in front of me. Lately I have not had such a view. When working, I mostly look outside at the chestnut trees which are still standing immodestly bare; a boring sight. I'm gazing at the bay, a little broader than that at Askevold, and one big ship crosses the other. You have only fishing boats to watch. Now, for instance, *"Nordstjernen"* is here, enjoying herself for a little while. She will stay here in the bay until next week, cheering up my depressed and melancholic spirit. Puff! Puff!—A corvette repeats this eight times after a similar salutation from the passing steamer.[85]

While there is no record of her drawing this scene, it would not be surprising to learn that she had been sitting in this room, which she loved, hoping her grandmother would not have to rent it out to students to make some money, as her grandmother had few resources to support her grandchildren. She wanted it for herself, so that she could sketch such scenes as this. In this account her eye for detail and color is obvious.

Urianienborg in 1850

She most often sketched in the evening as she sat around with the family and friends in the parlor. While she was in charge of the house in Askevold, because her aunt and uncle had to go to Bergen for a funeral, she described herself sitting with her uncle's vicar, Friis, drawing caricatures, as she called them.[86] While a caricature is different from a genre painting, it does take skill with the pen and eye to produce a likeness that exaggerates an outstanding feature of the subject. She and the vicar learned from one another as they practiced their art, refining their skills together.

She often sent these drawings along to friends and family in letters, so they might share the life of the family far away. Her first such letter with a drawing in it was to Hermann, a letter she sent on February 26, 1850, during her second stay in Askevold. What the scene was, she did not say. This began a lifetime of sending drawings to friends and family to enable them so they could picture the events of her life.

While she was returning from Bergen to Christiania, she began drawing as a way to deal with her boredom. "Even though Auntie is with me, I am terribly bored on the steamer—I talk to nobody and mope and draw and read."[87] As she prepared to leave Norway for America, her pencil became more active. She sketched a design for their parsonage in Wisconsin to send to the congregation there, hoping that their home would be ready for them when they arrived—a vain hope indeed. She also sketched favorite places and people that she would want to remember. "I just came from Glende, where I sketched the little place, and said good-bye to the loving old wife of the pastor, Aunt Breder. She stood by the stone fence and waved."[88] Only two months before the young couple left Norway, she wrote that she had wanted to make contact with Anders Askevold, the son of the cantor in her uncle's church in Askevold. At the age of thirteen he had gone to Bergen to study painting. Later, Askevold became a well-regarded Norwegian painter.

In the New World Linka continued these sketches, and the pastors' families in the new settlements enjoyed them and sent them from one family to another. On December 15, 1869, Elizabeth Hovde, the wife of their new associate Brynjolf Hovde (1839-1930) in Spring Prairie wrote a letter to "Bedstemoder," Grandmother Linka. She sent greetings from her family to Linka's and commented that she was a "master sketcher," that a sketch Linka had sent had made the rounds in the family. "Could you make a copy?"[89] We have no idea what subjects she had sketched in this drawing, but her skills were obviously admired. Early the next year, Caroline Koren, Elisabeth's second daughter, wrote to Linka thanking her for her drawings, "They are wonderful!"[90]

Teaching at Home

Teaching the young—until the boys went off to their Latin school education, or girls married—was typically the responsibility of the wives or unmarried women in the family; sometimes a tutor was hired for the older children. Thus a wife had to be well educated in order to begin the education of her children. Linka, taught by her aunt and university students in the area, was preparing to take up her vocation as a teacher in the home. She had learned much of the basics through home schooling at her grandmother's house. In Askevold she began a more intentional study of religion. At first she studied with her uncle's vicar Friis who instructed her in religion and prepared her for confirmation.[91]

Linka took up the task of teaching the younger children, her cousins, rather quickly. On March 26, 1845, she noted that she "started reading the small letters with Doris [Christie, her cousin], though she showed very little interest in this. I guess she would rather have me tell stories about wolves, or let her play with Wilhelm, her younger brother."[92] It is a brief note, but it indicates the difficulties of teaching children in the family. She was surprised to discover that she had undermined her authority as a teacher through bedtime stories about wolves. Having to discipline the children to do what she asked them and work at learning required a different relationship. At first Linka did not understand this, but she was wise enough to record the problem.

There was also the temptation to play with her younger siblings or younger cousins during these hours. She struggled with this on several occasions. It is easy to imagine why women had continued the tradition of having their children, especially their pubescent daughters, taught by someone who was not their mother or sister, since it was difficult even for Linka, an older cousin, to maintain order because her authority was not quite accepted by the children. In a letter to her Aunt Rosa after her return to her Grandmother Carlsen's home in Uranienborg some months later, Linka described her difficulties with the system. While preparing for another aunt's birthday, Linka had the girls make birthday gifts: embroidering handkerchiefs, knitting a sofa pillow, even embroidering a cushion. She specified, however, that they were not to do so for more than an hour every day. During that time of handwork, by command of their grandmother, they were to speak only German. Now Linka was the teacher.

The parlor was much like a one room schoolhouse on the frontier where the older students taught the younger, and the younger learned what the older were learning. When her aunt left her in full charge once, she laughed at Linka's fear about being in complete charge, saying, "Oh, don't worry about that, it will just do you good, dear child!" Linka, however, did not feel that things went as they should. In addition to regretting her untimely slaughter of the veal calf, she expressed her frustration at the way she handled the routine of the day, especially the teaching.

> The housekeeping was not the only thing; I was also a teacher and had to look to my duties concerning the teaching. Unfortunately, though, our reading and so on weren't going too well. The lessons couldn't always be held at the set time, and that made everything a mess.[93]

The young woman was discovering the importance of routine in the management of both the household and the classroom. When routine broke down, confusion reigned— something all new parents and teachers come to understand rather soon.

When her aunt came home from an extended visit in Bergen, on May 18, 1850, Linka happily turned the household back to her, pleased she had also found it possible to churn two tubs of butter for her. Her Aunt Rosa, however, did not praise her overmuch, except to repeat what she had said when she left, that it was good for her to be alone and learn how to manage the household by herself. Linka had learned a great deal

The marketplace in Christiania in 1830. This is the way the city looked as Linka was growing up. The cathedral is in the background to the left.

more about management of the household and instruction of the children during this time. This served her well in Wisconsin when she was all alone running the household for weeks on end.

Confirmation and Preparation for Religious Leadership

Linka's religious education is also a matter of some interest because she was being trained to be a spiritual leader in the family and the parish in Wisconsin. Upon arriving in Askevold, as was the custom, she began confirmation instruction with her uncle, Pastor Johan Carl Christie:

> January 18th was the first day this year that I started studying with Uncle. I got up at 6 a. m. and looked over some homework I was to be examined on from 6:30 to 7:30 p. m. When this work was somewhat done, I went down to have breakfast.[94]

Very likely she was memorizing some version of the *Explanation to Martin Luther's Small Catechism* prepared by Erik Pontoppidan (1695-1764), the Danish bishop and professor. Together with Wilhelm Andreas Wexels (1797-1866), a popular preacher and scholar whose preaching and writings drew many young theological students to him, Linka's father revised it and shortened the catechism. They wanted to make it easier and less terrifying for young people, but their work was not appreciated by the country folk, especially, who thought it too liberal. Linka's uncle may have taught that version out of kindness to the confirmands in his charge.

Linka did not mention her catechization lessons again until shortly before she was to be confirmed.

> From now until the last day of September, I studied religion with Friis in the afternoons. Before Uncle went to the city, he had asked him to do that. I can't deny that I was a bit anxious before we started studying together, but after the first afternoon, all this anxiety had flown away, since I liked him very much—not very much, but at least a lot. I also liked it when we were not studying, because I was not alone.[95]

The next day her uncle Christie returned and reviewed the lessons with her.

> Uncle came home, feeling quite good after having been in rather poor health during his stay in the city. He studied with me once, and when we were done he said a couple of words to me regarding my forthcoming confirmation.[96]

This exhortation from the pastor to the confirmand was strongly recommended by Pontoppidan. The conversation concerned spiritual things, the state of the confirmand's soul, his or her thoughts and beliefs about the coming day when they would promise as adults to keep their baptismal vows. After their promise to renounce the world, the flesh, and the devil, and to follow in their baptismal covenant, they were welcomed to the Lord's Table. Linka was sixteen years old and, by the clock of that time, soon ready for marriage and a family. The rite marked an important time for her. She wore

> a very long skirt for the first time. I think I stepped on it four or five times until I made it to my place. Because I had told Uncle that I had problems standing still for a long time, I had a chair brought into the church, on which I could sit when the hymns were sung and when Uncle was with the confirmands further down.[97]

Because her uncle began by examining the boys at the end of the row, asking them any question he thought appropriate for each student, she would have had to stand a long time. The Askevold church book records that there were ninety-five students in her class. This was a momentous occasion. Without passing through this examination, one could not enter

Adolph Tiedemand's Catechization

into the common life of the state as an adult, not even marry. About the ceremony she reported very little. The church book records in her uncle's hand testimony that she was a lovable (*elskeligt*) young woman.

Confirmation also meant a family party for the young woman, celebrating her passage into adult life, at which she received presents from family and friends. These items seem to have been more interesting to Linka than the serious promises she made that day. She entered into her diary a list of the gifts she had received—handkerchiefs, necklaces, earrings, a necklace with a diamond clasp, and a little ring from her father, one her mother had worn at her confirmation. Most significant, although it was last on the list, was the hymnal she received from her uncle. She did not say which hymnal it was, but it most likely was the *Guldberg-Hoegh Hymnal* of 1788, considered to be the more orthodox of the hymnals of her day. Several days later, on October 24, 1845, she recorded her first communion, "I went to God's table for the first time in my life."[98] Once again, she wrote very little about the emotion of the day, other than to note that it was her first time.

Linka, steeped in things Lutheran, continued her growth in the faith. She did not, however, seem especially devout until after her engagement to Hermann Preus on February 26, 1849, when she realized that she was indeed going to be a pastor's wife as she had declared three years before. Her future father-in-law, Paul Arctander Preus, reminded her of this announcement in his letter of congratulation to her on March 26, 1849. In it he asked her whether she had been thinking of his son at the time she said that she was going to marry a minister.[99] He then blessed her, invoking also the blessings of those "yonder [Linka's parents] who with heavenly rejoicing look down upon the eternal ties of their loved ones still on earth."[100]

When Linka left Hermann in Christiania for a short time to return to Askevold to help her Aunt Rosa care for her new baby, she received a sober letter from Hermann. He encouraged her to go forward "toward the cross" and her Savior, who had the "crown" to give her. With his letter he also sent a Bible with the hope that "in the hour of sorrow may it bring balm to your spirit; in seasons of joy, attune your heart to thanksgiving and praise to Him who gave it."[101]

As Linka and Hermann awaited the call they had been expecting from the Spring Prairie congregation in DeForest, Wisconsin, her thoughts turned more and more to the guidance of God for their future of great hope and uncertainty. After a few days in Askevold, her uncle, who now understood the seriousness of the young couple's plans, took Linka for a two-hour walk during which they discussed the marriage. First, she reported, he wanted to ascertain "if my thoughts were based on reason or if I was just captivated by youthful ideas."[102] Linka assured him of how deeply she and Hermann had committed themselves to the call. To her joy, he did not discourage her from accepting it. When she retired to her room after the conversation, she recorded in her diary that with the "firm hope that God will help me, even if I do not make the best decision, I finally fell asleep."[103]

From this time forth, her diary recorded pious thoughts and prayers that deepened as she left her home for America, and then as she met the difficulties there. When her grandmother Carlsen found it difficult to commend their plans to leave for America, Linka expressed her concern and concluded her entry with a prayer of thanks for the wisdom of her uncle Wilhelm Keyser with whom Hermann had spoken at length.

On New Year's Eve 1849, she wrote a long letter to her Uncle Wilhelm, thanking him for his kindness in caring for her and Hermann. She realized that in the short time since her engagement she had "become a grown-up old person," and that her plans for the future were setting her on an "irrevocable" course for which she could only pray "God grant it may all work together for good."[104] Her prayer for the New Year, that she might do something "truly good," began her annual journey into her own troubled heart. She prayed that she might defeat self-love and pride to keep from thinking she had done anything good. At the same time she prayed for guidance from the Lord.

Trying Out the Role

From the first she delighted in her chosen profession. When she began her duties at Askevold, she enjoyed the fact that even during her first stay at Askevold, "several people think I am the minister's wife."[105] After her return to Askevold, at the request of her uncle, she had been "godmother for little Oluf—the parsonage's temporary inhabitant. God knows what the future of this child is going to be! My best wishes be with him, Auntie, Uncle, and Mons were the other godparents."[106] She took very seriously the duty of the pastor's wife of bearing a baby to the baptismal font. This happened frequently in the New Land. People were separated from family and friends by great distances and the pastor's wife would often take on this role.[107]

Just before her twenty-first birthday she confided in her diary that things were different for her now. No longer was life an "unmixed joy."

As she celebrated the day with her family, the young woman was increasingly aware of her impending departure for America. All the joys of the event were colored by that sadness. Over the next weeks she contemplated more and more their coming departure. Was it the last time she would see Aunt Rosa, who had functioned as her mother over the years since her own mother's death? "When I think about her leaving me in a few days, my heart beats with a sad melancholy whose presence in a motherless, orphaned creature only can be compared to separation from a motherly friend."[108] When Linka bade Aunt Rosa farewell, she took comfort in Hermann's understanding of her sadness, and also in the hope for an ultimate reunion in heaven. That was the solace that many immigrants clung to as they left for America. "Forgive me, my God! If we remain faithful we shall one day be gathered with Thee!"[109]

As the day neared for them to leave, and for Hermann's ordination and their wedding, she anticipated the vocation of the pastor's wife in reading Hermann's examination sermon, the sermon he had to give before his ordination. She noted that it had an "arresting thought" which ran through the sermon and had been carefully worked out. Then she modestly admitted that she was no judge of such a matter, but noted that she could "at least say what impression it made on me." A day later she recorded her nervousness as she entered the chapel where Hermann was about to give his sermon. Part of the vocation of the pastor's wife was to advise her husband on his preaching. "No wonder then, that my emotions were stirred in a new and different way."[110] Linka often wondered how much a pastor's wife should advise her husband on his sermons and ministerial work. Being a colleague (and critic) was part of the job description of the pastors' wife, but what was its proper measure?

The Call

Hermann received his call from America on January 1, 1851. He rejoiced that with it in hand

> I had become a minister; I had a congregation! What significance, what responsibility, in those words! A congregation of souls was turning to me in matters pertaining to their salvation; their spiritual welfare rested on my heart.

For Hermann, the old Lutheran notion that one could not become a pastor without a call was why the call made him a pastor. The young candidate now sought a bishop to ordain him.[111] They were both shocked when Bishop Jens Lauritz Arup (1793-1874) of Oslo at first refused to ordain Hermann, on the grounds that he would not be under the supervision of the Norwegian church in America. Later he relented, and Hermann was ordained on April 23, 1851.[112] This struggle caused Linka to wrestle with her own soul. Not only was she worried about Hermann's ordination, but also her wedding, which would occur only after he had been ordained. As these events were unfolding, she remembered that on September 24, 1850, she visited her parents' graves, with a prayer that God would bless her. She trusted that "God does all things well! Every night I dream of ministers and discussion—America always in the background, day and night! Now good night, everyone!"[113]

Bishop Jens Lauritz Arup

Through the year of struggle about the call and ordination, Linka confided more and more in her diary her spiritual distress at what was going on and her prayers for relief. On April 17, 1851, she recorded that because Hermann's ordination had finally been approved, they could begin planning for their wedding. In a letter Hermann told her that the banns for their marriage were already being read in the Halden church. On hearing the news, she resolved to be a good wife. With that "resolution" she was reminded of the writings of Kierkegaard, who had written in his *Works of Love* on the very issue of Resolution and "how to preserve one's soul in patience, and how a resolution springing from a 'preserved soul' shall be carried out through patience."[114]

On May 5, 1851, the young couple was married. Before the marriage, Linka wrote a long farewell to her maidenhood and childhood, and her Independence as a young single woman. In it she expressed the certitudes of her time about the marriage relationship and what would become her profession as well, even as she heard an inner voice that is not completely convinced.

> Tell me, my cousin Independence, will I enjoy you more as a wife than as a girl? "No, as a wife you'll just be a slave." Oh, now I do not dare to marry! "Oh yes, I believe you should, as you may not even notice your slavery as a wife. Rather, you will think of what a woman's mission is and your love and common sense will teach you to follow its voice. Then you will remember me, your cousin Independence, no more, which will do you good, as I really belong to the man.[115]

She concluded these reflections hopefully, "May Wifehood never suffer in comparison with Girlhood."[116]

As the wedding day approached, she was troubled in her conscience, wondering whether she was fit to be a wife. Hermann had reassured her on many occasions that she would do just fine. She finally resolved this with a girlish jest: "Once I even told Hermann. 'I have second thoughts about becoming your wife; I do not think I can become the wife I am expected to be.' Hermann then comforted me for a long time, so it is really his own fault if he gets a wife who cannot make him happy. Right?"[117]

She then returned to a description of the actual wedding. The compiler of the first Norwegian hymnal, Magnus Brostrup Landstad (1802-1880), the pastor in Halden, and now beginning his work as an editor of the hymnal, officiated at the ceremony. Linka spoke kindly of him, although it is curious that later in America, when the Norwegian Synod was compiling a hymnal, Preus opposed the Landstad hymnal, because it was not Danish enough and used Norwegian words they did not think appropriate in a hymnal.

Magnus Brostrup Landstad

Hand in Hand We Meet the New World

On May 15, 1851, Hermann and Linka left Halden by ferry. Linka lingered over the last sight of her sisters as they boarded the ferry.

> God be with you, sisters! were the last words in my heart. The whole family is dear to me, but my sisters were the last ones in my prayer for all of their well-being. God knows if old Uncle's eyes will ever see us here again.[118]

From Halden they crossed the Oslo Fjord for Moss, and finally Kragerø, a small city not far from Porsgrund, nestled between the sea and mountains. It was a major port for many of the Telemark immigrants, a frequent destination for many from the inland regions of southern Norway, either for work in the thriving little city or as a port along the way to other places around the globe.

At Kragerø they boarded their ship, the *Columbus*, on May 21, 1851. When they went to bed that evening, Linka realized it was their last night in Norway, perhaps the last time they would ever see it. Linka bade her

Columbus, *the ship the Preuses took to America*

brother and sisters farewell in prayer again: "May the Lord keep you under His protecting wings! Good-bye, may life be good to you. I know you will remember your Linka."

The next morning the ship departed, after a number of emigrants from Telemark boarded, awakening the Preuses with their noisy arrival. As the boat finally began to leave Norway, she prayed that God would guide and lead them, make her a good wife, and Hermann a great leader. "Hand in hand we walk out into the world! Be with us always; we will always need Your help—You, almighty Father. Hear my prayers for the sake of Jesus Christ!"[119]

They were on their way to America. Soon the world of the ship closed around them, and the young couple began to establish themselves in a new world without any family near them. Despite her misgivings about her own worthiness to be a pastors' wife, Linka was ready. She could manage the household well and she had learned the finer arts expected of a pastor's wife: the languages of the day, writing, drawing, fine handwork, and music. Her religious education had prepared her for the trials of the new life they would share. Finding resources in the faith was something they knew well from their families. Now they would need whatever they had learned, and more. They had been well prepared.

Building the Preus Parsonage

When the young couple finally arrived in Spring Prairie, on August 18, 1851, they had to set up housekeeping from scratch—from building their home to furnishing it. Although there were some pastors' wives around and certainly other women in the parish whom she could ask about various situations that arose, Linka was more or less on her own. Her most valuable help was a book by Hanna Olava Winsnes (1789-1872), a pastor's wife in Vang, in Hedemark, Norway, of whom Linka was aware and probably knew. Winsnes was a successful writer of novels under the pseudonym Hugo Schwartz. What made her famous was her *Textbook on the Various Branches of Housekeeping* (*Lærebog i de forskjellige Grene af Huusholdningen*) print-

Hannah Olava Winsnes

ed in 1845. It was the standard book of advice on domestic science for the women of her day. Linka, Elisabeth Koren, Diderikke, and many of their colleagues used it faithfully and corresponded with each other on how they had consulted the book and whether or not the advice was helpful.

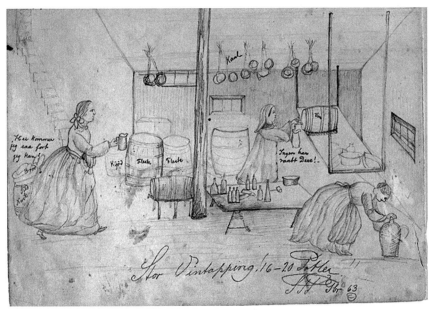

A big wine tapping! Sixteen to twenty jugs!! February 1863. K: I am coming as fast as I can! R: Yes mother, now Karine is coming. Can I come too? L: No one has called you. Norwegian herring, Bread, Meat, Pork, Cabbage, Wine.

Such books of advice had grown to be more and more necessary as people moved far away from their families to the frontier. Winsnes' book, a peculiarly effective and comforting book, gave the young wife a sense of confidence as she started out alone and far away. Hilde Diesen, in her biography of Winsnes, sees the book as being more than a book of advice. She strengthened the confidence of the reader by taking the reader into her thinking in an almost novelistic ways:

> When a calf that has never eaten anything but whole milk, is to be butchered, it must be given sweet milk, two or three hours before, and then one will find in its stomach something like white cheese; take it out and rinse it of straw and other impurities, wash the stomach and lay the cheese in it again, mixed with salt, and sew the stomach together and hang it in a warm place for it to dry. Such small bags are called Løbe; they are best when they are one to two years old.[120]

The writing is compelling and comforting. It helped women far away from their mothers and aunts learn how to do many things they needed to know on the frontier. Both Linka and Elisabeth Koren, who was related to Mrs. Winsnes, referred to her book frequently as they needed to know how to brew beer, vint wine, slaughter animals, make cheese, and deal with the many different situations that came up in their daily work of establishing a home and farm. It is difficult to imagine how primitive the situation appeared to this young couple when the parsonage land came into view that mid-August day in 1851.

Parsonage in Tvedt today

Upon arrival in Wisconsin the Preuses discovered the situation to be much worse than they, especially Linka, had expected. She had sent ahead a drawing of what she wanted the house to look like, but it seemed to no avail. "The unfinished parsonage was a depressing sight. Perhaps a tear hid my house-to-be from me, from seeing it the way it will look when it is done, with a nice interior, something in the future."[121] Even by September 7, 1851, she wrote "The parsonage is still nothing but a basement filled with water."[122]

Meanwhile, they were living at the home of the closest neighbor, Lars Møen, where Linka made do, describing their twelve-by-twelve room as best she could. It had one large bed, a sofa, tables, two chests of drawers, two easy chairs, and bookshelves on the walls, with other shelves for the tools. Their room, however, had no heat; the only warmth came from a stove on the other side of the house. As the temperature sank in November, she wrote mostly about the cold. She recalled how her father and mother would get them running back and forth in order to survive the cold in the parsonage back in Tvedt. This memory suggests that the difference between the Old Country and the New Land probably was not all that great. Life was primitive on both sides of the ocean. This made it easier for the young couple to manage in their straitened circumstances, while waiting for their own home to be finished. It would be another three months before the parsonage was finished, something about which she did not complain. She looked forward to its completion with the optimism of youth. She had lots of time alone to wonder about her role as wife and especially pastor's wife, while Hermann was away visiting and establishing new congregations in the area.

Women's Rights

When Linka left Norway, women's rights was not yet an issue at the fore of the society. As she thought about her role as a woman and now as a wife, with a fine education, alone on the prairie, she reflected on what exactly the vocation of a woman was. She did express a complaint that women needed very little formal education to do the work they were expected to do in the home. She was grateful for her education, but wondered what it was for. The idea that she should be an adornment to her husband struck her as useless.

When I feel that nature has been just as generous toward us, why should we not be allowed to develop our abilities without limitations? Nature did not give them to us only so that we could use them to salt the food and mend socks.[123]

It raised the question for her, What does a housewife need? She concluded that

her piety must be the foundation of her entire housekeeping. In that case, it can only be good, and her role has been filled; her consciousness bears witness to that, and with a light, humble heart, her spirit, soul and heart thank the Lord because He is "with her all days."[124]

But of what use is an education to do that, she continued. She was now thinking of her own education and its worth.

More than once I've been grateful that my parents let me go to school, where I learned quite a bit besides my religion. I can't claim to be such an honorable woman that I don't care about other books as long as I have my Bible. I'm afraid it happens quite often that I pick up the novel instead of the Bible, and leave the latter on the table in front of me. I'm so old fashioned that I have Walter Scott and Ingemann as friends, and they seem like decent people to me.[125]

"Mamas and Aunties evening enjoyments after the children are in bed. Playing the salmodikon."

As she continued, she described her education: languages, literature, history, geography, music, and sketching, all of which she needed to know as a member of her class in Norway. Now, sitting in her simple room in Wisconsin, she wondered how she could use any of what she had learned. At that time, the domestic chores of cleaning and cooking were minimal. Though she ironed Hermann's shirts, which she conceded was an unpleasant job, she still had a lot of time for her own pleasures: reading, sketching and embroidery, rather than sewing or darning.

The farm wives, she correctly observed, would not approve if they found her reading a novel rather than darning socks. Thus she had learned to pick up her sewing, even without a needle, when she heard footsteps coming toward her room.[126] Even this early in her career as a pastor's wife, she knew that she needed to make a good impression on the people. She understood full well that they would comment on her life style no matter what she did, so she made an accommodation to their expectations, with only a bit of grumbling. She would keep a bit of darning in her apron pocket so that she could grab it in case a guest would wonder why she was reading or doing fine work instead of something necessary.

Even though her chores were much reduced while they lived in this room, she did have Agnes, the cow, whose scant milk she churned into butter with "a paddle she whittled herself."[127] In addition to this chore, she helped their old friend and boarder, Ziølner, make sacks into which he could put the rye he was going to buy in Madison for making flour. By December 13 Linka had acquired two cows, three hogs, one calf, and a dog. Her conscience, or Hermann, may have urged her to be more "circumspect" in her acquisitions so as not to arouse resentment from the congregation. For they also had a young maid and a confirmand who was living with them and helping out while Linka taught him the catechism. Pastors' wives provided such instruction quite frequently. With these helpers, she noted in her diary, she had time for sketching, reading, and writing.

> When I am done with my duties, drawing is my reward. What about reading and writing? Reading is necessary, and writing, for example in this book, I also believe to be useful, as I get to know myself a lot better. I strive not to lie to myself— yes, I strive not to, but can I trust myself not to make this error? I'm afraid not—that dark selfishness, the one it seems like I can never suppress—oh God, forgive! Forgive!—is in my way here too.[128]

Not long after they arrived, "Kalla" (Johan Carl Keyser), Linka's only brother, wrote a teasing letter to Hermann inquiring as to how good Linka was as a cook. "Does she give me honor," Kalla asked, thinking of them in Spring Prairie, suggesting that she should slaughter a pig so that Preus would fatten up.[129] The letter must have amused them, although one wonders whether the questions caused Linka to reflect on what use her education was in the American parsonage.

Linka knew, however, that if she had to do all the work that the maid was doing,

> I would rather do without that [kitchen equipment] than without a maid—the only reason for me not to keep a maid would be to be able to pay back our debt sooner, but I'm not about to ruin my good health to do so. Keeping her doesn't make me feel guilty in any way, and neither does she contribute to any greater debt.[130]

The need for a maid came with her self-understanding of her role as mistress of the parsonage. Managing a maid was one of the responsibilities of the pastor's wife. It was part of her vocation, to have a maid and learn how to use her to the best of her ability.

Linka continued to be a reader, especially of American magazines and novels, in order to understand the New World better. Two years later, on April 6, 1853, the Preuses received a letter from the publisher Knud Fleisher, the publisher in LaCrosse, thanking them for their kind hospitality, especially Linka's. He added that "I am sorry I can't send you *Uncle Tom's Cabin*, maybe someday I can hand it over to you."[131] Linka was an avid reader and quite aware of the current American scene. The book had been published only the year before, in 1852.

The issue of slavery plagued the Preuses and the Norwegian Synod for many years. For Hermann and the others the question was whether or not the Bible said slavery was a sin, not whether slavery was wrong or a moral evil. If the Bible did not say it was a sin, they could not say it was a sin. This way of reading the Bible later generations would call biblicism.

That Linka reflected on whether it was a waste of time for women to read novels shows her to be aware of her new situation in America, where they lived much more closely with their people than they might have in Norway. She recognized the privations of the farmers as well as her own. While the Preuses could afford these helpers, just barely, she had seen from her close proximity to the farmers that her situation was viewed by them as privileged and often resented. She understood these judgments, but she knew her work was different from that of the ordinary farmer, even though she also had to run the parsonage farm.

She did berate herself some about this, but she was also able to bear the contradictions with good humor and a hearty appreciation for the work and her own interests. This was in sharp contrast to Engel Marie Johansdatter Brun Preus (1831-1860), the wife of Hermann's cousin, Adolph Carl Preus, who was unable to adapt. This may have been because of her poor health and her sense that she was in the wrong place, far away from home. Linka demonstrated unusual flexibility in adapting to the new situation. A number of other Norwegian pastors did not

Adolph Carl Preus

flourish and returned to Norway. Engel Bruun Preus died young in Wisconsin, in 1860.

Parsonage Completed

In the middle of January the young couple finally moved into their new parsonage, a primitive log cabin. Linka noted in her diary that it took "two huge oxen" to move all their stuff. When it was all placed around the new cabin, Linka worried that she took too much satisfaction in all

"Our parsonage from 1852-1856."

their possessions. "It will be fun, taking care of my own house," she concluded, before they retired for the evening.[132] While Linka did not openly express her dissatisfaction with the progress in the building of the parsonage, one wonders whether the members of the Spring Prairie congregation, long used to imperious pastors in Norway with certain legal powers over them, took a little satisfaction in delaying the completion of the parsonage. Neither Linka nor Hermann, however, complained much. Instead they expressed great joy when they finally came into their new home.

Almost immediately, she observed the difference between Norway and America. When Hermann had to leave for a Synod meeting and she was left alone with her thoughts, she made more entries in her diary. In addition to her prayers and spiritual self-examination, she thought about Hermann's role as pastor and her own role as pastor's wife in the New Land. She commented wryly that, even though Hermann and the other pastors were barely thirty, they had become so serious that their dignity made them seem like much older men.

"Hermann walking."

She had observed that the farmers were quick to agree with the pastors, not because they could not think for themselves, but because they trusted their leadership. They no longer called him "father" (*han fa'r*) she said, for the Norwegian immigrant "finds himself too clever to talk so simply and beautifully. Now it is only: Pastor, Minister, or Preus."[133]

Since Hermann was away from home often, Linka assumed the spiritual direction of the household, a role Luther had suggested for the head of the household. There was no church when Hermann was gone. She called the maid, Margit, her firstborn, Christian, and the confirmand—usually a neighbor boy who stayed with the pastor to study his catechism with the pastor's wife and help her with the chores—together for devotions. "I read them a sermon and sang for them. I am still not used to being a lecturer and lead singer." She was uneasy about her assumption of this office when she found it difficult to concentrate on the content while reading out loud to others and leading the singing. She concluded, "I want, every evening and Sunday morning when H. is away, to read God's word with the people working for me, as long as I am not ill or anything."[134] This understanding of the importance of continuing the worship of God on Sunday, while there was no preacher, was widely practiced in pious homes in Norway and throughout the settlements in America. Her son, Christian Keyser, remembered this practice fondly in a speech he gave to Symra, the literary society for men in Decorah, on growing up in the Spring Prairie parsonage.[135]

During her first winter Linka described making butter and cheese— for the first time she made the much maligned *gammelost*, or old cheese, and *primost*, a kind of whey cheese, brown and spreadable. She tried a new recipe for the *gammelost* "old cheese" in fourteen days, "when it's rotten" in that time, which she doubted was possible. In this, she was going against the advice of Mrs. Hanna Winsnes, Mrs. Winsnes advised that, to be good, old cheese should be forgotten for some time (*en Spand*). In her second recipe she said it should be aged for "at least one year."[136]

Winsnes' book includes many tips on how to keep and preserve milk by keeping it cool, how to make butter and cheeses of all sorts, how to slaughter animals and preserve them, and how to preserve vegetables. In her next entry, on March 28, 1852, Linka rejoiced that she had now received wooden milk bowls carved from cedar, for which she was thankful. In her chapter on how to care for milk, Mrs. Winsnes recommends that wooden bowls for milk could be made of either oak or birch or any hard wood that would not give the milk a strange taste.

Linka and Hermann visited with two other clergy families in their immediate vicinity on July 5, 1852—the Adolph C. Preus and Gustav F. Dietrichson families in Rock Prairie. From the diary entry we can infer that she was now five months pregnant. This may explain her fainting during the Easter church service, which she reported without giving a reason. (Women at that time would rarely discuss such matters publicly—or in mixed company.) The families stayed in a hotel in Janesville, where they were thrilled to find a piano. Mrs. Dietrichson played the piano while the others sang, a treat that they cherished, as none of them had had access to a piano since they had left Norway. For the next few years they saved money to buy one as soon as they could. Linka missed the piano more than almost anything else from Norway.

By the end of their first full summer, she had discovered that the soil was so rich that the seeds would lead to a good harvest. On August 28, 1852, she recorded that they had broken about two acres of land for their garden. They had planted pumpkins and watermelon, which she

"Here is our dear Spring Prairie, June 1, 1859. Papa, C.K., and Sina are going to work in the garden. I am working up by the fence in the hotbeds. From 1856-1861 our house looked like this."

observed grew much larger than back home. However they were not as tasty—a remark that reflected her particular loneliness for Norway. The soil, however, was so productive that it was much better for the growing of food than back in "delightful" Norway. It was so productive that they had to fence in part of the land to keep the pigs out. She enjoyed describing the comedy of keeping the pigs out of the garden and away from the dogs, not the least the occasional forays of Hermann and Ziølner who wearied of the game and called the fiercest dog to chase the pigs away. Linka, in this drawing, shows the flourishing farm that she has begun to manage through a summer. That included finding a way to preserve much of this bounty for the hard winter that she knew was coming, along with a new mouth to feed.

Just before Christian was born on October 13, 1852, Linka entered into her diary a long confession and prayer that seems especially dark for a young inexperienced woman who was quite devout. Contemporary readers miss that this is the practice of women before childbirth in the nineteenth century. The diaries of women from this time, and their letters, contain agonizing confessions as they prepare to meet their death in childbed. Claiming the promises of God which she knew from Scripture and hymns, she resolved to meet death calmly. With the old Lutheran hymn, which moderns cannot sing for its morbidity, "Who knows how near I am to dying?" (*Wer Weiss, wie nahe mir mein Ende*") she considered whether or not she could actually face the Angel of Death calmly and be prepared for it.

> Oh yes, I sincerely ask you my God, whatever time and place you call on me, let me be prepared to stand before You. Let me not be like the five virgins who had no oil left for their lamps when the bridegroom came! Let me love everything You have given me here on earth, but nothing, nothing like I love You—once more—"the spirit is willing but the flesh is weak."[137]

Birth of Christian

The birth of Christian Keyser Preus, Linka's first son, was uneventful. Her only problem was that she was now completely occupied with the new baby, and the house work was not going to get done. Apparently her maid, Margit, had found other employment, as Mrs. Dietrichsen had warned she would. Christian's first year passed quickly, it appears from Linka's diary, which understandably contains fewer and fewer entries.

She continued sketching, as time permitted, especially after she found a new maid who was company for her. Hermann was gone on longer and longer expeditions into the prairies and woodlands in Wisconsin, Minnesota, and Iowa. He established new congregations and scouted out new missions, while serving the needs of those he met along the way.

During this time, Linka's diary entries became more and more spiritual. They reveal her struggles with her sin, rebuking herself for her faults. While these comments make moderns queasy about her lack of self-esteem, she did not see it that way. These were her sins. She confessed them, and trusted in the mercies of God to forgive them so she could get on with her life. These insights also made her a valuable teacher of the faith in the home where she was alone, now much of the time, keeping the farm going, and seeing that they had enough food for the long winter.

The Parsonage Furnishings

On December 10, 1853, Linka recorded her anxiety about the imminent arrival of Pastor Ulrik Vilhelm Koren and his wife Elisabeth Hysing, another young married couple soon to become good friends. Linka had prepared chicken fricassee and was distressed by the Koren's tardy arrival. As she awaited them, she thought about how much the condition of her house had improved over the past year. Now she had a set of china, a serving tray, six chairs, chests, a table cloth, a tray which cost the forbidding sum of one and a half dollars, plus a set of twelve dinner plates and soup bowls. Most important of all, however, was that they now had a guest room added onto the kitchen, so that the bed could be taken out of the kitchen. This made it easier for them to receive guests, she observed, as she recalled hosting the recent meeting of the church council. Then the men all had to sit in the living room, while she and Engel Bruun Preus, who had been a guest with her for three months, had to make do in the study.

After the Korens' visit, the winter cold began to blast away at their small house. They moved into the study because the parsonage walls had not yet been plastered. There were gaps between the logs where the cold blew in, so much so that the stove could not keep the room warm. Linka spun wool to keep her feet warm by moving the treadle, but the effort was unsuccessful. Finally Hermann secured a buffalo robe and sheepskin. He put the robe on the floor for little Christian to play on and the sheepskin on the easy chair for him to sit on while he read and smoked his pipe, sheltered from the cold. On one wall they hung a quilt to keep out the wind, and over the door her heavy winter coat. They could put nothing they valued on the wall, for, when the wind came in through the logs during the rain, it ruined whatever was there. In addition the gaps between the logs were excellent hiding places for all kinds of vermin, especially bed bugs. Understandably they eagerly awaited new chinking and plaster for the house that next summer.

Linka described the design of the house in her diary, especially the bedroom, where the bed took up most of the room, plus the cradle and two chairs. At the foot of the bed, they had a small table; on the wall her bookshelf; on the window wall a shelf where she kept her drawing and painting supplies. Finally, on the wall partition, they had hung a portrait of Governor Christie, her Aunt Rosa's brother-in-law, a small sketch of Askevold, a hanger for their watches, a knit catchall for her key and scissors, as well as a ball of yarn.

While the New World was different, it shared some features with the old that made it possible for the young couple to adapt easily. A common challenge was how to deal with cold winters and how to build their homes to survive the long winter season. They built the parsonage according to their tradition. The house had a window facing south, and the study window faced east. The kitchen was placed along the north wall, the standard practice in cold climates, so the stove could warm the coldest room first. The west wall separating the kitchen and living room had a door and was a place where they hung pictures or etchings and a small mirror, one of her purchases in Wisconsin. The furnishings of the living room included a homemade sofa of aspen poles with cushions from her home in Norway and a towering bookshelf "containing a large number of handsomely bound books, slightly musty from the voyage across the Atlantic."[138] They had to keep their bookcases away from the wall, to keep the books dry in rainstorms. One can see in their plan for the parsonage how it was designed for a bitterly cold climate.

Maria Dahl Fleischer, in a memoir about growing up in the Hobøl parsonage in Norway, where a Preus family had lived a century before, noted that the kitchen was usually in the northern room in the house. It was the warmest room because of the stove, as well as being on the dark side of the home. Linka described the situation without much complaint about their privations. While this house was certainly primitive, so were the homes in Norway, and all of their parishioners lived in similar dwellings. One marvels that they got through their first winter, before the house could be plastered and the gaps between the logs filled, providing insulation to keep it somewhat warmer during the difficult winters. Linka expressed no feeling that she should have had it better, though she had

The Summer Kitchen. It was traditional to have a place outside for the stove so that the heat inside the house would not be unbearable. It was also a time to clean the pipes of creosote, something that was necessary to prevent chimney fires.

occasionally daydreamed of returning to Norway to see the good life they were having. Her longing for Norway faded as they got more settled and time went on.

In the summer of 1854, as she prepared for the birth of her second child, Rosina, Linka noted the work that was being done on the house. At last the congregation engaged a professional to plaster the bedroom and set mortar of lime and sand between the timbers. This would make the house much more comfortable during the next winter.

Because of Hermann's frequent and long absences, her responsibilities for the farm and home increased: She had to care for the domestic animals as well as till the garden and manage the farm. Linka had read good advice in Mrs. Winsnes' book on how to tend domestic animals, what to do for their various illnesses, how to prepare them for slaughter, how long it took to hatch various eggs, what to feed the chickens so they produced lots of eggs, etc.

In November 1855, Linka expressed regret over neglect of the diary. With two children and increased responsibilities on the farm, she pleaded weariness. She noted that she had to do much of the outside work because of Hermann's more frequent absences. In addition, she was without a nursemaid, although she had an older maid whose health was not good. This meant that she had to carry the baby with her, with Christian clinging to her skirts as she worked around the house. Her list of responsibilities were many:

> I've been both nursemaid and cook. I find that pretty tough, especially when you add that Hermann has been away more than at home, which means that I have had to watch the farm, too, with boys and workers—horses, cattle and pigs, sheep, and hens. No wonder I haven't had the time to write.[139]

Although she had some help, it was not enough. In August, during the wheat harvest and the haying, her maids preferred working for half a dollar a day in the fields; they were paid a pittance for the washing of kettles. However, they did do the milking in the morning and evening to pay for their board at the parsonage. In addition to keeping the house, she had to cultivate the garden. This was too much for the girls to do.

Linka had a very clear idea of how the garden was to be kept, for vegetables and fruit trees as well as flowers. Her grandson, in an afterward to her diary, tells how carefully the young couple planned the parsonage yard for both food and beauty. The parsonage was set in an oak savan-

Linka with neighbor ladies and her children giving the new baby, J. W. Preus, a bath. "Anga sees the possibility to take the tub away so that Doctor shrieks so that Mama cannot bathe him."

nah. To this the Preuses added various fruit trees and other popular trees, such as evergreens, maples, elms, birches, silver poplars, and ash. The garden, in the shape of a horseshoe, included a variety of flowers: pansies and mignonettes, lilies of the valley, narcissus, grape hyacinth, roses, peonies, and dahlias.

The parsonage gardens at home in Norway were examples of how to create such a landscape. Many of the Norwegian pastors followed the work of the botanist Carl Linneaus (1707-1778) in Sweden and began to cultivate gardens in certain traditional shapes. Linka's ancestor in the Hobøl parsonage had planned a garden in what was known as the French style, a rectangular pattern with its long side running west to east. Succeeding pastors continued that form and created a very large park-like garden with many flowers: fushia, asters, phlox, and lobelia. In the middle of the garden was a hotbed for rice, corn, hemp, and tobacco. Around that was an *allé* with climbing roses, jasmine, snowballs, and lilacs. Linka put into practice in the New Land what she had observed in the old.

Linka quickly learned that despite many similarities between the old and new world in climate and farming, there was a sharp difference in what she could expect from the help. Nothing shows that as well as her drawing of Henriette Neuberg cleaning the intestines of an animal they had just slaughtered. The drawing plays off the instructions of Mrs. Winsnes, who assumes the reader would have several servants on the farm to help her. Both Linka and Mrs. Koren made fun of Winsnes' instructions, because they assumed so much more help than they had on the prairie. Once Mrs. Koren told Linka about her attempt at salting down some beef. Her assistant, a young man who had never done it before, needed help himself as did the girl who was not very gifted at salting. Thus "mother" was in

> constant activity supplying a little more than I was used to when I did it the first time. But now I have the great joy to see the long links of sausage being smoked, and the shanty full of meat hanging on all of the walls. You also have made sausage together with your three girls and had so much to do that you haven't written to me for a long time.[140]

This reference to the "three girls" is most surely a sly reference to the advice of Mrs. Winsnes on how to manage the slaughter of animals on the farm. They must have laughed about this frequently when together. Mrs. Koren may have seen the sketch Linka had drawn of herself and Henriette as they were cleaning the intestines for sausage some years before, on October 1, 1862. With it Linka poked fun at her own situation. Under the picture, she wrote "In this slaughter, the wife and governess must themselves clean the intestines."

This obviously refers to what Mrs. Winsnes' suggestions for slaughter, especially the need for three girls to help. Both Linka and Elisabeth must have commented about this many times. The advice assumed a household full of servants and work enough to keep them busy. Before the slaughter, Mrs. Winsnes advised, one must be sure to have enough wooden vessels that are mended and tight, and to have stocked up on lime and other chemicals in order to make the work easier. "On the first day," she wrote, "you will need at least two girls simply to wash the intestines and stomach, and if you can find a third girl, that would be even better."[141] She then gave instruction on when to slaughter an animal: in the afternoon so they can clean the intestines by daylight on the next day. Of most importance, of course, was to make sure the intestines got very clean. One needed to rinse them several times in many different waters, and in the last rinse one should add some celery and leek leaves to draw off the smell.

Cleaning the intestines

In this sketch the wife and the governess must themselves clean the intestines. She has a good supply of buckets and she is holding the dull knife Mrs. Winsnes suggests. The spoon that is to be there is on the floor by Henriette. The young man entering the door on the right background may be one of the confirmands that stayed with the Preuses for instruction while helping the minister's family with their work. Mrs. Winsnes suggested that there be at least two boys to hang and cut the meat. But the boy's work was to be separate from the work of the women. That may be why in this sketch, he seems to feel that he has intruded. One can almost hear him say, "Oops!" and back quickly out of the door. It was difficult work, work women supervised in Norwegian parsonages. On the frontier, they had to do it themselves.

A sign of Linka's good humor is the way she makes fun of herself and Mrs. Winsnes at the same time, adapting to the frontier with grace. What mattered most to Linka's education as a pastor's wife on the frontier was the training she had received from her aunt. She learned how to manage the farm and household, with some help from Mrs. Winsnes. It stood her in good stead. Her education in the finer things, while an important part of her life, was not as crucial to their existence. Her aunt, however, wanted to be sure that her charges knew both the practical skills and the finer things. It was part of her vocation to make certain that they knew both. As the world became more and more modern, the education in the finer things became more important and the domestic skills less so.

CHAPTER FOUR

Outside Contemporary Influences on the Education of Women

When she [a woman] seeks to develop her intellect it is viewed as a sort of secondary matter, something useless that could never serve the world in any way—when these thoughts come to mind I often get bitter because I find it unfair.[142]

—Linka Preus

When Linka was growing up, the debate about Norwegian education and the education of girls was very lively. Because of her family's position in the leadership class, she observed much of that debate swirling around her. In the late 1830s and 1840s, several Norwegian pastors chose to send their daughters to the Moravian school in Christiansfeld, Denmark, which had become a well-regarded finishing school for girls from Norway. Although there were a few schools for girls in Norway, such as Jomfru Pharo's girls' school in Christiania, they did not have the solid reputation of Christiansfeld's school, which had begun in 1784 and continued until 1891. Its residential plan intensified the educational program

Christiansfeld Square

as the young girls lived and studied together in a community of students. By the 1850s, its dedication to teaching girls to be well-mannered ladies was so well established that young girls in Scandinavia were said to whisper to each other on meeting an unruly girl, "She is so ill-mannered her father is thinking of sending her to Christiansfeld."[143]

The school and its philosophy of education made it attractive to pastors looking to give their daughters what we might call today a junior college education. Among the first Scandinavian residential schools for girls, it had a powerful impact on the Luther College tradition. Its story needs to be told briefly, as it provides more context for what the pastors and their wives did to educate their daughters in America. Two of Luther College's most important founding mothers —Diderikke Brandt neé Ottesen (1827-1885) and her double cousin Christiane Hjort neé Ottesen (1833-1873)—attended the school in the late 1830s and 1840s.

Christiansfeld

The Moravians were granted a charter to establish Christiansfeld by the Danish king, Christian VII (1740-1808), in 1771. In this he followed

Johann Struensee

the advice of his doctor, Privy Cabinet Minister Johann Friedrich Struensee (1737-1772), the son of a Lutheran pietist theologian and minister serving in Altona, Slesvig, part of Denmark at the time. Struensee, brought to the court to treat the king's mental illness—probably schizophrenia—found a way to deal with the king and calm his rages. He gradually accumulated more and more power as the king, growing increasingly unstable and unequal to his office, ceded his authority to him.

Struensee essentially appointed himself Privy Cabinet Minister and ruled Denmark as dictator briefly, from 1770-1772, doing much to change Denmark. Struensee was a man of the Enlightenment. As regent he introduced many Enlightenment principles into practice in the kingdom of Denmark. He abolished torture, the Danish slave trade, and censorship of the press—all good things but perhaps done too quickly. His greatest mistake was that he fell in love with Christian's Queen Caroline Matilde (1751-1775), the sister of George III of England, and fathered a daughter by her. He was brutally executed for the crime of *lése majesté*.

Before Struensee's fall from power, Christian VII authorized the Moravians, whose spiritual leader had been Count Nicolai von Zinzendorf (1700-1760), to found Christiansfeld. In 1773 the community established its colony on the flat plains of southern Jutland, not far from Kolding, surrounded by rich farmland. In architecture and design it was almost an exact replica of Herrnhut, the motherhouse of Moravians, in southeastern Germany.

Count Zinzendorf, whose grandmother, Henrietta Catharina, Baroness Von Gersdorff (1648-1726), had been a biblical scholar with a command of Hebrew, Greek, and Latin, along with his mother, also a scholar, had favored the educational and spiritual development of women. Zinzendorf, a member of the European nobility and a radical pietist, spoke of the Holy Spirit as Mother and stressed the motherly aspects of God. This appealed to women, such as the Swedish hymn writer Lina Sandell (1832-1903), who found the emphasis an inspiration for some of her hymns.[144]

Count Zinzendorf

Zinzendorf's stress on the arts over dogma attracted women to his movement as it expanded from Saxony to the larger world. Among Moravian signature beliefs was the notion that men and women should write spiritual autobiographies in which they practiced self-examination, evaluating their spiritual progress. (Søren Kierkegaard grew up in a home influenced by Moravians and certainly knew of the practice when he wrote his *On Self-Examination* [*Til Selvprøvelse*] in 1851, one of his most popular books during his lifetime.)

Zinzendorf urged his followers at Herrnhut into a kind of communal living that separated the sexes from each other into choirs. Unmarried women lived together as did unmarried men. Adolescent girls and boys also lived separately as did widows. Even their graveyards, God's acres, were not arranged by families, but by sex, with the men buried on the one side and women on the other. Families, however, did live together on the estate. This mild form of communitarian living continued until the later eighteenth century.

For Moravians education for both men and women was important. The education of women was at least as significant as it was for men because women were the educators in the home. Women could be leaders in the community. For example, Zinzendorf's wife, Erdmuthe Dorothea, Countess of Zinzendorf, neé Countess of Reuss-Ebers-

dorf (1700-1756), took over Herrnhut while her husband was away on an extended exile. His daughter, Henrietta Benigna Justine Zinzendorf von Watteville (1725-1789), founded in 1742 the first boarding school for the education of girls in America, the Bethlehem Female Seminary of Bethlehem, Pennsylvania. The school was highly enough regarded that George Washington wanted his niece to attend it. This early emphasis on the education of women came with the motto: if you educate a woman, you educate a family.[145]

Benigna Zinzendorf

Moravianism in Scandinavia

Moravianism arrived in Scandinavia in the 1730s when Zinzendorf came to Denmark and interested the pious King Christian VI in sending missionaries to Greenland and the Danish Caribbean Islands, such as St. Croix. His religion of the heart won for him ecumenical friends among his many relatives in royal houses throughout Europe, from Catholics to radical pietists. His fellowship had begun on his estate in Bethelsdorf, Saxony, in 1722, when refugees from Moravia and Bohemia, followers of Jan Hus (1369-1415) and the *Unitas Fratum*, sought refuge on his land. He welcomed them to establish a place they called Herrnhut (the Lord's watchful care). They began living and worshiping together as a close community, with the usual annoying conflicts of such communities. During a service of communion, the community was visited by the Holy Spirit and a great awakening ensued. Afterwards, as they continued in conversation, prayer, and singing, Zinzendorf sent them food so they could continue what he called an Agape, or Love Feast. The feast became a signal event in the life of Moravians. Not sacramental, but an important marker of their identity, the participants drink coffee, tea, or lemonade, and eat sweet rolls while conversing together, singing hymns, and listening to music. Moravians around the world still observe August 13 as the birthday of their church.

Moravians were among some of the first Protestant Christians to establish missions around the world. Count von Zinzendorf went to these mission fields. After preaching in St. Croix to great acclaim, he came to America in 1741. There were already Moravian colonies in Pennsylvania and North Carolina modeled on Herrnhut with its communal living— outposts for mission to the Native Americans among others.

Officially, the Dano-Norwegian church viewed the Moravian movement with suspicion. They passed a Conventicle law in 1741, forbidding the ministry of women and unordained laity in leading a religious gathering. It was used to imprison Hans Nielsen Hauge for ten years. Gradually people took a more tolerant view of Moravianism. It was first the wealthy upper classes that were taken with the revival. They understood the religion to be a mildly pietistic Lutheranism and less legalistic than the radical pietist Hans Nielsen Hauge.

It was probably the influence of the popular Moravian pastor Niels Johannes Holm (1778-1845) who had come to Christiania in 1820 to serve the Moravian congregation that moderated the reputation of Moravians. He caused Norwegian pastors to view the Christiansfeld school favorably as appropriate for their daughters. An impressive number of Norwegian pastors' daughters appear on the list of students during the late 1830s and early 1840s—names such as Collett, or Arup, a daughter of the bishop who ordained Hermann. There are many others along with several girls from St. Croix and Jamaica where the Moravians had active missions.[146]

Hans Nielsen Hauge

Camilla Collett in Christiansfeld

Norway's first and most famous feminist writer, Camilla Wergeland Collett (1813-1895), sister of Norway's greatest poet, Henrik Wergeland (1808-1845), and daughter of Pastor Nicolai Wergeland (1780-1848), attended Christiansfeld for two years, from 1829-1831. In her book, *In the Long Nights* (*I de lange Nætter*) she provided a description of what it must have been like for Diderikke and Christiane Ottensen when they came as young girls to this very different place for school.[147] She recalled coming to Christiansfeld, knowing she had been sent there by a loving father, an Enlightenment man, who wanted her to receive all the benefits of a fine lady's education, somewhat on the order of Rousseau's *Emile*.[148]

Nicolai Wergeland

After enduring a rough journey by sea with a family that was bringing its daughters to Christiansfeld, Camilla arrived at the school in the little town in the southeastern part of Jutland, Denmark's western region.[149]

She met other girls from Denmark and the Islands, even girls of color from the Moravian mission in St. Croix. One of them, Anne Friborg, became a good friend of Camilla.[150]

When she arrived, Camilla was escorted to a large dormitory room where the girls lived together with their counselor, an older girl who had finished her schooling.[151] On her first day she was introduced to the straight, wide streets of the settlement, with the dorms for boys on one side of the city square and the girls on the other. The topography of flat Denmark, with its green fields stretching off toward the horizon, the ditches filled with wild rose bushes, and the milder climate, seemed very different to Collett who was accustomed to the mountainous regions of inland Norway. The city, with its graveyard arranged according to sex and the honey cakes made famous by the Moravian bakers, presented a new prospect to the young girl, one very different from her home. A fountain stood in the city square beside the church. Like the church in Herrnhut, the Christiansfeld church had the same long, white benches facing the long side of the rectangular building, with matching pews where the leaders sat facing them, with the image of the Lamb on a green field, holding a crown and a cross—all very different from what she knew. What she most hated was the food, especially the beer soup—never too little, but never enough.[152]

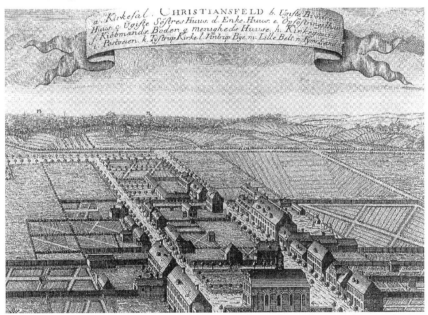

Birdseye view of Christiansfeld. The house where the girls stayed is marked c. in the middle left.

She felt herself to be in an alien environment, but following something of a hunger strike which threatened her life, she became close friends with a Danish girl, Christiane von Schoultz. This friendship rescued Camilla from her nearly terminal loneliness, but very soon after they became fast friends Christiane died suddenly, to Camilla's great grief.

Camilla later commended the instruction that she had received in Christiansfeld especially her religion teacher Pastor Roentgens. Her

parents, especially her father, were clear about what they expected of her when they sent her to Christiansfeld. He wrote to her on her fifteenth birthday, expressing his fond hope that she would prove herself worthy of their love and be a comfort and joy to them in their old age—which meant not that she would remain at home with them, but that she would marry well, so as to have

Camilla Collett

the means to care for them in her home. Her mother wished for the same, hoping that her daughter would marry someone appropriate from their class: a business man, a pastor, or even someone from the military with substantial enough income to make it possible for them to be cared for by her in the manner they expected.[153] As for most parents in these times, children, especially a well married daughter, were social security. Educating her to be a good wife, and thus able to attract a good husband, especially a financially independent one, contributed to their wellbeing as well as her own.

After a disastrous love affair with Norway's second greatest poet of the day, Johan Sebastian Cammermeyer Welhaven (1807-1873), her brother's sworn enemy in the national cultural debate, Camilla married

Peter Jonas Collet (1813-1851), a lawyer, politician, and professor, also of her class. Collett supported his wife in the feminist causes of the day and proved to be a soul mate. Together they had four sons, but his death after

Clavier at Christiansfeld

only ten years of marriage meant that Camilla had to support herself and her children with her own writing. Her novels, *The Governor's Daughters* (*Amtmandens Døttre* 1854-1855), the first "feminist" novels written in Norway, created a storm of interest for their portrayal of the way girls at the time were raised to submit to the will of their fathers and husbands in matters of marriage.

When Camilla thought of it later, she came to see that Christiansfeld had made a difference for her because of its focus on the place and spiritual freedom of women. Christiansfeld, and Moravianism in general, significantly influenced the women's movement in Scandinavia. According to Torril Steinfeld, "Feminism, which had promoted the idea that the two sexes were alike, but different, used the Moravian belief that women could have their own vocation without having to give account to a man."[154]

Christiansfeld's Educational Plan

Christiansfeld established its school for boys and girls with two goals in mind: 1) to educate the young for their earthly lives by giving them skills and an education appropriate for the finer things, or upper class milieu they would inhabit during their lives, and 2) to prepare them for their eternal life by teaching them the faith.

The curriculum for both the boys and the girls included what a good liberal arts education traditionally included: the biblical and ancient lan-

Girls' house in Christiansfeld

guages for the boys—Hebrew, Greek, and Latin. Like the girls, who did not learn the ancient languages, the boys also learned Danish, German, French, and English, vital for the success of anyone from a small country in Europe whose language was not widely understood. The parents could choose among the languages they thought most important to emphasize or to ignore. Camilla's father, a Francophile, expected her to learn French well, and to some extent ignore English. The boys and girls were taught not only to speak the languages fluently, but to write in good German, French, or English, especially letters, since correspondence was a valued skill for sophisticated gentlemen and ladies. This meant they also had to learn calligraphy, or penmanship. Both Diderikke Brandt neé Ottesen and Christiane Hjort neé Ottesen show in their letters that they had mastered these lessons, especially Diderikke. Her elegant Gothic cursive handwriting is nearly impossible to decipher for those not trained in reading the script.

They were also to learn world history, geography, some math, natural history, and science. Of the arts, attention was given to drawing—especially the human figure, then animals, landscapes, geometric shapes, and, finally, perspective—and music—especially the singing of music by the best composers, Mozart, Hayden, Handel. There were also private lessons in piano and violin, and, if possible, wind instruments. The students regularly performed in small concerts to edify each other. These skills were intended to be used not for public performances but, in the case of women, as they established their homes.

Christiansfeld's catalogue stated that education occurred not only in the classroom, but also from the students' time together with classmates and older companions who lived with them. In their communal experience students heard some of the best German literature read aloud to them while they engaged in sedentary activities. For the girls these activities centered around fine handiwork. They practiced knitting, tatting—lace making was a big business in southern Denmark at the time—crocheting, embroidery, and other fine needlework. The boys were expected to participate in vigorous gymnastics and sports, with free time to play outside. The girls less so, but they were also urged to take walks and otherwise exercise.

Punctuality was one of the main habits the school sought to instill in its students, along with a rigorous routine of devotions—an hour in the morning with singing, Scripture readings and homilies at the three meals of the day, and at bedtime. They were also expected to take part in the rituals of the Moravian congregation—funerals, weddings, and baptisms. They were to memorize Luther's Small Catechism, among other things.

Discipline was strict, but the punishments carefully meted out. And although parents might be tempted to send their children to the school to reform an unruly daughter or son, students who did not comply with the rules could be expelled. The catalogue made clear that the school was not to serve as a substitute for the home. Students could matriculate as early as their ninth birthday and as late as their fifteenth. In July, before they went home for summer break or left for good, they were examined to determine how well they had done. These evaluations were dutifully recorded in the record book for each student.

Diderikke Ottesen left home in 1838 when she was about eleven to attend this school; Christiane a few years later, in 1845. Like Camilla Collett, they probably came by boat from their home in Norway to a port on the northern shores of Jutland, Hirtshals, or Christianshavn, and then took some sort of horse-drawn carriage overland to the school. When they arrived, they were taken to the girls' building and assigned a young woman counselor, rather like a dorm counselor, who would stay with them in their "choirs" until they graduated.

Diderikke Ottesen Brandt

Christiansfeld church and square

What Diderikke thought of the place is not recorded until later, when she is said to have bragged a bit too much about her education there.[155] As a very young girl, like Camilla Collett, she must have felt she was in a very different place. Christiane remembered it fondly and spoke well of it. Louise "Lulla" Augusta Hjort (1856-1931), her first born, and Johan "J. C. K" Carl Keyser Preus (1881-1983), her grandchild, recalled later how much it had meant to her.[156] While there were several other pastors' daughters from Norway, they mostly spoke German, the language of instruction. Danish may have been the language of private conversations among the girls, but now they had to learn to speak and read German

well enough to succeed in their studies. As in a true finishing school, Diderikke had to study many things she had probably begun learning at home, but in which she needed further instruction, such as drawing, various kinds of handwork, literature, history, and music. Her grades indicate that, on the whole, she did best in German. The comments on her conduct noted a character that matched well the impression of the pastors' wives in America—rather undisciplined—and may indicate that she had been in need of more training in being cultured and well-mannered. Her sister had died in 1840 after a long illness, and Diderikke's parents may have felt she needed respite in another place. The record is not clear on that issue.

D. Ottesen —1839

Hand work	Good
French	Average
Writing	Not good, yet she makes an effort
Reckoning	Good in both grades
History	Good
Geography	Good

German Reading	Quite Good
Grammar	She is able to grasp it very well; very good
Music	In the last period seems really to make an effort
Drawing	Little talent
Conduct	Is never obedient without first raising objections and has no discipline; otherwise has several good qualities[157]

Her course of study was fairly standard for young women of the elite classes at the time. At Christiansfeld, Diderikke learned the domestic and womanly arts of the upper class pastor's daughter. In every form of schooling for girls, the pastors and pastors' wives recommended this curriculum for their daughters.

After Diderikke's schooling she took a tour of Europe with her siblings—to Germany, Holland, England and Denmark—the sources say. She was even presented to King Oscar, I, King of Norway and Sweden, probably on his visit to Christiansfeld about the time she was in school.[158] Her command of German was highly regarded. It helped when she and her husband Nils Brandt (1824-1921), and Jacob Aall Ottesen, her double cousin, visited some German American Lutheran seminaries seeking a school to educate future pastors until the Norwegian Synod could build its own seminary.

When Diderikke arrived on the frontier in 1856 after her marriage to Nils Brandt in Norway, her forceful personality impressed the Rock

Brandt's parsonage in Rock River, Wisconsin

River Congregation, near Oconomowoc, Wisconsin, where she and her husband began their married life. She took the lead in organizing ladies' aid societies that supported the young Norwegian students at Concordia Seminary by sewing clothes for them. Mrs. Caja Munch, in her letters home, scorned Diderikke's learning, reporting that they had visited with Brandt "and were received by his very talkative wife. I think she probably regards herself as quite erudite, but she is unable to sustain it. . . ."[159] Her aggressiveness, while not appealing to some women, is probably what drove Diderikke to organize assistance for the Norwegian students at Concordia. She spoke to the aid at Waupaca, Wisconsin, on the special needs of one of their students, "Anders" (Torger Andreas Torgerson). It was important to supply the boys with stockings, underpants, neckties, and even vests, which she thought they could exchange for stockings if they needed to, but most important:

Torger Andreas Torgerson

> That which we ought to do, and which at least in my case is not done enough—is to pray for these boys, for their progress and for the resources by which they can be brought onward. Oh, do let us do this, as well as we can even if imperfectly, dear Mrs. Preus; The Lord does not disdain the humblest prayer, if only it is sincere.[160]

Diderikke was fully devoted to her work as a pastor's wife. In addition, when she and her husband moved to Decorah, she became a legendary "mother" for the Luther College boys. She gave them a semblance of family life at the college, sewing and cooking for them, putting on parties, and remembering them in very many ways which endeared her to them. Her education, and her breeding perhaps, made her and her cousin Christiane among the first of the pastors' wives in the Synod on record who appear to have chafed somewhat at the restrictions of the role.[161] These stirrings clearly did not endear Diderikke to the other pastors' wives, who found her bossy, unfeminine, and wearisome, because she did not fulfill the role they expected of her. These were transgressions typical of the early feminists who wanted an education like their brothers and a more public role.

Her husband's work often involved long journeys away from the parsonage. Diderikke took advantage of his absences to attend a ladies' seminary in a nearby town of Fox River to improve her English.[162] When she was together with other pastors and their wives, she must have given the impression of a sense of superiority because of her education. In any event, Caja Munch, wife of Johann Storm Munch, reported in a letter that the group of pastors and wives "did not like her; she talked so much and was so informed and boasted about her many trips in Europe."[163] Even Linka, in several of her drawings, shows the forward Mrs. Brandt, and what Pastor Munch called her "oratorical endowments," wanting things to move more quickly.[164]

Linka's sketch of Mrs. Brandt at the dedication, urging the other woman to hurry drinking her coffee so others could partake

Diderikke seems to have wearied the wife of President Larsen, Karen, who was always in delicate health. They lived in such close proximity and were together regularly in their work. Mrs. Larsen commented: "Mrs. Brandt has been sick, but she still manages to talk. I cannot understand how she manages to talk so, but she could even talk when she was half dead, I'm sure."[165] Elisabeth Hysing Koren (1832-1918), not given to gossip, hinted in many letters that Diderikke was forceful, unladylike, and undisciplined, staying up all night sewing presents for the boys and playing games with them.

Peer Strømme (1856-1931) fondly portrayed Diderikke in his novel, *Halvor*. He essentially agreed with the women's assessments of her, but he viewed the same aspects of her personality positively:

> At the Christmas parties in the dining hall she was indispensable. If she was not there, the games fell flat. She knew any number of amusing and harmless ones, and she managed to see that none of the shy young boys were neglected. And she enjoyed it all as if she were one of them.[166]

In the long run, Didderikke became a fixture in the mythology of the Norwegian Synod, much revered for her work as a mother for the young students at the new college. However much some liked or did not like her, Didderikke's education at Christiansfeld was a model for the future education of their daughters in the New Land.

Educational Ferment

The decade of the 1840s was a time of much intellectual ferment that arose out of romantic nationalism sweeping through all of Europe. In Norway it took the form of a quest for a usable past. (Until 1814 Norway had been under Danish rule and was now under Swedish rule.) A philosophy of education and a curriculum suitable for Norwegians became the question of the decade. Should Norwegians keep the Danish language as their official language and use the Danish/German curriculum for their schools?

Johan Welhaven

Waves of romantic nationalism washed over Norway as the topic of education became more urgent. The major disputants at first were Norway's two major poets—Henrik Wergeland (1808-1845) and Johan Sebastian Cammermeyer Welhaven (1807-1873). The debate was essentially over which sources—linguistic, historical, and literary—to use: the Norwegian, that is, old Norse, or the Danish, and more German or continental sources of Danish language and literature.

Another major figure was Ivar Aasen (1813-1896) who had begun a campaign to make Norwegian a truly Norwegian language by returning to Old Norse and dialects closest to it. This resulted in the development of a language called Nynorsk, or New Norwegian (which was really old Norwegian!), a language still required, along with book Norwegian, in Norwegian schools today. The Norwegians especially took pride in their Viking past. Eventually the recognition of the shared culture of the Scandinavian countries even led to discussions of joining the countries together into one, as Germany and Italy did later in the nineteenth century. This did not replace the nationalism of Old Norway, however, which all the Scandinavian countries admired. Norway's history was their shared Viking history.

These debates came to a head about the time of the sudden death of Wergeland in 1845. At this time the men who would lead the Norwegian Synod in America were in Christiania studying to become pastors. Vilhelm Koren, a member of the first Norwegian glee club, had just returned from the Pan-Scandinavian Songfest in Copenhagen. There he had heard Grundtvig, Oehlenschläger, and countless other speakers whipping up the national fervor of Norwegians and Scandinavians. Immediately upon their return, in July 1845, the glee club sang for Wergeland's funeral. It was a period of deep mourning for the loss of their young and most gifted poet. Koren and most of his future colleagues who emigrated to serve congregations in America were in Christiania at the time and very likely attended the funeral events.

Koren—a student of Welhaven, with whom he walked the streets of Christiania discussing philosophy, hymnody, literature, and other cultural issues—was on the Danish side of the argument, as were Preus and the other early Norwegian Synod pastors. This was apparent later, when Koren prepared a hymnal for the Synod. He made choices which were consistent with Welhaven's thinking about a new Norwegian hymnal and its language. Both he and Preus opposed the use in America of the new Norwegian hymnal by Landstad. They thought it used too many Norwegianisms. This offended their Danish sense for the language (and also their elite status in the culture) which came from their Dano-Norwegian schooling.

What should not be surprising about these debates is that they had consequences for education. Rethinking their history and their language had serious implications for their educational systems. What made for a true patriotic Norwegian education? The debate raged on and on. In some ways it continues today, especially in regard to the requirement that all Norwegians learn both regular Norwegian (*bokmal*) and Nynorsk (which current Norwegian students have complained against as *spynorsk*—spitup Norwegian—a useless romantic effort that wastes time they could use to learn other skills). The founders of the Norwegian Synod were well aware of the debate when they arrived in America to begin their work as leaders of Norwegian-American churches and educational institutions.

Christian Nicolai Keyser

Linka's father, Christian Nicolai Keyser (1798-1846), played a central role in these debates. He moved in 1839 with his family to Christiania to teach at the university in the Sacred Theology department. As noted above, in 1840 he was named to a committee of three, also including Jens Matthias Pram Kaurin (1804-1863) and Wilhelm Andreas Wexels (1797-1866), to redo an explanation to Luther's Small Catechism on the model of Pontoppidan's *Explantion*. Their revision, associated mostly

Vor Frues church in Christiania about the time Hermann and Linka were there. They often went there to hear Wexels preach.

with the popular pastor and preacher Wexels, evoked strong opposition to its changes and suspected Grundtvigianism. Wexels, pastor at Our Savior's church, the cathedral in Christiania, whom Hermann and Linka went to hear many times, became the chief object of derision. Keyser also experienced some criticism for his association with the revision.

As a professor of sacred theology, with a special interest in education, Keyser continued to participate in the discussions. He became involved in the national debate about what to teach in schools. At the time the lines were drawn between the classical, often called Latin, schools and more practical schools, called *Realskoler*.

Keyser wrote a paper that, according to the historian Boyesen, is one of the most remarkable in the history of Norwegian education up to that point in time. Keyser's argument, a dissenting paper to the committee he was serving on, "went directly into the central issue, not just the fight between classicism and realism, but into the modern society's relationship to a country's national education system in its entirety."[167] The box below shows essentially what Keyser recommended the schools teach: sharing the same basic beginning courses, but branching out after the sixth year. Keyser thought this would make it possible for boys from either group to move into leadership from either the practical or classical side and not be prevented by a too practical education from doing so. A higher education (*gymnasium*) should prepare all students to be leaders. It would give them all a sense that they were to be servants of the native land—

Fædrelands Tjeneste—what might be called *noblesse oblige* although he did not use the term.[168] He did not want the two approaches mixed after the basic courses of the first six years, but rather side-by-side, with the students taking the basic courses together and then separating into the two different lines. This approach ultimately became the solution used by the Nissen school years after Keyser died.[169] He remained chair of the Sunday School Board in Christiania almost until his untimely death in 1846. His most compelling issue, however, was what kind of schooling Norwegian students should receive.

Nissen's Role in Educational Reform

Another development in the Norwegian society's attempt to educate girls, the school Linka would come to know best, was Nissen's School for Girls (*Nissens Pigeskole*) founded in 1849 in Christiania. Hartvig Nissen (1815-1874) was the pioneer in education in Norway at the time. He had devoted his studies to education and in 1842 founded the Nissen school for boys, a school that included both a Latin and a Scientific School; it offered an *Examen Artium*—something like an A.A. In 1849 he opened a school for girls, using

Hartvig Nissen

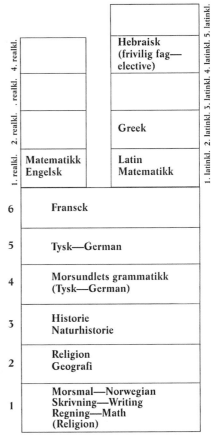

almost the same curriculum as for the boys' school, but omitting the classical languages. In the context of the need for a truly Norwegian schooling for students, Nissen had traveled to Denmark to study education. Education there was still dominated by German models; since Norway had been ruled by Denmark, Norwegian schools also reflected the German system.

Denmark was also evaluating its educational system, and one of the great reformers of education was Nicolai Fredrick Severin Grundtvig (1783-1872). Nissen came to know Grundtvig's work and admired his proposal for a more Nordic education based on Nordic roots, represented in his folk high schools. Grundtvig proposed in 1843 that teachers in Danish schools should seek to make the "mother tongue" come alive in the mouth of the people, based on knowledge of Danish history, poetry and stories, geography, and Danish law. This appealed to Nissen and many other reformers of education in Scandinavia.

In exploring possible models, Nissen wrote a small book on the schools in Scotland and later a comprehensive history of education in co-

NISSENS PIGESKOLE
OG
PRIVATSEMINAR

CHRISTIANIA
GRØNDAHL & SØNS BOGTRYKKERI
1900

Front cover of Nissen's girls' school catalogue

lonial America. To understand his innovations for the girls' curriculum, it is best to begin with the boys' school curriculum that he developed in 1842. The contrast was between the words classicism (*klassicisme*) and realism (*realisme*). Classicism meant the teaching of the classical languages and classical literature because the Greeks and Romans and their literature represented the "Golden Age of the Spirit."[170] To be well-educated one had to know this material, along with Hebrew and the modern languages of Europe, usually German, English, and French in that order. *Realisme* could more properly be called a scientific or commercial curriculum, including the rapidly developing natural sciences.

This came to be seen as the more practical of the two options in the discussions during the 1830s and 1840s.

Grundtvig called the classical schools "schools for death," since they taught a curriculum which was undemocratic (*ufolkelig*), not based on the national character of the country and in dead languages as well. His proposal for folk schools provided for the study not only of the mother tongue, but also its antecedent language, old Norsk, along with the legends and sagas of the past. A good education, in his view, meant that students learned the language, literature, and history of their culture and tradition— in other words their national heritage and character. Grundtvig called them folk

N. F. S. Grundtvig

schools, "schools for life." Many such schools were established both in Denmark and in Norway.

Nissen responded to this argument and made the mother tongue and literature fundamental to his plan. His innovation was that the boys from both the classical and scientific schools would be taught the same subjects together. After the sixth class they were divided into what might be called the Scientific and Classical lines. The diagram of the curricula shows Nissen's plan. One cannot help but notice in this diagram that the course of study at Luther College was much the same as that of the Nissen school. Often referred to as a Latin school, Luther College required Greek, Latin, and Hebrew of all students. Those heading for the ministry had to learn both Latin and German well enough to speak them in the classes they took at Concordia Seminary in St. Louis where they continued their professional study before Luther Seminary in Madison, Wisconsin, opened in 1876.[171] Later the study of Hebrew became optional. If a student took it, it usually meant that the student was headed for the ministry.

Nissen's school prospered and educated many boys from the upper classes in Christiania and from around the country. The innovation of the girls' curriculum was that it was the same as the boys' excepting Greek and Latin. Most significant was that it was not coed. They each studied at different schools, but Nissen argued that women needed to share what their husbands and sons knew. Every educated person should know such things. For Nissen it was something of a scandal that the country had not assured that all girls were educated with the same attention—and very similar curriculum—as the boys. Since men were to be educated to work away from the home and for the improvement of the state, women, no less important to the state, needed a good education, for while the

> man is wearied and exhausted by life's burdens and with the battles and strife there, the women in the home make a quiet reality, which not alone makes for a peaceful and happy source, where man can receive Peace for his heart and power and strength for his soul, and also the woman in raising the children, plants seeds that will bear fruit in the next generation.[172]

For that reason, Nissen concluded that the education of women was fundamentally important, not just for them as individuals, but also because it had so much to do with the development of family life and the flourishing of the next generation.[173] This was not a new argument, but now it had to do with the actual curriculum of a girls' school outside the home.

One hears Rousseau in Nissen's proposal. For Nissen, women had open and warm hearts and feelings, but that was not enough, "Since a woman's call is to be the man's support and help in his life's work, her education should teach her what she needs to know in order to understand the higher significance of things." That meant she had to be "led by her Christian faith and hope."[174] Both men and women students needed religious education in order to know the tenets of the Lutheran faith, Bible history, and geography. This was especially important for women who would teach the faith to their young children. Naturally the girls would also be learning the typical skills of the home: sewing, embroidery, housekeeping, etc. Nissen thought this was similar to a boy's education in the skills of his future trade. Given that, Nissen concluded, that "the girls school's curriculum should be pretty much the same as the boys."[175]

Nissen was especially concerned that the girls not be given a superficial introduction to history, but engage deeply with the context of major figures to understand the wider meaning of the era. This fit with his Grundtvigian nationalism: girls should be taught how individuals emerged from their nationality. To that end they needed to study the people's character, roots and customs, language, literature, and history, because these made up the basis of their spiritual lives and first experiences.[176] Linka would echo this idea later.

He then turned to the need for girls to learn languages, which helped them understand not only their own tradition, but the character and traditions of other cultures in Europe. Learning the geography and natural history of one's own country would also help one understand that of other countries. A good mother and housewife also needed to know something about math in order to run the household. More important was a sense for the beautiful: music and art. A woman should learn what was pleasing to the eye and ear as she kept her home and herself beautiful. The Nissen curriculum for girls included religion, history, the mother tongue (with some Swedish, its grammar and literature, given the dual monarchy of Norway and Sweden), literature, German, French, English, botany, natural history, rudimentary physics, mathematics, writing, music and drawing, along with handiwork and robust courses in physical education—different from the boys' curriculum in that it was without classics and added handiwork. The school offered girls the same degree as the boys earned in their *Examen Artium*. This was a first in Norway. In a sense it was the parlor brought into a more intense and higher plane of learning.

Many of the teachers Nissen hired were pioneers in Norwegian education. They wrote their own textbooks in Norwegian, which was necessary if Norwegians were to develop their own culture and language of instruction. Many instructors were trailblazers in establishing a course of study or expertise that continue into the future. A small country has to consider such issues as: how much of its national heritage should be taught, so that the students know who they are, and how much they need to know of the languages, especially, of the larger world, so that they can flourish outside of Norway. By cultivating their own tradition in the arts, they contributed to the wider world. The Nissen school, both for the girls and boys, hired

Johan Behrens (1820-1890) to teach music. He had established the first male choir in Norway in 1845 and was one of the founders of the patriotic male chorus tradition in Norway (*Sangerfest*) that also flourished in America. Both in Norway and America, these gatherings grew to involve thousands of participants. Along with the male choruses, the Norwegian-American church, led by F. Melius Christianson and Theodore Reimestad at Augsburg Seminary, established the Choral Union based on the same idea as the nationalistic male choruses, except they were mixed choruses that sang sacred music. (The male choruses in America such as Luren in Decorah are direct descendants of Behrens.) Behrens influenced what would become in America the male chorus and Norwegian Lutheran choral tradition. His students and students of his students started choirs in the colleges and later in the congregations. Vilhelm Koren belonged to the first Behrens group and never forgot what he had learned from him.[177]

Johan Behrens

Nissen's schools were the model schools many of the future leaders of the Norwegian-American community knew from experience. They had been involved in the debate and knew what these schools had as a mission. Several had attended or taught at the Nissen schools: Hermann Preus and Vilhelm Koren at the girls' school, Jacob Aall Ottesen at the boys' school. August Weenaas, first president of Augsburg College, and a little later, Georg Sverdrup, both attended the Nissen school. Surprisingly little scholarship has been done to examine the influence of this school as a model for Norwegian Lutheran colleges in America. There were parallels as well in the controversies that these young men experienced in founding colleges in the New Land and later in their attempts to educate their daughters.[178] Nissen's emphasis on languages and classical learning, in both branches of the schools, was innovative at the time. It remained fundamental to the way the founders of Luther College shaped their school.

The Nissen School for Girls was a new educational effort that Linka must have observed with existential interest. She surely heard arguments for and about the education of young women in her home as her father, brother, and future husband spoke about these questions in their daily conversations: what girls should learn, when, and in what context. Undoubtedly Linka became much more intimately acquainted with the school's goals when her uncles, Rudolph Keyser (1803-1864), professor of history, and Fredrick Vilhelm Keyser (1800-ca.1862), librarian, at the university, hired Hermann to teach Linka's younger sisters at home. (Some records indicate that Hermann actually lived in the same house with the Keyser girls, their grandmother, and uncles.)[179] The Keyser uncles had good reason to expect that Hermann was well suited to teach the young girls, since he was at the same time teaching at the Nissen School for Girls—*Nissen Pigeskolen*—while waiting for a call from America.

Linka's brother, Johan Carl Keyser (1828-1904), served for many years as the principal at Nissen School for Girls. Her proximity to these debates may have been the reason she would later reflect in her diary about why women even needed an education, given the housework that was expected of them and justified with language about the necessity of this being woman's work. Grateful that her parents had given her an education, Linka reflected in her diary on the thirst of a woman to receive an education[180] and in doing so echoes almost exactly the language Nissen and his followers used:

> When she seeks to develop her intellect it is viewed as a sort of secondary matter, something useless that could never serve the world in any way—when these thoughts come to mind, I often get bitter because I find it unfair. When I feel that nature has been just as generous toward us, why should we not be allowed to develop our abilities without limitations? Nature did not give them to us only so that we could use them to salt the food and mend socks....Won't it be useful for a woman to know something about the world, its past and present history, about human beings, their customs through different times, etc., etc.?[181]

Since both Koren and Preus had taught at the Nissen Girls' school, and Ottesen at the boys' school, and Ottesen's sister Christiane and double-cousin Diderikke had attended Christiansfeld school, they were intellectually well prepared to found schools. They understood educational philosophy from their experience as young teachers and pastors and their knowledge of the educational debates of their times. They had thought deeply about how to educate young men for the ministry and what young women needed to learn in order to be cultured and well-educated wives and mothers. They had a keen sense of their tradition and the differences that the American context made for them as they began to establish schools to educate their children, both girls and boys.

Catherine Beecher's Ideas

Catherine Beecher

The debate about how to educate women was also lively in the United States about the time the pastors arrived on the frontier. Perhaps the most important pioneer in women's education in America was Catherine Beecher (1800-1878), the oldest daughter of Lyman Beecher (1775-1863). She had a vision for establishing women's schools throughout the country, which she tirelessly promoted with the help of her much more practical sister, Harriet Beecher Stowe. Her preference was an education in how to be a successful wife and mother who knew the finer things of life. As a pastor's daughter herself, the sister of Harriet and Henry Ward Beecher, she had received a typical parsonage education in her home from her father. He was a fierce Calvinist, and Catherine adored him, but she could not reconcile herself to his Calvinism. When she was ten years old, her parents enrolled her in Miss Pierce's School, a finishing school that has educated many of America's most famous women, from Beecher to Barbara Bush. Young women learned the social graces there, preparing to be wives of professional men, especially graduates of the neighboring law school. What they were taught, according to her biographer Catherine Kish Sklar, were mainly the virtues that would make them "agreeable to their elders and their peers: Candor, Truth, Politeness, Industry, Patience, Charity and Religion."[182] Her plan for the education of women and their preparation to be mothers and teachers focused mostly on moral education. This meant the teaching of good habits and practices—good middle-class Yankee values. Her book on the skills necessary for domestic life is similar to Hannah Winsnes' book from Norway, without which Linka, Elisabeth, and their colleagues in the Norwegian American parsonages could not have managed as well as they did. Both books, written about the same time, met the need for daughters who had left the confines of their homes and gone far away from their mother's and aunt's advice. Both are filled with moral instructions, along with practical advice on how to run a home, farm, and kitchen.

Leaving the Farm

When one reads the letters of the early pastors' wives among Norwegians, one is struck with how much farming they actually did. In fact it was crucial for them to be shrewd farmers for mere survival. Thus they needed these books of advice, not only for how to treat illnesses, but also for how to preserve meat and other foodstuffs, and how to grow fruits and vegetables in the garden. Susan B. Anthony noted years later that the Industrial Revolution made many of the old chores unnecessary. Things had changed so much that "we were on the verge of an era of unmarried women."[183] The farm could no longer support its daughters, nor were the daughters needed there anymore.

Girls from the lower classes had it better, to some degree. Young, unattached Norwegian women in the peasant (*bønder*) class or the cotter (*husmand*) classes began to find jobs outside of the home. Norwegian law in 1843 gave them their majority rights at the age of twenty-five. Women from these classes were no longer crucial to the family's survival, since the textile mills were producing material more cheaply than the women could at home. This released many young women from such work, although on the frontiers of North America such work continued for some decades longer. Young, unmarried women without fathers or brothers to support them gradually began to enter occupations that gave them a chance to earn money on their own. Being a telegraph operator, for example, was a coveted occupation for women in the late 1860s and 1870s.

Beecher recognized the problem for upper-class women, writing in her most famous book, "The customs and prejudices of society forbid educated young women from engaging in socially useful employments making their suffering as keen as those of working class women. Their spirits were starved, instead of their bodies," she concluded.[184] What she wanted was an education for women that would consist of training in the Christian virtues, so that women could raise a well-bred family, ready to enter society. The job of the mother, she believed, along with most of the other educational thinkers at the time, was to educate her children for useful vocations. With the Moravians she believed that when one educated a woman, one educated a family.

The sense that upper-class women should not engage in socially useful employment caused difficulties for several single women daughters of the Norwegian-American clergy who had come to the United States unaccompanied by men and tried in vain to find their way to economic freedom without leaving their class. Henriette and Karine Neuberg, sisters of Karen Neuberg Larsen, found it difficult to survive as single women in America. They were dependent on their relatives and friends to give them room and board in exchange for their help in the home. Thus it is not surprising that the trail-blazing feminists at this time in Norway and America were women from the upper classes, women like Camilla Collett and Aasta Hansteen (1824-1908), a portrait painter of some note in Norway, or Lucretia Mott and Cady Stanton in America, all daughters of privilege.

One catches glimpses in her diary now and then of Linka's awareness of things having to do with the status of women. She wonders what the use of education is for a woman when she is expected to do mostly chores in the house. She indicates rather poignantly that she had aspirations beyond this. She supposes in her diary that a man has so many advantages over a woman, not because "he is more gifted than a woman, but that his mind has been better developed by many kinds of knowledge than has a woman's."[185]

Because she left Norway before the emergence of the women's movement—three years before Collett's first novels, which she may have read later—Linka does not refer to this issue much nor to the movement that was beginning to simmer in the culture. At first she clearly preferred romantic novels, like those of Scott or Dickens. The one place the young girls in Linka's class would soon feel something changing was in the building of schools appropriate for girls of their class to attend. The Nissen school was a pioneer in this. In giving girls the same education, they were being prepared for the same vocations as the boys, even if the argument was, as per Rousseau, that women needed to know the same things simply to converse with their husbands and teach their sons. It would change the debate, as Linka seemed to sense already.

The Arrival of Elisabeth and Ulrik Vilhelm Koren

As the Preuses were getting settled in Spring Prairie, the Korens, equally as lettered, were making preparations to come to the Little Iowa, or Washington Prairie, Congregation in northeast Iowa. While neither Elisabeth nor Vilhelm was raised in parsonages, they were from the same class and had many relatives among the clergy. Vilhelm Koren (1826-1910) grew up in Bergen. His father, a sea captain, died when Koren was young, and he left his family in poverty. Vilhelm determined to study for the ministry at the university in Christiania. There he met Preus and many of the future pastors with whom he would serve in the Norwegian Synod in America. Mrs. Koren, Else Elisabeth Hysing (1832-1918), was born in Larvik Norway, on May 24, 1832. Her

Ulrik Vilhelm Koren

father, Ahlert Hysing (1793-1879), was the headmaster at the "Real" school in Larvik. Her mother, Caroline Mathilde Koren (1801-1840), died after a long illness when Elisabeth was only eight. Caroline Koren was the daughter of one of Norway's first women writers, Christiane Birgitte Diدericksen Koren (1764-1815).

Elisabeth spent her childhood alone, given her mother's long illness and her tendency to deafness. She was sent to Copenhagen twice to find some treatment for her problem. Neither trip helped. Elisabeth learned to read and write English from Mary and Jane Archer, daughters of a Scottish family living in Larvik. Her deafness may have made learning to speak another language dif-

Map of Wisconsin and Iowa, showing where the Preuses and Korens lived and worked

ficult. Herman Amberg Preus, Jr. (1896-1995), grandson of Hermann and Linka, told me he remembered her voice as cultured, melodious, and beautiful to hear.

Elisabeth received a typical education for girls at the time—languages, history, and literature in her home. She was also fortunate that her father's colleagues at the Larvik Real School gave her private lessons. Other friends and family were also helpful, especially her father to whom she was especially close. Elisabeth spent many long hours with him in the garden learning horticulture. Her father, a distinguished leader in the country, served in Parliament in 1830 and was elected mayor of Larvik, a post he held for ten years. He had been a good teacher for his daughter.

Elisabeth Koren, 1853

Her education and good sense stood her in good stead in the Washington Prairie parsonage where as a pastor's wife she was expected to know about cures from the garden.

She married Koren on August 18, 1853. Very shortly after their wedding, they left Norway via steamship for Kiel. From there they took a train to Hamburg and set sail for New York. While on the boat, the young wife began a diary. She kept it faithfully until her first child was born, when the diary ends. Fortunately we do have a rich trove of the letters she wrote to Linka Preus (and her father) over the next thirty years.

As their ship, *The Rhein*, a three-mast bark, left Hamburg with 250 aboard, Elisabeth described their own situation in their first-class cabin. The fact that she was a pastor's wife was not foremost on her mind at the outset of their journey. It was a role she would have to study harder to fill than Linka, but her powers of observation give us rare insights into the life and profession she had entered. This description of a storm at sea shows her eye for detail and her own fierce mettle. Because her inner ear was not very sensitive, she was among the few who never really got sea sick.

> The storm raged all night. We could not sleep; it was impossible to stand. A little later in the day the storm subsided; but the strong ground swells are worse. To stand on deck in such a sea, when the ship dips fore and aft and the water is beautifully dark blue with white crests, is thrilling. It is a magnificent sight. [186]

During this time, Mrs. Koren finished Charles Dicken's novel, *Martin Chuzzlewitt* (1844), finding him to be more and more appealing to her than others of Dicken's characters. Then she began Washington Irving's *Sketch Book of Geoffrey Crayon, Gentleman* (1820,) also preferring the more romantic type of reading. She knit while reading and listened to Vilhelm read a Swedish poem by Esaias Tegner, "Frithjofs Saga" (1843) as she continued her tatting or crocheting. On Sunday, October 9, 1853, when they set sail for America. Koren, in his new role as pastor, read a sermon for their traveling companion, Mr. Juul, and Elisabeth, but seemed to feel no calling to preach for the entire ship as Hermann had done on their trip.

Elisabeth's literary adventures resembled those of Linka. She knew German, English, and probably a little French. The ship was very much a place where the typical evening entertainments of the parlor could be engaged in throughout the journey. She had no work to do, except her writing, reading, and handwork.

The first we see her in her vocation as a pastor's wife came on Thursday, October 20, 1853, when she had completed her "sick visits—the customary round I make every morning."[187] While she did not say that these visits were in fulfillment of her role as a pastor's wife, it was a familiar one for a pastor's wife. Later, in a brief reference to these visits, she

The guest room at Korens. Diderikke Brandt is on the bed, putting a new candle in the sconce. Mrs. Koren is holding the candle. She has been helping Linka with an eye problem.

wrote that "I have actually been comfortable during these stormy days, when indeed there is little that is agreeable, and have passed the time working, chatting, reading, and paying visits to the poor women." Later members of their parish in Washington Prairie would consult her about their illnesses and over time she became especially knowledgeable about diseases of the eye.[188] As the trip dragged on because of poor weather, and countervailing winds, the young pastor's wife made short notes on her visits. She continued to keep such records when they came to Iowa in December 1853 just before Christmas.

Assuming the Role of Pastor's Wife

As Mrs. Koren began to assume her role as pastor's wife on the frontier, she had some idea of her role. It did not come as naturally to her as to Linka, who had been raised in a parsonage. Elisabeth's own youth and upbringing without a mother seems to have made her insensitive to the obligations she was incurring in the homes where they lived. Nor did she quite grasp the new situation for the members of the congregation now in a free country that did not have a state church or state church pastors. The pastor in America had no legal authority over his parishioners as in Norway. He could not make demands on them as he had been able to back home. This major difference in their situation seemed to escape her at first. At the same time, her clear eye for the scene she observed reveals details that she may not have fully understood, but which give the readers a picture of what she was like.

This became clear as they took up residence with the Egge family in a cabin hardly as big as most bedrooms today. Elisabeth's sense of her vocational obligation to write letters and read did not sit well with her hostess, Helene Egge. It was not long before Elisabeth began to criticize their hostess for her lack of gentility. The young couple attended a Christmas party at the neighbor, Ingebret Haugen, partaking of many Christmas foods and rituals. When they returned to the Egges they found "Helene waiting for us with her pork" a meal that wearied Elisabeth.[189] She did help Helene sew curtains that were to be used as dividers on the beds. They were placed together on one side of the room, end to end. These curtains were necessary to give the two couples only the barest modicum of privacy. Elisabeth saw the need for them and helped Helene sew them, but left to visit another neighbor. When she returned later that evening, they had been completed. Elisabeth helped Helene hang them around the beds, after which she and Vilhelm continued reading

Inside the Egge cabin

and writing. Erik Egge, Helene's husband, read *Emigranten* (The Emigrant), one of the earliest newspapers of the Norwegians in America. Helene, Elisabeth reported, went straight to bed. Behind the newly hung curtain, Helene may have wondered how she was going to survive the next months until the parsonage was built. She had to serve not only her husband and children, but also wait on this young couple who did not show themselves to be very understanding of her situation. Their work consisted of reading, writing, preparing sermons, and doing fine handwork while she slaved to serve them.

As the year ended, Elisabeth sat in the Egge cabin writing away, recording invaluable details of their initial days in Iowa. In her writings we observe a very young lady sitting in this simple cabin on the edge of the frontier. She remembers the progress they had made from the beginning of the year, when she was "clad in bobbinet, dancing away with roses in my hair. This year I am sitting here with Vilhelm in this bare room, where tomorrow he is to conduct divine services for all these people who so long have lacked a pastor. Still, this is the best."[190]

Getting Into the Part

Through the next year, Mrs. Koren began to understand her vocation as a pastor's wife. The expectations of the people in her husband's congregations helped her see what her role was. New Year's Day found her enjoying the first worship service of the year, remarking on how wonderful it was to

> see our people in this foreign land streaming together from every direction, and to feel the devotion and attention with which they sing their hymns and listen to the pastor. It all has quite a different aspect from what I have been accustomed to.[191]

Through the next months, the Korens suffered a long period before their parsonage was finished by the Washington Prairie congregation. The process, similar to what happened to Linka and Hermann in Spring Prairie, seemed endless to the Korens. Even Elisabeth's considerable good humor and optimism were severely tested. Koren, in a speech on that year, said he only saw tears in her eyes but once.[192] Finally it was finished so they could move in. Her joy was diminished when a farmer brought a pig for slaughter so that they had to salt it down before they could do anything else. She took it in fairly good humor.

After the house was finished, Mrs Koren set out making it into a parsonage. It had a farm and a garden. Their home over time was graciously furnished and ready for many guests over the next decades. In 1854 their first child, Henriette Christiane Koren, was born. She was followed over the next twenty years by seven other children. Elisabeth soon had to be-

The first church building of Washington Prairie

gin schooling her young brood of children while keeping the farm going, which she seemed to have done with great equanimity.

The Home School

Every day this fall we sit together upstairs above the little girls' room from 10 to 12 and have school. It is very good for Ahlert in every way when he gets a little regular schooling.

—Elisabeth Koren to Linka Preus[193]

As the Koren family grew, Mrs. Koren managed the house and farm. Koren even referred to her as the farmer in the family. She began to provide the kind of medical advice and spiritual wisdom their parishioners expected, something new for her. What she knew how to do, the traditional work of a mother, now had to include teaching her children preschool, kindergarten, and primary school. We know she did this well and with good humor. She demonstrated in her own life what experts in women's education believed at the time: One educated a woman so she could educate her children and be a companion to her learned husband. It was part of her vocation as mother and, especially, pastor's wife. Koren described her teaching with all its challenges in this poem he wrote to her for their Golden Wedding anniversary:

I see in my mind, when they were all still small,
You bore one in your arms, another at your breast,
And when they soon were older, and we wondered what was best,
What we would do to teach them, to which school they would go,
Your love, it found the answer—I'll teach them all myself,
    you said,
It is like a fairy tale to think of how you did,
You gave them all your time, and you offered them your strength
A better faithful teacher has never yet been found,
One sat upon your lap, the other on the floor,
And tried to find out whether his little wooden horse
Could stand on only three legs.
Two studied German, yes, and English, one learned the alphabet,
And one learned to your joy that two and three were five,
But first of all you taught them to know their Lord,
And thank him and to pray to him and be reminded of his
    Word.[194]

The chaos of the scene, which Koren had observed many times, is vividly portrayed. The complicated teaching job of the young Mrs. Koren is clear as she tried to keep the home school under some kind of control as she taught a variety of subjects at a variety of levels.

Discipline was not her strong suit. The other wives noted on frequent occasions the Korens' failure to discipline their children appropriately. Karen Neuberg Larsen in a letter to her sister Henriette Neuberg (1840-1879) pitied poor Mrs. Koren alone "out there with six unmanageable children."[195] It is a bit surprising to hear this. Mrs. Koren wanted her servants to work hard, as she might have expected servants in Norway to do. Keeping servants was her most vexing problem.[196] She needed maids to relieve her of her cooking and cleaning responsibilities so she could teach. Since the classroom was usually in the kitchen, a mother could

Elisabeth Koren at 40

supervise the housework being done, or do it herself, while teaching her children.

Mrs. Koren's daughter, Caroline Mathilde Koren Naeseth also remembered their home school instructions that lasted every morning from nine until twelve. She taught

> much of the time with the youngest child on her arm. Of course, there had to be interruptions and she had to have help with the housekeeping; but I am constantly amazed that she had strength and endurance to do it. She instructed us in the ordinary school subjects, in religion, and in Norwegian, English and German. We read aloud, translated, wrote from dictation, and memorized hymns and poems in the various languages.[197]

Later, when they needed help with English, the Korens hired Synnøve Lomen. She was a local woman who helped the pastors' families with everything from teaching to housework. Afternoons, Caroline remembers, became a time for practicing skills they would need later: knitting, sewing, tatting, crocheting, various kinds of handiwork.

Evenings were when their father helped with the teaching. Koren, an accomplished singer, taught his children famous old songs from his time with the Behrens Quartet. He read to them from the great romantic literature of Scandinavia: sagas, poetry, and historical romances by the great Danish romantic poet Oehlenschläger. This was consistent with Grundtvig's theory of an education for life.

The Preus Home School

The Preus' home school was no different. Linka sketched some scenes that show her children sitting at her feet and learning what was age appropriate for them, very much like the scene Koren describes in his laudatory poem to his wife.

Rosina:"Ufda! I'll never learn world history!"

Christian: Now I have done my lessons. Can I go over to Jahn Anbjørns to go hunting?

Linka Yes, but be careful!

Doctor: Anga, now I have done the fourth commandment.

Anga: But I am doing the fives in subtraction.

It is a dramatic and knowing presentation of the drama of home school-ing and all its complications. She pictures her younger son, Johan Wilhelm, "J. W." or *Doktor*, memorizing the fourth commandment, "Honor thy father and mother," while sitting at his mother's feet. Rosina, whom we will meet later, struggles with world history, as she will later. The two younger children labor to learn their primary lessons. This is the home school: children studying at their various levels, handiwork continuing as the mothers teach and run the home. Christian, now a teenage boy, is edging out of the women's room to go hunting, another masculine activity that was a rite of passage for boys. It is not just accurate to the scene, but it is filled with a good sense for the ironies and contrasts of the moment, even the technological disruption that comes with the sewing machine. These are the best features of the one-room schoolhouse that built American character on the frontier.

The Hjort Parlor

THE PARSONAGE: A TEACHING SCHOOL

As the immigrants continued to move west into Iowa and north into Minnesota, Lansing, a river town on the Iowa shore of the Mississippi, became a landing point for many Norwegian immigrants. It had a pier for paddle wheels steaming north and south, and ferries crossing back and forth from DeSoto Landing in Wisconsin to the Iowa side. Many Norwegians settled in northeast Iowa. They traveled through Lansing on their way to claim the rich farmland awaiting them further west in Allamakee and Winneshiek counties. By the 1860s, there were Norwegian congregations being established across the northeast Iowa countryside. They were built under the pastoral leadership of Nils Brandt and Vilhelm Koren. These growing number of congregations called pastors from the clergy class of Norway.

For a while, the higher education of their young children seemed a distant problem. The pastors were confident in the ability of their wives and governesses to teach their younger children as they had done in Norway. After 1861 the sons of the Norwegian pastors in America could receive an education at Luther College. If they felt called into the ministry they could attend either Concordia Seminary in St. Louis or Fort Wayne in Indiana. Hans Gerhard Stub, the first Norwegian pastor's son born in America, attended Luther College, then Concordia Seminary, St. Louis, and returned to Norway to attend Bergen Cathedral School.

The Hjort parsonage in Paint Creek

The pastors' daughters did not have a place to go for further education, but in the New Land they could receive a good schooling from their aunts and mothers, as well as their fathers in the home. Their parents were concerned that their daughters further their education in the liberal arts and the fine arts, as they had a generation before at Christiansfeld and Nissen's School for Girls. In order to be worthy mates for the men they would marry, they needed to learn the subjects and skills their mothers had learned in the old country.

For the time being, the family parlor had to do as the schoolroom for the teenage girls. Every evening in the parlor, far out on the western frontier, every adult became a teacher of the young. Children reviewed their lessons for the next day, surrounded by adults and older siblings and cousins who could help them. There the young engaged in various solo activities such as reading or writing letters, reading books, or working on another lesson. They might have conversations in a number of languages, well known by their elders. Each worked on his or her own project while in the company of the family. If someone had trouble with some handiwork, such as tatting, crocheting, knitting, fancy needlework, someone in the room would be able to help. Should a young person want to learn to play the guitar or the piano, an older relative could teach them. Then, while doing their work, they sang together, folk songs and hymns, especially during evening devotions. The old practices of sending their daughters to an aunt continued in the New World. Mrs. Hjort, by Lulla's report, was the most sought-after teacher among them.

The Hjort parsonage, "Blaasenborg" [Castle of Winds] was some miles east of Waukon, Iowa, on a high ridge surrounded by rich fertile farms. The parsonage and barn are gone, but the landscape looks much as it did 150 years ago. The rolling hills stretch out across the landscape, with farm homes and little hamlets dotting the land. Below them Paint Creek meanders on its way to the Mississippi. The Norwegians built two congregations here known as East and West Paint Creek, both of which still survive and are actively serving many of the descendants of the original settlers.

To this early settlement came Ove Jakob Hjort (1827-1879) and Christiane Elisabeth Ottesen Hjort (1833-1873) with their family in 1863. Hjort had been an unlikely candidate to be a pastor. He had bad eyes and did not think school was in his best interest, so he became a gentleman farmer in Ringsaker, Norway. In 1855, he married Christiane, a pastor's daughter from nearby Toten, a sister of Pastor Jacob Aall Ottesen who was serving the congregation in Manitowoc, Wisconsin.

Together the young couple farmed without much zeal for farming, despite Hjort's having attended an agricultural college in Sweden.[198] Christiane got the "America fever" on reports from her brother, Jacob, and from Lauritz (Laur.) Larsen

Ove and Christiane Hjort, Otto, Lulla, and Dikka

(1833-1915), president of the fledgling Luther College. He had returned to Norway in 1860 to recruit pastors for the increasing number of Norwegian congregations on the frontier. Christiane's father encouraged the move, but Hjort's father opposed the move, given Hjort's dislike of school, his weak eyes, and the fact they now had three children, making it expensive for him to study theology.

The Hjorts soon gathered together their growing family and boarded the sailing ship *Droback*, for America. Lulla remembered their terrifying trip across the Atlantic in bad weather. The journey took eleven weeks, far longer than the usual six. They suffered a fire on board; fifteen passengers died of infectious diseases; many nearly starved to death, especially young children. One child was buried in a box Christiane provided the grieving family. When the ship was becalmed in a fog, the captain came to ask Hjort if they would share their water with the rest of the passengers in steerage, which he gladly did.

Lulla remembered many of these experiences vividly. Once she awakened and came on deck to see the sight of icebergs with their sparkling green light hemming in the ship. They sailed down the St. Lawrence River to Quebec, from which they traveled the rest of the way to Koshkonong, Wisconsin, by rail to stay with Christiane's brother, Jacob Aall Ottesen.

Not long after their arrival in Wisconsin, Hjorts left for a year in St. Louis at Concordia Seminary where he finished his theological degree. Given Hjort's bad eyesight, Christiane read his theological books aloud to him. This gave her a theological education as she studied the theological classics along with him. Lulla's memories of Missouri's patriarch Carl

Ferdinand Wilhelm Walther (1811-1887) were especially cordial. He took her into his own home to keep her from catching measles from her younger sister, Dikka. (She did, however, come down with the disease, so was taken home again.) Hjort finished his studies in 1861 just as Civil War hostilities broke out. Lulla, a six year old, remembered this as a time of soldiers and marching.

C. F. W. Walther

After his ordination, the Hjorts moved to Paint Creek. It was an exciting trip for the young Lulla, who described the train trip to Prairie du Chien and then a ferry boat to Lansing where they were met by members of the congregation. They were driven the ten miles to Paint Creek over a "nearly impassable road which went between woods, up hill and down, through the stony hills to their parsonage which had been built in the middle of thick woods, with a little stall and place enough to keep horses and a buggy."[199] Upon seeing the site of the parsonage, Lulla describes their surprise as the clearing where the parsonage stood in the middle of the forest appeared almost out of nowhere. Lulla says the family later delighted in the rich harvest of plums, grapes, berries, and various kind of nuts (walnuts, hazel, and hickory), plentiful in the woods around the parsonage and the homes where their members lived.

The farmers in the congregation brought food, as was the custom, of all kinds to the parsonage: sides of beef, a slab of pork, chickens, lamb, cream, butter, and many other food items in which the parsonage family delighted. The congregation, which grew to love the Hjort family, knew and approved of the Hjorts' generosity in hosting many Luther College students during the holidays and gladly supported them.

The Paint Creek parsonage, a convenient stopping point for those going further west, became a central gathering point for pastors traveling to Decorah for meetings. Korens lived only about twenty miles from Hjorts, and they visited each other often. Elisabeth Koren and Christiane Hjort became good friends over the next few years.

A pastoral mentor of many of these first pioneer pastors, Wilhelm Andreas Wexels, a colleague of Linka's father, had written a book, *Lecture on Pastoral Theology (Foredrag over Pastoraltheologien)*. They had attended his church in Christiania. In his book he suggested that the parsonage be "a

The Hjort parsonage

teaching school for men and women, boys and girls" on how to live the Christian life.[200] In her memoirs, Lulla described how her father and mother took this to heart. Many pious members of the congregation came as guests either to ask Hjort some question or simply see how they lived. This often resulted in long evenings of conversation and devotions. These evenings brought the congregation closer together as the Hjorts taught the lay people how to practice their faith. The congregation took care for the pastor and his family, while they served as a school.

Wilhelm Andreas Wexels

The culture of the parsonage involved both the Hjorts as teachers. Because there were no schools in the immediate area dedicated to the kind of education their girls needed at the time, Mrs. Hjort was frequently asked by other pastors' wives if she could take their daughters and teach them a little of everything (*lidt af hvert*). She had been well prepared to do this at Christiansfeld.[201] Despite her large family and her many other duties, Christiane was glad to help in the time-honored tradition of taking in a teenage daughter of a relative to teach them the necessary skills of domestic life. The Hjorts, according to Lulla, loved having young people around. They frequently invited Luther College students for longer periods, such as the Christmas holidays when the poorest did not have the money to travel home.

Lulla never forgot the falling of the evening light as her father gathered them around him to sing. "When we sang, we all sang with our whole hearts, and Mother sang descant. There seemed to be no end to all of the hymns and children's verses that my parents knew."[202]

Peer Strømme (1856-1931) who attended Luther College from 1869 to 1876, wrote a novel called *Halvor: How Halvor became a Pastor* (a roman á clef about his own experience at Luther College). In it he showed the Hjort parsonage to be culturally beyond his reach as a poor farm boy.[203] While Halvor was studying at Luther College preparing to be a pastor, he was invited to the Hjort's home, his first experience in a Christian home of high culture. Their politeness and good breeding astonished him. He marveled that people would treat family members with such courtesy. Their family devotions also impressed him.

> When the family gathered for prayers morning and evenings and Pastor Dahlby [aka Ove Hjort] read a chapter of the Bible in his rich bass voice, Halvor felt that he had discovered the wellspring of the love and happiness with which the home abounded.[204]

When pastors returning home from a trip to Norway passed through Paint Creek, many brought Mrs. Hjort a stack of sheet music from Norway. They gathered around the piano while she played and learned what was popular in Norway and the continent.

The Hjort parsonage and parlor was devoted to teaching and learning, admired by most of the other pastors and their wives. Mrs. Hjort had a calling. She would later call it a *Beruf* (profession) not only to teach her children, but also to teach young women how to teach.[205] This became a project for Mrs. Hjort when she took on the education of the Neuberg sisters, the younger sisters of Mrs. Laur. Larsen, Henriette and Karine Neuberg. They came to this country as single women intending to marry someone of their own class, but in the meantime had to earn their keep by working as governesses and otherwise helping housewives with their many household chores while caring for the children. The stories of both Henriette and Karine are important sources that show how the school in the parlor worked and how

Laur. and Karen Larsen's wedding picture, 1857

the group trained its future teachers. Like so many in their class, they were prepared to serve as governesses, something like apprentices, in the various clergy homes in the Synod until they found suitable husbands. As they taught, they would learn how to teach. If they did not find a husband, they usually continued governess work for the rest of their lives.

Teacher Training in the Parlor for the Parlor:
KARINE AND HENRIETTE NEUBERG AND THE HJORT PARLOR

I have been to the college land and think it is the most beautiful place in the west. It is too bad you can't go there.

—Karine Neuberg to Henriette Neuberg, November 4, 1864

There is a rich trove of letters written during these evenings from the pastors' wives and daughters in the Norwegian Synod describing what was happening around them while they were sitting in the parlor. They had learned from reading the many letters they got from their parents and friends how to describe vividly the lively scenes they were observing as they wrote. Henriette and Karine in their letters show the difficulties they experienced making a place for themselves as single women of their class. As Catherine Beecher had noted, single women of the upper classes found it difficult to find appropriate positions. Even if the old class lines had, for the most part, become irrelevant, in this small corner of America, among the pastors and their wives, it still lived and continued well into the twentieth century.

Henriette and Karine Neuberg, as they began a kind of internship as governesses, both learned what to teach and how to teach at the same

Evening entertainments in the parlor in Askevold

time. Trying to find a place and vocation in the New World, while still

operating on the assumptions and understandings of Old World traditions and customs, made for some difficult times. Even as they were partaking in this long tradition of being educated and teaching in the parlor, the New World impinged on them, especially the

Henriette Neuberg

Karine Neuberg

younger, Karine Neuberg, later Magelssen. Lulla remembered Karine as a wonderful friend and governess for whom she had great love and affection, but the letters give us a more complicated picture.[206]

A New Life in a New World

Why it was and how it was that Karine got permission from her father, Peder Janus Matthias Neuberg (1805-1877) sheriff in Bergen, to leave for America to be with her sisters, Henriette and Karen, we do not know. Their mother, Randine Christensen, was a dancer in one of the semi-private theaters of the day in Christiania. She had the temperament of an artist. Karen Larsen, in her biography of her father, Laur. Larsen, makes a cryptic note to the effect she "had neither the character nor the personality that might have made a really happy home for her large family."[207] Not reported in the book was that Randine had left their father for a military man.[208] This may be the reason almost all of her children came to America and gathered around Karen Larsen, their oldest sibling. Randine seems to have given her children not only their artistic and delicate temperaments, but also some emotional instability. Karen, Laur, Larsen's wife, was born in 1833, Henriette in 1840. She stayed with the Larsens during their time in St. Louis and many times later to help with the children. They had a brother, Hagbarth, who died in prison during the Civil War, born on October 13, 1841.[209] He came to America in 1859 with Henriette when she was nineteen, and Viktor, the younger brother (b. 1845), only thirteen at the time. He would later settle in Brooklyn. They had another sister, Thora, (b. 1842) two

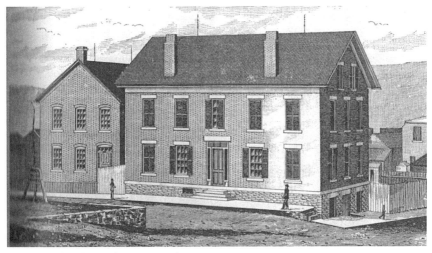

The St. Cloud Hotel in Decorah, Iowa

years younger than Henriette, and a brother Harald (b. 1847) who both remained in Norway. Their father expected Laur. Larsen to be legally responsible for the Neuberg sisters. It was the custom of the time, so he even sent Larsen money as part of the deal.

The Page School in Decorah

Karine left for America from Bergen in May of 1862. She jotted off a letter before she left to her sister Henriette, who was already working in the parsonages of their sister and their friends. Karine expressed her hopes for her life in the New World. She was planning on teaching "privately" she told Henriette. "I'm coming with heart and soul and life!"[210] Karine saw an opportunity with Henriette: They could start a school where she could "earn her keep."[211] The Larsens had just moved to Decorah from Halfway Creek in Wisconsin where the college had been for one year. About that same time, Karen Larsen wrote to Henriette, with whom she had probably discussed what they would do with their little sister when she arrived.

Karen Larsen

> I have begun to lay plans that you, Karine and Miss Jensen should open a girls' school here in Decorah. It is seriously needed—the little girls get such a different education here."

When Karine arrived, she brought with her several books of Norwegian history so she could study and teach one of the courses recommended for a young woman of her rank. Very soon, Karine found a school in Decorah, located near the St. Cloud Hotel where the Luther College students and faculty were housed. The Winneshiek Normal Institute was also known as the Page school, after Principal S. Page. Its aim was to make

> thorough, independent scholars. Superficial acquirements will not be allowed to take the place of sound mental culture. The discipline will be mild, but firm. Students are reminded that their business here is not pastime but study. Wholesome regulations will be instituted, and the pupils' sense of right appealed to in sustaining them. The School is under the supervision or patronage of no particular Sect or denomination. The morals and habits of students will be strictly guarded, and the religious opinions of all respected. Unless under the immediate supervision of parents, pupils will be required to attend some place of worship on the Sabbath. Tuition ranges from $3 to $5 per quarter. Penmanship, Vocal Music, and Normal Class each $1 extra. Instrumental music, $10. Incidentals, for fuel, lights, .25 cents. Board, including everything except lights, $2.00 per week.[212]

The Page school opened on August 28, 1862, not long after Karine arrived in Decorah. She convinced Larsen that she should attend it, given her stated career ambitions to be a teacher. Karine wrote a breathless letter to Henrietta in early September about her new situation: She had enrolled in the Page School. "I read English for one hour, wrote German translations; after we ate, I read about the Greeks, Romans and Phoenicians and that I enjoyed. At two I read French, then later I sewed a dress."[213]

Karen Larsen, who was watching Karine closely, realized her sister needed a strict schedule. It is not surprising she established a routine for her to give her an ordered life, one of the approved treatments at the time for nervous excitement. This normal school curriculum at its base seems to be rather like the curriculum of Nissen girls' school and Christiansfeld. For a so-called practical school, there was a fair amount of classical content to the education with its languages, history, and classical literature. The school did not want to appear sectarian, but it did require that the students attend the church of their choice regularly. Living with the Larsens in very cramped quarters in the St. Cloud Hotel in downtown Decorah put Karine in close proximity with the boys studying with Larsen and the other teachers. She would soon weary of their theological obsessions.

A week later Karine described her life at school more precisely.[214] School began at 7:30 a.m., went until 12:00, then resumed at 1:30, continuing until 4:30. Her studies included English grammar, spelling, reading, geography, arithmetic, accounting, using decimals; both ladies and gentlemen were among the students, which pleased Karine, who, we can infer from her letters, was "boy crazy." The day began with devotions from the *Book of Common Prayer* and a hymn. Karine worked hardest on her English accent; being with the English attracted her to

Decorah Episcopal Church

the Episcopal church, a new little congregation in Decorah. In following the requirement that they attend church, Karine had found a unique way to study English, find another denomination, and at the same time irritate her family and friends.

Soon she began attending the church, a move that appealed to her rebellious youthfulness and at the same time upset her community. In addition, she found it to be a refuge from the pure Lutheran doctrine (*die reine Lehre*) of the pastors and students around her. "I'm beginning English school," she wrote Henriette, "and think I'm going to be Episcopalian—at least it is a faith. I've read the Prayer Book."[215] In the previous letter she had lamented that Lauritz (Laur. Larsen) had sat her down to talk religion because he did not think she was serious about her beliefs. He and the pastors agreed that they needed to persist in their efforts to convince her she was wrong. Their methods were, on the whole, less than effective. She told Henriette, not unreasonably, these attempts just made her more rebellious. In a comment that reveals Henriette expected this would happen. "I can't do what you told me to do—read the Augsburg Confession. I have read it, but I read more shame than gift in it."[216] Not an uncommon response.

Karine needed to have an orthodox faith in order to get a job. All of her potential employers were Lutheran pastors and their wives. Her unbelief upset the women, to say nothing of the pastors. Karine described a conversation in which Larsen told her she was "naughty" for not believing the faith in an orthodox manner. This, frankly, did little to advance his case. When they visited the Korens some days later, the theological conversations continued, this time about the Trinity which she thought was not logical: "Three must be three," she concluded, once again not without some thought.

Her heterodox opinions and questions upset the group and caused the pastors to decree she could not teach their children. The consternation among the families was obvious. They always needed help. Karine had come to help them with household chores, child care, and especially teaching. Her restlessness, probably the result of some immaturity or emotional instability, made it impossible for her to stay focused on school. She wanted to escape. She traveled from family to family looking for respite from the theological attacks and a place where she could quiet her nerves.

After a time at Korens, where Elisabeth offered her refuge, she had galloped on her horse home from Washington Prairie to the Larsens in Decorah. "I rode on the great ridge that goes to Decorah, and I was happy. I wished I could ride to the end. You can believe that when I ride alone, I dream it is the olden days, with knights and ladies."[217] In a way, the old world of knights and ladies would have been better for her. There the roles of men and women were more clearly drawn. Her place and era, however, were different, something she knew from her own experiences.

Laur. Larsen's children

Despite her reports that she was doing quite well in school, especially spelling, things had come to a head for her: "Today I resigned from the school. What will become of me?"[218] For Karine this was not a mere rhetorical question. She was caught between the upper class expectations from her life in Norway, and the American sense that inherited privilege and class no longer obtained. Still the men and women in her group still operated, to a large extent, with the expectations of the Old World.

Shortly after the announcement that she had resigned, Karine wrote a long letter to Henriette. In it she regretted that her faith had once again disappeared, despite her attempts to revive it by reading three chapters of the Bible every day. She supposed it was her cold heart that caused this. As always her immediate future as a teacher hung in the balance. Her lack of faith, about which she was honest, was a career ender. She remonstrated with Henriette who was also casting about for a place in society. "I am almost mad at you for suggesting that you be a serving wench and I be a teacher. Fy!" A better solution she thought would be for them to buy a house together—with their father's help—and settle down in a small town where they could work, especially if they had a sewing machine.[219] That route, she realized, would not be quite appropriate for women from their class.

As she struggled to rekindle her faith, she tried attending church and had further conversations with the wives who treated her teenage rebellions with a bit more tolerance than the clergy. Mrs. Carolina Schmidt, the wife of Professor Fredrick August Schmidt (1837-1928), had not helped when she told Karine of a student who had seen the devil while they were still at Concordia just a couple of years before.[220] This caused Karine some nights of weeping and prayer, which resulted in her worrying that she would lose her faith again.[221] In an effort to remedy that situation, she resolved to read the New Testament, one chapter at a time. She also vowed to relearn Luther's Small Catechism and the Augsburg Confession. The Augsburg Confession, however, continued to repel her, probably as much because of her irritation with the young pastors who were not exactly winsome in their missionary efforts. The pastors were maybe still too young: Laur. Larsen was twenty-nine when Karine arrived in Decorah, Ulrik Vilhelm Koren thirty six, Hermann Amberg Preus thirty seven.

Karine does give us a unique insight into the world of pure doctrine the pastors were pushing. She described, as only a lively teenager could, the efforts of the young pastors to persuade her to accept the pure teaching of Lutheran doctrine. This came from their Missouri brethren, or teachers, such as Walther and Craemer (who were in many ways more like their fathers), since they were a generation older. From her reports, they followed her around the house, waiting to pounce on her to read long sections of the *Book of Concord* aloud to her, arguing that she should believe in it because it was right. Apparently, they could not find more winning ways. They poured it on more and more, with less than stellar results. She described sessions with Laur. Larsen in which they read one page of Luther every evening.

It drove her to despair. "Where can I find a pastor?" she cried, looking to find, not doctrinal surety, but someone who could deal with her very troubled soul.[222] Koren was no better. "Don't talk about Koren. I have no confidence in any pastor."[223] She concluded that when she was alone with the children the next day things would be better. She came to prefer them to their parents.[224] Even serene Mrs. Koren spoke with her about the issue, without forcing anything on her. The Korens decided not to ask Karine to teach their children because of her lack of faith.[225] While she realized that it was important for her to subscribe to the Lutheran faith in order to teach their children, she found the requirement onerous and irritating. She was forthright enough to say so, regardless of its consequences for her economic future.

After Christmas, she knew she was in some economic difficulty because of her refusal or inability to believe. She came to think that she would not find a place in the new world. She wrote Henriette that she could not be a servant, because the idea of getting paid offended her and made her afraid. What she wished was that she and Henriette could be their own "lords" (*Herrer*).[226] The reluctance to be paid is also a hint of the move from a familial set of expectations to a cash economy, which Karine found beneath her for traditional reasons.

Christmas Eve 1861 at Spring Prairie Parsonage (sketched March 26, 1862). Hermann is the man facing to the left; the man on the left is Laur. Larsen. Christian is playing with the cannon. Sina is the girl in the foreground. Anga is two, Johan Wilhelm Preus is six months, held by Linka, center left. Thora Larsen is probably facing Larsen. The woman next to Larsen is probably Karen. Henriette is probably the woman on the far right.

Larsen's Guest Room No. 8 at Luther College, Decorah, Iowa, October 1864. C. K. Preus and Professor Laur. Larsen. Linka is showing how little room there really was at the college. Notice the cruciform tree in the back center. Larsen saw it one day and took it as a blessing, in hoc signo vinces (in this sign will you conquer). Linka is making fun of Larsen's assurance there would be room for them when they came. There were only boards.

At the end of 1862, she was taken to be with the Preuses in Spring Prairie. The families gathered there to celebrate the season. Karine observed that she really felt better when she was not being hectored by adults and could just "think her own thoughts."[227] The idea of a career still bothered her. "I have no money and cannot travel into the wide world."[228] It was possible for people to survive without much money, as they lived off the land. She was helpless without a family where she could stay and live, exchanging her services for room and board. Most were close to the farm and got all they needed from it.

The problem for Karine, who failed at the Preuses and was taken back to Washington Prairie to stay with the Korens, was that her Old World sense of things and the American culture clashed in ways she could never reconcile. She could almost replicate the situation in Norway as these pastors' families were doing, but as a young single woman in the New World she also was looking for opportunities around her in America. She always wondered why she and Henriette could not avail themselves of these opportunities. She was becoming a problem for the entire community, all of whom felt they should do something for her. Given her spiritual state, they could not engage her to teach their children, and did not want her to influence them, spiritually. They could not have her in their homes for long periods of time. The process through which Karine was going is not unlike the typical professional training necessary for any candidate wishing to enter any profession.

The Civil War and Building the Main Building

This was also a very busy time for the young group of pastors and professors. They were building the new school. The Civil War was raging and occupying the minds of their laity, who were for the Union. They had sent numbers of volunteers to fight, especially the Fifteenth Regiment of Wisconsin, also known as the Scandinavian Regiment, largely from the area around Spring Prairie. Karine's brother Hagbarth had answered the call, as had many immigrants still not even American citizens, and joined the Illinois Volunteers.

On January 31, 1862, the Fifteenth Regiment of Wisconsin was mustered into service. It would see action and receive much glory for its participation in the victory on Island No. Ten, February to April 1862. It also suffered a bloody defeat at the battle of Chickamaugua in 1863.

Laying the cornerstone at Luther College, June 30, 1864. Craemer and Walther are seated at the left, watching the pastors of the Norwegian Synod, led by Preus and Larsen.

While the war was proceeding with its financial and personnel demands, the Main Building of Luther College was being built. All of the pastors and professors were involved in that project, none more than Laur. Larsen. Although Karine did stay a bit with the Larsens, it did not last long for many reasons, including the cramped space in the Larsen rooms. While she could be a companion to their children, the Larsens did not trust her to teach. They welcomed her into their cramped quarters for a season, until things broke down, which they inevitably did.

Fortunately for them all, not least Karine, she fell in love with a medical student, Jacob Wright Magelssen (1843-1931), probably the only man she could find who was not going to be a pastor! He knew that she wearied of all these clergy types. He had emigrated in 1863, one year after Karine, from Åfjord, Norway, not far from Trondheim. At that time he was about twenty. He had attended Nissen's school in Christiania, where he got to know Karine's brother, Harald. That he was able to attend Rush Medical School immediately upon arriving speaks well of his English abilities, although his record at the Nissen School was not distinguished.[229] Where Karine could have met him is not quite clear, although they were part of the same class and relationship. Jacob was not a Luther student, but he was a pastor's son and knew many of the families in the Norwegian Synod. His father was Hans Gynther Magelssen. Jacob's old-

Jacob Wright Magelssen

er brother, Kristian Magelssen (1839-1921), served Highland Prairie, Minnesota, near Rushford, the town where Jacob would later establish a practice. Wherever they had met, Karine and Jacob were in love and planned to marry. This served as a welcome reprieve for the young woman whose faith and temperament made her ill-suited for teaching, especially given the requirements of these orthodox pastors. In a way, Karine had flunked governess school and moved to the only other option for her at the time: being a wife!

The wives had come to the conclusion that Karine would do best at the Hjorts. They all believed Mrs. Hjort was one to best manage Karine's flightiness. Things would go well and then blow up. The religious question was still the most troubling for them all. Jacob Magelssen appeared to know this and sent her a letter on November 28, 1863, from Rush Medical School in Chicago wondering if she could hold out at the

The Hjort Parsonage at Paint Creek: "All the children are occupied with some nosy little pigs who have run all the way from Mama's garden where they were into something they should not have gotten into. The wife herself is following them and Father is going to spade a little wherever he finds it necessary."

Hjorts while she waited for him to marry her. Mrs. Hjort, apparently, brooked no nonsense from the flighty Karine who managed to stay with them for about nine months, but still the relationship and her vocation were still rather up and down. That winter and spring, things continued at the same kind of pace for her. Karen Larsen was glad that Karine was getting a place at Hjorts and Blaasenborg, because the Larsens could not take her, given their cramped space.[230] One hears a hint that Karine needed more care than she could give the children herself. Blaasenborg would be a good place for her, almost everyone agreed. Mrs. Hjort, with her common sense and sturdy character, seemed to be a good match for the restless young woman. In the Blaasenborg parlor, Karine could learn things a cultivated lady should know in order to establish a home regardless of whether she would teach. In a letter to Linka, Mrs. Koren discussed the situation at

Christiane Hjort

Ove J. Hjort

Paint Creek. The work there, she mused, was not as difficult as it was at other parsonages because they did not have much of a farm. They still had the help of three servants whom they had brought from Norway: Laura Knutson, Ludvig Larsen, and Carrie Hansen. All knew this was a credit to the Hjort family. Not many pastors had been so effective at keeping their servants with them.[231] At the time, Mrs. Hjort was expecting another child, but she could count on the help of the older girls, especially the oldest sister, the ten-year-old Lulla. The Hjorts by this time had five children and would have three more by the time Mrs Hjort died in 1873. There was lots of work to do for everyone in the parsonage.

As in most of her endeavors, Karine arrived at Blaasenborg with high hopes. Now she assured everyone she was ready to adapt to their situation and she would also be prepared to learn from the couple some of the fine arts required of wives in this culture. She could also help with the children while waiting to marry. Predictably, relations between Mrs. Hjort and Karine quickly deteriorated, however. "I've just told Mrs. Hjort I'm going to Decorah. She's been crying and carrying on so much I can't write."[232]

From Mrs. Hjort's point of view, however, things looked different, apparently, for about the same time she wrote, they had "two very capable girls helping us, so Karine and I could enjoy the company of our distinguished guest," probably Architect Charles Griese, from Cleveland. His work as architect of the Main Building brought him to Decorah frequently while the building was being finished.[233]

Four days later Karine wrote a long letter to Henriette exclaiming on the conditions at the Hjorts. As we read her letter, it is easy to set the scene. She was sitting in the parlor with the family, while Mrs. Hjort was sewing, Pastor Hjort was singing, Mrs. Hjort joining in with a descant as he accompanied them on the guitar. It is an autumn evening. One can see the young woman glaring at Mrs. Hjort as she writes her letter, "I am so restless," she says, "I sit and read hymns, the Gospel and epistles. I love hymn 319 (*"Du er jo kun et Menneske"* "You are only human, why do you want those things that only are in God's power?"). I would like to go out for a walk, but I can't get permission. I'm reading French and Walter Scott. . . . I want to be with you!"[234] The reference to the hymn is touching. The unknown author used the Norwegian equivalent of "You're only human" to express the singer's restlessness and sense of unhappiness. "What can all your worry do to help your situation? What can your sorrow solve?"[235] For many reasons, Karine found it comforting.

For the moment she was angry at the Hjorts, especially Christiane. Then, a week later, Karine wrote again to Henrietta, apologizing that she had made her think poorly of Mrs. Hjort because both of the Hjorts idolized Henriette. Then she noted that Hjort had a beautiful voice. She was probably listening even as she was writing: he "can sing the highest tenor, and lowest bass especially beautifully."[236]

These good feelings, however, did not last. Although we do not know what the issues were, not long after this letter, apparently things fell apart completely and she had to leave, either because she demanded it, or the Hjorts, driven to distraction, took her home to the Larsens who were still living in their cramped quarters in St. Cloud Hotel. Elisabeth Koren observed "Friday, Karine came to Larsens. Hjort drove her. . . . She needs lots of help."[237] Apparently, she found some respite there, helping the children with art projects, while trying to do her work, crocheting, and drawing. "I crochet until it is light and then read the New Testament and the hymnal. I think of all my trouble with the filthy boys. No one has as nice a boyfriend as I."[238] We can see from her report of her time at Larsens that she was given freedom to sit up all night, crocheting and reading. This was not good for her mental state because it got her off balance. Now that she was with Larsens, she once again had to contend with the college boys, whom she called filthy because of their failure to clean the common toilets.

The Larsens were obviously not equipped to handle the volatile moods of Karine, occupied as they were with their own family, Mrs. Larsen's delicate health, and Larsen's work as the foreman of the Main Building project. In addition he had to teach full time. It was not good for her, however, to sit up all night and get off schedule. If Mrs. Hjort, especially, knew anything about the treatment of this type of mental problem, it was the conventional, and probably helpful, treatment for young people with excitable nerves. Keeping a very strict schedule with little variation kept them from going off the rails. Larsens knew this but could not enforce the rules, so they sent her back to Hjorts.

By December 2, Karine was again sitting in the Hjort parlor sewing presents for Christmas, one of the common tasks in the parlor. In a letter to Henriette, who was with Linka to help her during her confinement at the birth of Carl Christie Preus (1864), Karine noted that they had heard

Preuses had gotten a piano. She wished were there. Mrs. Hjort had not given her permission "to put one finger" on their new piano, nor would she teach her how to play, even though Karine wanted to learn. She added that she had just heard from Jacob's parents, probably a letter welcoming her into the family. They told her that he was studying medicine now because he could neither be a farmer nor a pastor. She spoke with some satisfaction: she was going to marry a man of her station, something she had hoped to do. She had not seen many prospects outside of clergy who would not have been ideal for her.[239] This was the best thing that could have happened to her in the New World. It meant she had a place and things were going pretty much the way they might have in Norway.

New Year's Day, 1865, Karen Larsen said that Karine, who had been with them for Christmas, was returning to the Hjorts and hoped she was getting better. She also wished Karine would learn to be more polite. Karine had probably told them that Mrs. Hjort was too strict, and Karen had probably inferred from the report that Karine had not been exactly a model of good deportment. That same day, Karine wrote to Henriette to say that Mrs. Hjort had just had a baby, Jacob Aall (1864-1939), and that she, Karine, had written to Norway to tell her family of her engagement. Things appeared to be going smoothly. Not long after the birth, Karine returned to the Hjorts to help. In early February, Karine was teaching Ansoph, one of the younger Hjort girls, to embroider and draw, the first record we have of her actually doing any of the teaching she had been eager to do when she first started Page Academy three years before.[240]

Predictably, her stormy personality exploded. Two days later she complained that Mrs. Hjort thought she corresponded too often with Henriette. This she reported with what can only be called exasperation. In addition, she was reading world history, and learning to sing and play the *salmodikon*, a fretted instrument with one string played with a bow. (Linka drew a picture of it, which is on page 80.) It was fairly common among the Norwegian emigrants, especially for playing hymns. Again she praised Hjort for his lovely voice when he would sing during their evening entertainments.[24`] Karine tended to get on better with Pastor Hjort than Mrs. Hjort, probably because he was a man. He was much milder than his wife, although he had his opinions about her education as well. He did not approve of her reading novels, especially French novels, because of their bad morals and immoral influence on young women, hoping she did not read them "for the sake of the story, but only for the sake of the language."[242] This struck her as hilarious. It was a continuing suspicion of the clergy about women reading idle tales and romantic novels. In addition to its bad influence, he probably thought that for one with such an excitable temperament as Karine, a romance novel was about the worst thing she could read. In this same letter she reported that she longed to learn how to read notes so she could sing, at least, since they did not allow her the chance to learn how to play the piano.

Her exasperation continued when she perceived the families were trying to get her to take a shine to Professor Lyder Siewers (1830-1907), an elegant single man with the soul of a poet. He came to teach at the school in 1863. His frequent visits to the Hjorts when Karine was there made  them think he was taking an interest in her. The wives appeared to approve of such an arrangement. Karine, however, had no interest whatever in him as a potential mate, describing him only as "a bosom friend" (*Busenfreund*).[243] Two days later she was trying to read the New Testament through, one chapter at a time, working to relearn the catechism and read the Augsburg Confession again. In that same letter she reported on a meeting the day before in the congregation over the confession/absolution debate swirling around the young church body, which she thought to be mostly funny.

Lyder Siewers

Karine gives a rather different picture of the serious debates of the Synod pastors. She describes her attendance at the debates on absolution in Paint Creek Church which she observed from the balcony. "I thought it was wonderfully funny to watch the way they argued."[244] This comment is in direct contrast to the unrelieved seriousness we get of the pastors in the formal histories of the founding of the early institutions of the Norwegian American church. Karine, whose faith was always teetering between doubt and assurance, was not very serious about these arguments. They bristle in the official church histories. She was probably more representative of the large majority of church members than we may have pictured when we confine ourselves to the published histories of these early pastors riding into battle on a variety of dogmatic issues that seem, now, a somewhat extreme. Very seldom do we get a picture of them in real places making real arguments before a variety of people, including women.

In the same letter she told about teasing Mrs. Hjort by telling her how much Henriette liked Mrs. Brandt, which made Mrs. Hjort jealous. Karen Larsen had told Karine, in a typical defense of Diderikke, that "there's something wrong with all of us."[245] Even as she tried to stop Karine's

Diderikke Brandt

criticism, she herself admitted it was difficult to be with the boisterous Mrs. Brandt; she was simply too loud and forward, a criticism with which Elisabeth Koren agreed. On April 11, in a letter to Linka, Mrs. Koren noted that Mrs. Larsen was sick again, and then wondered how it was going with Karine with Henriette at the Preuses in Spring Prairie. She suggested that Karine might profit from a visit to Koshkonong where she could get help from Dr. Søren Johan Hanssen."[246] Dr. Hanssen (1820-1885) was valued by the immigrants as a "real" doctor from Norway, not the typical American quack. At their suggestion she did travel to Koshkonong and stayed with the Ottesens. While she was there Ottesen, also an accomplished musician, taught her to read and sing notes, something she had been hoping to learn at the Hjorts.[247]

Henriette by this time was a fairly permanent fixture at the Preuses, caring for the children and serving as a companion to Linka. She had been with Linka in February 1864 when Linka had lost her newborn baby, Carl Christie. She helped the midwife baptize him before he died. In the late summer of 1865, from the end of August, until October 14, and the dedication of the new building at the college, Hermann and Linka took a long trip to New York. They left the children with Henriette. She

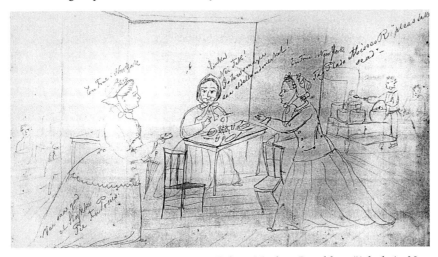

Linka eating oysters in a restaurant in Fulton Market, Brooklyn. "A lady in New York: Would you like a piece of pie, Mrs. Preus? Linka: No thanks, the oysters are so remarkably delicious. A lady in New York: Take a seat, Mrs. Preus."

took them to Decorah so they would be there when the Preuses returned just in time for the dedication service.

Karine wrote from Paint Creek on August 23, 1865, to inform Henriette that she was engaged to Jacob Magelssen. Her spiritual situation had improved enough for her to consider taking communion in church that next Sunday. To her surprise Hjort refused her when she came up to the rail, a rather shocking detail.[248] This little fact says about as much as can be said about the strict orthodoxy of the pastors who would not overlook their theological scruples simply to please a relative.

Dedication of the Main Building

With the dedication of the new Main Building scheduled for October 14, 1865, the attention of the entire group turned toward Decorah and the celebration planned for its completion. Laur. Larsen's leadership in the building of this impressive building during the Civil War had surprised everyone. Karen Larsen's biography of her father says that although he had no experience in building, working with architects, contractors, and the like, he had done well. He had managed despite the pressures of both teaching, running the school, and caring for his young family, and his wife, who was suffering a terminal illness.

Given all that, the two Neuberg sisters must have been too much for him at the time. As the male responsible for them, beside his own wife, he had many worries and responsibilities on account of them. While Karine

Luther College, October 14, 1865, Dedication

A view of the tables at the dedication. Larsen is shaking up an Irish boy and Mrs. Koren and Brandt are going around the tables speaking to people. Several thousand people—between 8,000 and 10,000—had been seated around the tables. "Farmwife: Yes, this is a fine arrangement, that's for sure! Mrs. Brandt: It was good to get coffee, for it is so cold, but let us hurry so others may eat. Professor Larsen: What are you doing that for, naughty boy! Scram, or you might get something more than cake! Irish boy: You may empty my pockets, and see all the cake I have stolen. Mrs. Koren: It is good when one can be so content with everything, Mr. Birkrem. Mr. Birkrem: Yes, dear Mrs. Koren. I am so please that we have this school ready and pleased to see the many people showing such interest in it. And then to have these 100 healthy and diligent boys seeking admission. Out of excitement, he accidentally spills his precious coffee on Mrs. Koren's dress."

was staying with the Hjorts, Larsen wrote Hjort about his trip to Cleveland, and also about Karine whose expenses needed to be paid. "You should receive 175 Specie dollars [a Specie dollar had about the same value as an American dollar at the time] from Norway. You should get something from Neuberg for Karine's expenses while she was ill."[249]

By the beginning of 1866, the fact of Karine's marriage to Jacob Magelssen began to sink in. Karen Larsen wrote to Henriette wondering if there really would be a wedding that summer, probably in light of the changeable moods and opinions of Karine, who was still at the Hjorts, where according to Karen, things between Mrs. Hjort and Karine were on the mend or at least for the time, better.[250] In January, Karine said things were getting better at Paint Creek. "Hjort apologized for the way he has been."[251]

Karine's wedding finally came to be seen as a reality for which they needed to prepare. Mrs. Koren reported to Linka that one of the Larsen girls, probably Thora (1857-1908), came to help sew a bridal present for Karine. By spring it was sure: Karine was going to marry Jacob in July, even as one can hear in the letters some wonderment as to whether Karine would keep her promises, given her known flightiness. Her visit to Dr. Hanssen in Koshkonong had resulted in some prescriptions that she tried to follow: "He says I should take no more pills, eat more, and take iron three times a day. I took a dose, but it didn't work yesterday. He's a great doctor."[252]

Jacob began his medical career in association with Hanssen and later took over the practice when Hanssen returned to Norway for his health.[253] So her trip to see Hanssen was probably a trip to visit Jacob as well. From the prescriptions Hanssen gave her, one can deduce that she had been constipated and maybe even anorexic. Karine drew a vivid pictures of her stomach problems, giving a surprising glimpse of how different life was at the time, telling how she vomited all night, which inconvenienced the Larsens in whose bed she was sleeping, along with them, a cramped apartment to be sure. Very few give such detail of their daily lives, showing the privations of the early pastors as they lived and worked in the new land.

When she came back to Blaasenborg, Karine reported that Jacob, who had probably brought her there, was with her and that she was fine. Jacob, known for his good humor and wit, caused Hjort to laugh so hard that Christiane commented that he had not laughed so much in her memory. The farmers called him "the laughing doctor."[254]

On February 2, 1866, Jacob and Hjort had visited the Larsens, maybe to determine what illness, exactly, Mrs. Larsen was suffering. About this time, Mrs. Larsen, always in delicate health, began a more rapid decline. Karen added that she hoped that things were okay with Karine now, probably hoping that she had done well in deciding to marry Jacob:."She's such a trusting person."[255] About this time, Karine in a rare moment of self-reflection noted that she had been with Jacob enough to know he was a good man, but that she "wished she were good enough for JWM and had Elisabeth Koren's patience and your love."[256] Noting that she could not be free with him the way she was with Henriette, she was now working on becoming a normal housewife and learning how to cook and otherwise keep house, "I've tried and learned how to make bread and brew beer."[257] Learning to be a housewife, even a doctor's wife, as we have already seen in the education of both Linka and Elisabeth, meant that one needed to know more than the fine arts. Karine still needed to learn how to run what we would consider today to be a farm.

Lulla Hjort

We cannot quite tell what the situation at the Hjorts really was. Karine's reports suggests that the time was as rocky as expected. Lulla, in her memoirs of growing up in the Paint Creek parsonage, recalled Karine's time with them as enjoyable and without trouble.[258] Whether Mrs. Hjort's feelings were accurately reported, Karine's reports concerning her relationship with Mrs. Hjort give us a pretty clear idea of what Karine needed to improve. Mrs. Hjort would not let Karine visit them at Easter, "as though Karine were not her own boss," wrote Karen.[259] There is a slight bit of criticism in the note, but it also shows Mrs. Hjort had some starch in her.

Some days later, Karine was still at Blaasenborg because Mrs. Hjort was in despair about having to train a new girl and hired man. She could not face it without Karine at the time, she said. Was Mrs. Hjort simply using that on the unsuspecting Karine to keep her there, or was she really exhausted? It is a bit difficult to tell. Things had begun to improve a bit because Karine reported that she was beginning to play the piano.[260] If Karine was suffering some kind of manic/depression syndrome, even if they did not have the medicines we do today, they did have a treatment for it: quiet and as little stimulation as possible. Mrs. Hjort knew this. It may be the reason she restricted Karine from many girlish amusements. That she had been allowed to play the piano means that she appeared to be improving.

By this time in the history of these pastors and their families, the issue of educating their daughters was beginning to press them. Things were changing as the generations began to change. The first generation of wives was still having babies, even as their oldest daughters grew into adolescence. By custom it was time to send their daughters to their "aunts" in the neighborhood to learn domestic skills, as the pastors' wives had done in Norway. Henriette Koren went to stay with the Preuses to help them and learn from Linka the special arts that she could teach: drawing, piano, German, among other disciplines, and maybe get to know Christian better, a ploy her mother may have used, but which did not work.[261] At the same time both women were much engaged in their teaching responsibilities for their younger children and some from their congregation as the parsonage served as school for needy children who could help with the work around the house and farm. Linka now had three boys to teach German every day, including Adolf Bredesen (1850-1913), a Luther student and friend of Christian, who would become a leading pastor in the next generation of pastors, along with Christian.[262]

Karine wrote from Blaasenborg that she, at the moment, liked it with the Hjorts and reported that there was a teacher available who would teach Norwegian for $15 a month and room and board.[263] At this same time, preparations for Karine's wedding on July 12, 1866, were in full swing. Mrs. Larsen had started sewing a wedding dress for Karine, whose marriage seemed to have been a relief to them all.[264] That she was marrying a doctor seemed very salutary since all three of the Neuberg sisters suffered delicate health, both mentally and physically. That he was not clergy was even better from Karine's point of view and probably the others. They did need a doctor: Karen's tuberculosis grew worse, and Henriette's nerves began to be a problem for the Preuses. A doctor in the family would be most welcome!

Through the summer of 1866, Hermann and Linka were preparing to leave for Norway for a kind of second honeymoon, fifteen years after arriving in America. Both were exhausted from their pioneering work, from establishing churches throughout Wisconsin, to building a parsonage, raising a family, and running a farm with much less of the help than they would have had in Norway, Hermann's invitation to give his "Seven Lectures on the Churchly Situation in America" at the Mission School in Christiania became a chance for a long rest among family and friends who could take care of them.[265] From here the letters become fewer and farther between as they prepared to leave for Norway with Henriette, who functioned frequently as a governess and "aunt" for the Preus children. About this time, however, something happened to Henriette's nerves. Hermann wrote Laur. Larsen that he was now worried about her, something Larsen would be interested in, given that she was his

Hermann Preus

sister-in-law. Just as they were leaving for Norway, in November 1866, Henriette had become too ill to travel with them. When they arrived in Europe, Hermann wrote Larsen telling him more about the situation with Henriette. Apparently she had been expected to go with the Preuses back to Norway, but, suddenly, for reasons they did not understand, she refused to go with them because she was afraid that her father would not be glad to see her, indicating some strain in the relationship. Magelssen had tried to stop her trip, thinking it better that she stay in Madison with Karine. Henriette's condition had forced the Preuses to sit up with her at night a lot.[266] By August 1867, Henriette had somehow made it back to Kristiansand, Norway, via Boston, and Hamburg. She wrote a letter to Linka who was now in Spring Prairie. She said that she would have loved to have seen her but had not enough money to make the trip to Halden. Linka was recovering from a difficult pregnancy that had resulted in the birth of Paul Arctander. Her condition had been so perilous that Preus even mused about leaving her there to recover while he returned home for the Synod meeting, something he fortunately was persuaded not to do.[265] Henriette would have liked to have been at Linka's side to nurse her, given their long friendship, but could not raise the money to come. She did report that Karine had had a big baby boy on July 21, and had been quite ill from it.[267] Both the Neuberg sisters, having struggled with their callings to be teachers, were now ready to become wives, but Henriette had not yet found a suitable beau. Karine's search for a vocation outside of marriage had come to a happy end.

Governess Problems

With the Neuberg sisters now effectively out of the picture as potential governesses and teachers in the home, the Preuses, Korens, Larsens, and Stubs, were still in need of help in the home with the education of their very young children as well as their adolescent daughters. When the Preuses returned from Norway to Spring Prairie in 1867, Elisabeth wrote to Linka welcoming her back from Norway and wondering about a mutual acquaintance of theirs, a Miss Magdalene Muhlenfort (b. 1850), a woman from Bergen, whom they considered to be a likely governess, except for her poor health. She came highly recommended by her friends in Norway. Mrs. Koren would have preferred her to any other and hoped she would not go to the Stubs in Big Canoe, given the unsettled nature of that household, which is never quite clearly explained. It is clear from the letters that Mrs. Koren was not close to the Stubs and looked askance at what she thought of as their recklessness and restlessness, moving back and forth from Norway to America, driving through storms and nearly drowning in swollen rivers, etc.[269] They had recently returned to America after a sojourn of several years in parishes around Bergen, Norway, while their son, Hans Gerhard (1849-1931), the scion of the Synod, attended Bergen's Cathedral School from 1861 to 1865. He would later be the first president of the Norwegian Lutheran Church in America.

As governesses and girls moved through the lives of the Korens and Preuses, we see that the wives continued to have chief responsibility to oversee, if not actually do, the teaching of the children. Mrs. Koren described the one-room schoolhouse in the kitchen in a letter she wrote to Linka, saying that as she sat writing, Henriette, her daughter, was sitting beside her, drawing, while Caroline "Lina" was playing a Danish folk song, *"Jeg gik mig ud i Lunden,"* on the piano, although all she could manage was the melody, something that upset her because she thought she would never learn to play with all her fingers.[270] Mrs. Koren needed additional help teaching the children, she realized, and questioned Linka to see if Miss Muhlenfort, who was with Linka at the time, would be able, without too much trouble, to help by writing to Lina and reassuring her that she would learn to play more than the melody soon. What was needed, Mrs. Koren, saw, was a better teacher, perhaps Miss Muhlenfort, teaching in the sketch, who was now in Spring Prairie, or at least in the

"Spring Prairie Parsonage in 1861, after we had lived in the old one for ten years."

Eggedosis. "Confusion at school because Mama has come in with eggedosis. Every birthday in the family is an eggedosis feast day when we have a plentiful supply of eggs and sugar. October 1869. M: Here I sit with the most serious thoughts and I am being disturbed. Come here right away. You first, Mymy, and then all the children afterward. A: Refreshing? It is so wonderfully fine that we will get eggedosis—eight and eleven are five—there you have a kick, Anga? Anga: You are a Hottentot, Doctor, you are! Careful— Mymy will see you! Rosina: The Hottentots? In Spring Prairie? I think. Lina: No, Sina, let me see—the Hottentots—I thought they were in South Africa Paul: Mymy, take, me, six, nine, four, eight. Muhlenfort: Listen, now Sina and Lina, where do the Hottentots live? There is always noise when you come in, who can manage when you carry on, Linka! Hermann: can I have a little? Linka: Excuse the band on my head, But I have a toothache today. My glasses have to sit on my nose, because I have eggedosis on my fingers."

Madison area where she could help Linka with the teaching. Mrs. Koren observed in her girls a longing to continue in school. It would be difficult for them when they were too old and no longer could attend school. She wondered whether or not Miss Muhlenfort could come up with a plan for a girls' school. Henriette Landmark, cousin to Professor Landmark and soon to become his wife after his first wife died in childbed, had given some hints that she would liked to open a school for girls, but Mrs. Koren, for private reasons, was not sure that she would like to have her educate her children.[271] "Tell me," she asked Linka, "would you want to have her educate your children if you could not be there? Neither would I," Mrs. Koren concluded, saying that she had "told Landmark both what she perceived to be her good sides and at the same time my hesitations about her."[272] While there is nothing in the record that indicates anything untoward about Landmark's behavior, or Henriette's, it is an obvious concern to the little group after the first Mrs. Landmark's death in 1870; it may have worried Mrs. Koren that the single woman, a cousin, was still living with Landmark and probably caring for his children, a not uncommon pattern at that time.

Linka Preus, 1860s

Marie Sivisind, another single woman whom they all considered to be a good help, who appeared frequently in the lives of the pastors' wives, would have been much better, Mrs. Koren concluded, if only she had a stronger constitution and could work more. Now that Johan Koren wanted to learn to play the piano, she thought he should begin soon, a big factor in the teaching of any young person to play an instrument. They both knew that Rosina had not exhibited much interest in the piano over the past months, something about which the two women chatted frequently in their letters, when they spoke of their children.[273] As Elisabeth concluded her letter, she noted that it was time to go help the little boys who needed her to teach them English: "I should be a passably good Mother and give up my desire to write you any longer."[274] Teaching the children had grown to be more and more complicated for these women now approaching middle age, with older children as well as babies.

Vocation of the Pastor's Wife

As Mrs. Koren and Mrs. Preus began to achieve a good sense for their vocations as pastors' wives on the frontier, they were confident of their roles and place in the scheme of things. They had to be managers of the farm and household, skills they had both learned well at home and adapted in the New Land. They had learned enough to teach their children and be a colleague to their husbands, helping them bear the burdens of their work, often isolated from their brother pastors. Vilhelm Koren often referred to his wife as his "colleague," with whom he shared every-thing as he did his work and whose wisdom he trusted about many things in the parish.[275] Frequently she shared her feelings about things required of her in the role. Not often did she complain, but once she reacted to a question about the role of the pastor's wife that Linka had asked her. She had quoted from a book on pastoral the-ology which had discussed the role of the pastor's wife. Whatever it was, Elisabeth reacted against it rather strongly, agreeing with Linka's apparent thoughts.

*Linka Preus
in middle age*

> I have not read the awful book you speak of, nor his memoirs, but you can believe that I take your part against the author when he says such. When you come this summer you will hear more from me on the subject. Wexels knows better how the pastor's wife should be—I have it here and you can read his *Pastoral Theology* when you come. For example I think that being a pastor here one is so taken up by the congregation and all that the church expects that their time and thought concerning their wife and children is very little. There is something wrong with that—the congregation first and last and house and children only the little they can get. It is also true in the Missouri Synod. What good is it? Can it be entirely right to care for Indians, schoolboys, and whatever and not find time to look after their own children? Can you beat that?[276]

Wexels in his *Pastoral Theology* book had spoken clearly about what kind of a person would make the best pastor's wife.

> Happy the pastor who has found a wife who without having to step into his calling, understands it so she can do what is possible to ease his sorrows, and his burdens; a housewife who as a worthy pastor's wife is like a servant of the Lord in the domestic sanctuary. . . . She spreads abroad the gentle virtues.[277]

Wexels encouraged the pastor's wife to be something of a colleague to her husband. This was not unusual; Luther certainly found a colleague in Katie, who took care for his welfare, both spiritually and physically. Other pastoral theology books and, later, books of advice on being a pastor's wife, suggested that the wife was to be the pastor to the pastor, a vocation that many wives in later years did not care to sign up for.

Elisabeth had read somewhere, probably in Walther, that pastor's families should be ideal Christians and in their own lives demonstrate the ideal Christian family. Potential pastors were to consider what sort of woman would be a good pastor's wife before they were married.[278] The idea that the pastor's family should be something of an ideal Christian family could be too much for some family members in the parsonage, but this was not an unusual way of thinking at the time.

This topic was not written about or discussed in the first pastoral theology handbooks. Most everyone knew the job description. The question came to be a subject treated in many of the pastoral theology books of the late nineteenth century well into the twentieth. Something not mentioned in Linka's or Elisabeth's letters is the touchy subject of the care of the parsonage. What was the responsibility of the pastor's family to keep it up for the sake of the congregation, so that the expenses of the congregation were worth it? The upkeep of the parsonage became maybe more of an issue in the New Land. The home was the responsibility of the congregation, part of the pastor's renumeration. Boards of Trustees watched the way the pastor's wife kept the house. Did she provide a clean and restful home for the pastor? If she left it a mess and the property deteriorated, it was expensive for the parish.

Pastors' families together in Koren's living room in 1858—the Brandts, Preuses, and Korens

Especially for Scandinavians, a filthy house with an unkempt housewife and unwashed children would be a sign of moral and religious decay. In an essay on the pastor's wife, Koren, who had traveled extensively among congregations and stayed in countless parsonages. He graphically portrayed what it was like to come into such an unkempt home where the wife

> had not learned to use soap and water or how to use brushes and brooms, or a comb for her hair, she is a bad housewife, something one immediately marks on stepping into the house, where there has been no sweeping or it has not been aired properly and there is an unappetizing table with a dirty tablecloth and a housewife with half done up hair and unwashed children, wearing a untidy, dirty and slatternly house dress as she is trying to clean up.[279]

He concluded this rather vivid essay with a scathing attack on a pastor's wife who gossips. Expanding on the language in the Epistle of James 3:7-8: "For no human being can tame the tongue. It is a restless evil, full of deadly pain," he concluded that if one had a wife who was a gossip, your greatest enemy lived with you. Koren had a trustworthy colleague in Elisabeth. She was careful about what she disclosed to her correspondents.

From the beginning church leaders were concerned that the pastor's marriage be to the benefit of both parsonage and parish. A poorly chosen mate could ruin a pastorate as could an undisciplined and slovenly pastor exhaust a gifted and talented wife. Often by dint of her work she could cover many of the pastor's weaknesses. As pastors' wives became more eager to step out into their own careers and lives, this became more vexing to all concerned.

Stormy Times on the Women Question

Most of the letters written during the 1850s and 1860s give us a bucolic picture of life in the parsonage. Few of the wives chafed at their roles as wives. After the Civil War, however, the debate in America over the Thirteenth and Fourteenth Amendments to the Constitution began to rise to a fever pitch. These guaranteed the black male his civil rights, but not women. Women of all ranks were beginning to look outside the home for further education that might get them positions of public employment, almost unthinkable before the war.

The Norwegian Synod pastors, especially Preus and Larsen, watched closely for the encroachment of feminism into their communities. Every issue of *Kirkelig Maanedstidene* (*Monthly Times of the Church*) the paper of the Norwegian Synod, featured a brief column, "Church Chronicles." It reported news items from around the world and especially in America. The editors watched the battle for women's rights especially closely. *Kirketidende* printed a news release from August 1, 1869, *Lehre und Wehre*, a journal of the German Missouri Synod Lutherans. It concerned Mrs. Margaret (Maggie) Newton Van Cott (1830-1914), who had just been licensed by the Methodists to preach, the first woman to be licensed by the Methodists. The editor of *Lehre and Wehre* hoped that this would not be "An example that many will follow in the women's rights movement that at the moment is raging through the whole country."[280]

Mrs. Margaret (Maggie) Newton Van Cott

How hotly the struggle for women's suffrage was raging can be inferred from the *Decorah Republican*. It reported on several Lyceum speeches scheduled for the coming year. Among coming attractions was a speech by the redoubtable Elizabeth Cady Stanton (1815-1902). It was scheduled for March 21, 1870. Even though, by this time, the railroad had come to Decorah, Stanton could not travel by train because of a blizzard. Nevertheless, she enjoyed riding a sleigh between snowbound villages in Northern Iowa in order to meet her engagements. That she did make it to the small villages of northeastern Iowa seems miraculous. The month before she had to cancel her speaking engagements because she had come down with pneumonia.

One would have hoped that Laur. Larsen had gone to hear Stanton. Were there others from the college or church leadership at the lecture? Larsen, a Democrat in Republican Decorah, had good relations with the English community of Decorah, but there is no record of his having gone to hear Mrs. Stanton. At this time, in addition to leading the college, he was tending his wife, Karen. He had to sit up many nights with her as she struggled with the tuberculosis that would soon take her life.

His daughter comments that he was very fond of women and preferred them as conversational companions. This did not mean, however, that Larsen would sympathize with the women's suffrage movement as it was developing. Whether he was there or not, we do have his comments on her speech. According to the *Decorah Republican* Mrs. Stanton's speech was based on John Stuart Mill's statement, "The worst tyranny in the world is that of man to woman." The statement only proved to the editor of the church paper that great minds could say foolish things. Nor did he approve of Mrs. Stanton's witty retort to Horace Greeley who had objected to female suffrage because women could never be drafted to fight the nation's wars. She had replied to him that a woman in such circumstances could do exactly what Greeley had done: send a substitute, a volunteer bought for some $300.

The editor continued that what she had not addressed was the one incontrovertible fact of nature that women were able to bear children and were, thus, the guardians of the race. If women could vote and take on political jobs, abortions were sure to increase, the paper argued.[281] It was the typical argument against Mrs. Stanton who had come to expect such accusations from the press and the church.

The *Decorah Republican*'s editorial was not the only notice her speech received. On May 1, 1870, two months after Stanton's appearance in Decorah, Hermann Preus came out in the church paper blasting such women and their cause. It is a fierce piece of prose and makes one wonder whether he attended to lecture. He knows the gist of the argument.

> One of the day's watchwords is women's vote that once again stands in strong relation to women's emancipation and liberation from her bonds, with which God has bound her to her husband and family, and liberation from God and his law.[282]

Preus went on to say he had read a new book by Mrs. Eleanore Kirke, *Up Broadway*. In it Kirke argued that divorce should be easier to get and that women should be bound by their marriage oath only so long as they continued to love their husbands. Calling such an attitude nothing but prostitution (*horeri*), Preus continued, "We have here before us not just a shameless woman's cackling, but a speech which is favorably received by many. . . . And it is recommended that all housewives and maidens read the religious papers of the Congregational Church, the *Independent*."[283] This was Henry Ward Beecher's paper, which Preus followed closely because Beecher was the most famous pastor in the country. Beecher also favored the cause of women's suffrage. Next to radical feminists, Beecher was more conservative, something Preus and Larsen did not see. Preus also saw in this statement that the feminists were rejecting the orders of creation theology.

It is the old Christ hatred that cries we will not have any dominion over us. Away with Christ and family life and marriage, school. Let everything be heathen and the golden ages will come again. . . . Surely we live in the latter days. Things will get worse and worse, such as we have not dreamt of. Brothers! It is time to wake up and let Christ be our light. Let his light shine in the darkness.[284]

In August 1871, the *Kirkelig Maanedstidende*, the editor selected a news note from *Lehre und Wehre* from April 20, 1871, quoting Beecher's paper. It concerned a conservative Baptist pastor in Boston who reported that he had been in the presence of a women who prayed movingly (breaking St. Paul's proscription of women speaking in church). He observed that her prayer was to the "comfort and edification of us all—whatever the Apostle Paul had to say about women speaking in church." The pastor then went on to say he really could not say what Paul thought about women speaking in church because on the one hand he said, no, on the other hand, they should not prophecy with their heads uncovered. Larsen remarked dryly in a editorial comment, "that was the last time Paul had been quoted in that room."[285]

Henry Ward Beecher

Not long after that Victoria Woodhull went before the Congress of the United States to urge the passage of the Woman's Suffrage Amendment. She was the first woman ever to speak to Congress and made a considerable splash. Later many in the movement came to think of it as a tactical error. Both Susan Anthony and Cady Stanton agreed in later years that Woodhull's espousal of such radical ideas turned people off to the whole idea of women voting. She was everything conservative men said women would become if they got equal rights.

Victoria Woodhull

To Preus and others, not only was she immoral in her behavior, she also espoused religious and moral ideals that no good Christian woman could espouse. She defended the right of women to divorce when they no longer loved their husbands. She vigorously espoused Marxism, a subject she had come to know by translating Marx's *Communist Manifesto*, a translation still used. American church people reacted with horror on hearing her ideas. To strike a blow against the hypocrisy of the churches, she accused Henry Ward Beecher of having had an illicit relationship with Libby Tilton, the rather silly wife of the newspaper publisher, Theodore Tilton. The revelation rocked the American church. Everybody had to take sides for or against Beecher who did not acquit himself well in the proceedings. Worst of all was that Beecher, a charismatic divine of the age, had been a champion of the women's movement. He was president of the more conservative group of women working

Libby Tilton

for women's emancipation. His fall proved everything the Norwegian Synod pastors feared about the movement. It also complicated the work of Anthony especially. She thought it imprudent for their cause to be as radical as Cady Stanton.

One would have to say that the scandal made more people aware of the uproar that women's emancipation would cause. The worst thing about it was that Woodhull, instead of lambasting Beecher, embraced him as a brother, a scoffer at silly old-fashioned bonds like marriage. It was, among others, an embrace he could ill afford. What effect that case had on the Norwegian immigrants is not certain from the journals except that they seemed to be watching the American scene closely for news on the women's issue after that.

Although this movement caused the pastors of the Norwegian Synod some anxiety, there is little mention of its impact on their own daughters, born in the 1850s. They were now approaching marriageable age. One can read in letter after letter the increasing concern about what to do to give their daughters a finishing school education. As the wives begin fretting about how they are going to give their daughters something akin to finishing school, or high school, they had many ideas and resources that they proposed to each other in the letters.

As Elisabeth Koren saw the situation, things were getting serious. Her oldest daughter, Henriette, was beginning to help with the housework, cooking, baking, serving the guests when they came. Caroline "Lina" was fourteen and filled with the typical emotional turmoil of a young teenage girl. Mrs. Koren found this troubling, but hoped her difficulties were simply the result of being in the teary stages of adolescence. She had been studying with her aunt, Mrs. Koren noted, during the summer. Which "aunt" is not clear, but it most likely was Mrs. Brandt in Decorah, about whom Mrs. Koren was skeptical. She hoped it would go well, but she did not care much for the two friends Lina had there, Marie Reque and Margretha Brandt, and hoped it had not done her any harm to be with them. "This is nothing to write about, but could be much to talk about," she concluded with her usual concern for saying anything in a letter which could be found and read and then misunderstood.[286]

As the new decade of the 1870s dawned we can sense that things are about to change for the entire community, especially the girls. Karine and Henriette Neuberg, who had now and again served as something like apprentice governesses in the old world, were no longer available. Now there was no one to take their place, not even their older daughters. While the women were taking stock of the situation, the men were seeing the beginning of a feminist movement arising in the east, and, as we have seen, they did not like it. What their wives thought was not entirely clear.

✝ The Death of KAREN NEUBERG LARSEN

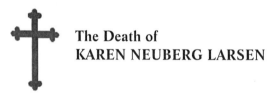

On February 6, 1871, after her long illness, Mrs. Karen Neuberg Larsen, died. She was the first of the wives in this group to perish.[287] Her trip to Norway to seek medical treatment for her tuberculosis had been in vain. Larsen had tended her, the great love of his life, through her long illness with patience and care. Considered by many to be almost too fine for the rough life of the frontier, she had done well until she contracted TB. Against that she was helpless and suffered a long and debilitating decline. Her death struck the pastors' families hard, as we can hear in Mrs. Koren's letter to Linka describing the death and funeral. In it we get a vivid account of the rituals of the Luther community as it faced death. Mrs. Koren is eager to report to Linka all that she had seen and heard.

Little Iowa parsonage
February 12, 1871

Dear Aunt Linka!

This noon we came back from Decorah and I thought that the first thing I should do was write you. I know you are eager to hear more about Mrs. Larsen's last days. I've been terribly upset that I could not be in Decorah with her during the last ten days she lived. I'm not sure I've written to you since I last spoke with her—It was 2 weeks before her funeral—on Thursday at noon Koren came from Decorah and said that her stomach had been so bad that they expected that it would soon be over for her. But before Koren left town, he got a note from Larsen saying that everything was better, she had both eaten and talked, and wished that I would come. I left immediately--it was remarkable how quick she was that evening. She spoke about Norway and things there, of our pastors and their situations, she spoke now and then in her old manner, quick and clear. I watched that night, until two. She was still and quiet, but then again her stomach bothered her, with much pain. At daybreak she got a little sleep. When Marie [Sivisind] dressed Herman that morning he said to her, time after time—wouldn't it be better if Mama went to heaven than to be so sick here. I will never forget the look with which she looked at the young children when they came in that evening in their night clothes to say goodnight, especially Herman (Herman, the youngest child, a favorite of his mother.) He was so sweet when he stood there, kissing and hugging her. She spoke very little that day, but improved a bit after dinner—and sat as usual in her rocking chair. After dinner, I had to go home. It was the last I saw her. And then I had spoken very little with her—she moved now and then and held my hand, and looked at me, but said nothing. She seemed not to be thinking death was so near, and God be praised, the time was not yet there.

I was not well after I came home. I got worse and worse, my throat was very sore and I could not go out.

On Sunday, we had a group of pastors and Mrs. Magelssen here [Karine Neuberg Magelssen, Mrs. Larsen's sister].

Monday we got the death announcement. I was so sick that Koren would not take me in to Decorah Tuesday. Mrs. Magelssen went with him (he was home Monday with a terrible cold). Wednesday morning early I went with the girls and later the three oldest boys came in with one of the neighbors.

Preus asked me to tell you a little about the funeral for he will not be coming home soon, but first let me tell you a little of what I know you long most to hear—about the last day and night that our dear Tante Larsen lived. You know she suffered terribly in her last days—her attacks were difficult, but God heard her prayers that she would not die during one. The heavy sweat and hard fever wore her out and so she was so tired, so tired. She could not get rest. She could not sleep and sat with her pillows first this way and then that in her rocking chair. The last day she could speak only with difficulty, her throat was so sore. Sunday she was a bit better all day. She ate cereal in the morning, later in the forenoon, I think it was, she said, "Now surely I am dying." She had the bed moved into the front room, as she had earlier said it should be. She wanted it to be so when she realized that it would soon be over. At dinner she spoke with the children, first blessing and exhorting the three youngest, especially Herman. Larsen told me this himself as we stood by her casket. She could do no more then, but later she called Lulla[288] and blessed and admonished her. Then she said farewell to Marie [Sivisind], Elisabeth Lommen, and sent greetings to all her friends. That evening she fell asleep and lay, as before, sitting high in the bed. Larsen sat beside her the whole time, reading and talking to her. She had struggled and fought so, but that day and night there were no shadows or fear and uneasiness about her, only peace and quiet. Every time Larsen asked her a question about her faith and assurance of salvation, she answered clearly and freely, "Yes." At three a.m. she slept, without struggle, as peaceful and trusting as a child would lie sleeping in her mother's arms. God be praised and thanked for all his grace. She was very little changed in death—It was not immediately, but a bit later, that a look of pain came over her eyes and mouth.

I covered her at the last with her flowers, all her own. I had only bleeding hearts from Norway to give her. My flowers are still at East Prairie. Larsen asked that she get as many flowers as possible. The cross which lay on her breast I wove out of the same small flowers that she had made into a cross for Mrs. Landsverk. Myrtle greens and bleeding hearts. Minken [her oldest daughter, Thora] stood by me the whole time. She was pleased that her Mama should be so lovely and when she saw the lovely green wreaths, she said Mama loved these, won't you take them.

The three little ones went in and out with me and stood by the bier and kissed their Mama on her forehead and cheeks. It was good they were along for all of that. Then six of the young pastors took the casket into the chapel which was overflowing. The altar was lovely.

Brandt had the first talk on the text, "Do not sorrow as those without hope." Then Preus spoke on behalf of the church. He spoke warmly of her as a woman, wife, and mother. Koren spoke last, especially to Larsen, on the text of Martha and Mary. "The Master is here and he calls to you." Between each talk, the students sang. Brandt or Hjort had written words for a special song. Little Herman sat in Marie's arms and slept nearly the whole time. But he woke in time to give his mother one last kiss. Then many people processed around the coffin. It took a long time. We went down again to the stairs where the six oldest pastors came with the casket and took it out. I did not get permission to go to the graveyard on account of my cold and stayed at the school for a while. You can't believe how empty and difficult it was. Then they came back. Koren, Preus, Ottesen, Brandt, all together with Larsen for a while in the dining room. That evening all of them went to Brandt's. I stayed at Larsen's and was glad for that since Larsen thought it was good I stayed with them. We sat in the dining room, Larsen, the children, Marie, and I the entire evening. Larsen spoke frequently of his wife. I think his main feeling that evening was thankfulness over her blessed death. It was such a consolation to be with him and hear what he had to say. But his loss will most likely be more and more keenly felt. It was good that Preus stayed until one today and that not all the pastors left at once. Minken is the one of the children who I think will grieve the most. She is a girl with a sensitive spirit.

They read the hymnal a great deal, she and the little one. The morning after the funeral, they stood and read at least four times the funeral hymn of Landstad, the one in the new hymnal ("I know of a sleep in Jesus' name"). Minken said it seemed to be written just for us. Lulla, the poor thing, is quiet and still. She will feel the loss keenly.

Marie Sivisind will be there for the first few days. When it gets milder it is thought that Aunt Anna will come. It is good that Mrs. Larsen was happy to see Brandt who visited her often. Mrs. Brandt was also very kind and helpful, but Koren is going now, so farewell. [Mrs. Koren often ends her letters to say that she must quit writing, unfortunately, because someone needs to take the letter to mail it in town.]

Write soon. Greet your children.

Affectionately, E. Koren[290]

Larsen would marry Ingeborg Astrup, the next year, in 1872, after he met her while on a trip to Norway. Their daughter, Karen Larsen, his biographer, noted how deeply her father had loved his first wife. "The very fact that he never could quite break down the reserve between them gave to his attachment an intensity that approached pain."[290] Karen had a much lighter sensibility and tried to temper his seriousness, and his unbending orthodoxy, rather like her sister Karine. As Karen neared death, Larsen wrote her:

> I wish to God that you were sitting like a fresh blossom in the midst of it all, but just as we are beginning to get things pretty, your strength is broken. For me there is left only the precious joy of trying to do a little to care for you. But alas, my efforts are not very successful. I am best fitted to keep account and read proof. I cannot be of much comfort and cheer to anyone, and I don't improve even though I weep in my sorrow. May God give you joy; I can do so little; But he will do it—perhaps on earth and surely in heaven.[291]

An ordinary sleigh, rather than an "ugly hearse," by her request, bore her to the Decorah graveyard where she was buried. Her loss, in some ways, closed the door of a deeply sensitive part of Larsen's soul, that never really opened again. One can wonder if she would have softened some of Larsen's ferocity as he took the lead in the wrenching theological and churchly conflicts that would tear the Synod apart in the next decades.

CHAPTER FIVE

Building Schools That Served Both Men And Women

Will there never be a time in one's life when it is useful to know which way the wind blows beyond our range of vision? Won't it be useful for a woman to know something about the world, its past and present history, about human beings, their customs through different times, etc., etc.?

—*Linka's Diary*[292]

While the higher education of their daughters was not the immediate concern of the pastors and their wives when they settled in Wisconsin and Iowa, the New World confronted them with issues about the education of their children. The record shows that the pastors participated in debates about education, and women's place in society more vigorously than we might have supposed. To understand their efforts to educate their daughters it is helpful to examine the concerns they were immediately confronted with in the churchly and political context in America.

Very soon, they realized that the New Land was different, something the French sociologist, Alexis de Tocqueville, had noted in 1840 in his book, *Democracy in America:*

I have been frequently surprised, and almost frightened, at the singular address and happy boldness with which young women in America contrive to manage their thoughts and their language, amid all the difficulties of stimulating conversation; a philosopher would have stumbled at every step along the narrow path which they trod without accidents and without effort. It is easy indeed to perceive that, even amid the independence of early youth, an Amer-

Alexis de Tocqueville

ican woman is always mistress of herself; she indulges in all permitted pleasures, without yielding herself up to any of them; and her reason never allows the rules of self-guidance to drop, though it often seems to hold them loosely.[293]

Because the Industrial Revolution in both Europe and America drew many daughters of farmers to mills and factories in cities, the education they received, if any, was practical—the three Rs—most likely taught at home or in fledgling primary schools. Harriet Martineau (1802-1876), the English travel writer and early sociologist, noted in 1836 that the only occupations open to American women at the time were teaching, needlework, keeping boarders, working in cotton mills, book-binding, typesetting, and housework.[294] The situation for upper class women was different. Catherine Beecher had suggested that upper class young women like Karine and Henriette Neuberg could not expect, nor could they quite imagine, being gainfully employed in such vocations. There were special schools for them, often called Ladies' Seminaries, already some decades before the Civil War. These schools prepared young women to teach their own children at home, or as governesses in the homes of others or, less likely, in the one room schools on the frontier.

Norwegian immigration grew exponentially in the 1850s, before the Civil War just as towns and counties were founding Common [Public] Schools to take up the responsibilities of a republic. Thomas Jefferson urged

the division of each county into wards, or "little republics," and the creation therein of elementary schools into which "all the free children, male and female," would be admitted without charge. These publicly supported elementary schools would equip all citizens with the basic literacy and computational skills they would need in order to manage their own affairs.[295]

For Jefferson the elementary schools were necessary to establish a democratic republic with a citizenry that could govern themselves. For the Puritans it had been the God-given duty of the father and mother to assure that their children could read and write and do their numbers. The Norwegian pastors' practice of home schooling, what we might call primary or elementary school, fit nicely with both the necessities of the day and the Protestant tradition.

Thomas Jefferson

When the Norwegian pastors came to minister among their country-men and women in this New World, they anticipated continuity with life in Norway, along with increased economic opportunities. They had come to serve their people on the frontier, not evangelize non-Norwegians. The culture of the New Land did not have a significant impact on their own families as they were establishing their parsonages and seeking to establish Norwegian churches among the settlers.

Their parishioners had a different attitude. When the emigrants left their home and families in Norway for America, they, of course, brought their Norwegian culture and religions with them, but they were in some sense already Americans. They wanted their children to be American in language and training. The pastors recognized this. They realized that they had to educate their boys and girls in the language and culture of the new land to enable them to flourish in America. They were also convinced that the immigrant children needed to know the language and traditions of their past. The question was how, when, and what to teach. About this they had many strong and well-informed opinions.

Faced with the need to educate their young men and women, the congregations, and the pastors, began to replicate the pattern they knew from the Old Country. In the year 1827 Norway had passed a law requiring all communities to build a schoolhouse near the local church, since church and state were one. Communities organized and operated local elementary schools where religious instruction was foundational. The lay assistant and music teacher, or *klokker*, if he was not the main

schoolteacher in the community, helped the pastor with religious education. He prepared the students for confirmation. In Norway this was a rite required by the state after which young adults could enter into the public life of the state. This involved rigorous instruction in Martin Luther's Small Catechism as taught in Pontoppidan's *Explanation*. This included Pontoppidan's 759 questions and answers on the five parts of Luther's catechism, supported by relevant Bible verses.

Erick Pontoppidan

The school morning opening exercises include the singing of Lutheran hymns appropriate to the church liturgical season and time of the day. This model made sense to the pastors because it is what they knew.

On the American frontier they found an undeveloped, minimally established system of common schools required by law—in Wisconsin, for example, after it became a state in 1848. The same was true in Iowa and Minnesota and all the states on the frontier. The Northwest Ordinance of 1787 established townships of six square miles, each divided into thirty-six sections of 640 acres apiece. Section number sixteen was set aside for a schoolhouse. The money raised from the sale of the other sections provided for the school. This system was in place and beginning to work when the Norwegian pastors arrived.

The pastors, however, were not impressed with the quality of the education, and wanted to build better schools for the general education of their children, even if they could not teach their Lutheran faith in them. By heritage they understood that it was a responsibility of the congregation to teach the faith in and alongside the regular school. The founding immigrant pastors, such as Elling Eielsen (1804-1883) and Johan Wilhelm Christian Dietrichson (1815-1883), had accepted the common schools, which could not teach their Lutheran faith, given the enormous challenges of their own work. Dietrichson, who had also been a teacher, on seeing the problem, quickly organized a district school and saw to it that the Muskego congregation also built a school to instruct children in their Lutheran faith.

Elling Eielsen

Johan Wilhelm Christian Dietrichson

The 1853 Norwegian Synod Constitution stated: "It is the Christian and churchly duty of every congregation belonging to the church to establish and maintain religious schools to secure for the young instruction in the fundamentals of Christianity."[296] These were essentially the catechism schools from the old country where the lay assistant (*forsanger, klokker, cantor*) had the responsibility of teaching the children—who knew how to read and write from their elementary school work—the Scriptures, Martin Luther's Small Catechism as explained by Pontoppidan's *Explanation*, and the hymnal. This was what the immigrants called with great affection the "children's teaching" (*børnelærdom*).

The pastors understood that the teaching of the faith was the church's responsibility. The problem in the New Land was that they could not do this in the regular primary school, or common school. This was completely new for them. Europeans, over centuries, were accustomed to state churches which naturally taught religion. In the New Land the pastors had to organize a church separate from the state and provide for religious education separate from the public school. This resulted in a lengthy debate concerning the stance of the church toward the common schools. Even as the Synod was husbanding its resources to build the Main Building at Luther College in Decorah to educate its young men, the question of the common schools and the relation of the church to them came to be an occasion for bitter arguments over whether the common schools were "heathen" or "religionless." What lay at the bottom of the fight was as much a cultural question as religious. How could one remain Norwegian and Lutheran by using the common schools, and how should the church organize its educational, and cultural, activities in the face of the Yankee schools.

The pastors who arrived after Dietrichson viewed the common schools much more critically than he did. Pastor Hans Andreas Stub (1823-1907), for example, who came to serve the Muskego, Wisconsin, congregation in 1848, considered the public schools utterly inadequate for the children, not only academically, but spiritually and culturally. He warned that the common school would lead to children losing their language, their heritage and faith, and, worst of all, causing them to marry outside the tribe.[297]

Hans Andreas Stub

In 1851, some of the Norwegian Synod pastors drew up a list of requirements for educating and examining parochial school teacher candidates who could teach both the basics of elementary school—reading, writing, arithmetic—and the slightly more advanced religious education of the parish school. While they did not oppose teaching children English, they thought it crucial their children learn first to read and write in their mother tongue, Norwegian, and then learn to function well in English, the language of their future.

They may have intended these congregational schools to be a stopgap until a better system could be devised or the common schools improved. However, the newly arrived pastors, all highly educated and sophisticated theologians, began looking to the Missouri Synod's parochial school system as preferable to the public common school. Although it is clear that they wanted to teach the Lutheran faith along with the regular schooling the students were to receive in the common schools, their concerns seemed to be as much cultural as spiritual. The pastors, used to their Norwegian system of church and state, found this debate difficult to untangle in the New Land.

At a busy Synod conference in Coon Prairie, Wisconsin, during the first week of July, 1858, the pastors addressed the situation. Adolph Carl Preus (1814-1878), the president of the young church, opposed the rapid Americanization "idolized by the Norwegian [settlers]." He suggested that the parish schools could teach the subjects found in the common schools, with the added benefit of teaching the faith in "the mother tongue [which] is the language of their heart."[298] This was the beginning of the parochial school (*omgangsskoler*) movement which met in farmhouses in the parish, or later in the common school buildings when the school term had ended and they stood empty.[299]

Adolph Carl Preus

Olaus Duus (1824-1893), a pastor in Waupaca, Wisconsin, was appalled when he became acquainted with a "clever American schoolteacher who did not even know the Lord's Prayer; so conditions are really terrible in respect to religion."[300] Adolph Preus answered a stinging attack on the

Meeting of the pastors in June 1858 at Coon Prairie

Norwegian Synod's attempts to build a parochial school system like that of the Missouri Synod by arguing that the

> the condition of the American schools . . . are as bad as it is possible for them to be and still deserve the name of schools. Why? Because nine out of ten teachers are totally incapable of conducting a decent school.[301]

The poor quality of the common school was not, however, the chief problem, according to some newly arrived Synod pastors. By the summer of 1859 Ottesen, Stub, Adolph, and Hermann Preus issued a pamphlet, "On Schools and Language Conditions." They conceded that their children needed to know English well enough to flourish in the new land and that the freedom of religion guaranteed by the Bill of Rights was a good thing. They then interpreted that freedom to mean that they were free to educate their people in the old language and faith. If they did not do so, they argued, their children would stray from the Lutheran church.[302] They saw clearly the dilemma of every immigrant family—the likelihood that their children would prefer the new culture to the old and the loss their communities would experience when that happened. The controversy seemed to have been on hold during the Civil War both among the pastors and their parishioners who were preoccupied with the war and by their stand on the question of slavery.

After the Civil War had ended, the school debate resurfaced. In 1866 President Laur. Larsen, Pastor Brandt and Professor Schmidt drafted a report, the Manitowoc Statement, which they presented to the Norwegian Synod annual meeting in Manitowoc, Wisconsin. It recommended that the Norwegian Synod supplant the common schools with its own parochial schools, much as the Missouri Synod had. The major issue for Preus, who agreed with the report, was that the common school was "religionless," an argument he continued to make whenever he spoke on the issue.

Hermann Preus delivered "Seven Lectures on the Religious Situation Among Norwegians in America in February, 1867," at the Mission school in Oslo. He reported that it was clear to him that the "congregations themselves must therefore provide for instruction in religion" as they had in Norway. It was his hope

> to arrange things with our congregational schools in such a way as to render the public, English schools superfluous on the part of the members of our congregations. Naturally this

will happen only if we in the congregational schools pick up the subjects taught in the English schools, first and foremost the English language, then arithmetic, geography, and a bit of history.[303]

Preus acknowledged that this would be an extra burden for congregations, since their membership was already paying taxes to support the public schools. At the same time they were building churches and parsonages and establishing their own farms, "but we must still work toward that end."[304]

Bernt Julius Muus

Pastor Bernt Julius Muus (1832-1900), when he came to Minnesota in 1859, entered into the discussion with as much vigor and sharpness as the others. His arguments and attacks on the common schools soon made him the center of the controversy. In 1869 he opened, briefly, a school in Northfield, Minnesota, after publishing an article titled "Schools and a Good School." In the essay he argued that the "common school was an institution 'which because of its essential principle must work in opposition to the kingdom of God.'"[305] He used the Preus argument that the schools were "religionless," saying with understatement, that schools "in which there is no religion, and that religion, in which there is no Christianity, I love not overmuch."[306] He had detected a kind of religion in the schools,

Bernt Julius Muus

perhaps a form of civic religion, but more in the line of Deism than Christianity. Catholics and later scholars agreed with his observation.[307] Muus' rather shrill arguments caused an uproar in Norwegian-American communities. They had come to accept the common schools and value them for how they were educating their children—not least because they were paying for them with their taxes.

Muus, although of equal distinction in background and class, never quite hit it off with the other pastors, perhaps because of his tendency toward pietism. His decision to join the Norwegian Synod was said to have surprised Professor Carl Paul Caspari (1814-1892), beloved Old Testament professor at the University in Oslo, who had taught most of the

Norwegian pastors who emigrated to America. Muus, however, was wel-

comed to the Synod and his leadership skills were commended by the Norwegian Synod pastors. Mrs. Koren spoke in friendly terms of the Muus family, especially Mrs. Oline Muus, although she worried about Muus' pietism. The proximity of the Muus family to the Korens, relatively speaking, made her feel as though they were not so alone on the frontier as they had been. Despite their initial camaraderie,

Professor Caspari   however, Muus and the Synod leadership later came to be at sixes and sevens.

In opposition to building parochial schools, Rasmus Bjørn Anderson (1846-1936) formed a group called the Scandinavian Lutheran Education Society. They held their first meeting on March 4, 1869. The society agreed on the need for education in their own traditions and language, but thought it better to do this later in academies or universities where professors in Nordic languages, culture, and literature could teach the subjects. At a meeting the day after the society's meeting, on March 5, 1869, the Synod pastors met and agreed that their culture had a place in higher education, but it needed to be taught at the elementary level as well. Both sides of the debate shared a commitment to educate children in their linguistic and cultural traditions. Preus suggested that a girls' school should be part of the school plan the pastors were meeting to discuss.[308]

Preus' concerns were not only for girls, however. He knew that serious attention needed to be paid to the education of all the children of the Synod, especially their religious instruction. To that end he contributed a series of about one hundred assertions (*satser*) on the school questions before them. It was an exhaustive set of theses regarding the school issue and the church and shows his logical mind. He concluded that the responsibility of the Norwegian Synod to educate its children in the faith needed to be addressed in certain ways. Preus' chief concern was how to provide religious instruction for the children. His conclusions and recommendations show his seriousness in the matter. He argued that the Norwegian Synod should:

1) enlarge and complete the teacher education division (the Normal department) in Decorah;

2) seek to found Lutheran academies or buoy up the Common schools where the Norwegians are most populous;

3) work to prepare and find good Lutheran teachers in the Norwegian language in the state universities and American colleges that are especially populous in Norwegian students;

4) raise up our young to educate themselves to be Norwegian-English teachers and offer themselves to such positions as a life calling;

5) strongly support with means those who are willing to train to take up such vocations;

6) pray that God will bless all of these our struggles.

These conclusions, especially the idea to found Lutheran academies in many ways became the preferred way that Norwegian-Americans, especially the Norwegian Synod, sought to educate its young. Several colleges of the Norwegian-Americans developed out of those institutions.

As the idea of academies developed, their curriculum became something like college prep schools for students needing what we might call today the last years of high school. They would school their young in Christianity, Norwegian, English, science, and history—a course of study rather like the scientific schools (*Realskole*) of Norway, or like the normal schools in the new land. They may even have been influenced by the folk high schools of Grundtvig since they also taught the culture and religion of Norway. These academies blossomed around the Midwest and served as feeder schools for Luther College or the other Norwegian-American Lutheran colleges.

Muus' Holden Academy

In 1870 Muus opened Holden Academy in Northfield in the basement of the parsonage; Thorsten Jesme was the teacher. In preparing a curriculum, Muus used the ideas of the Norwegian Synod pastors about what the academies should teach, more along the line of what the Norwegians called the scientific (*Realskole*) line: Bible, Christian faith and doctrine, church history, English, Norwegian, geography, history, penmanship, arithmetic, physics, geometry, drawing, and singing. The courses in history, drawing, and singing made the curriculum look a bit fancier than the kind of curriculum Karine Neuberg experienced at the Page school in Decorah. There the emphasis was on what came to be called a "commercial" course of study, but it could easily become a normal school and later maybe even a liberal arts college. Typically these schools began with a preparatory course and then specializations: commercial or teachers' education (Normal). Women could find employment on the basis of such courses of study. The Holden school began with three students and expected five for the second term. Only three appeared, making the school unsustainable. Benson, a historian of St. Olaf College, supposes the need for help on the farms as they were getting established made it impossible for the school to attract enough students at the time.[309] The failure drove Muus back to the drawing board.

The founders of St. Olaf thought it important to admit women because Americans, especially on the frontier, were aware that they needed the skills of both men and women. Women were increasingly needed in certain professions, such as teaching, nursing, and some clerical work. Married men were twice as expensive as single women teachers. This followed from the logic of the day that single women did not have a family to house, feed, and clothe.

B. J. Muus

Although Muus' first attempt at founding a school failed, he was not one to quit. He continued his efforts without any official support from the Synod. Finally in 1874, he and several Northfield businessmen and pastors got St. Olaf's School incorporated. His purpose was to have a school "in which the youth of the congregations could acquire a better education than could be obtained in our parochial and common schools."[310]

The success of Muus' school increased pressure on the Synod to provide educational opportunities for all of its children, men and women, at the high school or junior college level. Most desirable was such a school in close proximity to their homes, so that children would not have to travel so far to attend school. Benson argues in his book on the history of St. Olaf College that this variety of approaches actually made the Norwegian Lutherans in America richer in educational institutions than they would have been with a uniform program.[311]

The urgency for the Synod to build a girls' school for its daughters was somewhat mitigated by coeducation at St. Olaf's School which began classes in January 1875. The Synod pastors supported it, if not officially, at least with their participation. Laur. Larsen sent his daughters there during its first years, H. A. Preus preached and lay the cornerstone of the Main Building on July 4, 1877, and Laur. Larsen and Koren both spoke informally at the festivities. Preus dedicated the building on November 6, 1878, and Larsen brought greetings from Luther College.

Caroline Koren

The Synod had not agreed to support St. Olaf's School financially, a school it must have regarded in some sense as an upstart institution. Nonetheless the relationship between Synod leaders and the school remained cordial. Koren's daughter, Caroline, was head preceptress and taught music in the 1879-1880 academic year. As it moved to become a college, Mohn described the goal of the school to be an American school with strong Norwegian Lutheran roots. While it would not be a religion school, it would be profoundly religious in its teachings and culture. Mohn was not interested in transplanting the old Latin school from Norway. He wanted to design an educational experience that prepared students for the American

Thorbjørn Mohn

context for participation in the society as citizens. This required that they have good command of English and be knowledgeable about American culture and history.[312] The general purpose was "to advance the education of pupils from fifteen years of age and upwards, as a college, preserve the pupils in the true Christian faith, as taught by the Evangelical Lutheran Church." This contrasted with Luther College whose primary purpose was to prepare theological students for seminary.

The Synod at this time was occupied with planning a seminary in Madison, Wisconsin, so that its students would no longer have to go to Concordia Seminary in St. Louis to study theology. It opened Luther Seminary in 1876. This effort, vital in their eyes, drew support away from the kind of work Muus was doing in Minnesota. Thus Muus and Thorbjørn Mohn, president of St. Olaf's School solicited support from communities around Northfield to get the school going. On November 6, 1874, St. Olaf's School was incorporated.

Sverdrup Answers

Observing these debates about the common school and academies, in 1876 Georg Sverdrup (in *Kvartal Skrift*) joined the debate about whether to provide Lutheran parochial schools after the model of Missouri. He had seen Preus' propositions (*satser*) in the *Kirkelig Maanedstidende* and wanted to address the issue himself, partly to oppose the Synod most likely, and partly to understand his new world. He did not agree with the

Synod's suspicions that the American common school was "heathen" or "religionless." For Sverdrup, who had done his usual careful scholarship on the common school in America before he wrote his articles, the common schools were neither.

Georg Sverdrup

From Martin Luther's writings, admittedly within a state church context, Sverdrup tracked Luther's thinking on primary schools for children. He was surprised at what he discovered. "I had thought," he confessed, "when I began this study that I would find that [Martin] Luther would have suggested a civil school built on a religious foundation and that the congregation should have every part of the instruction of children under its supervision." Luther, however, proposed civil schools for civil instruction and religious schools for religious instruction.[313]

Sverdrup commended the American system of common schools and encouraged congregations to build their own system of religious instruction for teaching Luther's Small Catechism, especially. He suggested that congregations establish parochial schools that would meet in the summer after the regular school session, an early version of Vacation Bible School. The teachers were young women trained in this same system, who probably taught regular terms in the common schools. They very likely had some normal school education as well. They taught Bible stories, songs, and the Small Catechism—the *Børnelærdom*. It took a while for the immigrants to sort through all these issues. However, Sverdrup's ideas became the norm toward the end of the century and into the next.

Seminary and Academy in Madison

When the Synod opened its seminary in Madison, Wisconsin, on the banks of Lake Monona, it was naturally a school exclusively for men. Establishing and building it took most of the attention of the leaders of the Synod. H. G. Stub would be professor of Old Testament and president. In that same building they also made provisions for an academy. When the Synod voted to buy the Orphans' Home in Madison to house its seminary, the

H. G. Stub

delegates understood that the extra rooms in the building would be used for an academy for both girls and boys.

The academy opened the same year as the seminary. Professor Ole Bugge Asperheim (1846-1891) came to Madison in 1876 to teach at the seminary. He had helped to establish the Norwegian Seamen's Mission in Brooklyn and had previously taught at the Missouri Synod's practical seminary in Fort Wayne, Indiana. On arriving in Madison, he quickly became the director of the academy, known as the Monona Academy. The school enrolled seventy-nine students, a good number at the time. Unfortunately, when the seminary discovered it needed all of the rooms in the building for its theological students, the academy closed after only two years. This ended for a time the Synod's provision for educating its young women.

American Politics and Feminism

The Synod pastors as avid readers of American newspapers and literature had been watching closely the early feminists from Cady Stanton to Henry Ward Beecher. Through this period the pastors were watching closely the debates about women and women's rights, which occurred as they were preparing to build a school for their daughters.

In the 1870s, the country was struggling with three political issues: the passing of the amendments to the Constitution that guaranteed black males suffrage, women's suffrage, and temperance. Most immediate to the Norwegians was temperance and women's

Elizabeth Cady Stanton

suffrage. At this time, liquor was a women's issue. If one approved of women's suffrage, it was fairly likely that one would be against demon rum. This was the case with Sverdrup and Oftedal at Augsburg Seminary, staunch temperance men.

For the Norwegian Synod pastors, however, there were other factors when it came to women's rights; they had observed the discussion as it developed in Norway. There the culture was becoming increasingly secular, resulting in growing hostility between the church and the culture. The secularists fought the church because of what they perceived to be the anti-woman stance of the church and Bible. Most of the Synod pastors' families had left Norway in the 1850s, when the culture war was not as bitter and anti-Christian as it would come to be, especially on the topic of women's rights.

Just after the publication of Ibsen's *A Doll's House* in 1879, (the most performed play around the world for some decades after its debut), the hostility between church and culture in Norway increased its sharper and more corrosive debates. To be for women's suffrage often meant to be against the church and the establishment at a very deep level. These church leaders were beginning to mark the strong anti-church rhetoric of the feminist forces in Norway. The debate was not only in the public sphere; it had made inroads into their daily lives. Linka's sense of being treated as inferior to a man was a mild expression of sympathy with those fighting for women's emancipation. However, she would not have approved of the virulent anti-Christian stance of many of the supporters of women's emancipation.

Lucretia Mott

In America the women's movement coincided with the abolitionist movement. Two of the most important early nineteenth century feminists, Lucretia Mott (1793-1880) and Elizabeth Cady Stanton (1815-1902), attended the World Anti-Slavery Convention in London in 1840. When they were not seated because they were women, they walked about London plotting the first Woman's Rights Convention in America, held on July 19-20, 1848, in Seneca Falls, New York.

Frederick Douglass

The two causes shared many of the same supporters. Almost every feminist of the mid-century was in some way or another involved in the opposition to slavery. Frederick Douglass (1818-1895), the former slave whose oratory furthered the cause of abolition, was also for women's emancipation. He gave a stirring speech at the Seneca Falls convention urging that women get the vote, something that had not been in their first proposals. The most important reform they had wanted was a change in the inheritance laws for married women, although the right to vote would soon become the main "cause," as Susan B. Anthony began to call it. As legislatures began to grant women the right to their own inheritance, the two causes became the same with the ultimate goal being suffrage for women of property, if not universal suffrage.

Tragically, their coalition was rent apart after the Civil War, when the campaign for the Thirteenth, Fourteenth, and Fifteenth Amendments were being waged. Unfortunately, these campaigns pitted the black man against the upper class white woman, who believed her education and status gave her more right to the vote than an illiterate black man. This was the Negro's hour, their former supporters in the abolition movement told the women.

Linka Preus watched these raging debates with an incisive sense for the place of women in the controversy. When she and Hermann visited Norway in 1866-1867, she sketched a scene showing her brother taunting Hermann on his position that slavery was not a sin, but a moral evil. The sketch reveals the intersection between the two sides in the debate as it must have arisen in her own home. Implicit in the sketch is what might be thought of as her feminist perspective on the debate. Linka made her statement by depicting herself talking to her brother, Kalla, about one of Herman's lectures. She called attention to his unfortunate and ill-advised defense of the Synod's position on slavery: that slavery, a moral evil, was not a sin, since the Bible assumed it and had no proscription again it.

To be clear on this, Preus and his colleagues in the Synod were not really pro-slavery. Their concern was that when people said, with justification, that slavery was a sin, they were making the Bible say something it did not. No place in the Bible says that. In fact many people in the Bible owned slaves. It was part of the society. Preus' lecture in which he once again tried to explain that nuanced opinion enflamed the Norwegian press again, as people scoffed at what they thought was a distinction without a difference. In the sketch Linka's brother is telling her that Herman's argument is pure sophistry (*bare snakk*). Hans Fredrik Bang (1820-1890), her brother-in-law, a businessman in Drammen, remarked that Linka appeared to be a better theologian than Herman.

Hermann Preus, 1867

An evening party at Hanchen and Bang's September 1867 Kalla: "This 'slavery in and of itself' as you say, that is sophistry. The slavery you have in America is sin. Give in, brother-in-law. On this point your wife has peculiarly enough, the right on her side. She is a better theologian than you. What do you think, Linka? I respect you, my sister." Bang: "Bang Bang. It is impossible for you to defend your theory."

To my knowledge there is no other record of a Norwegian Synod pastor's wife of Linka's stature expressing an opinion about the Synod's stance on slavery, either for or against. Ladies at the time were not supposed to express themselves on politics or religion. This sketch indicates that Linka and Hermann had discussed this issue enough so that she had made it clear to him and to her brother that she disagreed with Hermann and the Synod's position on slavery. She did not make public what she thought. Bang said what he thought she had said. While this is not surprising, the comment by her brother-in-law that she was a better theologian than her husband brings up the woman's cause as well and has a bit of a stiletto in it. It fits the conventional notion that women tended to be pro abolition. It also makes a feminist statement that she has theological abilities and can make such arguments. Is she showing us that she agrees with the women who were abolitionists and feminists? Is she saying that she is her husband's equal? Did she make these arguments in letters to her brother, or was it simply a discussion in the Bang parlor that she thought worth depicting? It raises as many questions as it answers, but there it is.

Ladies Aids and Women Missionaries

The woman's movement found its first expression in Norway and Norwegian America in the churches. In both countries it was the ladies aids that gave women voting privileges, while raising significant funds for the physical needs of their congregation, needs in the area, and worldwide missions.[314] Whatever their view of radical feminists like Victoria Woodhull, who loudly opposed religion, it did not stop Norwegian-Americans from organizing ladies aids. The church papers, whose editors marked the growth of ladies aids within their own congregations, give us an insight into the thinking of the pastors as they faced this new thing. As in Norway, so in America, the women got the vote in the church ladies aids long before they did in civil society. Each church body viewed the issue somewhat differently and not always predictably. The Norwegian Synod leader, Hermann Preus, unwavering in his opposition to women's leadership in the church, resisted the establishment of a ladies aid in his Spring Prairie congregation until after 1880, the year Linka died.

The Norwegian-Danish Conference and Augsburg

It was a slightly different story, however, for the Norwegian-Danish Conference gathered around Augsburg Seminary. In 1871 August Weenaas (1835-1924), president of the fledgling seminary located in Marshall, Wisconsin, hired a woman to teach English to the students, probably a first in the schools of the Norwegian-Americans. He was also editor of the conference's new paper, *Lutheraneren*, and in a note on the growth of women's organizations in the churches of the conference, he gave women advice on how to establish and run a woman's organization in the church. Weenaas' wife, Valborg Iversen (1837-1874), cared for the twelve to twenty boys at the new school, all of whom lived in their home, sleeping in the attic and expecting

Valborg Iversen Weenaas meals from her every day. At the twenty-fifth anniversary of the school, Pastor Johan Arndt Bergh (1847-1927), who had been a student at the time, remembered her fondly, marveling at the work she had done. He remarked that without her strength and perseverance, Augsburg Seminary would never have endured.[315]

In an article in *Lutheraneren*, Weenaas expressed appreciation for the contributions of women in the building of the new American church. He commended them for their care for widows and orphans and for their fundraising support for the mission of the church. He added suggestions for maintaining order and rule in establishing organizations for women, indicating his confidence that women were fully capable of doing this. His suggested rules were: 1) have a regularly elected board, 2) rules for running the meetings, 3) agree how often to meet; 4) begin in Je-

The Weenaas parsonage in Marshall, Wisconsin

sus' name; 5) do the work you came to do—a mild suggestion not to eat and gossip; 6) read edifying literature during the meeting; 7) begin and end with a hymn and prayer. He went on to say

> If no woman dares to pray—which should happen at the beginning and end of every meeting—she could read a prayer. A man, a pastor or teacher, should be at every meeting to close with prayer and keep things moving.[316]

The article is open to the idea of women's societies and women voting in their organizations, if not in the congregation, despite the suggestion that a man should be there to lead if things did not go well. Women who read *Lutheraneren* must have felt encouraged by the article, despite the lingering patriarchy.

As the Augsburg group began organizing its own education plan, it proposed that the academy it was building should serve as both a theological preparatory school and one that would "educate capable men and women to be teachers for the common school, in order to impart to young men and women the most important knowledge necessary for ordinary people to learn."[317] This was voted

August Weenaas

down at a meeting in Racine, Wisconsin, on October 29, 1870. It was replaced by "The Academy should serve as a preparatory school for the theological seminary."[318] This effectively stopped co-education in the Augsburg community until 1921. They chose the way of the Synod by establishing Oak Grove Lutheran Ladies' Seminary in 1906 in Fargo, North Dakota, to educate girls from the countryside who needed further education. Thus, they also had two separate schools for boys and for girls.

The Hauge Synod

While one can find significant suspicion of ladies aids and women's leadership in the church among Hauge Synod pastors, they found themselves unable to resist when the women organized to support missions at home and around the world. Hans Nielsen Hauge had included women in his leadership councils and even approved women preaching, although not women pastors. It was something not all of his followers could quite stomach. Although they feared that women would only eat and gossip in their aid meetings, they ultimately did not oppose them. However, they suggested strict constitutions which included clear language proscribing too much food (and gossip) at the meetings, and assuring that Bible study was the main activity, under the tutelage of the pastor. No matter how much these pastors may have disliked the fact that women got together on their own, they recognized the significance of their gifts to support projects both locally and in far away missions. There were women there who needed to hear the gospel of Jesus Christ.

The Hauge Synod's *Budbæreren,* in reporting on women in the larger religious scene in America, expressed closer affinity with evangelicals such as Dwight Moody than with the liberal Congregationalists like Beecher. In March 1871, *Budbæreren* included a note on the KwaZulu mission, a favorite of Norwegians around the world because of the work of Bishop Hans Paluden Smith Schreuder (1817-1882), the storied missionary from Norway to the Zulu. It noted fourteen women workers were serving in that mission.[319] In October that year, the paper included a historical report on the fiftieth anniversary of the mission on the Sandwich Islands (Hawaii) their vivid descrip-

Bishop Hans Paluden Smith Schreuder

tions of the brutal conditions for native women, of the violence of their religion with its human sacrifice and cannibalism, and of the joy with which the natives received the liberating gospel of Jesus Christ.[320]

These women had good warrants for their work. Not only could they claim inspiration from Scripture and the inclusion of Phoebe, Dorcas, and Lydia as workers in the church. They also cited the work in Norway of Gustava Kielland (1800-1889), the pastor's wife who founded the first Norwegian ladies sewing circle in Stavanger in 1844. Finally they claimed a higher cause that was almost impossible for the men to oppose: the saving of millions of souls.[321] In imitation of their English and American sisters, they could send women missionaries to far-off lands with the gospel, something the

Gustava Kielland

Haugeans did in 1891 when they sent Thea Rønning (1865-1899) and her future sister-in-law, Hannah Rorem Rønning (1871-1907), to China. One of the ironies of foreign missions was that women could claim a higher calling and travel to far-away lands where they might function really like pastors.[322] They were, however, careful not to suggest to church leadership that women should become pastors. This was beginning to happen in the Yankee churches in other parts of the country. It was also on the mind of the various editors of church newspapers. Most of them assumed that it was a consequence of the women's suffrage movement which was developing in the east.

Hannah Rorem Rønning

Women's Emancipation Among the Yankees

The March 15, 1872, edition of the *Kirkelig Maanendstidende*, contained a long piece in the "Church Chronicle" (*Kirkekronike*) section which reported that a Quaker woman had preached from a Presbyterian pulpit. As the piece went on, the editor was quite explicit as to what troubled him about this. "As our readers know there has been a long war to get women their rights—and not just women, but many well-spoken men, and among them not a few of the so-called popular preachers, are for it."[323] The program of these radicals, the editors went on to say, was 1) easier divorce, or free love; and 2) suffrage for women in church and state.[324]

As far as the editors of almost all these papers were concerned, the Bible did not allow women to speak in church. *Kirkelig Maanedstidende* reported, with interest, a discussion in a Brooklyn church, most likely near Beecher's Plymouth Church, about the Presbyterian position on women preaching and what the Bible said. As the conversation was reported, the conclusion was that even if women did prophesy in the early churches, Paul had still forbidden women to speak in the church. One person, a Mr. Patton, commented that though many things were not forbidden, they were still not permitted. The meeting concluded with the decision by an overwhelming vote that women could get together by themselves, pray together, maybe even preach, but they could not, under any circumstances, speak when both sexes were present. *Kirkelig Maanedstidende* regarded this as a good sign, noting that with such a large vote to keep women in their place, there was little danger of having women in the pulpit.[325] Two months later, however, there were new alarms

Laur. Larsen

sounded in the editor's report of the statistics on women pastors (*pastorinder*), not pastors' wives, but

> ordained Ladies, who preach, baptize, marry, bury, etc. In 1871 there were 76 female reverends. What is wrong with these male reverends who ordain women, who set themselves at the feet of these women pastors—to be ruled!! How sorrowful it is when folk lose their sense of the created order.[326]

The editor was Laur. Larsen.

The temperance movement, which was growing in this decade, was consistent with Haugean pietist values. Already in Norway people who participated in the Haugean revival considered alcohol to be a woman's issue because of the scourge of liquor on their husbands and families. Frances Willard (1839-1898), the founder of the Women's Christian Temperance Union, a shrewd organizer of people, favored women's suffrage as much as temperance. She thought that if women got the vote they would very quickly vote the saloons out. Everyone who took the

Women's Christian Temperance Union marchers also argued for the vote.

temperance pledge had to sign on the dotted line that they would be for women's suffrage.

By March 1874 *Budbæreren* was publishing frequent reports on the growing power of temperance. In June 1874, the paper carried an editorial describing the work of women in Manchester, England, against liquor, even as they were also agitating for the vote. This was followed by another note in which the editor commented, "The Christian woman is given her place in the family by God. She will be saved by childbirth [Timothy 2:3]. She was the first to fall, she should be the first to lead the young to the cross."[327] (1 Timothy 2:3 has confounded scholars for centuries, but it was still used.) In any event, the Haugeans supported the temperance movement and tended to be more open to women's leadership than the more conservative Synod.

CHAPTER SIX

Comitia Dumriana

Assembly of the Silly Fair Ones

At 8:30 the girls go to Larsen's and have history class, then back
to Brandt's where we talk and sew our handwork. Tuesdays we
have German from 1-2, English from 4-5, so we march down
to Korens to eat supper. Wednesday, history from 3-4, English
from 4:30-5:30. When we have eaten and Larsen has finished
devotions, we went to sing for Aunt Koren.

—Rosina to Linka[328]

The question of what the Norwegian Synod pastors should do for
their own teenage daughters' education continued to worry them. They
did not have the options they had had in Norway: a girl's school like the

*Left to right, seated: Caroline Koren, Henriette Koren, Lulla Hjort, Mathilde
Stub. Standing: Thora Larsen, Marie Reque, Margrethe Brandt, Emma
Larsen, Rosina Preus*

Nissen Girls' School or Christiansfeld in Denmark. There were repeated suggestions about opening a girls' school in Decorah—the first from Mrs. Karen Larsen to her sister Karine Neuberg, that she should start a girls' school when she got to Decorah. There was an obvious market among the daughters of professors and pastors located there, she thought.

Laur. Larsen had once dreamed of opening a school for girls, even to the point of writing down a possible curriculum, before he emigrated. He thought he would be an effective teacher for them, although his experience was limited. He had "taught for a short time in a school for girls. . . . I am confident that if I am capable of instructing boys, I can succeed with little girls as well."[329] Unfortunately, his notes on such a curriculum are not to be found.

Larsen realized from the first that America was a different place and praised it for its treatment of women:

> Women are certainly better off here than in Norway, and the Yankees, to their credit, always treat them with a deference that is seldom seen at home. A servant girl, in fact any decently dressed woman, would everywhere pass ahead of even the President of the United States.[330]

After he became president and professor of the Synod's school, the beginning of Luther College, his work turned exclusively to the education of boys, since there was no expectation at the time that women might become pastors or have professional careers.[331] Besides teaching and administering the young school, he served as a pastor at the Norwegian Lutheran Church in Decorah and edited the church paper, *Kirkelig Maanedstidende*. In addition, he managed the construction of the first part of the Main Building finished in 1865. By 1872, the school had grown large enough so it needed to add the south wing of the Main Building.[332]

When Larsen's first wife, Karen, died in 1871, he had three daughters—Thora (1857-1908), Marie (1863-1899), and Elisabeth Henriette (1864-1904)—for whose education he was responsible. His second wife, Ingeborg Astrup, whom he married in 1872, was their tutor for some years, but upon maturity they needed further schooling. What should it be? Perhaps some kind of finishing school, similar to the education Christiane and Diderikke experienced at Christiansfeld?

Although the pastors and their wives wanted their daughters educated as they had been, this was a new age. The education of Linka Preus and Elisabeth Koren on how to manage a household as a unit of produc-

Scene from the parlor, February 1868. Christian: "Mama, I have done my lessons and written what I had to before Papa comes home. Can I go over to Ambjorns and hunt?" Linka: "Yes, but be careful, Christian." Anga: "But I am doing the fives in subtraction." Doctor: "Anga, now I have done the Fourth Commandment." Rosina: "Uffda, this world history! I will never learn it!" Petra Brevig knits. "Paul is the loveliest boy in the world." Da da da da Misses Johnson sews on my machine. Mrs. Christensen holds the yarn.

tion was less important as social conditions changed. Now, whenever the pastors traveled to cities such as Chicago, their wives drew up shopping lists of dry goods and other amenities—cloth, yarn, dresses, stockings, hats—most of which they could themselves make, but now found it easier to buy. These possibilities lightened the work of more and more of the women in the country. Still, the home remained a major unit of production for a surprisingly long time. Karen Larsen, daughter of Laur. Larsen and his second wife, Ingeborg, referring to her mother's home in Norway, noted that even in the 1870s, homes were places

> where shoemaking, candle-making, curing meat, not to mention weaving and all manner of needlework, were still carried on in the home under the supervision of the women of the family, who had to be well trained in all the domestic arts.[333]

As the century wore on there was a gradual easing of the manual labor in the home with inventions such as the sewing machine. Linka's drawings show how things were changing. Her sketch of the parlor in which she is both running the home school and spinning yarn while other women are sewing using a new sewing machine, gives a comprehensive picture of a home school surrounded by the activities which provide for the needs of the family—now with the added efficiency of the sewing machine.

It was a common practice for these homes to employ what they called sewing girls (*sypiker*) when they had weddings or other festive events to dress for. Misses Johnson, sitting at the sewing machine trying it out, may have been such a person. The machine made their work much more efficient.

When Mrs. Karen Larsen wrote that she had begun sewing Karine's wedding dress in May 1866, all she had was her two hands, a needle, material, and nimble fingers—a daunting task for most seamstresses even today. Although the sewing machine had been invented in the late eighteenth century, it was not common in home use until after the Civil War. Then more and more women were able to purchase the machine, making it possible to sew a shirt, which normally took fourteen hours, in an hour.

Once the daughters of these mid-nineteenth century immigrant pastors were approaching maturity, it was time for them to learn the fine arts, especially music and the piano. Almost all of their mothers had gone to a special music teacher in Norway to develop their skills on the instrument. Where were their daughters on the frontier to go? The question became more and more urgent to them as they watched their daughters growing into fine young ladies. What they needed now was a finishing school like Christiansfeld or the Nissen School for Girls.

Theories of Women's Physiology and Psychology

About this time, there were changes in the understanding of the physiology and psychology of women that affected the way the culture understood education for girls. Upper class women had more problems finding a place for themselves in the economy than women of the working classes did. That was a problem for the pastors' daughters in the Norwegian Synod. They needed a liberal education, not to enter the work force, but to prepare for their role as wives, often pastors' wives.

About the time that the older daughters from the Norwegian Synod parsonages approached the typical age for higher education, the early 1870s, there was a shift in how women were understood and understood themselves, especially the women of the leadership classes. They were to be decorative and sentimental, no longer so much producers as consumers trying to please their husbands with their beauty and abilities to make the home a refuge. Rousseau had urged this in his book *Emile*. Ann Douglas' book, *The Feminization of American Culture*, shows this to be a dominant theme in the literature of mid-nineteenth century America, such as the novels of Harriet Beecher Stowe, among many others, novels which the pastors' wives were reading with interest.[334]

Henriette and Karine Neuberg had encountered the beginnings of this change as they struggled to find a productive role in their society before marriage. They could not work for money—it was beneath them. At the same time the frontier required them to be strong and capable of hard physical work, even in the parsonage, something their delicate health could not endure. Later descriptions of them as lovely women who, by their presences, added elegance and finery to the rough life on the frontier, use the language of decoration and sentimentality. David Nelson, author of the Luther College centennial history, noted that Karen Neuberg was "an attractive, if somewhat retired woman, for whom the hardships of early pioneering proved too strong."[335] Ottesen said something similar about the refinement of the Neuberg sisters: They were fine additions to the clergy families' common life, but not strong enough to meet the rigors of the frontier.

The View of Women at the Time

This view of women—especially of the upper classes—intensified in the 1870s as a kind of patina over the older notion of the orders of creation which placed women under the headship of their husbands. Now, in the new, more secular, world, as women were moving from being productive members of the family to consumers, this theory of the female came be regarded as scientific fact, something the popular medical books of the day argued. Oddly, as the actual labor of women was less needed, the theory of women restricted them almost exclusively to their biology, which meant motherhood and homemaking.

Hardly any other book was as influential among the educated classes than that of Doctor Edward H. Clarke, a professor of Materia Medica in Harvard College. He wrote *Sex in Education; or, a Fair Chance for Girls*, a book that became gospel in the education of girls. Its theories of the biology of young women especially affected women who hoped to become doctors, lawyers, or pastors. It gave scientific warrant for restricting the entrance of women into professions traditionally reserved for men. Based on Darwinian evolutionary theories, it argued that the education of young women needed to allow for the development of girls' sexual organs and sexuality. Their blood should go to feed their developing sexual organs, not their brains. If not given "a sufficient opportunity for the healthy development of the ovaries and their accessory organs, and for the establishment of their periodical functions" teenage girls could become sterile.

Edward H. Clarke

Another doctor wrote that the young women who took no care for their reproductive system as teenagers would have female organs that remained germinal, or undeveloped. If they "graduated from school or college [as] excellent scholars, [they would do so] with undeveloped ovaries. Later, they married, and were sterile," he concluded.[336]

While this may strike today's feminists as medicine or science backing up pure misogyny, it should be noted that this was widely accepted scientific advice from the highest secular authorities of the day and not the church. These works were accepted by the medical community of the day as unimpeachable, and it served to make the lives of many, especially upper class, women miserable. Part of this notion was the idea of the "wandering womb" which could only be cured by pregnancy. It served as the diagnosis for women suffering for everything from appendicitis to abdominal cancer, hysteria, and mental illness.

While there is no record of the Norwegian Synod pastors or their wives using these categories specifically in their discussions of the education of their daughters, they can be seen in a variety of incidents. Any member of the elite would have heard these arguments simply by virtue of keeping up with the times and the latest science. There are echoes of it in the proscription of strenuous and "unlady"-like exercise for girls and even the mental exercise of reading novels that inappropriately excited the imaginations and bodies of young women. Karine Neuberg expressed her exasperation with Hjort's dictum that she should not read lurid novels or secular literature because of its bad moral influences—inappropriate for girls. Karen Larsen's mother, Ingeborg Astrup, told her that when she was young and her older brother Nils found her reading Ibsen's *Peer Gynt* he took it from her saying it was "horrid stuff not fit for girls to read."[337]

These theories did not stop the pastors' wives around Decorah from looking for some way to give their daughters a higher education, or

The Preus family arriving in Norway, greeting their family there after fifteen years in America. Rosina is in the foreground, meeting her uncle Kalla.

finishing school. They sought something similar to what they had experienced in their youth—not for careers outside of the home, but for the managing and leading of a gracious and flourishing home. This was to be something more than the school that Mrs. Hjort had established in her parlor in Paint Creek. They were continuing a tradition of education as old as the Lutheran parsonage.

By the middle of the 1870s several of the young teenage pastors' daughters of the Norwegian Synod had traveled to Norway with their families or friends either to study with capable aunts or in girls' schools, as their mothers had done. Rosina Preus accompanied her family on their trip to Norway in 1866-1867, when the Preus family returned for an extended visit.

Karen Larsen left Decorah to visit her father and family in Bergen, so that she could receive better medical treatment. There is a record of her visit to the baths in Sandefjord in June 1868, a common destination for those suffering everything from TB to arthritis. She took her three daughters—Thora, Marie, and Henriette—and toddler Herman (1867-1895) along. Later, the girls, using an inheritance from their grandfather,

Peter Neuberg, returned to Norway for some further schooling.[330] When and where is not clear. Thora may have received further education in 1875 when she traveled with her aunt Karine Neuberg Magelssen to Norway. Their father advised them not only to study music, but also to hear lectures at the school. It may have been Nissens Girls' School that he recommended, but that is not documented.

When Mrs. Larsen announced her intentions to take the trip home for medical advice, Diderikke Brandt decided that it was a good time for her to return home as well. Thus she and her four children—Edel Margrethe (1857-1926), Realf Ottesen (1859-1927), Olaf Elias (1862-1940), and John Elias (1864-)—accompanied Mrs. Larsen. The Hjorts saw an opportunity in this trip and sent Lulla, their oldest daughter, along with Mrs. Larsen and her aunt, Mrs. Brandt. They were escorted by Professor Lyder Siewers. Given their penury, they had to take  steerage. They boarded ship in Quebec on April 9, 1868. It was a difficult journey for Mrs. Larsen and Lulla who were seasick most of the time. Mrs. Koren commented in a letter to Linka,

Mrs. Diderikke Brandt

> Hututu, how hideous it must have been in steerage! Mrs. Larsen had no help so she was terribly weary. Only wished they would soon be off in Liverpool. Mrs. Brandt also wrote that it hadn't been all that bad. But I believe I would rather see it from Mrs. Larsen's point of view.[339]

When they arrived in Liverpool for their transit across England on their way to Hull to board the ship to Norway, Siewers was suspected of being a Mormon with two wives. That caused the mild-mannered man to erupt in anger.[340]

Lulla spent some time with her aunts and grandparents, retired Pastor Otto Christian Ottesen and his wife Diderrike Aall, in Porsgrund, near Skien. Christiane Hjort, in a letter to Linka, remarked on Lulla's going so far away for school, but recalled that she had done the same when she went to Christiansfeld as a young girl, and there everyone was a stranger. Lulla's parents had sent her to Norway specifically for training so that she could "later teach the young here."[341] Christiane lamented that she was growing weary of being a teacher and would rather keep house, since she was not a good teacher, an opinion not shared by any of the pastors' wives. Part of the reason, she said, was that their home was becoming very crowded with their own family.[342]

What the various daughters did, exactly, during their time in Norway is a bit murky and not very well described in the letters of the women to one another during the time abroad. One can assume a large part of their reason for going was traditional. Their mothers had studied with their aunts, so also should their daughters. In this case, they were to learn something about their families, grandparents, and cousins, and learn more about how to manage a home along with further instruction in the arts of fine handiwork, music, and drawing. Even Karen Larsen's well-regarded biography of her father gives us few dates and not even the names of her half-sisters who were sent to Norway. These traditional attempts to educate their daughters seemed insufficient. Without a girls' school in the area, the pastors and their wives had to provide for their daughters' higher education in another way.

The Koren Parsonage Burns Down

Then a crisis occurred that gave the pastors' wives an opportunity they were quick to seize. In November 1872, on a cold autumn Sunday evening in the Washington Prairie parsonage, the Korens were sitting in their living room enjoying the late evening. Their colleague, Frants Einar Wulfsburg (1841-1906), noticed smoke in the upstairs office where he was working on the hymnal Koren was preparing for the Synod.[343] He called to them, and they were able to save the children who were sleeping upstairs, along with some furniture and a few books and papers.[344] The parsonage was the one

Frants Einar Wulfsburg

Elisabeth and Vilhelm had planned and built after their first year in America, and its loss was wrenching for them. Rosina "Sina" Preus, who was in Decorah studying with a Luther College professor at the time, wrote her mother a vivid account of Mrs. Koren catching nine-year old Paul Koren as he jumped from a window. Caroline "Lina" ran out without any clothes. Because the parsonage and the church were out in the country, there was no help nearby. Neighbors in the area may well have seen the fire, but, by the time they got there, it was too late for much of anything to be saved. The Korens lost nearly everything: clothes, furniture, books, and papers. Thus the long extended hymnal project, *Synodens Salmebog*, had to be postponed for yet another year.

The Chicken Coop on the Luther College campus

The Korens needed to find housing in Decorah, quickly. After a journey of about eight miles, in the cold without winter clothing, they came to Decorah in the middle of the night and had to find temporary accommodations at once. Because of the large enrollment at the college that year, space was hard to find. Eighteen students were housed in the Chicken Coop, a two-story brick building on the campus, recently converted to dormitory space. The only place for the family to stay was one of the guest rooms at the college, one-room apartments in the Main Building reserved for professors' guests. There the Korens stayed for a few days, but they needed to find a house quickly for their large family, not an easy thing in the small, new town.

The Korens had recently returned from an extended trip to Norway, where they had renewed contacts with their families and colleagues in the church. Henriette and Caroline were of an age for some kind of higher education or finishing school, and they had probably seen a possibility for it at their grandfather's school in Larvik. The Brandts had a daughter, Edel Margrethe (1857-1925), a little younger than Rosina Preus and Lulla Hjort. Laur. Larsen's Thora was now ready for such a school. With the Koren family there, the professors' constituted a large family of cousins all living together at the school. One can imagine a conversation among the wives that late November, while sitting together in the parlor doing their handiwork, discussing what they could do to further the education of their daughters. Why not organize a school for them now that they were going to be in the same place for some time? Perhaps the Luther professors could be persuaded to teach their daughters during their free time—a laughable notion considering how busy they already were with their overcrowded schedules.

Luther College professors, 1869: Standing left to right: Friedrich A. Schmidt, Nils Brandt. Seated: Gabriel Landmark, Lyder Siewers, Knut E. Bergh, Laur. Larsen

As noted before, Koren and Preus had taught at the Nissen School for Girls, and Larsen had also taught young girls, thus they and their competent wives had ideas about such an education. What they wanted their girls to study followed rather closely the curriculum of Nissen's School for Girls and Christiansfeld—without instruction in fine needlework, which they had learned and would continue to learn from their mothers and aunts as they sat around the fire at night. Music instruction would be provided by their uncles—Brandt, Schmidt, and Koren—who led the singing instruction. Karen Larsen indicated in a note how important music was to women students at the time of her mother's education, "They must, of course, be experts in all domestic arts, and they must be able to play the piano."[345] Even if a number of their mothers and aunts were capable pianists, it was common for girls to leave home to study music with the best piano teachers available. Ingeborg Astrup Larsen had done this for a year in Christiania before her marriage in the fall of 1872 to Laur. Larsen. Now that the Korens were living in town, it was only Mathilda Stub from nearby Big Canoe who needed a place to stay. Rosina Preus was already there, as was Lulla Hjort, learning piano and other skills from some of her "aunts." The girls could live together in the Brandt parsonage, a spacious building which already housed three bachelor professors, plus some college students in the attic. It seemed like a happy and fortunate opportunity, and they began

Rosina "Sina" Preus

immediately. While it would be in the context of the men's school, their classes would not be co-educational, rather, still segregated by sex, even if they were often the very same courses.

The Luther professors had been teaching the girls on an individual basis at the time. Rosina was studying writing with Professor Jacobsen. She had private lessons from other professors and a Miss Halla Gylling, who had come to Decorah from Milwaukee for a time to teach. Rosina complained about some of the assignments and criticized Miss Gylling for not knowing the English author William Thackeray.[346] That she did not know this, even though she had come highly recommended by Elise Hovde in Bergen, troubled Rosina. Miss Hovde had written to Linka from Norway, informing her that Miss Gylling was hoping to establish a school for girls in Decorah.[347] Apparently she had heard of the need for some kind of girls' school there, especially for the pastors' and professors' daughters. She wrote to Linka, asking if she could find some Norwegian children to teach at Decorah. She would be there, she said, in the middle of January.[348]

Who Miss Gylling was, other than a Swedish woman wanting to open a school in Decorah or teach at Milwaukee Downers College, is difficult to determine. Milwaukee did have a female seminary at the time, founded by Catherine Beecher. Gylling may well have been teaching there and looking to extend her work in Decorah, which she could have heard of through various contacts in Milwaukee. Downers was a common source of women teachers through the end of the century. Christiane Hjort, who knew whereof she spoke from her three years at Christiansfeld, commented on Miss Gylling's plan for a girls' school, noting that it would not be Norwegian, but rather "the whole plan would be European." That probably meant that it would be more German in its language and curriculum, as Christiansfeld had been, in contrast to Nissen's plan for a nationalistic curriculum that taught the girls their Nordic heritage.

Christiane observed that the tuition Miss Gylling was going to charge for such a school was quite expensive. While the pastors and their families had some means, cash was hard to come by. In the past when their daughters had gone to an aunt to study, they had exchanged their work in the home for room and board. Christiane had been pleased Lulla could go stay with the Brandts while she learned French from Professor Lyder Siewers, a language important for her musical ambitions as a singer. Now the possibility of the men teaching their daughters in a classroom situation seemed much more attractive. It was surely less expensive, since their daughters could stay with their cousins in Decorah at the college for free.[349] What they paid for instruction is never mentioned in the letters, but there are some hints they did have to pay something. Mrs. Koren had taken some classes from the male faculty in Larvik. She must have remembered this as they were discussing possibilities and may have been the one who recognized the opportunity first, given her experience in her father's school in Larvik.

There is no mention of who made the proposal and why it became a reality so quickly, but it happened with astonishing speed. Whoever pressed the overworked professors to teach the girls must have been persuasive. Taking on these bright young women students must have stretched them to the point of breaking.

There were several fine teachers in the Luther faculty, including Jacob Daniel Jacobsen (1847-1881), who had recently married and lived on campus with his wife. Jacobsen had been one of the first Norwegian immigrant students to study at Concordia Seminary in St. Louis in 1858. In 1873-1874 he was teaching English and Latin, German and Greek, as well as logic, mathematics, and religion. A gifted man who loved beauty and great literature, he became a valued faculty member who paid attention to the physical campus and its care, the first to do so.

Professor Jacob Daniel Jacobsen

Professor Lyder Siewers, for whom Siewers Springs, a small park southeast of Decorah, is named, became a beloved fixture in the community. He also had a rugged teaching schedule: twenty-three hours of teaching each week during this year. He taught German, Greek, Latin, geography, penmanship, Norwegian, mathematics, natural history, and history. Siewers had studied at the University of Oslo and in Germany. He had married in 1868, after his futile courtship of Karine Neuberg. Gabriel Landmark, who had remarried in 1871 after the death of his first wife in 1870, shared the responsibility of teaching the girls. He was already teaching twenty-four hours a week, plus serving as the librarian.

Professor Gabriel Landmark

The average of six hours a day in class, while a normal day of teaching at the time, was a heavy load for any teacher, without the addition of extra classes for the girls. Jacobsen, who taught English, logic, and rhetoric, with all the themes and grading involved in those disciplines, had the heaviest load. These three bore the brunt of teaching both the young men and women, with the help of some other instructors, such as Brandt and Koren in music, and Larsen, who taught some Norwegian.[350] Jacobsen became the librarian in 1874. He died young from tuberculosis, in 1881, after having essentially given his life for the furtherance of the college.

School Begins

The year of 1873, despite the financial panic that sank the world into a depression of some years, was a very busy, but fulfilling, year for the church and the community. The panic, however, derailed any possibility of the church founding a parallel system of Lutheran primary school education, no matter how desirable.[351] The following year small divisions in the church signaled fissures that would become complete schisms in the next decade. The common school debate continued unabated as did questions about establishing academies into the fall of 1874.

Hermann Preus continued to support his proposal for a girls' school (*Pigeskole*) to be built by the Synod in Red Wing. It was most likely an offhand remark to O. K. Simmons, his good friend in Red Wing, while they were discussing a gift of land and money that a man in Red Wing had made to the Synod (which it did not, finally, accept). What exactly Preus meant by that has never been clear, although, given his name for it, *Pigeskole*[352] (girl's school) he may have been thinking of Rosina and Comitia Dumriana and looking back to Nissens *Pigeskolen* where he had begun his teaching career a quarter century earlier, just before he left for Wisconsin with Linka. Linka's brother, Johan Carl Keyser, was now the rector of the Nissen Girls' School so the term was well known to them.

In addition to his normal teaching and administrative duties at the college, along with editing the church paper, *Kirkelig Maanedstidende*, President Larsen was now occupied with the addition of the second wing of the Main Building. He oversaw this project from the drawings to the requisition slips of every kind. It was scheduled to be finished by October 1874, but, despite all the work, it was not ready for the Founder's Day gathering on October 14. The dedication had to be postponed until December 1874.

Despite all these compelling responsibilities, the already overworked professors agreed to teach the girls during their free hours—their normal teaching load with the boys started at the crack of dawn. The girls, at least the ones we know of—Thora Larsen, Henriette Christiane Koren (1854-

1939) and Caroline Mathilde Koren (1856-1945), Margrethe Brandt, Rosina Preus, Lulla Hjort, Mathilda Stub (1857-1900), Marie Reque, and Emma Larsen (not a daughter of Laur. Larsen)—began classes together just before Christmas 1872. The classes continued until the end of the spring semester in 1874.[353] Their class came to be called affectionately *Comitia Dumriana* (an assembly of the silly, fair ones).

During their course of studies (1872-1874), they studied German, French, English, Norwegian, history, and music. These days of living together at the college with each others' families, whom they already knew well, solidified the close connections and sisterly feelings which they maintained throughout the rest of their lives. The girls' presence on the men-only campus created, for over a year and a half, a completely different environment for the boys. Peer Strømme (1856-1921,) a student at Luther during this time, described the difference the girls made in his novel, *Halvor*.

Peer Strømme

> Almost all these young ladies were so pleasant and attractive that they made poor Halvor's heart ache. When this bevy of girls or *Comitia Dumriana*, as they were called, strolled down the road, he could not keep his eyes off them.[354]

Not surprisingly many marriages resulted from the girls being on the campus![355]

Rosina, who was a good observer, wrote many letters home to her mother describing scenes from their life together at the college. She also reported on how her mother's good friends were doing, especially Mrs. Koren, who at the time was under the stress that comes with losing one's home and nearly all possessions. The Koren family had to move frequently, since homes available in Decorah to rent temporarily were sparse.[356] Rosina observed that she liked practicing the piano, but was not making fast enough progress to suit her. This may have caused Linka to smile, given Rosina's reluctance, at first, to practice.[357]

Because the school began just before Christmas in 1872, the girls experienced the festivities of the season together with the boys at the college. Their first party, however, celebrated the second marriage of President Laur. Larsen. He visited Norway after the death of his first wife, Karen. While there he met and married Ingeborg Astrup (1846-1923). She was a sister of Nils Astrup (1843-1919), missionary to the KwaZulu in South Africa. The daughter of a judge, Ingeborg had the usual education in the finer things both at home and at a school in Christiana where she had music lessons.

The girls of the *Comita Dumriana,* led by Rosina, purchased a wedding gift for the Larsens, a silver service set. In addition Rosina gave them engraved silver napkin rings to go with the set. While the marriage was to be expected—Larsen needed help raising his children and hosting events at the college—it was a bit delicate for the community, especially his own children, to fully

Ingeborg and Laur. Larsen on their wedding day

accept another in the place of their mother, Karen. Marriage, however, particularly in these situations, with young children needing care, was as much a necessity as a matter of falling in love.

Mrs. Koren, who had lost a dear friend in Karen Larsen, wondered with Linka what she thought of the new wife. She assumed that she would be a first-rate housewife, but she was not sure how it would go with the children. She thought it would be good if Henriette Neuberg, Karen's sister and beloved aunt of the Larsen children, would come and be with the children that spring. Perhaps Marie Sivisind, one of their frequent helpers, would come in the winter to help with their lessons. Henriette would please the children, as well as the other pastors' wives, but how Ingeborg would like it was another issue to which Mrs. Koren was sensitive.[358] Now that the Korens lived temporarily in Decorah in close proximity to the new Mrs. Larsen, Elisabeth had a good sense for how things were going, and her letters to Linka give us a detailed picture of the activities of the faculty families and the young people.

Christmas 1872

Because travel was difficult and expensive for most of the students, many remained at the college over the holidays. The Hjorts made a practice of inviting most of the students left behind during the holidays to spend Christmas with them at Paint Creek, driving them on sleighs from the college. Lulla recalled that sometimes they had hosted as many as fifty students at Blaasenborg, the parsonage at Paint Creek.[359] These were celebrations Per Strømme never forgot. He memorialized them in his novel, *How Halvor Became a Pastor*. The faculty families strove to make sure the boys did not spend the time alone. This year, however, with the girls and their families living on campus or in Decorah, most of the festivities were held at the college, not Paint Creek.

Rosina, in a chatty letter to her mother, described some of the events of the holiday. Brandt, who was both a teacher at the college and pastor of what became First Lutheran Church in Decorah, had preached at the Christmas service. During the processional offering, an expected part of yearly compensation and taken up for the pastor and *klokker* on holidays, Rosina gave the pastor twenty-five cents and the *klokker*, Gulbrand Lommen, fifteen cents.[360] She also described the Christmas festivities at the college, coming down into the dining room for the Christmas dinner that had been beautifully set. Lulla had gotten a rare book of musical selections from some Germans in Lansing, and she was eager to play them. Mrs. Hjort, knowing that her daughter was gifted musically, always sought to find a good teacher and good music for her.[361]

Mrs. Koren, ever keen to notice new things and mark changes in the old rites and rituals, had heard a conversation showing that something was changing, a change she did not approve. One evening, as the wives sat together in the Brandt parlor doing handiwork, the two double cousins, Mrs. Brandt and Mrs. Hjort, began discussing the amount the Hjorts should pay Linka for taking Lulla into her home and teaching her the many domestic skills necessary to be a wife, especially a pastor's wife—the traditional custom. Although Lulla later married Christian Preus and became Linka's daughter-in-law, at the time it was not clear who was going to marry whom. Mrs. Koren listened to the conversation and their concerns for paying room and board for Lulla. She found it to be so different from traditional practice that it seemed to her laughable.

> It struck me so comical to think that I should be paid for having Sina or Lulla or any of the children in the house, that I almost began to laugh out loud, until I started to think that maybe I should have asked you what you wanted for the week when Caroline "Lina" stayed with you, and then I thought you might have laughed as well.[362]

She then went on to ask Linka if she had now become a good gossip. She had, however, not laughed out loud, because she was too "stiff," something Linka had apparently noted about her. "Am I too formal? I must have an unconscious formal instinct," she concluded.[363]

Mrs. Koren knew that she was taken to be somewhat forbidding by those who did not know her well. One can see in fact in her photographs an aspect of tensile steel grace. It is clear that one would not toy with her. Her sharp wit and careful observations (which make her diary and letters so rich) are evident in the above comment in which she noted the beginning of an ending to the practice of aunts teaching their nieces. It was a slight move toward a cash economy, no longer the barter system the families had used for generations as they helped each other with the education of daughters.

Elisabeth Koren at 40

Just after Christmas 1872, Elisabeth described the new rooms into which they had just moved. It had been one of the coldest Christmases they had experienced since 1864, when the college's Main Building was under construction. The boys had warm stones from the stove to put in their beds, an old remedy which helped, and the three youngest had slept with the Korens in their bedroom, where the stove in the living room gave them some heat. The college rooms did not have storm windows. According to Karen Larsen, they had been "miserably cold."[364]

Home School Continues

The pastors' wives, now in their late thirties, were not yet done with babies or preschoolers. Christiane Hjort, home in Paint Creek after visiting Lulla for Christmas, wrote Linka that "we have begun school full steam ahead. It is not always fun. In the afternoon they study English, then I have Thinka [Cathinka, their five year old and youngest daughter] alone."[365] Although the education of the older girls was the main concern at this juncture, life did not stop. The wives still had the task of teaching their youngest children, and now they could get some help from their older daughters. While they did not regard this as drudgery, one can see hints of their yearning for another life. Christiane had written a plaintive note to Linka, once, wishing she had a *Beruf* (German for profession or calling) like Diderikke, working and living at the college, but then said, Ove Hjort, her husband had comforted her by saying her *Beruf* was taking care of the children and their home.[366] This missed what she was saying.

Her tone is one of resignation. She had obviously enjoyed the holiday at the college with the students and observed closely Diderikke's work as something of a dorm mother. She may have seen possibilities for herself, no less well-educated than her cousin. She had, after all, studied for three years at Christiansfeld and probably had as much ambition as her cousin. She knew she was acknowledged by the entire community to be one of their best teachers, and she had been running a school in her parlor, as noted in the last chapter. Her comment seems to imply she felt somewhat constricted by her role as pastor's wife and mother. Her ambitions appear to be more outside of the home than in it. Her husband's comments did not really meet her concerns. He was only expecting what pastors had always expected of their wives in this system.

Back in Class

> History is worst. I can't remember names or dates. Lulla Hjort is just as scared as I am in class.
>
> —Rosina Preus to her mother

Studies continued for the girls at the college. Rosina "Sina" told her mother about her schoolwork and gave her a vivid picture of her English assignment and her own struggles as a student: "I have written in my theme book. I checked it over hundreds of time, but I didn't get a better mark. I can't explain everything about a snowstorm. I'm glad no one else can either." She went on to describe the other classes. For their English literature classes, taught by Jacobsen, they could choose between *Robinson Crusoe* and another book. "History is worst. I can't remember names or dates. Lulla Hjort is just as scared as I am in class. Larsen is kind, but we can barely answer him. I study as much as I can—twice as much as the others." (Rosina is shown in Linka's drawings as not being good at history.) She concluded that the Reque girl was the best student of histo-

Rosina Preus

ry. Homework took seven hours a week. This took time from her piano practicing, probably her chief focus.[367]

A woman teacher, Miss Kristine (Stine) Wråmann (b. 1839), had come to teach music for the girls and, apparently, the boys. Although we know little about her, Miss Wråmann was a daughter of pastor Hans Nicolai Wråmann from Borge in Lofoten. She appears in the Norwegian census in 1865 as a private school teacher. She had come to America with her sister Louise sometime after the Civil War. Her sister, whom the census of 1870 names as Vrooman, taught in the Hans A. Stub home in Big Canoe and later married an American and stayed. Kristine is mentioned occasionally in the letters as an itinerant musician, staying now with the Stubs, then appearing a bit too much at the school—in the opinion of Mrs. Brandt.[368] Miss Wråmann appears to have been a true itinerant teacher. After leaving Decorah for Chicago, she disappeared from the American scene. She later turned up in the 1880s in Christiania, advertising in the evening paper, *Aftenposten*, her private school for girls which she ran with a woman named Blakstad.[369]

With all their homework, which it appears the instructors did not spare them, the girls also had fun like any teenagers. Not surprisingly, Sina reported on more than their studies. She complained about the rigors of Jacobsen's writing assignments, but shows herself to be an able reporter of their common life at the school. Apparently there had been a silver thaw in the little city—not uncommon in Decorah, hardly anything is more beautiful and treacherous. Sina described watching one of the students, Bjørn Haatvedt, (later Bjørn Edwards), skiing behind the college, where they were skating. Since the silver thaw made it virtually impossible to navigate, they fell helplessly over one another, slipping and sliding, laughing and squealing like typical girls their age.[370] Linka must have smiled reading this, remembering a sketch she had done of just such an adventure ten years before, with Henriette, Karine, Christian, and Rosina walking on the icy snow, laughing and squealing.

Rosina also reported to her mother more about their studies, probably because it was still new to all of them. School had begun again after Christmas, and now they had Norwegian lessons from Larsen at 7:30 a.m. Larsen had not agreed to teach much, given his pressing schedule. The fact that he taught them Norwegian shows that they were using a curriculum like that of the Nissen Girls' School. In that plan, the mother tongue was viewed as a basic and fundamental part of one's heritage.[371]

The Norwegian of the second generation tends to be less agile in diction and grammar than that of their accomplished parents. It was mixed

Walking through the snow, a Sunday morning pleasure with Hennrietta, Karine, Christian, Sina. March '63

with anglicisms, as is natural for the children of any immigrants, even for those as sophisticated as these young people were, but it was their heart language which they used most of the time. All agreed, however, that English was the language of the future and their children needed to know it well to flourish in America. To that end, the English composition from Jacobsen required more time and concentration.

After classes one cold January day the group took Koren's sleigh to Washington Prairie to view the burned out parsonage. On the way home, they stopped at Dunning's Springs, a spring near the college, and had another great evening of fun. Christian came along, Rosina reported, as well as Henriette and Caroline Koren, Lulla Hjort, Emma Larsen, and Thora Larsen.[372] The boys were experiencing the pleasure of girls being around, although not in their classes. (No one suggested they study along with the boys, which might have spared the teachers some precious time.) They knew the girls as well as they knew their sisters, but it was completely different from what school had been like for them over the past ten years.

Christian Keyser Preus

Mrs. Koren, who seemed to enjoy the teenagers, observed that the young people had been together just before the beginning of the second term at the Larsens, and "the whole room was full of youth." Tomorrow, she noted, the new term would begin again. "The young girls did their best in their exams," she concluded. Before classes resumed the girls had been invited to hear the first class of boys giving dramatic readings of Shakespeare.[373] This was not all that different from the parlor gatherings, such as Linka described in her first entries in her diary, where the family would perform or read plays for each other. Although the boys and the girls were experiencing something close to co-educational college life, it was not the same. Their classes were still separate. One wonders if any professor, pressed to teach two lessons of the same content to both boys and girls, might have suggested the classes meet together. It did not come up. There is only the briefest indication that the church council had noticed the girls were studying with the Luther professors. In the minutes of the church council, there is a note that they needed to hire another professor because the "always larger lower classes had to be divided into two parallel classes.[374]

They believed the sexes should be apart during instruction. With girls in the classes, the boys' education would no longer be as tough as they believed it should be. They could, however, enjoy each other's company after school in the general activities of the school, rather like in Christiansfeld.

Mrs. Koren had not been out to see the parsonage for some time, partly because of the weather, and partly because it was too much for her to take to see the burned out carcass of the home she had planned and loved.

The Koren parsonage in 1858 when the Preuses visited them. Hermann and Linka are walking toward it with Rosina and Christian.

In March 1873, when spring made travel easier, she finally went to see it. She sent Linka warm thanks for having given them copies of her sketches of the "dear old parsonage" in Washington Prairie. The children had been trying to remember it and draw it themselves. They could never get theirs right, nor could Elisabeth draw a picture of the parsonage to their satisfaction. "Aunt Linka is much more clever than Mama," Elisabeth quoted them as saying, as they began to look closely at the drawings to see if the windows were right, and found that the kitchen had a window.[375]

Linka and perhaps Christiane Hjort were the best teachers of drawing and piano, though the camera was beginning to encroach on their art. Still the girls wanted to learn to draw because they enjoyed Tante Linka's witty drawings. They captured not just the appearances of people, but also interpreted their characters in dramatic scenes which often were very telling. A course in drawing, however, did not appear in the curriculum

of the fledgling college. Apparently the boys were not being taught the art in their home schools either, or if they were, not as seriously as the girls. The Luther College professors did not teach it to the girls although it had been a significant part of the curriculum at the Nissen schools for boys and girls. This may have been as much for the lack of someone who could teach it as their not thinking it necessary. Everyone knew that Tante Linka was the best at the art and probably the best teacher, but the instruction was informal and in the parlor. And she was not there.

Elisabeth Koren in her 70s

On March 10, 1873, the Korens had to move a third time. Mrs. Koren was not pleased to have to do so, because of all the extra work involved in moving. Given the few empty houses available in the small town, space large enough for the family was temporary at best. She had wanted to move into the Dayton house, an old house of note in the small city. It was the only house they would have liked in West Decorah. However, it was not available, so they moved back in with the Larsens for a short time again. The rebuilding of the Koren parsonage had been slow to get started, given the hard winter and the time it took to draw up plans for a new home. It was now beginning in earnest. Koren had asked all of the girls to go with him to the burned-down parsonage, after which they came back and ate their evening meal at the Korens in Decorah.

At about this same time, Mrs. Jacobsen wrote Linka a warm and friendly letter, telling her a bit about their living conditions in such close quarters. Sina had an unpleasant experience with the Brandts and needed to move. According to Mrs. Jacobsen, Sina moved in briefly with the Larsens. She thought Mrs. Larsen, whom she had not come to know very well in the few months she had been in their midst, would be a much better hostess for Sina than Diderikke. Mrs. Jacobsen regretted that even

though they lived in the same house, they were almost strangers to each other. They had their own lives to live with children and family, but they did have to deal with each other in more intimate ways, since they lived close to one another in apartments in the college building. One can well imagine that these strong-willed men and women, accustomed to their private lives, found accommodating to the others a bit difficult. Mrs. Koren had agreed with Mrs. Jacobsen on the move, and all were praying it would help the situation, though Mrs. Brandt was apparently quite put out by the situation.[376]

Professor Jacobsen

While the girls were receiving a good education in this rather unusual arrangement, the mothers still longed for something more permanent and institutional. Hermann and the other pastors agreed on this. No wonder, then, that about this time Hermann Preus is said to have proposed a girls' school in Red Wing.[377] It may well have been the gathering of the girls in Decorah that prompted his suggestion. Co-education at Luther was not imagined, given their belief in the superiority of segregated schooling. Still, the Synod knew it had to provide its daughters some kind of higher education. There continued to be talk of what to do for their girls beyond *Comitia Dumriana*. Christiane Hjort, remembering her education at Christiansfeld, wrote to Linka that the idea for a girls' school was good but not yet feasible. Lulla would have to come home in May, perhaps because of the costs. She still needed a teacher, however, for further instruction.[378] Elise Hovde, who watched for possible teachers from Norway, wrote to Linka that she had heard from Henriette Neuberg in Norway that a Miss Magdalene Muhlenfort (b. 1850) was teaching music and English in Norway and longed to return to America. She had been with the families some time before this and would return again.

Passing on the Tradition

We can observe through these letters how the lives of these young women were developing. They, of course, did not realize it as they were writing their letters. On March 10, 1873, Sina described another party with Mrs. Brandt, where Jørgen Nordby (her future husband), Nils Forde, and Styrk Reque appeared and sang together for them all. This is the first concert on record at the college. Christian Preus' job, as manager, was to provide beaten eggs and sugar (*eggedosis*, what the British would call an "egg flip," or eggnog without the alcohol) for the singers.[379] Christian took his work as manager seriously. The event provided great merriment for the assembled students, now including the girls.

The Brandt family in front of the parsonage on the Luther campus

> The teacher's desk was removed from the platform, and a shawl was stretched from a pole on one corner of the platform to the wall on the right sight [which] hid the singers from the public gaze between the numbers. . . . Physics was not studied at the college at that time; therefore, a lamp was placed on a small table close to a shawl, which screened the performers, and between the numbers the audience was entertained hugely by moving pictures on the wall back of the stage in which gigantic spoons were conveyed to enormous mouths. It is reported that the troupe was required by the authorities to return the proceeds of the concert to the audience.[380]

Two weeks later, on April 6, there was a concert for a mixed chorus. They charged a dime. The sopranos were Lulla Hjort, Marie Reque, Lina Koren, altos were Realf Brandt and Johannes Thorbjørnson Ylvisaker, tenors Nils Forde and Fingar Jørgensen, and basses, L. S. Reque (who himself was a part-time instructor during this year) and Christian Preus. They sang hymns like "O Sacred Head, Now Wounded," Christian told his mother.[381] This concert of mixed voices has not made the official histories, but it is a first mixed choir concert given at the college. Although Luther students would be asked to sing in the First Lutheran Church Choir, the possibility for a mixed choir with men and women would not be possible for the next sixty years.

Every evening the pastors would have devotions with their families and other charges, each of them in their own living quarters. Hans B. Thorgrimsen, an Icelandic emigrant who lived as a hired man with the Preuses and who married Mathilde Stub, came to Luther College at the time the girls were there. His description of devotions in the Brandt parsonage gives a vivid glimpse of the way the parsonage functioned in the life of the college, especially during the time of the *Comitia Dumriana*.

> When I think of Rev. N. Brandt, I always at the same time, think of Mrs. Brandt, the excellent wife of this worthy pastor. Rev. Brandt was then pastor [of the Norwegian Lutheran Church in Decorah] and also a member of the faculty, and Fru Brandt, there, as were, ex-officio, a sort of a mother of the student body. She was always very interested in the students and very sympathetic. Rev. Brandt's residence was close by the College, the red brick building—the old historic parsonage stands there yet; it always talks to me when I go by it. This home was, to a great extent, our home. This contains a world of good things which I could say about it.

Thorgrimsen described the fatherly and motherly correction and encouragement he received from both Pastor and Mrs. Brandt. He found it to be a great "edifying influence" that could not really be valued properly. Their parsonage, "this genuine Norwegian-American Lutheran refined parsonage" made a profound difference to the students. Mrs. Brandt was memorable for decorating the Christmas tree. She cooked the festive meals for the holidays. It was in this home, Thorgrimsen says, where *Comitia Dumriana* took their classes. It was where the traditions of the parsonage were passed on to both the boys and the girls, who would soon be establishing their own homes around the Synod.

Music was as important to the school as it had been at Nissen's school. Several of the pastors would teach singing. Brandt was assigned the task. He set about drilling the entire community in song so they would learn the hymns of their tradition. Thorgrimsen thought Brandt's method of lining out the hymns, singing one line at a time which the students would sing back, seemed a bit odd at the beginning, but it helped them learn the hymns by heart without having to have hymnals. It did aid them in memorization and made them pay attention to the text, he concluded. Koren had the most training from his time with the Behren's Quartette.

As the school prepared for its next big celebration, the dedication of the new wing of the Main Building, Koren, by Mrs. Koren's report, was preparing the students to sing for it. From what we can tell, he was writing the hymn they would sing for the dedication of the new wing. "It was the hymn he wanted for the dedication, if we only had some instruments, she exclaimed."[382]

We know that the college did not acquire band instruments until 1878, so Mrs. Koren was expressing a desire that had been in their minds for some time. The hymn that Koren was rehearsing with the girls was very likely the hymn that Koren wrote, "Oh, Sing Jubilee" (*Al verden nu raabe*)

which appeared in the Synod's hymnal (*Synodesn Salmebog*) published in 1874, in time for the dedication service that December.[383] Mrs. Koren told Linka that Lulla Hjort was learning to sing well for strangers and was going to sing a solo for the May 17 party that

Behren's choir, 1845. Koren is the second from the left; Behrens is sitting in the middle.

was coming soon. She was very good, Mrs. Koren noted.[384] Sina had not been very well. Mrs. Koren thought she spent too much time sitting and studying. She wondered if it had not been too much for her to sit so still for so long.[385] This is an echo of the notion that study was bad for girls because their female organs were developing at the time. Linka relied on the sharp eyes of Mrs. Koren for reports on the health of her two children, Christian and Rosina, both studying at Luther.

The piano continued to be the main instrument of musical instruction for the girls. In a letter describing for Linka the May 17, 1873, Norwegian Constitution Day celebration in Decorah, Mrs. Koren said they were going to buy a piano for their new house. The celebration included speeches and music with lots of food prepared by the competent hand of Mrs. Brandt.

Life was full for these pastors now in robust middle age. Not only were they seeing around them in their growing families and homes the flowering of their dreams, but also in the communities, churches, and college being built around them, now flourishing because of their dedication and hard work. The boisterous life of students and pastors' families during these times must have seemed like a dream years later, as they thought back to these days. The Norwegian Synod under their leadership had grown from seventeen pastors in 1862 to seventy-four in 1873 with 335 congregations with 75,000 members, more than twice as many members than the other Norwegian-American Lutheran church bodies combined. One could not blame them for a bit of pride. They had built well for the next generation, and they continued to do so.

The Death of
CHRISTIANE OTTESEN HJORT

After the end of the semester, in the spring of 1873, the girls went home to their parents for the summer, planning to come back in the fall. That summer of 1873, however, the close-knit group of pastors' fami-

lies experienced an almost unbearable tragedy that affected their educational plans: the death of Mrs. Hjort in a fire. Pastor Hjort had gone to Norway to a mission conference as a representative from the Synod. According to the story, as Mrs. Hjort was making punch for the hired hands on their farm, the alcohol caught fire. To save the house from burning down, she had walked out of the house carrying the burning material and had burned herself so badly that she died soon thereafter. Mrs. Koren's letter describing the situation to Linka is one of her most moving missives. In it we see the closeness of the families and their shared grief as they react to Christiane's death.

Paint Creek Parsonage

July 12, 1873

Dear Aunt Linka!

How is it going with you now, and how it is with your little Paul?[386] Our last report was on July 7. Are you still sitting by your dear little boy's bed, or has God, in his grace, healed him, or at least made him better. How I wish I knew how he was!

Thank you for your few lines and thank Sina for making you write. Dear Linka, write soon and often, just a few words so I can know how you are. I am afraid that you are exhausted now, but God gives us great strength when it is needed.

I would have written you before this, but the reason I have not written is so sad that I hardly dare to say it now, for you are weak and have so many cares of your own. But yesterday afternoon, just after Koren had finished evening devotions, Larsen came in and said that a message had come from Hjorts that Mrs. Hjort had been burned in an accident and that either Koren or Larsen should come. [The Korens were still living at the college.] Larsen was on his way anyway, in the morning, and Koren was totally exhausted. They decided Larsen should leave immediately that night. I did not receive permission to go with, as I wanted. We were to leave on Friday morning. [The Korens had been planning a trip to Paint Creek.] Larsen took Thora [his daughter] along. It was terrible to know as much as we did and yet so little that next day, until Larsen's letter came at evening and fulfilled our worst fears: Mrs. Hjort died at 5 o'clock that afternoon.

I am sitting here in Hjort's office writing this. Poor, poor Hjort, how will he take it? I can barely write, but I do want to write something to you so you will hear properly about the accident and not by rumor first.

Wednesday morning Mrs. Hjort was making some warm drinks for the hired help as it was so cold and rainy. She was heating some alcohol on the stove in a dipper and spilled a few drops, which set the rest of it on fire. She became panicky and ran with the burning dipper in her hand through the door to the kitchen where she fell and spilled the burning liquid over herself. At the same time, she threw the dipper saying: "I threw it too late." When she got up, she ran from the kitchen toward the house; Lulla caught her and held her around the waist while Marie got a quilt and threw it over her. Smeby got some water, and put the fire out quickly. They carried her into the bedroom. Her clothes were almost all burned up. They wrapped her in cotton, but when the doctor came he said right away there was no hope. She seemed to be okay and spoke clearly about everything, but then suddenly she knew she was dying. This happened Wednesday forenoon, July 9, at around 10 o'clock. At 5 in the afternoon she was dead. She died peacefully and quietly, without a struggle. She was conscious the entire time, and was peaceful and composed, sorrowing for her husband and children, leaving them in God's hand and praying eagerly to die quickly. Blessed be the name of the Lord. I cannot write about all of the details I have heard, but it shows me once again God's mercy: the Lord giveth and the Lord taketh away, blessed be the name of the Lord!

Just think how Lulla stood by her and held her, feeling the great heat in her body, both she and Marie [Sivesind] wiping her brow. Lulla's hands were both burned, though not seriously. Johanna (11) fell under her Mama, the paper in the hall burned, and there is soot on the walls and on the porch.

Yesterday at 2 o'clock she was buried. Koren, Brandt, Henriette, Lina, and I left home at 5 in the morning. Just before the burial the Ottesens came. That was good. There was a huge crowd of people from all of the congregations. They had decorated the church with black crepe and green foliage. Mrs. Hjort was highly respected in the congregation. You should have seen them, especially the old people when they went by the casket, how they stood there and touched her on the forehead and cheeks. Koren spoke in the church, Brandt at the graveyard, as well as Ottesen.

Poor Lulla! She is bearing her sorrow quietly and honorably. Praise God that Hjort has her. All of the other children are rather lively today. Jacob will go home with the Ottesens.[387] All of the others will stay home. Lulla thinks it would be best. And the congregation would be so bereft if everything were to be torn apart. They are showing their love in every possible way. Ola Storla [Hjort's neighbor] has been like a father to them. Ottesen is writing to Hjort now, first and foremost to Tinn. [The place in Norway where he was.] If only the papers do not report it first, but we have done what we can to get the news to him before he reads it in the papers.

Hjort, dear me. How will it be with him? God is merciful, and will help him to bear this cross. We hope he does not leave Norway right away and be all alone with his sorrow on his return, leaving Otto [their first born son who was in Norway at the time].[388] Marie [Sivesind] is here, How good it is to have her. Tomorrow Koren will preach here. We had all—not least the youngsters—rejoiced in the trip [the Korens had been planning to visit Christiane at that time]—and now—Wednesday we are going home, leaving Henriette [Koren's eldest daughter] here with Lulla for a time. After that Lina [Caroline Koren] can come. It is strange to see little Kathinka [five] running around so happy and pleased with herself. The Stub's children are here as well, and it is good for the children to have each other.

One of the last evenings before Mrs. Hjort's death, we all sat on the porch while she spoke of how good she felt and how next summer she was going to go to Norway to bring Otto home. She was getting things ready now, so that things would run smoothly while she was gone. . . .

Now I have told you the most important things and can write no more. How loving Lulla is; praise God they have her!

You must write soon. God strengthen you in both sorrow and gladness. Yes, God have mercy on us all for Jesus' sake!

Yours, Elisabeth Koren

Greet Sina and Christian from all of the girls here and greet your dear little Paul from Johan and Eleis and all of the children.

Regardless of the tragedy, life had to go on, the children needed home schooling, and the girls would return to the college for their last year of school. After the death of Mrs. Hjort, Mrs. Koren wrote more frequently to Linka to report on how things were going with the Hjort family, especially Lulla. As something of an extended family, Mrs. Koren rightly felt it was her duty and responsibility to keep Linka informed of her future daughter-in-law's progress. Lulla was an unusual girl, Mrs. Koren concluded, after telling how the children, with only the direction of Lulla and Dikka, the next oldest girl, resumed activity in the parsonage garden and farm. Lulla effectively took over as mother of her younger siblings after the death of her mother. Mrs. Koren was glad that Lulla had survived the tragedy without too much injury—she could have been seriously burned when she held her mother as she was engulfed in flames. It had threatened them all. Mrs. Koren did note that the sorrow of the young woman seemed almost too much for her to bear.[389] Now Lulla would have to be the teacher in the home school once considered the best of the Synod.

Later, Mrs. Koren added detail to her description of the tragedy at Blaasenborg, while she remembered it. While Larsen had told them in the letter they had received immediately after the accident that she was making drinks for the hired men in which she used liqueur, that was not quite the case. She had been making an almond liqueur which she had served the pastors when they were last together. In keeping with her expertise in medications, part of her role as a pastors' wife, Mrs. Hjort used the liquor as a medicine for her cold. Given the terrible rainstorm that day, she may have thought it would be good for everyone to have some.

> What was Dear Aunt Hjort thinking, when she did not, as she always used to, take the grog away from the stove, when she put the alcohol in the sugar. We don't quite understand what she did, but I would like for you to have a good grasp of what happened; here most people are asking if she was making punch.[390]

Mrs. Koren also told Linka how Mrs. Hjort looked in the casket: peaceful and calm. She had thrown a thick coat over her head when she ran out of the hallway into the yard, so her face and head were spared burning, Mrs. Koren reported. Although the Synod pastors and professors were not teetotalers, they were careful to keep behaviors such as dancing and drinking private, and it may have been for this reason that Mrs. Koren issued the correction. While it was okay to use alcohol for medicinal purposes, the notion that she was making "punch" had probably caused some negative comments to circulate in the small community.

Mrs. Koren reported six weeks after the tragedy that Lulla, now seventeen, was staying with them in Washington Prairie. She was trying to find some peace and quiet as she had earlier in the old parsonage, but, exclaimed Mrs. Koren, "Here there is no peace!"[391] Lulla had just heard from her father and was anxiously awaiting his return. Mrs. Koren commented on how the next oldest, Dikka (13) and Johanna (11) were doing rather well, and the youngest, Cathinka (5) very well. This was not surprising, she noted, since Lulla, as the oldest daughter, had already been something of a mother to the younger children. Almost a week later, Mrs.

Koren wrote to Linka that Lulla had heard from her father that he would be home within the week. This Mrs. Koren, thought, would take a great burden off Lulla's shoulders, since she was functioning as the housewife, as she had been trained to do.[392]

Though we do not hear that Mrs. Koren is in the first months of her pregnancy with Marie, her youngest, it explains some of her weariness. Still, she had to keep thinking of the education of both the youngest and the oldest of the children. When the pastors wrote Hjort in Norway, they suggested that he bring his fifteen-year old son, Otto, back home from Norway where he was attending school. They also recommended he find a governess who could teach the children at home.[393] They needed someone to provide an education for their younger children and to teach the older girls the piano. Mrs. Koren mentioned that Miss Muhlenfort had written to the young girls from Bergen, her home town, after she had heard one of the Luther

F. A. Schmidt

professors, Fredrik A. Schmidt, preach in fluent Norwegian. This had impressed the people in Bergen.[394] Schmidt had also been in Norway for a meeting of the Norwegian Mission Society and most certainly had spoken with Miss Muhlenfort about returning to Decorah as a teacher for these busy families.

Rosina needed more training in the life of the parsonage at this point in her education. The Preuses wanted her to live with the Korens to learn from Mrs. Koren how to run a home, in the traditional manner, just as Linka had gone to Askevold to learn a generation before. Mrs. Koren was glad to have her, but in the reduced circumstances of their rented house in Decorah, she was not sure they had a place for her to sleep or to read and study. There was little space in the dining room which was like a hallway, and very unhandy. Sina could be with them while she attended school, but it would be difficult.

The curriculum for the girls also concerned Mrs. Koren. Mrs. Brandt, educated at Christiansfeld with its strong emphasis on German, had believed that they should take history from Landmark, English and arithmetic from Narvesen, and perhaps Jacobsen would give them a German lesson now and then. Maybe Siewers would teach an hour of French so they could understand a little French and not stumble around with just a few words.[395]

Elisabeth had discussed the Preuses' proposal with Koren, and they decided that they could sleep in the small girls' room, and the older girls could share the bed if they could stand to be three in a bed. The room was too cold for Mrs. Koren to tolerate, and she wondered if Sina would be able to stand it. There was no place in the dining room, because the stove took up the space. The only place left was the office, and that was better for the small boys. They would manage if Sina wanted to be with them, she said. These privations indicate how very different life then was from today.

The girls had just finished their first introduction to French and history, of which they would have four hours a week before Christmas. They would also receive piano instruction from Miss Wråmaan, who needed a place to stay. People were not eager to have her in their home, for reasons Mrs. Koren did not clearly state, though one can infer that she was not to be trusted.[396] Miss Wråmaan had found a place to live near them in Decorah. Despite this, the pastors' wives decided they needed someone they liked better than Miss Wråmann.

About this time they welcomed a new family to the faculty at the school, an Icelandic pastor, Jon Bjarnason (1845-1914). He had recently emigrated from Iceland and could speak some Danish but no Norwegian, and he was difficult to understand. Mrs. Koren held out little hope that he would be acceptable as a teacher, given his accent. However, his wife, Laura Gudjohnson,[397] was very gifted and surprised them with her ability to speak fluent Danish.[398] She was thirty-one, had a good mind, *Professor Bjarnason* was well educated, and could play the piano and the guitar and could sing. She was Icelandic in heart and soul and dressed in her Icelandic national costume winter and summer. It was her musical gifts and her potential as a teacher that impressed and interested Mrs. Koren, ever on the lookout for a good music teacher.[399]

Though Mrs. Koren was realistic enough to understand the demands of the teachers on the students, but she also knew when enough was enough. After Jacobsen had given the girls too hard a lesson, she had gone directly to him and protested on behalf of all the mothers. His wife agreed that he had been too demanding, but what he did to relieve the situation is not clear.[400]

The ubiquity of the piano in Decorah so far out on the frontier has an interesting story that involves the little town. After the 1850's, when companies like the Kimball Company of Chicago figured out how to market pianos on the frontier, a piano became a fairly common thing in the parlors of people on the frontier. William Wallace Kimball (1828-1904), who made pianos available to the people of the Midwest, had started out in Decorah as a land entrepreneur. He left Decorah just before the crash of 1857 and was going to Chicago to make his fortune. On his way there, he came upon a man who had four pianos to sell and he traded his Decorah land for them. Kimball told his biographer that when he considered whether or not to sell his land in Decorah, he remembered that there was only one old beat up piano in Decorah and that it belonged to a Norwegian family. They continued to be some of his best customers. The piano company apparently did a land office business with the likes of the Korens and their compatriots.

The story of the piano teacher gives a glimpse into the life of the itinerant woman musician and her trials. Mrs. Koren told Linka that her Caroline "Lina" had wished that Linka could have been her teacher, because Miss Wråmann did not drive her hard enough. Furthermore she did not play very much and when she did it was not fine music. Lina thought that Miss Muhlenfort was a better piano teacher. When Miss Wråmann left for her summer vacation, she proposed leaving her piano with the Korens. Koren, however, did not want it. He much preferred to have an organ, given his interest in hymnody.[401] On April 10, 1874, Sina wrote to tell her mother that Miss Wråmann had suddenly decided to leave for Chicago where she could get a job as an organist in a church and teach piano on the side.[402]

When Mrs. Koren announced the birth of Marie, she made a side comment on the sad situation of Miss Wråmann. She had left abruptly for Chicago, according to Sina, but Mrs. Koren assumed she would go home to Norway directly.[403] It may be too easy to speculate about what had happened to the music teacher, but we have no information available other than this slight hint of some indiscretion on Miss Wråmann's part. This was one of the difficulties of a single woman teacher out on her own. How she managed to take the piano with her is another question. It may be that it was one that could be set up on a stand, like the one Linka had purchased for her home.

That May, six weeks after the birth of Marie, Mrs. Koren wrote that they were finally going to get a piano from Chicago. The girls had just heard from Miss Muhlenfort, who was probably in Milwaukee, and appeared to be in good health, since she was giving six hours of lessons every day.[404] In a letter to her mother, Sina complained that they were having history and English lessons that day. Two weeks later she wrote to protest the comment of Mrs. Koren that she read too much and it was not good for her. "It's a sin to say that." They had only three history lectures left, she concluded, "Then we are done."[405] Sina had the determination she needed to finish. Does one hear a bit of the language about young women studying too much and destroying their reproductive organs here? Hard to say. Mrs. Koren is always thinking Sina is working to hard for her health.

Lulla found it easy to be with Mrs. Koren, because she and her mother had been very good friends. After the death of Mrs. Hjort, Mrs. Koren missed Christiane a great deal since they had been together frequently and got on much better than she did with Mrs. Brandt. By now Lulla had become the head of the household at Blaasenborg. She was, however, still a girl, much sobered by her great loss. The oral history of the Preus family maintains that she never really recovered from the shock of this death. Still Lulla participated with the other girls fully. Along with the others, she spent time at the Brandts, her aunt and uncle, because they had a piano. By this time the budding romance between Lulla and Christian had become clear, and Lulla began to regard Linka as her mother. In a warm letter to Linka, Lulla reported on her own health much strained by her grief. She had not felt well, she said, and had spent some time in bed, grieving, when Linka's letter came and cheered her up. "I have had bilious fever, the doctor said, but now, God be praised," she was almost well again and had washed some clothes without much strain.[406] The week before, when their girl had gone home to help with the farm, Thora Larsen came and took care of her and the managing of the house.

> I'm sorry that I always come to you with complaints, dear Aunt Linka. You must be as weary of me who only complains. Thora is so very sweet and kind. She helps me with everything. I don't know what kind of housekeeping there would have been here if she had not come. [407]

What she was most happy about was that she would be staying in Spring Prairie with Linka for a long time. With that she thanked her dear Aunt Linka for writing so often to her as it was a great comfort to her.[408]

Elisabeth continued to watch closely over Lulla. Poor Lulla, Mrs. Koren exclaimed, "I wish she were stronger! But it has been good for her to have Thora Larsen there, she is always fun when there is work for two around and she is so fond of Lulla." Thora Larsen would be the last of the girls to imitate her aunts Henriette and Karine in helping the various parsonage families with both housework and teaching. She began to find work or at least positions where her good spirit and robust health—rather different from her delicate mother Karen—made her a great companion and indefatigable helper in the parsonages around them.

Some months later, in one of the few letters we have from Linka, Linka wrote a motherly missive to Lulla hoping that she would think of her as a mother and would write and talk to her as if she were one. This same letter also dealt delicately with an issue that probably disturbed Lulla as well: her father's decision to marry Henriette Neuberg while he was on a trip to Norway that summer.[409] Although Henriette would not be in Paint Creek until March or April of the next year, Hjort told Larsen on December 14, 1874, that Henriette was visiting Hjort's relatives in Norway that January, as a kind of pre-nuptial meeting with the family.[410] While it was no quicker than many second marriages, especially when the husband needed help with young children, it grieved Lulla, who was very close to her mother and father. Henriette would now take her mother's place. Linka urged her to accept the marriage. She mentioned that both Mrs. Koren and Lulla's mother thought that, even though Larsen had remarried too quickly, it was for the best. Probably her own father's surprising marriage to Henriette seemed too soon to Lulla.

Graduation

The year 1874 was filled with signal events for the young church and the pastors' families. In March, Mrs. Koren gave birth to her last child, Marie, twenty years after the birth of her first, Henriette in 1854. Koren finished editing the hymnal, *Synodens Salmebog*, which appeared in 1874, a signal accomplishment for a man so far away on the outposts of the frontier. The south wing of the Main Building was dedicated on December 4, concluding a fulfilling and busy year.

The work of the immigrants was enervating for those who did not share the good health of the pastors. Teaching the boys a full day of classes and then the girls caused Jacobsen, whose wife had just given birth, to become so ill he had to cut down his teaching of the girls to only two hours.[411] While the pastors lived to be quite old and seemed to have robust good health, Jacobsen from the beginning suffered from what later was diagnosed as TB. He was increasingly unable to do the work demanded of him by the college.

The classes of the *Comitia Dumriana* ended in the summer of 1874. There is no record of a ceremony of graduation or any such festivities, but the girls had a wonderful time going to school and being together with each other, with the boys, as well as with the other pastors' families. The pastors' daughters were soon ready to take up their vocations. Like their mothers before them, some of them would take some time away from home before marrying, to study music more intensely. Rosina and Lulla did this, supplementing their mother's and aunts' instruction with more advanced teachers in Milwaukee after their year and half at Luther. Milwaukee, a very German town, had at the time an Opera House and a sumptuous Academy of Music that seated 1600. Lulla stayed with Pastor Sebastian Theodor Geelmuyden (1837-1923) and his family, but where she studied is not named. It could well have been Downer School for Ladies. Later their younger sisters, Anga Preus (Agnes Wilhelmine Rudolpha Keyser—1859-1927) and Linka Hjort (Maren Pauline Ovidia—1865-1954) also went to Milwaukee for a year of study living with the Eisfeldt family, where they learned German. Following that, they traveled to Norway to live for an extended period with aunts and uncles, as their mothers and older sisters before them had done.

Getting Back to School

Luther College now focused its attentions on its main purpose: the education of the boys studying for the ministry or other such professions. Nonetheless the question of how to educate their daughters—and not

only their own, but all the girls in the Synod— became more and more pressing. When Bernt J. Muus, pastor of Holden Congregation in Minnesota planned his school, one that would include women, he found it difficult to get help from the Decorah pastors, Their attention was focused entirely on the second wing of the Main Building, just dedicated. It watched with some suspicions the efforts of Muus to establish his academy, after the generous offer by Harald Thorson of a plot of land worth $1,500 and a gift of $500 for the establishment of a school. On hearing of the gift, the Synod at its meeting in Holden congregation passed a resolution thanking Thorson for the offer.

Harald Thorson

The Synod expresses to the merchant Harald Thorson of Northfield its gratitude for the generous contribution he has offered to make toward an academy in Northfield. With joy and thanksgiving to God the Synod expresses the wish that such a academy may be founded.[412]

These words seem to indicate the Synod would support the college with its gifts and prayers. To the disappointment of the St. Olaf's School supporters, that did not happen.

At the beginning of 1875, in January, St. Olaf's School in Northfield, opened, announcing that it would accept both boys and girls. Although things still seemed fairly settled in Decorah in respect to the education of women, things were bubbling under the surface that would lead to the most turbulent decade in Norwegian-American history. The year 1874 proved to be a very important and stressful year for the Norwegian Synod, with many harbingers of what would come in the next decade. Many troubles would, in one way or another, involve questions about the place of women in the society.

On April 29, 1875, about two years after the death of Christiane Hjort, Henriette Neuberg arrived in New York on the ship *Jupiter* in the company of Diderikke (Dikka) Hjord (15), and Caroline Magelssen (Karine Neuberg) with her son Hans and daughter Karen. Henriette had written to Linka from Bergen that she could still not believe that she was going to marry Hjort.[413] Some months before, at the end of the term of the *Comitia Dumriana*, Karine had gone to Norway with Thora Larsen, her niece (Laur. Larsen's oldest daughter), her two children, and Dikka Hjort, who would become Henriette's step-daughter shortly. Hjort had written to Larsen in December saying that the Neuberg sisters and his daughter planned to come in March or April, after visiting some of Hjort's relatives in Oslo. Lulla anticipated Henriette's coming with some dread, which she expressed openly to Linka: "I hope we can get along. Maybe I can be like a sister to her, as I was to Mama. But the old Adam in me rebels against God. I must always say God has done this."[414] Lulla in her memoirs many years later commended Karine as a good companion, but says nothing about Henriette, which may indicate her initial hurt had remained.

Paint Creek and Blaasenborg Again

When Henriette Neuberg married Hjort, Blaasenborg began once again to be a gathering place for the pastor's families, but now the teacher was Henriette, not Christiane, who had been Henriette's mentor. The family in the parlor continued to read, write, listen, and sing together as a means of learning, but it was a different time. Thora Larsen (1857-

1908), now eighteen, wrote to Linka that during their evening time, Jacob Magelssen, Karine's husband, had read Ibsen's *Peer Gynt* to the group as they sat sewing and writing letters in the dusk. Ibsen had not yet

written *A Doll's House*, but would shortly, and that play, along with the new secular and anti-church feminism, would radically change the debate about women and their place in society. While Thora sat listening, she had mended a pair of gloves and made four aprons for "Aunt Koren." Thora was now living and working for her Aunt Henriette Neuberg Hjort, who was ill at the time. She was most likely closer to Henriette than she was to her father's new wife, Ingeborg. She wrote that they had all been out picking up hickory nuts, and that

Henrik Ibsen

she had washed socks and other woolen clothes in preparation for the winter. She had baked, cooked, and made dinner since Henriette was ill, and even made sure that the cellar was cleaned while she was there. This made her feel good. When Karine had another baby, Henriette traveled to Rushford and North Prairie to see to Karine's health. Karine did not look well and would probably not get old, she wrote some time in 1876. Karine did die young, in February 1881. Later Magelssen married Thora, on December 20, 1882.

On January 4, 1876, Henriette Hjort neé Neuberg, wrote to Linka to wish her a happy New Year and express her joy in the coming marriage of Christian and Lulla. Christian had been with them for Christmas, and Henriette noted that it must have pained Linka's motherly heart not to have her older son with her for Christmas. Now she and Lulla were teaching the younger children. According to her, Henriette taught religion and Lulla music.

By now the Korens were living in their newly built parsonage in Washington Prairie, and in a letter to Linka Mrs. Koren looked back with pleasure on their nearly two years in Decorah, close to the center of events. Thora Larsen was on her way to see Karine, to help preserve crabapples and plums. From there she would go to the Stubs to help them put up food. Thora was as helpful as her aunts had been when they were single. She seemed to enjoy doing the kind of work that needed to be done in the house. In addition to helping with chores and the teaching, Thora, who had her father's robust health, brought a good-humored presence to each home she visited.[415]

About the same time, on July 22, 1876, Henriette gave birth to a still-born baby. Hjort wrote Larsen that if it had been a girl they had intended to name the baby Christiane Elisabeth, but, after twenty-four hours of hard labor, the baby had been born dead. In answer to Hjort's letter, on August 4, 1876, Larsen grieved with him, but rejoiced that Henriette had lived through the labor. Then he inquired whether Hjort needed a governess. Why he asked this is not quite clear, but Larsen was now the father of children with his second wife, and Hjort also had four children under sixteen—Johanna (15), Jacob (13), Paulina (11) and Cathinka (9)—who all needed an education. While the next older daughter, Did-rikke, was seventeen, the children needed more than an older sister to teach them, something Larsen probably understood.

Thora wrote to her father asking when she could come home. She reported that she had visited a doctor who had said she had a little spot on both lungs. The left was worse, a troubling reminder of her mother's death. Larsen responded that he could do nothing for it but advised that she be quiet, get fresh air, and not run around the farm too strenuous-ly— advice in line with the idea of a girl not working too hard. She had taken his prescribed medicine for it, which helped some. In that same letter she noted that Christian Preus had come to them in Paint Creek and surprised them. He was ill so that he could eat only wheat meal and crackers, probably the recommended prescription for his anxiety, a condition he seemed to be suffering at this time. Elisabeth Koren had earlier mentioned this as the prescription Henriette Koren had gotten for her anxiety some years before. She also noted that Anga Preus, Linka's younger daughter, had come all the way with Christian in order to play at a musical exhibition in Lansing the next evening.[416]

Late in the evening of October 22, 1877, Laur. Larsen wrote a friendly letter to Hjort with whom he felt a deep connection, probably because in some respects they were now brothers-in-law given Hjort's marriage to Henriette, his first wife's sis-ter. He apologized that he had not written much before, but he had very little time. He told about his long acquaintance with the Neuberg family, whom he had known from student days in Bergen. His father had been close to Neuberg, the sheriff, and he had met them almost daily when he visited Mrs. Neuberg in the hospital. In addition, he had been

Laur. Larsen

close to Karen's brothers, Peter and Herman, long before he had met her. "I wish I could sit and talk with Karine and Henriette about all the good God has given us," he concluded. Not long after that, Larsen heard that Henriette had gone to be with Karine, very likely to help with a new baby. Thora, who might have provided help, had gone to Norway to study, using the inheritance from her grandfather. At the time she was in Bergen, on her way to Christiania after a visit in Valdres.[417]

St. Olaf's School

In 1878, St. Olaf's School dedicated its new building. Laur. Larsen attended the event. By this time Larsen had decided Luther College would remain a men's school, but he was concerned about his daughters' education. To that end he sent two of his daughters to St. Olaf's School, where they did well, but found the conditions at the new school, "worse than primitive."[418] Larsen did not forget the education of girls during this time, busy as he was. From his first arrival in the country, he had thought parochial schools on the model of the Missouri Synod were the answer, and that Luther College could provide teachers for these schools. Meanwhile, life pressed the small group of pastors' families with tragedy.

At the end of February 1879, Hjort, in a hastily written letter informed Larsen that Henriette had just given birth to another stillborn baby, and that she would probably not survive either. Appended to that letter was the confirmation of his worst fears. Henriette had died. It struck the pastor hard, as it did Larsen and Karine and the rest of the pastors' families. Henriette had been aunt and sister, mother and cousin, plus teacher, to most of the wives and children. She was a beautiful, cultured woman of refined sensibilities who elevated the tone of the group, but, like her sisters, she was not strong enough to survive the demands of the frontier.

From sheer grief Hjort left Paint Creek and moved to a house in Decorah which he had purchased in the spring of 1872 for $1,500. His purchase may have been an effort to encourage Christiane in the hope that one day they would be able to assist at the college as Diderikke had. His own illness alarmed Larsen, who urged him to rest, first take the cure in LaCrosse, and then come to Decorah. "Our three girls are gone, and Marie Sivesind is alone, so there would be room. You need a good doctor," he concluded.[419] Hjort's move to Decorah marked the end of the old parsonage tradition in Paint Creek, especially its place in the cultivation of the young pastors and their future wives. Hjort died as much of a broken heart as a bad heart on December 14, 1879.

Things were changing. The older generation was giving way to the younger, and the country where they were living was beginning to ask more urgent questions about the education of women. The old system, while still somewhat in place, was not quite enough. While the parlor had served its purposes, and they had been fortunate to find teachers for their daughters at Luther, their daughters did not have degrees or professional standing. Still, one must commend what they had done. The pastors' wives had transplanted the parlor school or Christiansfeld into a college setting for a brief moment. Although several generations would pass until their daughters could attend Luther College, it was a beginning, deeply rooted in their experiences, and it became a model for another attempt to educate their daughters. Their experiences in Norway and their sense of how to build a girls' school are little remembered today, but the story of *Comitia Dumriana* was affectionately remembered by all those who attended classes together as a golden time for them. It was the highest level of education available to the pastors' daughters at this time. It served these daughters of privilege well. The next generation, however, had many more choices and difficulties in educating and finding vocations for them other than that of a pastor's wife.

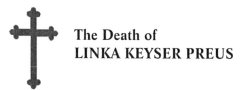

The Death of
LINKA KEYSER PREUS

On September 19, 1880, Linka Preus died, after a long illness. She wrote few letters and drew few sketches after 1876, when she suffered a stroke. While her friends still wrote to her, and Mrs. Koren attempted to  be as faithful a correspondent as she could manage, Linka rarely responded. The obituary in the church paper said that after that first stroke, the family knew it would not be long until the end. The stroke has weakened her ability to recognize things, but she would brighten up when a family member came near. The writer of the obituary noted, as was common in the genre of the obituary of the time, the state of her soul. As she languished, her faith became stronger.

Before thoughts of death would have troubled her, but after her stroke, she peacefully awaited the time for the Lord to come and take her up. Her dearest readings came from our church's beloved hymns and edifying books, especially Scriver's *Treasury of the Soul*.[420]

The obituary also drew attention to the fact that Linka had been a teacher, especially to the Christie family in Askevold, one of whom now lived in Alexandria, Minnesota. Beloved by both family and members of the congregation, her funeral filled the church as it had rarely been before. Not so many pastors and their families could attend, but the professors at the seminary in Madison were there. President Han G. Stub, of Luther Seminary in Madison, spoke in the home, around the casket, remembering her as a faithful wife and loving mother. "Preus, deeply moved, thanked her for the great love she had given him and their dear children. Words were few, but made a powerful impact."[421] Pastor Hvistendal preached the funeral sermon, and Professsor Johannes Ylvisaker spoke at the committal service beside the grave. Because DeForest was near Madison, it was possible to have the seminary choir sing, making the hymn singing especially moving.

> The weather was sunny and bright. The church was filled to overflowing, and a great many stood outside by the open windows. Many hundreds took the opportunity to see once more that dear face. Many tears flowed and all seemed to agree that the mourners were as deeply moved as at any time.[422]

When she died she left behind a flourishing family, many of whom became leaders in the church that she and Hermann had been instrumental in founding. Her older son, Christian Keyser Preus, served as president of Luther College. J. W. was pastor in Minneapolis at Our Saviors. Her daughters, Rosina and Anga, married pastors who were also leaders in the church they loved and served. Her most enduring legacy, beside her accomplished family, is her diary and her sketches of the early pioneer days, some of the earliest visual records we have of that time. These records provide a woman's view of a world long since disappeared. She made that world vivid in her sketches.

Anga Preus Kvaas

Linka died when many issues concerning the rights of women were coming to the fore—issues such as the notorious Muus divorce case, the visit of Bjørnstjerne Bjørnson and Kristofer Janson, the women's suffrage movement, and the beginnings of the ladies aids in the church. Of the first generation of pastors' wives, she was the most articulate about her sense of vocation, both its pleasures and its privations. She was sensitive to her desire for and lack of access to a good education. She and Hermann provided a good education for their two daughters, for which they had a good model from *Nissen Pigeskole* in Oslo. In teaching the faith to her household by reading sermons, singing hymns, and teaching the catechism, she handed down to her family a rich tradition of Lutheran piety and practice. As was common in her generation, she often thought of death. Like the Baroque poets and pastors before her, she pondered her death as a pious exercise because it brought her into a closer relationship with God. Part of that exercise was the drawing

Linka's death mask. "When I am dead I will look like this. I look a little more lively with my eyes open."

of her own death mask that appears among her sketches. In sum, she left a faithful and pious legacy.

She left her sketch book, which gives us an intimate picture of life in the parsonage.

> I will bequeath you this book, but I am not in shape to remember if it was Doctor or Anga I promised it to after my death. Now for the seven of you there are seven to share. Take half of them that are not bound as the bound were.

Norwegian Supporters of Women's Suffrage Arrive

In 1879 one of the great Norwegian-American champions of women's emancipation, Kristofer Janson (1841-1917), a pastor from Norway, arrived in this country and began to preach. He was followed by Norway's literary provocateur, and literary giant, Bjørnstjerne Bjørnson in 1880, who was attracted to the women's movement as well.

Kristofer Janson was already a well-known writer and thinker in Norway when he came to this country in 1879 for a lecture tour. He later settled in Minneapolis, after being ordained into the Unitarian church on November 25, 1881, a ceremony even *Budbæreren* noted in one of its church news notes.[423] Janson was greeted with great fervor and appreciation by a great many of his countrymen throughout America. There was a glittering banquet in his honor in Chicago on October 14, 1879, at which Pastor Vilhelm Koren, hardly a free thinker, toasted him on behalf of the newspaper *Norden*.

Kristofer Janson

Janson's reputation as a "freethinker" was not yet known, although he opposed the rigid orthodoxy of the Synod. He remarked once that he had traveled to America with Hans Gerhard Stub (1849-1931), son of Hans Andreas Stub (1822-1907), a Norwegian Synod pastor, and Sven Oftedal. Though they were both suspicious of him, Stub and he got along, Janson reported. Oftedal avoided them both. Oftedal shared with Janson an interest in the cause of women's suffrage but grew apart as Janson grew more radical.

That is an interesting detail, for Oftedal, by persuasion a feminist, introduced the weekly edition of *Folkebladet* (the paper of Augsburg Seminary) in 1880 with the statement that the paper would have three causes: 1) unity in the church; 2) temperance; 3) and women's place among us.[424] Oftedal was an ebullient type; why he did not speak with either of the clergymen we cannot tell. Oftedal would have good reason to feel uncomfortable with Stub since he had issued a "Public Declaration" (*Aapen Erklaring*) against the Norwegian Synod in 1873, after arriving in Minneapolis to begin teaching at Augsburg Seminary. It was published in *Skandinaven* on January 30, 1874. Its intemperate attack on the Norwegian Synod and its pastors for their Catholicism, universalism, and pastoral despotism made Oftedal a pariah, even among his own colleagues. August Weenaas, president of Augsburg Seminary, who had signed the declaration, withdrew his support. It raged against the Synod's stand on lay preaching, slavery, the common school, and its theology of absolution.

A pietist from Norway whose family was liberal, Oftedal kept firmly to those convictions politically as well as religiously in this country. His bosom friend and colleague, Georg Sverdrup, came from the Center

Party, the left, in Norway; Sverdrup's uncle Johan Sverdrup was prime minister in the 1880s; Oftedal's brother Lars was a representative from the Liberal party to Parliament after 1883. Janson and Oftedal were much closer politically than they were doctrinally, and this made it difficult for Oftedal, who never gave up his commitment to women's suffrage. A gifted orator, linguist, and character, Oftedal was the emotional half of the Sverdrup-Oftedal team.

While his ebullience and quick wit won him friendships from those in his circle, Oftedal is a hard man to read at this distance, since we have few reports on what he was like in person. Elisabeth Koren, with her keen eye for personalities, gave her impression of Oftedal, who came to Decorah in the summer of 1874, not long after his piece had been printed and

reviewed with scathing retorts by Preus and others. She criticized him mostly for his breezy rudeness, though she practiced restraint on most topics, especially personalities. She expressed disdain for Oftedal's manners during his visit to Decorah. She wrote she had never met anyone so unpleasant and ill-mannered. "I don't fight against persons, he had said." Mrs. Koren thought this to be untrue. "No, hardly!" (*Nei, langt fra!*) The entire Luther College community had taken umbrage at his unseemly at-

Sven Oftedal

tack and did not forget it. Even the young boys, she continued, had stood along the street to watch him leave, and Lina (her daughter Caroline) had informed her that she would not have greeted him even under compulsion. The bad feelings here would only increase.

As Janson traveled around the Midwest he followed the women's movement carefully. October 8-10, 1879, he attended the Seventh Congress of the Association for the Advancement of Women in Madison, Wisconsin. The congress, attended by women from all over the United States, received front page coverage in many of the Chicago papers. Janson was amazed at the freedom and poise of the women and became an avid supporter of women's emancipation. His favorite suffragette was the outrageous Victoria Woodhull, whom he inquired about wherever he went. During a visit with Henry Wadsworth Longfellow in Cambridge, Massachusetts, he asked the famous, but conservative poet about her and watched as the man sadly shook his head resignedly.[425] Later he attended the Free Love Conference, where he hoped to meet her, but did not, though he did meet many of her friends.

It did not take long for the Norwegian Lutheran pastors to sniff out a natural affinity between his being a Unitarian, or what they would have seen as rationalism, and being a feminist. On March 3, 1880, Janson was the guest of Laur. Larsen in Decorah, where he spoke on the education of women. Laur. Larsen's daughter, Thora, in a letter to her father, asked what he thought of Janson.[426] His answer, unfortunately, is lost to us.

The Muus' Divorce Case

The issue of women's place, if not their rights or education, was about to explode in the Norwegian-American community. Janson's feminism may not have seemed so threatening to the Norwegian-Americans had it not been that at this very time Mrs. Oline Pind Muus (1838-1922) and her husband, B. J. Muus (1832-1900), were involved in a nasty legal dispute about her inheritance. In December 1879 she had sued her husband for the inheritance her father had left her. Muus, using the law of Norway, said it was his. Mrs. Muus needed it to care for their children. Her complaint was that Muus had given her a mere $15 a month for household expenses and, as the family expanded to six children, it no longer was enough. She needed the money, she said, to relieve her poverty and help her care for the family. The legal case was clear: Did the *Mrs. Oline Pind Muus* Muus couple operate by Norwegian or American law? They were still Norwegian citizens. Norway still ruled that the woman's inheritance went to her husband. American law had changed over the years to say that women could inherit money on their own.

This issue was at the heart of the feminist movement as it had begun at Seneca Falls in 1848. Did marriage make a woman "civilly dead?" The Muus case quickly became a Rorschach test for all the commentators. How they saw it depended on their attitudes toward the women's movement. Like all difficult legal cases, however, this was messy. Scarcely a temperate word was spoken about the case, and the Norwegian-American immigrant papers along with the church journals entered into the fray with predictable points of view.

What really happened between the couple is almost impossible to discover. The laws in America were in Mrs. Muus' favor. However, the District Court in Red Wing ruled that the statute of limitations had run out on the first payment from the estate. The court did reward her the second payment of $1118.05. When Muus appealed it, the Minnesota Supreme Court upheld the lower court's decision. The legal process was long and complicated but famous. Papers in Norway and America had been watching closely and reported on it with delight. *Tromsøstifsttidene* reported on October 23, 1881, that the court had found in favor of Mrs. Muus. When Mrs. Muus sued for divorce, in January 1882, Norwegian papers from Christiania's *Aftenposten* to Bergen's *Adressecontoirs Efterretninger*, printed, with no comment, "Mrs. Muus has left her husband and will begin divorce proceedings against him. Attorney Ueland will take the case for her."[427] She did not win the case. However, in January 1883, she won a legal separation (Ueland called it a "limited divorce") with alimony from Muus. The alimony was $150 a year for ten years and a repayment of $2500 from Muus for her father's estate. He was given custody of the children.[428]

The Church Debate on the Muus' Case

The leaders of the Norwegian Synod and members of the Holden congregation were scandalized by the suit. Everyone in the Norwegian-American community formed an opinion of this affair, and the papers led the way. The Synod paper, *Evangelisk Luthersk Kirketidende*, remained quiet on the issue until November. Then Preus, Koren, and Frich issued an accounting of the events thus far and a conclusion, something Holden congregation had asked them to do. Their statement ("*Redegjørelse fra Holden Menighed, Minn.*") described the churchly process from its beginning.[429] It is a helpful accounting of the facts of the case, whether one agrees with their conclusion.

J. B. Frich

They began by noting the scandal had been a heavy cross for all involved. After Muus had been summoned to court by his wife to resolve the issue of her inheritance in late 1879, the congregation had met on February 18, 1880. The purpose of the meeting was to determine what effect Mrs. Muus' complaint against Muus had on his position as pastor of Holden and the many sister congregations in the area he served. The meeting had been called and led by Marcus Bøckman (1849-1942), in the absence of President Preus. Over 1,000 people were said to have attended.[430] After the proceedings, the congregation voted unanimously, excepting one vote, to retain Muus as pastor. This did not end the case. Muus called another meeting of the congregation on March 10-11, 1880. Its purpose was to determine whether his wife had failed to "follow the duties of a housewife to her husband" according to Ephesians 5:24: "Just as the church is subject to Christ, so also wives ought to be, in everything, subject to their husbands." For Muus it was a matter of church discipline.

Mrs. Muus refused to attend the meeting unless she could read, or have read, her complaint against Muus. In it she rebutted her husband's argument.

> I feel no heavy reproach in placing myself in opposition to the Synod's teaching concerning a wife's blind and unconditional obedience to her husband; I can never accept this teaching, and I will not be a hypocrite. If God created woman to be her husband's slave in every manner, He would not have given her the ability to act and think for herself.[431]

The statement went on, with vivid accounts by Mrs. Muus of her husband's ill treatment of her. Among her most memorable complaints was that her bedroom was cold and damp, "with water dripping on her bed." Most often repeated was the account of Muus' failure to get her to a doctor when she broke her leg in 1877.[432] According to her, Muus had replied, when she asked him to get a doctor, that she would have to "butter myself with patience until the doctor came."[433]

The congregation listened, in rapt attention, to these shocking allegations against the pastor whose services they had nearly unanimously voted to retain. Mrs. Muus chose a neighboring pastor, Ludvig M. Biørn, to read her statement. After it was presented, Bøckman, the chairman, waxed eloquent on the nature of marriage, concluding that a wife might even be called "a slave, but not in the bad sense of the word. 'Obedience for her should be a dear duty.'"[434] Such language, given the Synod's issue with slavery, was ill ad-

Marcus Bøckman

vised. Biørn interpreted the Ephesians text "in everything" to mean less than all things. Muus challenged him.

The press went wild, focusing mostly on Bøckman's notion that a wife was nearly a slave. This could hardly have been expected to help. Janson and Bjørnson both stoutly defended Mrs. Muus. Bjørnson wrote Ueland on April 16, 1880, to say he had followed with disgust the case of Mrs. Oline Muus; I have seen with regret how she is captured in the foolish dogma of these ignorant priests (which they call spiritual liberation!) how she sprawls in the net without being able to emancipate herself from twenty years' imprisonment.[435]

The congregation concluded, after these fireworks, it should have another meeting with advice from the Synod leadership. Koren, Preus, and Frich were asked to be present. Once again the congregation gathered on May 12-13, 1880. With the Synod leadership in attendance, several people spoke regarding Mrs. Muus' charge that Muus had not been quick to find her a doctor for her broken leg. After hearing the charges and the defense, those present voted 57-1 that the charges had not been proved. On the second day, as the proceedings dragged on, Koren suggested a committee of fifteen to investigate the charges.[436] It had become clear to Koren that the larger group could not appropriately investigate the charges and counter-charges.

The group of fifteen met in early June. Mrs. Muus did not agree to witness before them until the court had ruled, nor would she name her witnesses. She issued new accusations against her husband as well as against the congregation and the Synod. Her behavior did not impress the committee. Little was concluded at the meeting, but the case did come before the Minnesota District's annual meeting. Muus was president of the district, so the question of his leadership presented itself again. The district had to decide what Muus' place was in the church as an almost divorced clergyman, something forbidden by their code of ethics. The district decided to retain him since Mrs. Muus' accusations had not been proven and one had been disproved.

Holden held yet another meeting July 7-9, 1880. Preus led it. The meeting reprimanded Mrs. Muus for making false accusations again Muus, the congregation, and the Synod.[4379] Muus was asked to defend his failure to speak with his wife over a period of two years, except in the most necessary moments. Muus defended himself, but this detail bothered many.

The Synod leaders found the whole thing distasteful, especially the notice it was getting from opponents of the faith. Marcus Thrane (1817-1890), a Norwegian writer and provocateur living in Chicago, seized on Muus' line about patience. He wrote a three-act play, *Holden, or, Anoint Yourself with Patience.* (*Holden, eller Smør Dig med Taalmodighet*) featuring a stern pastor named Bernt.

Finally the Synod leadership issued a statement in November 1880, printed in the church paper. The tone of the report is serious and not inflammatory. However, their conclusions inflamed those supporting Mrs. Muus.

> The congregation and pastor have striven to assure that this unhappy case would be treated as God's Word says, with seriousness, fairness, and carefulness. It has been their wish as well as ours that the matter could have been brought to a speedy conclusion and the scandal forgotten. But Mrs. Muus' refusal to meet with us and to bring us witnesses or simply give us their names before the case went before the court has made it necessary for the congregation to delay its final decision until after that time.[438]

This language against Mrs. Muus outraged many, especially those in the Augsburg Seminary community. Oftedal's comments in *Folkebladet* were typically shrill in his support of Mrs. Muus, consistent with *Folkebladet*'s official stance on suffrage. What Sverdrup and Oftedal criticized was that the meeting at the Holden church became, in the eyes of the congregation, a regular court of law. That meant, to them that Mrs. Muus had been tried without due process. Oftedal complained

Georg Sverdrup

that there had not been one word of concern or love toward poor Mrs. Muus.[439] In December, Sverdrup responded to the statement in *Lutheraneren*. No one hearing about the case could escape feeling a deep sorrow. After reading the statement, Sverdrup could not agree that Muus was not guilty. Muus had not followed the word in 1 Timothy 5:8: "But if anyone does not provide for his relatives, and especially for members of his household, he has denied the faith and is worse than an unbeliever." Sverdrup thought that Muus' failure to generously support his wife and their children meant that he was not able to lead a congregation.

Secondly, and much worse, Sverdrup continued, was the way Muus admitted treating his wife. He had not spoken to her unless absolutely necessary for two or three years. Muus should ask why he had not found the grace to speak with his wife, Sverdrup said. Just hearing that he had done this would open the ears of the deaf and the eyes of the blind. "But these three presidents, Preus and Koren and Frich, they have not heard or not seen or not spoken, but they have sent these heartrending words out into the world as a witness to Pastor Muus' and his own scandal."[440] Sverdrup concluded: "The question before the congregation and the Synod was now: Can Pastor Muus really serve his congregation to its edification and growth? We must answer, No."[441]

Finally, *Evangelisk Luthersk Kirketidende* had to answer its critics, especially the comment by Bøckman saying a wife should be a "dear" slave, language about which they were naturally touchy.

> Is a woman her husband's slave? The world has heard that Pastor Bøckman said that. But they can laugh. Why do worldly people have worse trouble with marriage than church people? There can be resemblances between wife and a slave. The world does not believe that women should obey and no one has heard Bøckman right.[442]

This language would be difficult to call back as much as the Synod tried to nuance it.

No õne who had to do with the case emerged unscathed, except maybe Andreas Ueland (1853-1931), the young Minneapolis lawyer who established his considerable reputation defending Mrs. Muus in the case concerning her inheritance. The case went all the way to the Minnesota Supreme Court that ruled she should receive what he had received in the previous six years. Not until she sued for a limited divorce, with alimony, did she recover the remainder of her inheritance.[443]

Andreas Ueland

On September 12, 1881, Holden congregation celebrated its twenty-fifth anniversary. Officials of the Synod were there along with some 2,000 others gathered for a celebratory picnic on the church grounds. Sven Oftedal could not refrain from commenting that all this celebrating happened

> while his [Muus'] own wife sits inside with a broken heart and bowed down spirit. There are heavy, bitter tears in that house. Is it not time for Pastor Muus to bring some gladness into his own house? Does not God's Word say that a servant of the Lord, a bishop, has some responsibility for his house and his family?

The case dragged on in the church. About this time, Preus, embarrassed by Muus' behavior, asked him to step down as president of the Minnesota District of the Norwegian Synod. Preus had agreed with the district council's advice that he do so "on account of the very grievous offenses in your household."[444] Muus refused, but he was not re-elected as president in 1883.

Muus did not relent. Again on October 12, 1881, Mrs. Muus had to appear before the congregation and face the charge that she had denied the authority of the Bible by refusing to obey her husband in all things. She agreed that for the sake of peace in the household, a woman should obey reasonable demands, but not unreasonable ones. Muus thought this was yet another attack on the authority of the Bible (and probably his own rights) and wanted to press further to have her excommunicated. The congregation did not want to do so. Finally, Chairman Langemo questioned her on several issues, among them the accusation that the Synod held that a woman was her husband's slave. She allowed that she did not know what the Synod's position on the matter was and said it was a sin to falsely accuse the leaders of something about which she was not certain. Then she asked the congregation for forgiveness. This satisfied both pastor and congregation. The meeting ended. But it must have been wrenching for Mrs. Muus, who withdrew her membership from the congregation shortly afterwards.

Later, in December 1881 and then through January and February 1882, Holden congregation continued to meet to decide the future of Muus as their pastor. Finally, at its last meeting on the subject, in early February, the congregation voted 73 to 37 to retain him. As Joseph Shaw notes in his biography of Muus, the vote showed growing sympathy for Mrs. Muus and a decline in Muus' support.[445]

Bjørnson found Mrs. Muus to be less sympathetic upon meeting her. Then, like many in the face of a conflicted situation, he shrank from the person he had defended. In a letter to his wife, Karoline, he gave a vivid portrait of the woman:

> I met Mrs. Muus. . . . She is big, robust, plump, has been very pretty, still is; black-haired, lively, but a real mountain troll all the way through. God Almighty, how he must have struggled with that female, who

Bjørnstjerne Bjørnson

is all worldliness, indifference, defiance, intelligence, craving for fun, and in her way as strong as he is. She was so dirty that her underclothing stank, so I had to smoke a cigar to be able to talk with her. She started by pretending to be nice and pious and quiet; but I saw the lay of the land at once and made fun of the Bible and Muus and holiness—and she laughed uproariously and was full of gaiety at once.[446]

Bjørnson spoke of trying to reconcile the pair, but granted that, while most of the fault in the conflict rested with Muus, he did have a formidable opponent in his wife.

The Muus' case gives us insight into what the Synod pastors thought theologically about women and marriage. They maintained their biblicism on this issue as they had on slavery. They could accept the judgment of Holden congregation that Mrs. Muus had not been truthful in her charges against Muus. Some of the charges, however, appalled them, especially her accusation that Muus had not spoken to her, unless absolutely necessary, for two or three years. His defense that it was the best he could do persuaded few. We can see growing sympathy for her in the congregation as their meetings continued. In his missive asking Muus to step down as president of the Minnesota District, Preus made clear that he had come to agree that no matter who was more guilty in the case, Muus shared the blame and had failed to keep his home peaceful as Scripture had admonished bishops to do.

Ultimately, this nasty case did nothing for the cause of women's emancipation among the Lutheran clergy, especially the Synod pastors. That Janson and Bjørnson supported Mrs. Muus was also not helpful. They were both considered rationalists or "freethinkers" by churchmen in Norwegian-America communities, and she herself appeared to have been something of a freethinker, if we are to believe Bjørnson's report. (Others, like Shaw, maintain she remained a devoutly orthodox Lutheran.) Their constant response to any appeal from the feminists was to say, "The Bible says . . ." and then quote it against any and all arguments from the feminists. Their thinking lent grounds to the suspicion on both sides that emancipation for women was something that could come to pass only outside the church. Cady Stanton had long since arrived at this conclusion. Her acrimony toward the churches for their enslavement of women continued to grow. Women in the church who longed for emancipation did have the women's missionary society or temperance causes to support. Churchwomen, especially Norwegian Lutheran church women, who supported women's emancipation in the public sphere were rare indeed.

One small detail: Oftedal and Sverdrup, out of concern for Mrs. Muus' situation, gave her housing at Augsburg and supported her until she began receiving her inheritance payments. She remained in the Augsburg community until 1888.[447] She never forgot this. She even left some of her personal letters with Oftedal, now in his papers in the Augsburg archives.

Women's Emancipation at the Time of the Muus Case

The excitement generated by the women's movement caused Bjørnson to form the same opinion of American women as Janson. He attended a Woman's Emancipation Conference in Boston on October 16, 1880, and could not get over the grand experience it was. He wrote home

> I sat as if in the future, and I had difficulty controlling my emotion. The finest women of America, with a cultural background equal to that of the best men, well-traveled and well-read, several of them with university degrees . . . arose one after the other to express their views on the matter at hand with ability, sincerity and moving conviction.[448]

After that experience he concluded that he should oppose the Norwegian Synod on the issue of divorce and women's rights. As he traveled throughout the Upper Midwest, he continued his move away from Lutheran orthodoxy toward a more rationalistic religion. It did not help that he began to defend Ingersoll and Beecher wherever he went. This was further proof to his critics that the women's movement was dangerously heterodox and unChristian, to say nothing of unLutheran.

It was not only the Norwegian Synod that noted the heretical tendencies in the women's movement. Oftedal, in the November 18, 1881, issue of *Folkebladet* sneered that "when Beecher and Ingersoll shook each other's hands in friendship it was called advanced Christendom in America. But it was something else in Norway: rationalism." Carl Chrislock, in his book *From Fjord to Freeway*, a history of Augsburg College, quotes *Folkebladet* as saying about Janson

> it is disconcerting to see a Norse champion of freedom become a clergyman in the U.S. for the purpose of advocating a doctrine of rationalism that was preached by those who imprisoned Hans Nielsen Hauge.[449]

Many Norwegian-American pastors and theologians viewed these freethinkers as nothing more than the old rationalists of the Enlightenment. They missed how anti-religious they were. Oftedal recognized the same old rationalism of the past in the freethinking of Janson, but he must have found it difficult to differentiate his own thinking on women, temperance, and the Norwegian Synod from Janson's. Oftedal's commitments on emancipation and prohibition were in agreement with other reformers in America, and this caused him some worry.

Not only did Janson stand for the rationalism which repelled Oftedal, but he also advocated the ordination of women, a bridge too far for Oftedal. Later Janson's wife, Drude, increasingly unhappy about her marriage, wrote a novel titled *The Saloonkeeper's Daughter*. It told the story of a woman, encouraged by Bjørnson, who left a rather miserable home life and marriage to become a Unitarian pastor. The story ends with her ordination. Janson was not alone in seeing the way the movement toward emancipation would lead to many new things. The novel joins the two reform movements of women's emancipation and temperance in a way similar to the combination of abolition and women's rights in the program of Frances Willard, the founder of the Women's Christian Temperance Union.

Kristofer Janson could not refrain from using the Muus case for his own purposes. In 1884, Janson wrote a novel titled *Wives, Submit Yourselves Unto Your Husbands*, which attacked the Norwegian Synod's treatment of the Muus' case. Oftedal, once again, had to draw a line, deeply offended as he was by Janson's story, though he was no defender of the Synod. He thought the novel was a total misreading of the Ephesians text that admonished husbands to love their wives as Christ loved the church.[450] Oftedal's more liberal politics moved him to be more liberal on the social issues that would plague the Norwegian Synod; at the same time he stood firmly against anything smacking of rationalism or "freethinking." His politics brought him into conflict with his own biblical thinking and convictions, and he never really resolved it.

It was not only the Synod pastors who were troubled by Janson, however. Several Hauge and Conference pastors agreed with the Norwegian Synod on this issue and prepared a document on January 16, 1884. Some of these pastors were Ole Juul (1838-1903), Nils Christian Brun (1847-1919), Jens Iversen Welo, and Christian O. Brøhaugh (1841-1908), from both the Norwegian and Hauge Synods. They accused Janson of "throwing over Christian faith. He reads the Bible very carelessly or else he would know that St. Paul said more than 1,800 years ago that women shall be under men in everything."[451] For many it was much harder walking the middle road where Oftedal was trying to walk.

In 1885. *Budbæreren* clucked that

> Kristofer Janson has advertised in a paper in Norway for theological students—young men and women—to come to America and study in Pennsylvania and then come out west to work among Scandinavians. Young women can be pastors in Janson's mixed up congregation.[452]

In 1885 the Women's Suffrage Association held its convention in Minneapolis. Drude Janson wrote to Bjørnson, whom she had known from Norway, that it was the greatest experience of her life. She could not get over the impact that the preaching of Lucy Stone had on her and how deeply captivated she was by the Universalist Church.[453]

The next year, in 1886, when Janson and his wife were invited to dinner in Madison at the home of Rasmus B. Anderson, they became reacquainted with Luther Seminary President Hans Gerhard Stub (1849-1931) and met his new wife, Valborg Hovind Stub (1860-1901). Valborg, the second Mrs. Stub, was an accomplished singer from Norway. Stub had met her in 1883 in Leipzig, Germany, when he was there on his sabbatical. He wrote Larsen to tell him of Valborg, who was unlike many other artists of the day. She was a devout Christian. A cultivated woman, she was said to have found being the wife of a theological professor in Midwestern towns like Madison, Robbinsdale, and St. Paul, somewhat stifling. She and Mrs. Janson became close friends. When the Stubs moved to Minnesota, where he taught at Luther Seminary, located then in Robbinsdale, Minnesota, Mrs. Stub and Mrs. Janson ran something of a salon for cultivated talk and musicales. Oline Muus, a violin and piano player, found her way into the musicales.[454] One can be sure that some free-thinking about the role of women entered their conversations, including discussions about divorce. The group broke up when Mrs. Stub returned to Norway for better medical treatment.

Hans G. Stub, his wife Valborg, and child Ingolf, 1885

Women's Suffrage in the Church

The cause of women in the church received an important push from an unexpected quarter. One of the most important years for women in the church was 1888, the year of the Centennial of World Mission. Gathering in London, the conference featured the contributions of women, and several American women made a great impact on the rest of the convention with their strong defense of the place of women as missionaries.

Lutheraneren of the Norwegian-Danish Conference reported on the convention in an article written by a Norwegian churchman, Lars Dahle (1843-1925), secretary of the Norwegian Mission Society. He remarked with amazement on the poise with which the American women spoke and presented their cases. Although it was a new idea, he thought it acceptable since he knew of some Norwegian women's societies which were considering sending their first women missionaries to China. This was in response to the work of Hudson Taylor whose call for missionaries attracted thousands of young people, especially women, from Europe and America. Although Janson and Bjørnson had kicked up a lot of dust on the issue of women's rights, it was considered to be a battle more outside the church than within it, except insofar as women could take leadership roles as missionaries in churches far away.

Lars Dahle

Red Wing Lutheran Ladies' Seminary

It was in the context of these arguments that the question of the building of a school especially for Norwegian Synod women, similar to its Luther College for men, became urgent. Clearly the academies and other colleges founded by Norwegian immigrant groups at the time were not what the Synod pastors had dreamed of for their girls. In the early winter of 1889, a group of Red Wing pastors and business leaders gathered to determine whether they could realize the dream of Hermann Preus to establish a ladies' seminary in their city. Pastor Knud Bjørgo and eleven other men from the city formed a corporation for such a school.[455]

In its context the accomplishment of these men in Red Wing is admirable. The previous year had been one of unmitigated disaster for the Synod. Because of the disagreement on election, the Synod had split.

Muus and other leaders around him in Northfield had formed a small group called the Anti-Missourian Brotherhood. Led by Frederick A. Schmidt, (1837-1922), Muus, Ludvig Marinus Biørn (1835-1928), and Peter A. Rasmussen (1828-1898), they rejected the position on election of the older generation of Norwegian Synod leaders, a position much influenced by the patriarchs of Missouri. The opposition viewed the stance of Missouri and the Norwegian Synod as Calvinistic and not Lutheran. The reaction swept through the churches and caused a split that left the Synod decimated in numbers and young supporters.

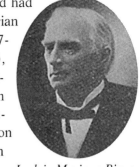

Ludvig Marinus Biørn

The question of a girls' school for the Norwegian Synod briefly moved to Sioux Falls. In 1889 the Norwegian Synod pastors established a Normal School in Sioux Falls (not to be confused with the school of the Norwegian-Danish Augustana Synod)that would later merge with Augustana, which was in part at least an attempt to provide education for girls. The purpose of the school was to prepare teachers, either for the parochial schools of congregations, which offered religious education alongside the local primary schools, or for the comprehensive schools sponsored by some of the Synod congregations.[456]

The preparation of such teachers had been a concern of the young Synod from the first. In 1865 Luther College established a department called the normal school line for preparing its young men to teach in such a Norwegian primary school or in an English school. Although it closed this department in 1886, it was clear that the Synod could not abandon this effort.

Three years later, the Synod's normal school opened in Sioux Falls with fifty students, twenty-seven boys and twenty-three girls. It began with two departments: one to prepare teachers for Norwegian-English schools and another for teachers in exclusively English schools. Many parents saw it as a place to send their confirmed children in the winter months, when they were not needed on the farm. Apparently Norwegian was still common enough that they closed the English department in 1893, but continued the bilingual department. This included a short course in Norwegian alone, for those who expected to teach only in the congregational schools. Those in the Norwegian-English department required more preparation, since they needed English to teach in the common or public schools.

This distinction between a "congregational" school and a public school recalls a common practice of that time. Parochial school included instruction in religious Norwegian, the Bible, hymns, and the catechism, with Pontoppidan's *Explanation* to Luther's Small Catechism. This was a required part of catechetical instruction in the Norwegian church from 1739 until the 1850s. A shorter version of it continued in the Norwegian-American churches until the 1950s. For this a short course in the summer was almost a necessity for struggling students. The combination of general and religious education is evident in the resolution the Synod adopted in 1896, recommending "that the students in our academies who want to be further educated for teaching be invited or called upon to go to Sioux Falls for at least one year, to receive the practical preparation necessary for teaching students."[457]

The leader of the school for its first five years was Pastor Amund Mikkelson (1835-1930). When his health gave way, he was succeeded by others on the faculty, such as Helje Aanestand (b. 1844), Johan Anton Blilie (1852-1935) and Ole Olsen Sando (1849-1903). This institution, whose first "lady principal" was Helga Bedeler, attracted women students and prepared them for teaching in both the church and public schools. One might think that answered the Norwegian Synod's need to provide higher education for its daughters.

Armund Mikkelson

Lutheran Normal School, Sioux Falls, South Dakota

The turmoil of the 1880s in the Norwegian-American Lutheran churches preoccupied all of the leadership. In many ways, the conflicts, while enervating to the older generation, left later generations with many more schools than there would have been without these bitter conflicts about theological and educational questions.

Norwegian-American women could now receive equal educational opportunities at St. Olaf and the normal school in Sioux Falls. By 1889, the year after the Anti-Missourian Brotherhood left the Norwegian Synod, there were schools available for women. The Synod had the Normal School in Sioux Falls, but it was a concession to those who wanted co-education. Their dream of a girls' school was not satisfied by the school in Sioux Falls. They wanted a girls' school on the model of the Nissen School for Girls or Christiansfeld. It would have come true sooner had there not been the fire that destroyed the Main Building in Decorah on April 19, 1889.

The Death of
DIDERIKKE OTTESON BRANDT

On January 21, 1885, the venerable Diderikke Brandt died. As she died she cried out in German, "Enter not into judgment with your servant, for no one living is righteous before you" (Psalm 143:2). It was a  sad ending to a remarkable life. Her husband Nils, after an incident at the college, abruptly resigned as professor at the college and pastor of the Norwegian Lutheran congregation in Decorah. On May 14, 1882, he gave his farewell sermon at his church and left for Norway. The official news report said he had to resign on account of his health. Furthermore, it said, he was planning to move back to Norway without Diderikke.[458] He returned to America on October 6, 1883, to live with his son Pastor Olaf Elias Brandt (1862-1940) in Cleveland, Ohio. In the winter of 1884 Diderikke, with her youngest daughter, Katherine, left Decorah to join him. Reports written to explain her sudden death indicated that her doctor in Decorah had thought her heart had been failing for some time.

Nils Brandt

Immediately after her death, her body was brought to Decorah, where funeral arrangements were made for January 25. A small group of friends and family gathered in the parsonage where she had lived with her family for sixteen years. They sang some hymns and President Laur. Larsen spoke a few words based on Hebrews 13:14: "For here we have no abiding city, but we seek the city that is to come." From there the cortege to First Lutheran Church began. A large group of students followed the funeral coach.

When they arrived, the church was already packed to overflowing. Never since its dedication had it been so full or so well decorated with flowers.[459] Pastor Koren preached the funeral sermon on John 11:20-28, the story of Martha's confession of faith. Larsen stood beside the casket and spoke on Proverbs 31, on the qualities of a good wife. Then, while the college band played, the entire congregation passed by the coffin to give their farewells and gaze for the last time on Diderikke's face.

The entire congregation followed her casket to the Lutheran cemetery in Decorah. There Pastor Thore Eggen (b. 1859) spoke a few words of commendation and committed her body to the earth, casting soil on the casket while reciting the traditional, "Earth to earth, ashes to ashes, dust to dust." Soon after the burial, a monument was raised in her honor, the largest of any in the cemetery at the time, with the inscription, "This monument is put here by the students of Luther College and members of First Lutheran Church" with a favorite hymn verse, "Christ's blood and righteousness/Are all I will be covered with;/With that alone I will stand before God/when I shall enter heaven."

First Lutheran Church, Decorah, Iowa

Diderikke was a powerful force in the work of the Synod. From the time of her arrival in 1856 as a newlywed at the Ixonia, Wisconsin, congregation she overshadowed her husband. The Brandts moved to the college in 1865, just after the completion of the Main Building, and into the parsonage when it was completed in 1867. Pastor Brandt had received a combined call to be pastor of the Lutheran congregation in Decorah and pastor and professor at the college. The parsonage, completed after their arrival, was on the edge of the campus at the time. It became central to the life of the college, with Diderikke as social director and mother away from home for the students. She planned parties, mended clothes, and nursed the ill. While the other pastors' wives wearied of her energy and what they perceived to be her undisciplined life, the students found her tireless work on their behalf to be a solace and support for them. Some of them were quite young, and most had not been away from home for an extended time before.

It is no wonder that Diderikke was featured as the most important woman in the life of the college in the many extant commendations following her death. All agreed that the college was much the better for her work among the students. Each report told a personal story that showed her concerns for the college and its students. The most reliable yet fulsome of the accounts appeared in Gisle Bothne's history of Luther College, *Det Norske Luther College, 1861-1897.* Bothne, married to Katherine Elise Brandt, Diderikke's youngest daughter, knew whereof he spoke.

Gisle Bothne

> This woman's name is so deeply knit to the history of Luther College that her biography is rightly included in this history, despite the fact that neither she nor any other woman has been a teacher at the school. But her vocation, as long as she was a pastor's wife in Decorah, was also in many respects a learning experience for the young people who were educated at Luther College despite her not having taught one class there.[460]

Bothne included in his encomium for Diderikke several important documents from the eulogies surrounding her death.

Laur. Larsen's eulogy, which also appeared in the *Evangelisk Luthersk Kirketidende*, noted the same personal qualities that the wives had remarked on when they met her, but he put a charitable construction on her life and work. He praised her for the very same qualities that irritated many of the other pastors' wives and contemporaries.

The first impression one got of Mrs. Brandt was that of her sacrificial character. She needed little rest; she always had to find something to do. Her activity always served to help, succor and give joy to others. Where there was need, she held nothing back, and no work was so poor or demeaning that she would in any way hold back from doing it. If there was someone nearby who was sick in bed, she was there; she understood how to nurse the sick. If anyone needed to be helped with money, or clothes or anything else, she was indescribably inventive in finding a way to get them help; or she would find ways by means of her own efforts, often working through the night to give help. She found an especially rich mission field for her talents when she moved to Decorah and began a relationship with the college just when the new Main Building opened and the number of students grew. When a large number of young people have to live together, eat at a common table, and have something of a common home, that large home necessarily will come to need several things to remind students a little of their family's blessings and joys. The leader, who should act like the father in the home, cannot really meet the needs of every

J. A. Schmidt.
E. Siewers.
K. Chrondsen.
J. D. Jacobsen
Diderikke Brandt.
K. E. Bergh.
U. Brandt.
G. H. Landmark.

Diderikke's inclusion in this picture of professors at the college is evidence of her importance to the school from its beginning.

single one in his large flock, like the father in the family, even if there are many of them. And who shall take the place of the mother? No one can fully do that; but if it will happen to any degree, it will depend on whether there is, in the families that are connected with the school, a woman who is rightly placed and rightly trained and who will offer something more than the ordinary measure of her time and thoughts to do so. And such a woman was Mrs. Brandt. She had, of course, her own home and her own children to watch over, and her youngest child was born at the college, where the family lived from its beginning. But she still found time and the occasion to care for the large flock of students that surrounded her. After her children grew up, and her three sons became students at the college, they also became a strong connection between her and the rest of the pupils. She founded a society of women in the Decorah congregation who gladly met together, not like other ladies aids to sew new clothes to sell, but to do a much less glorious work, and that was to mend the students' clothes. She baked communion wafers and made the pastor's clerical ruffs, not to earn money for herself, but to give it all away to the needy students. If one could reckon the money she had saved for the students, so they could use their clothes for a longer time, and what she would have otherwise done with her work to help them it would have really amounted to a very large sum. But the best is not the worth of what she gave in money, but the impression she gave that affected the hearts of the young and the example they saw in her, that one should learn to live for others, not only for one's self.

Her efforts were not restricted to only those things that were profitable. She had herself one of those minds that was always young. She understood that youth also needed a little support and enjoyment and she sought therefore to do what she could to fulfill these needs in an appropriate manner. She often invited students to her home; at other times she sought to create enjoyment for them at the college. In all the festival arrangements she took the most active part both at the college and in the congregation. Briefly put, at so many occasions she seemed indispensable.[461]

In 1883, after Nils left for Norway, the college alumni association commissioned, in her honor, a portrait of her to be done by Gausta, By fall, it was completed and given a place of honor in the college buildings. H. B. Thorgrimson observed that a copy of this portrait was always included in the annuals of the school. In 1884, the college and church sponsored an ingathering of funds to give her as she left for Cleveland. H. G. Stub the leader of the drive wrote:

> Dear Mrs. Brandt! We hope that you will receive this sum as a testimony to the love shared by so many who during their studies at our dear Luther College have received unforgettable memories of all that you have meant to them and who have, in many ways, had the occasion to receive good from your friendship and hospitality. Your name is indelibly united with the Decorah College and when our thoughts return to our Alma mater, they also bring thoughts of you, who with our Alma mater were a *mater* (mother).[462]

These tributes expressed the true affection the students had for her and maybe their unexpressed, but clear, concern that she should be comforted in her loss by their strong feelings for and approval of her work. Those who knew the story—and it is difficult not to think everyone did given the small community they lived in—knew that she was probably trying to exonerate her husband, but after a certain amount of time, her cry at his death continued to be reported but little understood. In fact, it mystified later admirers that one so good should feel so guilty.

For her it was a double tragedy, not only for her husband, but for her own career, which was inextricably linked to his and now over. She had known from the first that the profession of pastor's wife would be a suitable outlet for her drive and many talents. It was the only career open to such a woman, and she came to it late. She was 27 when Nils returned to Norway from his first years in America, looking for a wife. Her education at Christiansfeld had prepared her for such a vocation, and she took it up with energy when she came to America. As time went on and the role of women began to change, she saw opportunities in her place at the college. She may have chafed at the restrictions put on her by the other pastors' wives, who frowned on her "unladylike" ambitions. Like all pioneers, she was difficult and forceful; she did what she had to do to get the necessary work done. She could do this, secure in the position she had as wife. When Nils resigned his position, she lost hers as well. Although she continued to live in the parsonage for over a year, her own health had declined so much she was not able to do much.

The Synod leadership had recently lived through the disastrous Muus' trial and separation, for which they had been excoriated because of their treatment of Mrs. Muus. Another such difficulty involving a woman would have been too much. Diderikke had no other place to go but to her son. The overweening praise she received hinted ever so slightly that the school and church were embarrassed about the situation and wanted to make clear to her that she was still important and would always be remembered. They could do that for her, even as she had to leave, for her own sense of honor and theirs. What the story shows as much as anything is the fragile place of a woman without a husband in this society. That it should be Diderikke who suffered the most from this has its ironies. It gives us a view of the place of women in a society long gone. Ten years later another school would appear, the fulfillment of Christiane's dream for a girls' school where the church could prepare ladies as they had been so well prepared at Christiansfeld.

CHAPTER SEVEN

Lutheran Ladies' Seminary
at Red Wing, Minnesota

…we want you all to be ladies in the true sense of the word; for a true lady is nothing but a true woman, a woman who can make a home. And the woman who can do that will be the crown and the glory and the sunshine of mankind; she will be the blessing for which men willingly will shed their heart-blood.[463]

—Pastor Andreas K. Sagen

It was in the context of the bitter theological debates and break away of the Anti-Missourians from the Norwegian Synod in 1888 that members of the Norwegian Synod began to plan a school for their daughters. None of the schools described above fulfilled the dreams of Preus and others for a ladies' seminary, or what Preus in 1869 had called a girl's school (*en Pigeskole*)—rather like the *Nissen Pigeskole* he knew from Norway. It would be a place where "Out of a due consideration for the place woman occupies as sister but especially as wife and mother, we should consider providing our girls with an opportunity for more enlightenment than is generally the case now."[464] Such a school needed three teachers, Preus suggested, and the courses should be first, religion, next Norwegian, English, then natural history and history. This curriculum was very like that of Nissen's School for Girls where Preus began teaching in 1849.

After 1886, St. Olaf Seminary was established, built for students and pastors who could no longer agree with the Synod seminary and pastors. The split of the St. Olaf Anti-Missourians from the Synod was bitter. Muus had publicly disagreed with the Synod position on election, causing Preus to demand a retraction from Muus in the fiercest terms. The bitterness of this fight made the attendance of their daughters at St. Olaf unthinkable. Preus' dream for such a girls' school, at least what was remembered by those who actually built the school, was not the same as

Muus' slightly more practical school. (The courses were much the same; it was the intentions of the plan that stood behind the choices of courses that differs: St. Olaf would be aggressively American, Red Wing's Ladies' Seminary more Scandinavian and upper class.)

When Preus made his proposal for a girls' school, he wanted to educate girls to be ladies, housewives, and mothers, to provide them something like the finishing school at Christiansfeld, to complement the home schooling of the parlor, or like the Nissen's Girls School he knew so well.

Hermann Amberg Preus

After 1889 and the secession of the Anti-Missourian Brotherhood from the Synod, Synod pastors would have found it difficult to agree with almost anything from the St. Olaf side. After that break, and few breaks are as bitter as those within families, it would have been near treason to send one's daughter to the competing school. A daughter marrying outside of the church family, while not quite a tragedy, could be troublesome. Girls at the Synod's ladies' seminary discovered this when they fell in love with Hauge Synod theological students. Sigrid Harrisville experienced this when she fell in love with and married Roy Harrisville, Sr., although by then the churches had merged into the NLCA (1917). The traditions of the various schools still made a difference to people.

A Year of Recovery
Luther Seminary in Robbinsdale

Despite all this turmoil, the year 1889 was a busy and constructive year for the Synod. It was recouping its losses from the splits and controversies surrounding the acrimonious theological debate about predestination (election) with the men gathered around St. Olaf College. Having decided to move Luther Seminary from Madison to Minnesota, they were completing the new building for the seminary in Robbinsdale, Minnesota, which was to be dedicated in the fall of 1889, at the beginning of the new school year. The normal school in Sioux Falls, built for the Synod to educate men and women for teaching and other vocations, opened its doors in 1889, as did Aaberg Academy in Devils Lake, North Dakota, and Bruflat Academy and Business Institute, Portland, North Dakota. The latter two were local schools established by Synod pastors

Luther Seminary in Robbinsdale, Minnesota

and leaders in their respective areas. Luther Seminary and Luther College, as official schools of the Norwegian Synod, received funding from the entire church. The other schools, while not discouraged from building, found their support mostly in the local communities where they were to be built. The driving forces behind them were not the old pioneer pastors, but their heirs and students. Although the leadership of the Synod was old and shaken by the split and bitter controversy over predestination, it still had the will to move forward.

Red Wing Organizes

In Red Wing, the plans for a girl's school went forward under the leadership of Pastor Knut Knutsen Bjørgo (1847-1935), who had just

taken the call in 1888 to Trinity Lutheran Church, the Norwegian Synod congregation in Red Wing. The Hauge Synod Seminary in Red Wing was well established, having been there since 1879, and the leaders of the Red Wing community wanted another school in their city. Hamline College had begun its work in Red Wing in 1854, but in 1869 moved to St. Paul; St. Ansgar's Academy,

Knut Bjørgo

which became Gustavus Adolphus College, had built its first school in Red Wing in 1862, but left the next year. The town fathers clearly thought another school would be to their economic advantage and pledged renewed support for a school.

On April 10, 1889, Bjørgo called together six or seven local business-men from the Red Wing area to discuss the idea of building a girls' school there. After some discussion, the group voted unanimously that such a school for girls was needed—both for the girls and for the city—and agreed to incorporate themselves as "The Red Wing Lutheran Ladies' Seminary Corporation." Fourteen men joined the corporation, and the group began a drive to raise the needed money. With the unanimous de-cision to proceed, six of the men contributed $1,000 and bought sixteen acres on a high bluff at the southern edge of Red Wing with a panoramic view of the Mississippi. Martha Reishus Langemo, in her brief history of the school, described the spot as being

> a hundred and fifty-six feet above the majestic Mississippi River where boats could be seen plying their cargoes up and down the beautiful waters. Level stretches and sloping meadows, the view of the lakes and the rugged woods on the Wisconsin side—all unsurpassed beauty and grandeur—a perfect setting for the proposed Ladies Seminary.[465]

With the property bought and the decision made to build, the group had to raise enough money to pay for it—which would come to $40,000. According to their reports, the appeal was going rather well (*med ikke saa lidet Held*) but then tragedy struck. On May 19, 1889, the Main Building in Decorah was totally destroyed by fire, the bane of so many buildings

Luther College's Main Building burning down, May 1889

of the Norwegian Synod.[466] Built in 1865, it had been the first visible emblem of the young church and held a special place in the hearts of many who had worked so hard to raise it up out of nothing. Watching it burn down, despite heroic efforts to douse the flames, hearing the bell fall to the ground and cease ringing was a death blow to the Luther College and Decorah community.[467] Understandably, the attention, energy, and funds of the Synod membership turned immediately from building the Ladies' Seminary toward rebuilding the College building as soon as possible.

With the exception of Preus, the Synod leadership all lived in Decorah or very nearby, and its publishing house was there. Koren, in nearby Washington Prairie, had bought the original plot of land, and the townspeople had great affection for the school. Decorah was the axis around which the Synod turned. Still, even if the Lutheran Ladies' Seminary was not an official project of the Synod, it may as well have been, given its constituency. Its many building projects, including the seminary building in Robbinsdale, had depleted the pockets of the supporters of the Synod. Not surprisingly, the Ladies' Seminary was put on hold while the Synod turned its energies to rebuilding the college building and finishing the seminary building in Robbinsdale.

Stay in Decorah?

Several questions had to be answered, however, before the reconstruction of the Main Building in Decorah could begin. First was whether the school should be rebuilt in Decorah, so far away from any city. As the papers reported, the center of the Norwegian population had been gradually shifting north and west, so that Minneapolis was now the center of the Norwegian-American people. Students and younger faculty supported relocation, and the board initially agreed. The committee to rebuild looked favorably upon a proposal to move the school to St. Paul Park, some eight miles south of the capitol city near the banks of the Mississippi River. They even voted to accept its proposal. However, after further examination of the St. Paul Park offer, it failed to get much popular support. One of the attractions of the proposal was that more students might be able to come to the school, raising the numbers of students to 200, some fifty more than they had at the time. LaCrosse, Wisconsin, also made a serious bid for the school. Even Madison, Wisconsin, made some noises about an invitation.[468]

As these proposals came in, Koren rallied the townspeople in Decorah to keep the college there. In September 1889 the board reconsidered its decision to move when the city of Decorah agreed to extend the water mains up to the college land—water to fight fires and serve the needs of the college for clean water and sanitation. The board voted to stay in Decorah. Soon enough money came in so they could rebuild in Decorah, free of debt. The cost, $50,000, was considerably less than the $95,000 the first building had cost, and many agreed the new building was much more beautiful and comfortable.

When the new Main Building was dedicated on October 14, it evoked some of the same excitement and pride the young church had felt at the dedication of its first building in 1865. The Red Wing contingent had generously sent $1,200 of its ingathered money toward the rebuilding. Ole K. Simmons of Red Wing offered to supervise the construction of the new Main Building free of charge.

Laur. Larsen

Upon the completion of the new college building, the Red Wing board could turn its attention again to the Ladies' Seminary. The architect who had designed the new Main Building in Decorah, Augustus F. Gauger (1852-1929) of St. Paul, had impressed people with his design, so the Red Wing board hired him to plan the Ladies' Seminary building.

Luther College's new Main Building, 1890.

During the time between the fire and the new Main Building at Luther, there had been a serious proposal that Luther become co-educational, but it was defeated, to the satisfaction of Laur. Larsen, who felt the school's original purpose as a classical school for boys should be maintained. The cost of making the school ready for women students and faculty—making living quarters for women and hiring women faculty—seemed to him to be financially impossible as well.[469] It may have been that, when the Ladies' Seminary board resumed its work, the pressure for co-education also was relieved. The Red Wing board went forward. By the spring of 1892, it had enough money to begin the building project.

Panic of 1893

Between the time the Red Wing board voted to build and the first evidence of a building on what came to be known as Seminary Hill, the women's suffrage movement had celebrated its Silver Anniversary in January with extensive press coverage of the major actors, Cady Stanton and Susan B. Anthony. Newspapers were filled with stories of the progress of the movement, and how women were gradually getting the vote in municipal and state elections. People of all stripes knew the world was changing, especially in regard to the role of women. Anthony was quoted as saying that things had changed so much that "we were on the verge of an era of unmarried women."[470] The farm could no longer support its daughters, nor were they needed anymore. "Young women used to have to spin, weave, make carpets and soap, and now all that is done in factories."[471] Even though the women in the parsonage still could do many of these things, and did, the need was no longer as great for them to do so. This meant a change from centuries of traditional work for women.

Susan B. Anthony and Elizabeth Cady Stanton

In July 1892 work had commenced on the Ladies' Seminary building, with hopes that it would be enclosed by the fall so it could be finished during the year and opened in the fall of 1893. It was not to be. The Panic of 1893, which began just shortly before the laying of the cornerstone that

May, meant that people had very little money to give for its completion. Despite that, the community loyally supported the school with as much as it could, but the gifts were few. The president of the Ladies' Seminary, Hans Allen (1863-1934), in his report to the 1903 Jubilee celebration of the Norwegian Synod, suggested that the rest of the church found it easy to forget the work in Red Wing, for their gifts were *"ganske smaa"* (very little). The board had, however, persevered and was now ready to continue the building.

Cornerstone Laying

By Ascension Day, May 11, 1893, the building was far enough along to lay the cornerstone. Pastor Vilhelm Koren, vice president of the Synod, presided and preached. That morning began with drizzle, which kept the crowd smaller than it might have been, said one report, and the day was a work day when farmers were working in the fields, planting. The ceremonies began at 1:30, led by President Bjørgo. After an opening prayer, he read a brief history of the efforts made to get the school built, from the first meetings in 1889 to the buying of the sixteen acres of land, and the struggle to get it built after the fire in Decorah. Then Koren gave the main address and dedicated the cornerstone,

Vilhelm Koren

putting into it several documents typical of the day: an English Bible, the *Book of Concord, Synodens Salmebog,* an English Lutheran hymnal, and a copy of several issues of church journals, the *Kirketidende,* the *Lutheran Witness* and the several newspapers, the *Red Wing Republican* and *Amerika,* one of the Norwegian-American newspapers of the day, plus some silver coins.

After this, representatives of various groups in Red Wing spoke—Pastor Edward Albrecht in German; Pastor G. Rast, of the Swedish Augustana Lutheran Church in Red Wing, in Swedish; and Pastor Ole P. Vangsness of Minneapolis in English. The event was made more festive by the band from the Red Wing Reform School and a joint choir of the Swedish and Norwegian congregations in Red Wing. Those who spoke, especially Koren, had thought quite a bit about this new kind of school and wanted to clarify its mission. What did it mean that this school would be called a *Ladies'* Seminary? When Preus had called for a school for girls (*pigeskol*) in Red Wing twenty years before, he intended it to be the "first English Norwegian girls' school" in the country.[472] Did he mean it should have the title Ladies' Seminary? It is difficult to tell.

How it had come to be called a Ladies' Seminary, rather than a girls' school, was never clarified, but it seems to have bothered some of the leaders of the church, so they set about clarifying the name. It was not an unusual name for a girls' school. At the time there were several models for women's schools in the American context using the name. As previously noted, the idea of the ladies' seminary in America had become somewhat common. The first of the Seven Sisters colleges in New England, Mt. Holyoke Ladies' Seminary, was not the first to use the name in America. Bethlehem Female Seminary (now Moravian College), founded by Zinzendorf's daughter in 1742, was the first. Todd Walsh in his history which is the most respectable research on the school, argued that Rockford Female Seminary in Rockford, Illinois, where Jane Addams attended, was the model the Synod pastors had in mind.[473] While that is possible, Christiansfeld and the Nissen school were just as likely the models Preus had in mind when he made his suggestion for a school. The difference between Nissen's school and the school in Red Wing was that it would be residential, like Christiansfeld, a place they also knew well.

The Norwegian Synod pastors believed, not only from their own wives and daughters in the family parlors, and from their own schooling and experience as teachers at Norway, that their daughters needed to know their own mother tongue and culture, along with other modern languages, arts, music and English literature in order to become well-educated ladies. They also needed to learn the art of hospitality and gracious living and, most of all, the religious foundations of their church. So although the title "Ladies' Seminary" had currency at the time, what it meant for the Synod and its daughters was not quite clear—even to them. Seminary, these well-educated men knew, meant nursery, or a place of nurture, appropriate for young women as well as for men in theological training schools. Americans might understand it better as a finishing school, where the girls received a more complete education than they had received at home. Koren's speech at the laying of the cornerstone reveals much about the ideas of the Synod regarding the place of women in the church and society. These ideas fit well with the "finishing" school concept. He tried valiantly to answer the question in his sermon that warm day in May as they lay the cornerstone. It is helpful to follow his rather long argument to see what he was thinking about as he prepared the sermon—something we can detect in the subtext of the speech.

For Koren and the entire leadership of the Synod, the question of women's rights within the church, and not just in the secular society, had grown more and more pressing; the missionary movement was sending Norwegian-American Lutheran women to faraway places. Women were getting the right to vote at the Synod's archenemy, Trinity Congregation, the mother congregation of the Friends of Augsburg, later the Lutheran Free Church.

These debates were thrumming beneath the speech of Koren. The women's suffrage movement was gaining strength in both the church and the secular world. The fight for the vote and women's emancipation were included by the Republican Party in its platforms from 1892 on. The Populist Movement, most fierce on the prairies, and led in Minnesota by Ignatius Donnelly who wrote the Omaha platform of the Populist Party in 1892, was spouting all sorts of attacks on the establishment for its captivity to the Eastern establishment, the fat cats, the banks and railroads. Mary Ellen Lease (1850-1933) of Kansas, a suffragist and strong supporter of temperance called for Kansas "to raise more hell and less corn." She, like other populists, was calling for an eight-hour workday plus the nationalization of the railroads, the telegraph, and telephone. Women began to see in the Populist Movement a chance to hitch their wagon to a movement that would give them the vote. Several states in the West, Wyoming in 1859 and Colorado in 1893, had given women equal suffrage in the state, and Montana women were given school suffrage in 1889, meaning women could vote in local school elections. Montana, through which Koren had traveled on the Great Northern, was among the most populist of states and would elect the first woman to the House of Representatives. The struggle was everywhere evident to anyone reading newspapers and participating in the civil life of the country.

Mary Ellen Lease

The high water, and ending, of the Populist Movement was in 1896, when the party agreed to nominate, along with the Democrats, William Jennings Bryan, for president on the Democratic ticket. All of these issues were clearly in Koren's mind as he was preparing his sermon, especially the women's suffrage movement. Just the week before, the Women's Pavilion at the Chicago Fair opened to great fanfare on May 1, 1893. Stanton and Anthony and many of the first suffragettes were there receiving much acclaim and notoriety in the press. Nothing much like it had happened before in the country and especially in the Midwest.

As we study Koren's speech we can detect all those concerns crowding together in his mind. He was now sixty-seven. In his capacity as vice president of the Synod, he traveled widely in order to visit the new congregations and leaders throughout the nation. He read widely in American papers and knew well the state of the country and its issues. As the Great Northern Railway began its service from St. Paul to Seattle that January, he would be able to visit the churches as they grew in the West. Koren could see the burgeoning of the new country, the expansion of the Norwegians across the northern tier of states. In his travels he may also have sensed the beginning of the Panic, which was first felt by the railroads. Railroad centers and shipping ports in towns like Red Wing were already beginning to suffer. The stock market would be at its lowest the week after the ceremony, and labor unrest would grow until the Pullman Strike in the next year.

Almost in contradiction to the collapse of the economy was the White City, the Columbian Exposition, or World's Fair, in Chicago. The event had been deemed important enough for the Synod to commission Pastor

J. A. Ottesen to write a brief history of the Norwegian Synod and Luther College to be distributed at the exposition. Among the several subjects he treated was the building of the Ladies' Seminary, which would address "a long and sorely felt need in our church, a place where young women will receive regular academic learning and the kind of education which is especially necessary for women to know."[474] He also noted, as many others would over time, that it would be the most beautiful building of the Synod and located in the most beautiful setting. The fact

Jacob Aall Ottesen

that he wrote this pamphlet and got it published shows how important the World's Fair was to all of America. The Red Wing papers reported regularly on the Minnesota exhibit at the fair and offered railroad tickets at a premium. Few people in the Upper Midwest could escape the excitement of the event, despite the economic hardships they were experiencing. Society news in all the major and minor papers marked who, when, how, and where the local mavens of society in the regions went to the fair.

Two of the most remarked-on exhibits in the Women's Pavilion were the statues of Cady Stanton and Susan B. Anthony. We have seen that the Synod pastors had followed these women with interest over the years, especially now as the debate about women's suffrage was at its most vociferous. An avid reader of American magazines and newspapers, Koren was well aware of what was going on in society, and, as he remarked in the sermon, a speech on women and women's rights at the National Association for Women Suffrage (NAWS) gathered in Washington had clearly bothered him.

Koren's Sermon

Koren began by remembering that it was Ascension Day when Christ's disciples had been promised the gift of the Holy Spirit. He went on to elaborate on the notion of "gift." While it was a good thing, he argued, we have come to the place where people no longer receive good things as gifts, but as "rights." So instead of gratitude for gifts from God, we hear demands, he lamented, thinking of the rising populist and labor movement:

> Demands of the poor, or demands for the poor. Demands of the workers, or for the workers. Demands of the women, or for the women. Many means are sought in order to assure that these demands will be fulfilled, among other things the overthrow of all those orders that keep those making these demands from receiving their right.[475]

In addition to the subtext on the political situation and the burgeoning of populism in the states around them, one also hears the conventional Lutheran language of the orders of creation—that after the Fall God created family and government with hierarchies to keep things going (i.e., that because Adam was first, he ruled over Eve, and she, after him, ruled the children)—Koren suggested that "those orders" were being overthrown, to the actual detriment of the society. As an orthodox Lutheran, much influenced by the fathers of the Missouri Synod, Koren found some comfort in the orders of creation theology, a traditional Lutheran way of understanding the orders of life and its hierarchies.

By the third paragraph he had set up the notion that he would go on to develop through the rest of the speech: the difference between God's gifts and our rights. Most of the demands of the law were from God, who could make demands on us, Koren argued, so we can make them on each other in God's name for the good of our common life. This sent Koren to the Upper Room and what followed in the Book of Acts after the outpouring of the Spirit. Although the early disciples chose to hold all things in common, it was not God's demand, Koren said—obviously referencing the specter of Marxism—but rather something the disciples decided to do and demanded of each other. Ever sensitive to the notion that because one is a Christian one is bound to follow a set of laws such as not drinking, dancing, playing cards, etc.—a use of the law strongly condemned by the Missouri Synod and the Norwegian Synod—Koren carefully laid out the difference between what God required and what we can require of each other in the Christian community.

Christians did have an example of how to treat the poor in Jesus' washing of the disciples' feet, when he showed us what true love was. We are to love the poor and see in them the face of Christ, Koren continued. He then proceeded to speak of those crying out on behalf of the workers in this country and the need to help the poor, which he did not oppose, even if he thought the relationship between owner and worker had changed since he had first arrived in the country forty years before. Koren did think it was an unfair accusation against the rich, but conceded that it was true that the poor may well have had much to bemoan. He then began to speak warmly of the United States, where the poorest could come and do well within a short time, so workers did deserve respect.

> I remember well, when I first came to this country, how it struck me as a young man that all honorable work no matter how lowly was honored here more than in any other place I knew, and I was deeply glad to see it. But that was forty years ago. Has there been a change for the worse, not only among the newcomers, but others?[476]

The question sounds plaintive from a man well into his seventh decade. Koren, while from the elite like his colleagues, admired the Norwegian peasant stock both in Norway and America for the strength and ability to work, even though legend has it that he exercised his upper class privilege over them. Whether he did or not, his aristocratic mien affected those around him. Hans Thorgrimsen, a Luther student from 1874-1879, reported in his memoir of the leaders of the Synod, that this characteristic seemed to be a cross for Koren, but it was who he was.[477] Koren's words, however, show his great admiration for the workers. What he is saying here, however, may reveal an old man's sense that things were better back when.[478]

He then returned to Scripture and the menial work of Paul as a tent-maker, and his co-workers Aquila and Priscilla, by Koren's reasoning, the first pastor's wife. In God's Word, he continued, we learn that hard work is honored and the difference between the lord and the servant is not observed as Jesus taught us when he washed the disciples' feet. So all work is valuable. Here he was not arguing for "the worker" but was beginning to justify the domestic labor of wives and submission that would have enraged Cady Stanton. While it is true that Christians are all to be submissive to Christ and to one another, this is a common move in this context: to use Scripture to reinforce his argument for the submission of women in the Bible. Stanton had given a bitter response to such talk as far back as the Seneca Falls meeting in July 1848.

> I think a man who, under such conditions, has the moral hardihood to take an education at the hands of women, and at such expense to her, should, as soon as he graduates, with all his honors thick upon him, take the first ship for Turkey, and there pass his days in earnest efforts to rouse the inmates of the harems to a true sense of degradation, and not, as is his custom, immediately enter our pulpits to tell us of his superiority to us, "weaker vessels"—prerogative to command, ours to obey, his duty to preach, ours to keep silence.[479]

Koren may well have known her argument, but his answer to it was of a piece with what Stanton reacted to. He acknowledged from Galatians 3:28 that in God's kingdom "there is neither Jew nor Greek, slave nor free, man or woman, for all are one in Christ." Quickly, as though he knew how he would be heard, he noted this did not mean to imply they were the same. Women like Martha, Mary, Priscilla, Dorcas, Lois, and Eunice were good examples of women glad to fulfill their duties as women. In God's kingdom, all were equal, no matter what their work even as this idea seemed to be using theology to approve of women doing menial work—or at least work they were required to do simply because they were women.

He then asked—and once again we can sense the specter of Karl Marx who had died ten years before—what difference it would make if the school were a place where there were no longer rich or poor, where everything was held in common or everyone owned the same, where there were no longer lord and servants, where no one has to command or to obey, and where men and women's work had become completely the same. Such an ideal, Koren said, was not possible. It would be heaven on earth, and, although desirable, sin had spoiled this possibility. All we could do was struggle against the consequences of sin by working for a better place for our neighbors. For that, Koren argued, all we have is love. It was love that built the Ladies' Seminary and love that had been the force behind the idea for it. "For my part," Koren said, "I am thankful for the work of those who have begun this work. It is a great thing we find here."[480]

Karl Marx

Koren once again seemed to have some version of Marxism on his mind and needed to dispute its claims. Is this just an aside because of what he has recently read in the press? It is clearly bothering him. Love is the right Christian answer to the question; it does help us fight sin and the consequences of sin, although his audience has not been making these arguments. They had, of course, heard in the outside world the arguments that he seems to be addressing most directly.

Koren went on to wonder about the kind of education the girls would receive at the school. "How is it that we will educate and raise our daughters here?" Clearly the goal was to produce ladies, since that was the name of the school. With that he began to wonder what the word "ladies" meant. He knew that it was a popular expression of the day, but what did it mean, what was its intention? Like the French word *"dame,"* Lady was preferred by some as being higher than "woman," and it goes well with the phrase, ladies and gentlemen, he agreed. While in itself, he continued, it was a noble word, it had changed to refer to distinctions between people. It seemed to suggest money enough for idleness, fine clothes, knowledge of party manners, and corresponding pretensions over those who did not have same standing.

> Is it this kind of person you are hoping to raise up from this school. If it is this kind of person, I hope that not many of you will work along with us for such a result. We have enough of that type of person.[481]

Here Koren derided the notion that women were decorative consumers. This was one of the ideas that Rousseau had about women and that

Ann Douglas in her book cited as an increasingly common problem for women of this class and status.

The church and world, he continued, rather needed women who feared God; who loved their domestic duties; and who, with an educated and developed spirit, could fulfill their place in life, decorated not with jewels, but with God's Spirit, as characterized by St. Peter said in 1 Peter 3:1-5.

> Likewise, wives, be subject to your own husbands, so that even if some do not obey the rod, they may be won without a word by the conduct of their wives, when they see your respectful and pure conduct. Do not let your adorning be external—the braiding of hair and the putting on of gold jewelry, or the clothing you wear—but let your adorning be the hidden person of the heart with the imperishable beauty of a gentle and quiet spirit, which in God's sight is very precious. For this is how the holy women who hoped in God used to adorn themselves, by submitting to their own husband, as Sarah obeyed Abraham, calling him lord.

For Koren, Scripture was clear: Woman's call was to be holy and submissive, celebrated for the conduct of her life. For him, and the writer of 1 Peter, submission was adornment. Such a woman, decorated with the Spirit, would instill respect and awareness in others; her behavior would calm the wild and raw natures of men.

> I hope that we can fill these rooms that are now being built with young women from our congregations whom we will welcome with joy from far and wide. The important thing in such an institution is to think forward twenty or thirty years from now when a great number of us will be gone from this earth. Where will these many hundreds of young women be, those whom we have raised up, how will their characters have developed, and how will they have strengthened the spiritual emphasis of our group?[482]

Koren asked, looking over the crowd of the older pioneers who were gradually fading away and on to the next generation standing in the wings ready to take over.

> A great many of them will be housewives and mothers. Can there be any greater work than to be a housewife? Think of the powers we put in the hands of women, from the young and the family who will receive their first impressions and im-

pulses for good or evil. This should never be forgotten. If they have been of the right kind, they will be able to stand against the worst temptations with more than the simple giving of rules. The truth is that in this life the men and women who in the church and civil life have left behind them the best memories are those who could point back to those who led them into the right ways. To teach and lead the next generation, to educate their senses and give them the right goals—where is there a higher work than that of the mother? And into whose hands is given more worthy powers?

Think of the effect of a mother reading Scripture to her son, how much fruit that will bear, rather than the woman who is tempted to elbow her way forward through strife and rank in the world in order to receive one of the positions into which so many women feel is their place before the little home.[483]

This was standard issue nineteenth century talk about the difference between men and women, the holy vocation of wife and mother, the reason for a school for girls only. One could not expect anything else from Koren.

Then he moved to the women who had not married, probably thinking of his two daughters, Henriette and Marie, who still lived at home, unmarried, with their single brother Paul. For that he had a solution: They could care for their aging parents! Think of the joy and comfort that would give them! What is better than such a daughter? He mentioned Florence Nightingale, something of a living saint at the time, who certainly must have been such a joy to her parents before she went out into the world. He did not know or at least admit to knowing how Nightingale had in fact clearly disobeyed and disappointed her parents by refusing to marry for many of the

Florence Nightingale

reasons Koren was holding up. She especially disapproved of the fact that marriage would deprive her of her civil rights, especially the right to inherit the substantial fortune of her family. Such a viewpoint would have offended Koren. For him, being a good daughter prepared one to be a good mother. It also helped her if she had to earn her own keep in the world.

Finally, there were women, he had to admit, who could not be mothers or good daughters able to stay in their parents' homes and serve them. Many women, he admitted, were independent and self-sufficient and open to careers in the world, careers from which they had been banned in the past. We can be glad that these careers are now open to women, though there are many who work to hurt women's positions in the world rather than praise them. He then told of a speech he had just read, given at the annual meeting of National American Women Suffrage Association that January and in other venues around the country, by Mrs. Ruth G. D. Havens. That he knew of it shows his awareness of the women's movement at the time. Haven's speech "gave a picture of the 'girl of the future.'"

> She could take her place in the professions, she would monopolize the lower callings, and fill the majority of the government's positions, she would be the manager of the department, bureau chief, a consul, she will be in the Civil Service commission, on the board of immigration, the Inaugurations committee, on the college faculties, she would become a Representative, senator, governor, and even President! What a man's position is to be in this picture we can't tell. We can smile at that, but it has to be taken seriously. There is in the spirit of the age a tendency to attack God's orders, and the relationship he has put between men and women. We see that within this understanding there is truth mixed in with a lie which makes it much more dangerous. For that reason it is needful that our young women have Christian guides with clear eyes for the truth who have the skills to separate gold from dross, or common sense, to teach others the same, and love enough to seek the best for the young.

> Pray that he, our heavenly ascended Savior, who himself is the way, the truth and the life, will pour out upon this school such teachers who will become blessings for our daughters to raise them up to a holy calling and life.[484]

Koren's speech displays his well-deserved reputation for polemics and also eloquence. He had seen what he regarded to be the dangers of the women's movement and made them clear as he worked to explain the need for such a school.[485] Did Elisabeth agree with him? He was describing her life quite well. At her funeral, C. K. Preus said clearly that she had no time for the women's movement and thought her home was her place. From my reading of the relationship, Koren would not often disagree with her, frequently calling her his closest colleague. His suggestion that unmarried daughters stay home and care for their parents describes his two

single daughters, Henriette and Marie, who were probably in the audience. Henriette as a teenager had been high strung and nervous, and there is little evidence that her personality changed much. Marie, twenty years younger, did have something of a public vocation. She studied music and hymnody with her father and knew enough about hymnody to support his hymnological efforts in the revision of the 1903 *Synodens Salmebog*. In an introduction to the *Koralbog* she defended the rhythmic chorale with the skill of a learned scholar, a skill she probably learned from her accomplished father.[486]

Mrs. Elisabeth Koren

For all his eloquence and polemical capacities, the speech is fairly conventional and entirely within the scope of the role of women he had known from his childhood. Using Jesus' example of service to justify keeping women doing their domestic chores happily was an argument that enraged many feminists. While Koren was especially considerate of his wife and not alien to housework, something he hinted at in his essay on the pastor's wife, his argument is typical.[487] Except for the notion that some women might have to work outside the home to support themselves, the idea that they could be executives of the official class as he knew it in Norway only caused him to smile.

Not surprisingly, as Koren was a biblicist on slavery, he was also one on women. If the Bible said women should be submissive and silent in church, despite some equally important verses on the other side, he followed the tradition and what the Bible said. One could hardly expect him to be a radical feminist. The changes that were occurring, which he well knew, obviously caused him some discomfort. However, he would be the last person to recommend a change in the conventional biblical understanding of what a woman's place was as helpmeet and companion, going back to Eve.

The festivities concluded with tours around the foundations of the new building, descriptions of its dimensions and rooms, and a banquet. Now the children of those pioneer pastors took charge of the project. There is no record of what they said to him in response except that the speech was praised in the church paper, *Evangelisk Luthersk Kirketidende*, as being the best argument for the school and why students should attend it.[488]

The First Months of School

The school opened its doors in November 1894, a hinge year for the leadership of the Synod. The second generation of the Synod had begun to assume leadership. While the old guard was still there, they were fading. Preus died on July 2, 1894, just before the school opened. Koren, vice president of the Synod, a vigorous sixty-eight years of age, took over as president after Preus' death and served effectively until his death in 1910. However, he was also giving way to the younger generation, to such persons as Professors Johannes T. Ylvisaker and Hans G. Stub. J. A. Ottesen's health prevented him from too much activity; he moved to Decorah in 1894, where he lived for ten more years. Nils Brandt had long since retired to live with his son, Pastor Realf Ottesen Brandt (1859-1927). Hans Andreas Stub, the elder, at the time of the cornerstone laying, was in Norway for a brief stint working for the Norwegian Innermission in Bergen.

Hans Gerhard Stub

He returned in 1894 with his son, Professor H. G. Stub, his wife Valborg and their son Ingolf. Larsen, the youngest in the original circle of leadership, was in his late middle age, but still fully occupied with Luther College.

The Mission of the School

Given the financial downturn of 1893, the worst since 1873, it took until 1894 before the building was completed. If the men who were leading the effort had not had the courage and strength to keep on, President Allen said later, nothing would have come of their beginning because things had looked very dark indeed. The building was ready for school to begin on November 5, 1894, slightly later than they had hoped, but finally it stood ready for students. The expenses of building the school had put the corporation into debt. It owed some $34,000, for which it issued bonds worth $25,000 and found friends in Red Wing to cover the rest.[489] It was not until 1903 that Allen reported to the church the final retirement of the debt. The assessed value of the school at that point was $80,000.

When the school opened, the first goal of its mission was to give the girls "a thorough and practical education on a Christian basis."[490] The

Red Wing Lutheran Ladies' Seminary, with Hans Allen's home

school's curriculum, originally intended to be two years, rather like a junior college, very much resembled the first two years of the liberal arts colleges for men in the area, especially Luther College. One difference was the inclusion of normal and business departments that made the education more practical. Unique to the Ladies' Seminary course of studies was the domestic economy department that had subjects all of the girls could take; all were required to do some kind of needlework.

Like Luther College, the ladies' seminary followed the motto, "A Sound Mind in a Sound Body." This second goal of the seminary meant the girls were expected, as they had been in Christiansfeld, to participate in exercise and activities both in the school and around it, given Red Wing's many opportunities for physical activities. Girls were encouraged to play basketball, lawn tennis, croquet, rowing on the Mississippi, hiking, and swimming during the fall and spring. During the winter, except for outdoor sports such as skating, tobogganing, and skiing on the hills around the seminary, most ac-

Hans Allen, president

tivities took place in a room above the dining room which the school had designated as a gym. For their course in Physical Culture and Hygiene, the students were required to find uniforms made of navy blue serge skirts, eight inches from the floor, attached to a sailor blouse. When the Music Hall was built later, it included space for a bowling alley.

Most important, however, was the third goal of the seminary's curriculum: To teach students to live their lives in a true Christian spirit. This was basic to the educational philosophy of the school, because, as its literature made clear, "Christian women will build Christian homes and these will wield a decided influence, which will be felt even to future generations."[491] Koren had stressed this as the goal of the school in his sermon. It was the essence of the entire program. This principle, assumed, with some concessions, that the future of women's vocation was to be confined to the home. The graduates could train to teach or work in commercial concerns, but only before marriage. If the woman did not marry, then she would be prepared to support herself.

To be admitted, students made direct application to the president. In their applications—which had to be in their own handwriting—they had to show they were willing and able to complete the course of studies upon which they embarked. They needed recommendations from both their pastor and their physician. In order to shape the character of its students, the school consciously worked to instill certain basic virtues. Like Christiansfeld, with its emphasis on punctuality and good stewardship of

Chapel at Red Wing Lutheran Ladies' Seminary, 1900

Front door to Red Wing Lutheran Ladies' Seminary main building

time—important habits that shaped a good character—the seminary ran on a strict schedule in which almost every part of life was rigidly organized, from morning bell to evening lights out. This made it possible for the school to make sure no student escaped its almost minute-by-minute oversight. After the last class of the day all students reported to the chapel again, where roll was taken and the students counted. This great care was to assure the safety—and chastity—of the girls.

A letter written home by a student gives us a clear sense of life at the school and its clear restrictions. Alma Engelbert, a student around 1905, gave a detailed description of their time.

> Dear Aunt Lena:
>
> As this is the only free after-noon I have (except Mondays) I thought I would write letters. Your wish certainly has come true when you wished I would be home-sick. I always kept bragging that I would not be home-sick, but I got it pretty bad. I have a pretty hard program. I take two piano lessons per week and have four practice periods per day (40 minutes each) and besides that I take sewing, cooking, needle-work, English, History of music (very hard), Harmony, German Bible, Luther lecture, analysis of music and painting. So have hardly any time for myself.

I have to get up at half past six every morning, then we have breakfast at seven (a bell rings five minutes before meal time and then we all have to assemble in the hall, when the five minutes are over we all go into the dining room and then the doors are locked and nobody is allowed to enter, many of the girls had to go hungry till the next meal) Then we have till 7:45 to clean our rooms and then the lessons begin.

I have a very nice room and there are three beds in my room, two singles and a double bed. I have first pick, and I took a single bed near two big windows, have a dresser, wash-stand and table for my use. I have three room-mates, one a German, Alma Bleckman, from Iowa, one a Swede, Frances Torwell, from South Dakota, and one a Norwegian, Cornelia Solberg, from North Dakota, so I have all the nationalities in my room, but they are all three very nice.

We have to study at seven, but have Saturday evenings and Monday eve free, then all the girls run around like wild (about 200 to 225 girls). The lights are turned out at ten. We have to go to church twice on Sundays and have chapel twice on all the other days, at 9:40 in the morning and 7:00 in the evening.

Sundays are the lonesomest [sic] days. It would be alright if we could go down town but we are only allowed to go down Monday afternoons. My arms and finger hurt just terrible after practicing all day.

Will have to close now. Will write to Alma soon, also to grandpa and grandma. Give them and uncle my love. Also love to you and Alma.

Alma

Ans. real soon.[492]

The meals were also a place where the students were closely watched. The lovely furnishing of the dining room may have fostered better behavior simply by its handsome appearance, with its handmade mahogany buffet and mirrors, reflecting the handmade china designed at the seminary and fired at the Red Wing pottery factory. Many commented on how lovely the dining room tables looked, set with fine white linen, china, silverware, and crystal. The rules on how to use one's silverware, not to

Red Wing Lutheran Ladies' Seminary dining room

speak with a mouthful, what subjects were appropriate to discuss at table were made clear to the students. The teachers ate with the girls, schooling them in the manners they may have lacked on coming to the school. However, enough of them came from fine homes, so they probably did

not need further instruction, but this was one of the duties of a finishing school. If the teachers at their table saw ill-mannered behavior, they would leave a note under the plate of the student who would find it at the next meal—"don't talk with your mouth full," etc. A matron was hired to look after the "bodily comfort, and needs of the pupils and guide them with a mother's love and watchful care."[493] The first matron was Ingerid Egge Markhus (1848-1918), who saw to it that the rules were followed and discipline maintained. While this would seem outrageous to students today, the deans of women at most colleges thought it was their calling to enforce such rules until the 1960s, when the rules broke down.[494]

Ingerid Egge Markhus

The Physical Plant

The main building was supplemented by a music building in 1906. Both were three stories high. The basement in the main building had good light and spacious rooms, making it an appropriate setting for the dining room. Between the two buildings there were "vestibules," which made it easy for the girls to move from one building to another without having to go outdoors. All of the rooms were large, with plenty of light, good ventilation, and many modern improvements. President Allen was proud of the steam heat that kept the entire building warm and comfortable. The heating system used gas, and the lights were powered by electricity generated by the school's own plant. There was room enough in the newly built school for 125 students to live in separate rooms. Occupancy could be increased to 250 and more by doubling up. Probably because of the economic downturn and the late opening, in the first year only eighty-six girls registered and completed the year.[495] Tuition was $160 a year, and enrollment continued to increase through the first ten years.

Without a doubt, there was more of Catherine Beecher's domestic feminism at the Ladies' Seminary than Cady Stanton's. While the school in some ways might have seemed a breakthrough for women, it did not teach anything revolutionary. It was designed to be a new place to teach the old courses and values that the girls had learned in the home schools and parlors of the past—a finishing school for the old ways. The school was what one scholar called a "factory of pastors' wives."[496] To that end, Allen determined that the school would have a "faculty of ministers," either clergy or pastors' sons or daughters, and most of them either graduates or the daughters of graduates of Luther College.[497] This was in line with the promises the school made to the parents and what they expected from it. As Reishus noted, the parents of the girls attending the seminary wanted a place that would be safe for the daughters and strongly Lutheran. It should also be noted that men could teach the girls, with some help from matrons and a few other women instructors, but the boys, except for Diderikke, were taught by men only.

Over the next few years, Allen attracted a stellar faculty to teach the girls.[498] Men such as Nils Ylvisaker Clausen came to be registrar and teacher of Latin and French. Like many other faculty, his background boasted a variety of well-known schools from the eastern United States to Europe. Theodore Graebner (1876-1950) taught German and English; Edward O. Kaasa (d. 1916) history and science.

Most significantly, Jacob Lauritz Hjort (1864-1939) taught vocal music, the most valued part of the education for the girls. He had grown up in the Paint Creek parlor of his parents, Christiane and Ove Hjort. He was a clear link with the parsonage parlor tradition now being passed on at the school. He had a colorful and wide-ranging career, but was well prepared for his work, not only from home, but from his travels around the world. He had studied with Arturo Mareschalchi (1869-1955) in Chicago, then with the well-regarded bass-baritone and first conductor of the Boston Symphony, and Georg Henschel (1850-1934), a good friend of Johannes Brahms. At the time Hjort studied with him, he was in London, where he received a certificate in 1902. Hjort left Red Wing about 1906 to teach in Minneapolis and then moved to Rider, North Dakota, where he farmed and served as a member of the North Dakota legislature. He brought a special kind of brilliance to the faculty and community in Red Wing. The Hjort Ladies Octette that he directed traveled extensively around the area for concerts and established the school as a worthy conservatory.

Jacob Lauritz Hjort

Hjort was followed in 1907 by Professor Bernard Frank Laukandt (1870-1958) as director of the Conservatory of Music. Laukandt brought with him distinguished musical credentials from his alma mater, the New York Conservatory, that helped to make the Red Wing Music Conservatory one of the best around. It fit the expectation of the pastors and their families and other parents who sent their daughters to the Ladies' Seminary.

The Curriculum

The main departments were Preparatory, Seminary, Classical, Normal, Domestic Economy, Business, Conservatory of Music, Art, and Elocution. Preparatory, which took two years of instruction, prepared the girls for further studies, something like a high school course with its introduction to religion, arithmetic, history, and English, plus some courses in domestic economy.[499] The course in domestic economy taught the young women the finer arts in homemaking: needlework of various kinds, dressmaking, and cooking, either plain or gourmet. The teacher was Marie Gellerup from Copenhagen, who was said to have worked as a cook in the Royal Palace there. She came with her daughter and served as housekeeper and teacher of cooking for many years. Gellerup's "motherly soul" and her regal bearing impressed the students despite her being rather deaf, a fact Allen's daughter described in some detail.

Marie Gellerup

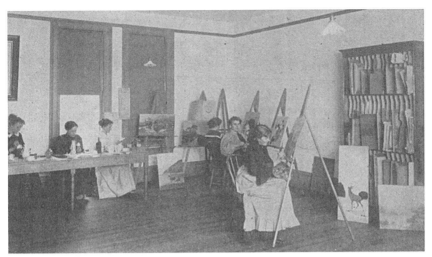

The Art Studio

Art was also considered to be important, as it had been in the parsonage home school. Here the girls learned to draw, paint, and do etchings on wood. One of their special interests was painting on china, a skill that made it possible for the school to have its own china fired at the Red Wing pottery factory. All students were expected to take something in the fine arts, especially painting. As the catalogue put it,

> A picture from the Artist's hand representing sublimity, grace and harmony, will teach beautiful and holy lessons both to the present and future generations. Art is the Child of Nature and by studying nature in its different aspects we cannot help but see the handiwork of God therein."[500]

On occasion the graduates would exhibit the results of their handiwork: shaded, white and Mountmellis cross stitch, Madeira embroidery, drawn work, Hardangerseam, Battenberg, Flemish and Point lace with basketry, Teneriff lace, among many other specialties the girls had learned to do in their domestic economy classes. By 1907 Mrs. Langemo reported, the Home Economics Department offered a course in the Bible, plus two other subjects in literature. A board member had noticed that many of the girls in the department would probably marry ministers and that it might be "profitable for them to 'take up' some literary subjects too, so they can rise up to their appropriate station (*Saa de kan komme op til sin stand*)." This showed how important the refinement of the upper class was to the school, as it sought to educate a potential pastor's wife for her vocation.[501]

The Seminary and Classical Departments were the center of the curriculum. The Seminary Department involved instruction in Bible, English, geometry, history, civics, and physics. The Classical Department taught languages: Norwegian, French, Spanish, German, Latin, and even Greek, although the call for Greek was minimal. This was revolutionary. Latin could now become a woman's discipline, and many women did become Latin teachers after the turn of the century. The Normal Department prepared girls to be teachers, offering teaching methods along with other subjects in preparation for a teaching career. In the Business Department, girls took the expected courses in typing, shorthand, and bookkeeping, preparing to become secretaries before marriage. Elocution, what we would know as speech, involved the memorizing of great literature as well as performing declamations and speeches for festive occasions. "Of all the fine arts, Elocution can best be applied to our daily lives. What accomplishment is as great as that of being able to express one's ideas fluently, with grace and beauty of speech."[502] All of the festival events of the Ladies' Seminary included orations and declamations of great literature and famous speeches from the past—ancient, from Cicero, or Nordic classics, and recent, usually great American speeches such as the Gettysburg Address.

It was the Conservatory of Music that especially distinguished the school, not surprising given the paramount place of music in the parsonage. In 1905 the name of the school was changed to Lutheran Ladies' Seminary and Conservatory of Music. The conservatory included three

The Music Room

departments: piano, pipe organ, and vocal culture. Completing the course took five years. It involved being proficient on one instrument beside piano, the most important instrument, and in music history, composition, and theory. In organ there were three divisions: one preparatory, one for certification as a teacher, and one a graduate course. The vocal culture department taught singing, so that when the girls married pastors they would be able to lead the singing in the congregation and the choir. It also had various levels that progressed toward graduate studies. Every student was required to sing in the school chorus and devote herself to the

Axel Skovgaard

groups' two concerts a year. If a girl majored in the Conservatory of Music, she was required to give a solo recital once a year. Residents of Red Wing were pleased to take advantage of these recitals, and often did, swelling the audiences during the year. In addition it attracted world famous artists such as the Danish violinist virtuoso, Axel Skovgaard (b. 1875), known as the Danish Ole Bull. His playing, enhanced by his Stradivarius violin, made him a popular draw for the Lyceum concert series throughout the Upper Midwest. For such concerts and attractions trains were chartered for Twin Citians to attend the performances.

While these various departments at Red Wing were more extensive than the courses at Christiansfeld or Nissen's School, the core of both of them were present. Christianity first, and then modern languages, literature, history, the arts, and music, plus the domestic arts, were central at both schools. Two things were different: the Normal and Business Departments, something of a concession to the needs of students to find a job in teaching or the business world. Red Wing Lutheran Ladies' Seminary had the added benefit of being a residential school where students, living together in a small community, could, as at Christiansfeld, learn together as they lived together. It was an elegant place to grow up.

Assuring the Morality of the Girls

The school had to reassure parents that their daughters would be safe during their time on campus. It was something all its literature promised, and the school was bound to keep that promise. As at Christiansfeld, there were some unruly girls whose parents sent them there to reform them. Walsh suggests this was more prevalent than we might think, but it stands to reason that parents, desperate to keep their daughters safe from their own worst impulses, might turn to the school. Girls in Norway had whispered that Christiansfeld was a last resort for parents wanting a well-mannered, gracious daughter, and a similar assumption circulated about Red Wing. Parents did send daughters there to reform their behavior, without always good results. The rules for deportment were strict and assured that the girls were rarely alone or on their own.

To assure the good behavior and safety of the girls, the following rules were enforced.

1) Rooms must be orderly by 7:45 every morning. Sweepings from the floors must be deposited in the baskets provided for that purpose. Nothing whatever must be thrown out the windows.

2) No visiting, talking, laughing, playing or loitering in the halls will be allowed during the hours set apart for study and recitations, that is from 7:45 to 12:05 and from 2:15 to 4:55 and from 7:00 to 9:30.

3) Pupils are absolutely forbidden to study during free hours: that is from 12:05 to 2:15 and from 4:55 to 7:00. Students are earnestly requested and expected to be outdoors during the hours above mentioned whenever the weather will permit.

4) Pupils are permitted to visit each other and to come together to sing and play during all hours not set aside for study.

5) Window shades must be drawn after lights are turned on.

6) When the first signal is given at 9:45, students must prepare for retiring at once, and after 10:00 p.m., when the lights are turned out, all must be in bed and quiet.

7) When ill, all pupils must obtain from the Nurse excuses for absences from classes, lessons, chapel exercises and church. All other permissions and excuses must be obtained from the Preceptress.

8) Pupils are allowed to go to the city once a week. This includes all shopping and visiting. Permission must be obtained from the Preceptress in every case.

9) Visits to the city must be made Mondays from 1:00-4:00 p.m., other days from 12:30-2:15 p.m. PUPILS ARE NOT ALLOWED OFF THE CAMPUS WITHOUT PROPER ESCORT.

10) Pupils are not allowed to use the telephone, except by special permission, and only in the presence of the President, Preceptress, or Assistant Preceptress.

11) Pupils must not make any changes in their programs unless permitted to do so by the President of the school.

12) All pupils must wait on the tables. All pupils except seniors must take their turn waiting on the tables. Seniors in attendance one year only must act as waiters one semester.

13) Every pupil must pay for damage done by her to building, furniture, reference books, books drawn from the library, etc.

14) Trunks must not be taken to the rooms nor into the corridors, but must be unpacked and stored in the trunk room.

15) WALLS MUST NOT BE DEFACED BY PASTING ON PICTURES OR PAPERS, OR BY DRIVING NAILS OR PINS INTO THEM.

16) Leaning out of and talking from windows is a sign of ill-breeding.

17) PUPILS MUST APPEAR PROMPTLY FOR MEALS. Dishes must not be taken from dining hall to the rooms.

18) Under no circumstances will pupils be allowed to carry victuals to their rooms except in case of sickness, when permission must be obtained from the Nurse.

19) Pupils are not allowed to read dime novels and other pernicious literature and are advised to consult the teachers in regard to reading matter.

20) Wardrobes, beds, chairs or tables must not be removed from the rooms except by special permission.

The rules having to do with housekeeping are reasonable and typically Scandinavian in their emphasis on cleanliness. However, the strict scheduling and restrictions on dime novels, leaning out of the windows, or

Panoramic view of the Red Wing area from the water tower of the school

using the telephone without permission clearly have one thing in mind: to keep students from destructive behaviors the parents had sent them to the school to avoid. Unmentioned in the list of rules, but anyone can see it writ large in them, is the need to keep the girls from getting pregnant out of wedlock—a tragedy that, almost without question, ruined a young girl's future. At the time the young man who seduced the girl would probably do the honorable thing and marry her, but that meant the end of her education and in many cases not the best marriage partner. This often caused the woman a life of bitterness at what she had lost. Although the school—or even the most vigilant parents—could not totally prevent a young woman's wild behavior, at least it could try. This was a major reason for the strictness of rules.

Procession to church

The regimen helped create not only orderly minds, but well-disciplined young women. At least that was the hope of the school's leaders, as it was at Christiansfeld. The attractions of Red Wing, with its side-wheel boats and trains, seen from Seminary Hill, were self-evident to the students who enjoyed traipsing in the woods around the school. However, their off-campus excursions were strictly supervised. Even the walk to Trinity Church in downtown Red Wing involved something of an enforced parade. The girls marched two by two or three by three down the hill to the church, a procession which caused the heart of many a young man in Red Wing, some of them Hauge Synod seminary students, to skip a few beats.

The picture of the girls in procession provides a view of what these rules meant in actual life. As Martha Reishus Langemo wrote, almost as if to show they had fun despite the rules:

> A merrier group than those getting ready for church is hard to imagine. It is indeed true that the girls "came and went" in a body with a chaperone fore and aft, but that did not prevent them from having a jolly good time. This was not the only time the girls were allowed "out"—they were permitted to go down town once per week. Naturally there was shopping to be done. Lovely stores beckoned them, Grondahl Brothers, Hulberg, the Jeweler, The Red Wing Bakery that always smelled so good.[503]

Today's young women might find it strange, but curiously attractive, this picture of a procession of women in long dresses and wide hats bustling off to church from the school with teachers surrounding them to make sure they did not stray.

The values and courses of the school had connections with the parsonage school in the kitchen or in the parlor. In addition, it did have some practical lines, combining the course of studies that Karine Neuberg had taken at the Page School in Decorah, with the requirement of the fine arts. The elegance of the place, its rules and course of study for the girls prepared many a young woman to be a polished pastor's wife anywhere in the country. Remnants of the effect of such training continued not so long ago in some small towns in the Midwest, where a pastor's wife saw to that the children of the town received piano lessons and learned to sing sacred music of high culture in their choirs, both in the congregation and public schools.

Dedication

The school's first graduation ceremony, on June 6, 1895, was also the occasion of the dedication of the new building and the school. The service afforded townspeople, Norwegian Synod pastors and their families, the parents of the students, and other curious onlookers a chance to see what the founders had wrought. Everyone had said that the location of the building was the most beautiful site that could be imagined: the green lawns sweeping across the campus down to the natural amphitheater, the lovely view of the river, and the woods across on the Wisconsin side. On the day of graduation, the press of women in large hats and elegant summer dresses accompanying men in their best suits, added sartorial elegance to the scene. The day was a typical June day in Minnesota, sunny and warm. The ceremonies were delayed an hour as people were slow in arriving, so the crowd, serenaded by the Red Wing Band, enjoyed visiting with each other while waiting for things to start. The dedication service took place in the amphitheater on the grounds because the weather was so fine. Despite the success of this festival event, the *Evangelisk Luthersk Kirketidende* in its report regretted there had not been as many there as one could have wished.[504]

Pastor Bjørgo began the meeting with a prayer of heartfelt thanks that they had finally finished the building with the gracious help of God. Three other men spoke. Vice president of the Eastern District of the Synod, LaCrosse Pastor Andreas Kittelsen Sagen (1851-1907), gave a quickly prepared speech in English on the kind of women the school was expected to prepare—ladies who understood their place as the guardians in the home, just the kind the church and society needed, exactly as the mission statement had said.

My young friends who frequent this institution of learning, your school is called a ladies' seminary; we want you all to be ladies in the true sense of the word; for a true lady is nothing but a true woman, a woman who can make a home. And the woman who can do that will be the crown and the glory and the sunshine of mankind; she will be the blessing for which men willingly will shed their heart-blood. Such a woman will be the sun from which good morals, lofty sentiments, purity and happiness are eradiated.[505]

Andreas K. Sagen

This sounds like Rousseau on the need for a woman to get an education to complement her husband, or the common Victorian assumptions about the nineteenth century woman as decorative with an education that made them fit for homemaking.

The major address, a sermon, was given by Dr. Johannes Thorbjørnson Ylvisaker (1845-1917), a professor of New Testament at Luther Seminary, who had just concluded a term as editor of the *Evangelisk Luthersk Kirkestidende* (1889-1893). His editorial comments over time on various news notes from the wider church on the rights of women had been sharp and trenchant, and not at all friendly to women's emancipation. His sermon shows him to be a skilled rhetorician and a learned man of the Word. His text is from Matthew 5:13-14, the passage in the Sermon on the Mount in which Jesus calls his disciples the salt of the earth and the light of the world. After some brief exegesis of the text, he began the body of his speech (published in its entirety in English the next day in the *Red Wing Republican*) noting that they lived in troubled times, as unrest and conflict were unsettling both the church and the civil world. He had good reason to feel that.

The Pullman Strike had, by this time, created much strife especially in the Midwest, and the economy had not yet recovered from the Panic of '93. Populists were still making headway in the Upper Midwest and West, fomenting rebellion. The Republican members of the House of Representatives, whose party had been founded to fight slavery and polygamy, had submitted what would become the Nineteenth Amendment to the Constitution, allowing women to vote every year since 1878, but it had been voted down by the Democrats every year thereafter. That Republicans were on the side of women's suffrage made Ylvisaker and others, who were staunch conservatives, somewhat reluctant to oppose women's rights, but the issue was not political for them, it was biblical: The Bible said women were to submit. Ylvisaker had been observing closely the speeches and writing of Cady Stanton and her colleague Susan B. Anthony. He also knew about the situation in Norway where Bjørnstjerne Bjørnson and his ilk increasingly maligned the church for its thinking about the place and role of women, divorce, and other feminist causes that seemed to them to strike at the Bible and the heart of Christianity.

Many of the leaders in the fight on the woman question in Norway were personal acquaintances of these pastors and professors. H. G. Stub's brother in-law was Hagbard Emmanuel Berner (1839-1920), the founder of *Dagbladet*, Norway's liberal newspaper. It consistently supported the most progressive causes. Berner, who would become mayor of Oslo, was a feminist, although not quite for the vote yet, as was his wife Selma Hovind (1846-1919). Valborg's sister, she was the first woman to wear bloomers in Norway. Ylvisaker had been with Stub in Leipzig on sabbatical when Stub had met Valborg Hovind and fallen in love her. He had also marked the suffering Stub

Hagbard Berner

experienced because of Valborg's deteriorating health and mental condition during their seventeen years of marriage. At this time, she was growing more and more ill and needed more medical expertise than she could receive in Minnesota. She would leave the next summer for Scandinavia to get better medical help on the advice of Dr. Hoegh, one of the more highly regarded doctors among the immigrants.

Ylvisaker's Sermon

Ylvisaker, a sophisticated and learned man, with a good sense for the spirit of the age, began with the statement that the question of women's place in society, both in church and state, had created much disagreement and conflict. He began, indeed, at the very beginning: A woman was the first to listen to the voice of the serpent in Paradise! He made an interesting argument out of that, however strange it sounds for the beginning of a speech to dedicate a ladies' seminary. Because of the Fall, all women had suffered terribly. He listed the terrors of a woman's life in heathen religions caused by Eve's rebellion without the mediating influence of

Christianity, which had been much better for women than any other religion. He even appeared to defend, or at least understand, a woman who killed her daughter in a heathen land because she wanted to spare her the sorrow of a woman's life. While these things were terrible and a result of the Fall, in Christian nations the fate of a woman was much better.

Now, however, as the society's leaders were abandoning the faith, they were missing the "middle way" of Christianity, in which women would sometime come to suffer from the mistreatment of men, but in a different way. Only Christianity guaranteed a woman her full personhood, if he could use such a word. Only at this school, which would be thoroughly Christian, could a woman, through God's Word and her own flesh and spiritual nature, mature into a pious woman. Only in Christianity were men and women more alike than different as indicated by the Apostle Paul in Galatians 3:28. In Christianity a woman, like a man, was a joint heir with Christ of God's riches. Both were equal in their humanity.

Dr. Johannes Thorbjørnson Ylvisaker

This begins to sound rather contemporary. It is when he gets to the relationship of the sexes, however, that he brings up the notion of man being over woman, the weaker sex. "In relationship to the man she is not made to rule, but to be submissive. He is her head, as Christ is the head of the congregation." Therefore man should be head both in the church and state, in the pulpit, in the judge's bench, in the legislature, and in war. Woman has been given a finer, but no less important, work, which fits her entire being. She is also to rule, but her sphere is within the home where her authority is rightly exercised. It is here that she achieves her nobility and honor. The Lord has given her this realm which will bring rich blessings to both church and state. Once again, like Koren, this is classic nineteenth century thought about the woman at home ruling the hearth and the man ruling in the public sphere. This is what the school had been teaching and would continue to teach until its demise.

After this exegesis Ylvisaker began to rhapsodize on the home, a typical meme at the time, and perhaps made more poignant by the fact that most of his generation sitting there had left their mothers in far-off Norway and would never see them again.

Women are like plants that flourish in their own greenhouse and give off lovely scents and colors, but when they are moved out of their place, they wilt and die. Only women can keep the home alive and good. She does this as a servant girl, a pious daughter, as a teacher for the young and even more as a god fearing housewife and mother whose work can never be overestimated.[506]

For Ylvisaker, and most everyone there, the home was something only a woman could create. "In this light and friendly kingdom on earth women will be both queen and priest, there she will stoke the holy flame at the home altar, there she will, as a daughter, be her parents' and sibling's help and joy, as a wife her husband's helpmeet, and as mother her children's closest parent."[507] From there he continued with comments from great men like John Adams and Abraham Lincoln on the importance of a pious mother. He continued in this line for some more paragraphs and then applied it to the school. "We expect that this school will bring the light of understanding to women's high and glorious calling and help those who come here to live out their callings."[508] It would be bad reasoning, he said, as if hearing the argument against him, to think that a mother did not need an education. This is not so, for those who expected a daughter or wife to be more than a servant would be gladdened to see what comes from this place. If, however, she must work, outside the home, we hope her education here can help and not bring harm. "We wish as little to create emancipated women as effeminate men. We already have more than enough of both kinds!"[509] This was another reason to keep men and women apart. Real men could only be created by the rigor of a classical education. Co-education would mark the end of puberty rites that made real men, they thought.

For Ylvisaker, who feared the brutality of paganism for women far off in a pagan country, Christianity was the best religion for women everywhere.

Many recalled this dedication speech with fondness. Lydia Bredesen Sundby, who graduated in 1902 and became a leader in the Women's Missionary Federation (WMF) of the Evangelical Lutheran Church, quoted approvingly what she considered to be his most important passage:

It is true that Christianity alone gives the true conception of the true place of man and woman in society, and it alone can elevate her to that place where she can fully enjoy the happiness God has intended for her, when she can both bless and be blessed. Christianity has been compared to a friendly angel that has opened the prison doors and now invited her to come out and enjoy the sunshine of the truth and inhale the strengthening atmosphere of freedom.[510]

Ylvisaker summed up his address with references back to the biblical text, hoping that the women they sent out from the school would be salt and light to the world. These women would have a character that was their own, not like a man's, "if this school is to be a blessing for this church and our people."[511]

Finally, he concluded, we hope that the students who apply here are not coming for "fun," but to be educated for their important calls in life. He then wished that

both the teachers and the students each time the lights are lit will shine in the darkness so that they will be reminded of their own calls to be salt and light, and that they shall be like a city on a hill in a more spiritual understanding than earthly."

And with that he concluded, announcing the school to be an evangelical Lutheran education institution for young women, a Lutheran Ladies' Seminary, in the name of the Father, Son and Holy Spirit![512]

The speech shows Ylvisaker, who sent his all daughters to the school, at his best— biblically literate, culturally aware, socially conservative and eloquent, aware of, but far from, the thinking of feminists like Cady Stanton.[513] Although the young women graduates would be capable of taking professional jobs in the society of the time, there was something about such jobs that was a bit beneath them. They had a higher calling, they were told, and that was being a wife and mother. Suffragettes heard in this kind of talk biblical warrants for keeping them in the home, doing what they considered to be menial tasks.

The question of the worth of a woman's education had persisted ever since women began receiving almost the same education as men. Linka had wondered in her diary, as she began keeping house in Wisconsin, why she needed an education to do these chores. She did not wonder about her education when it came to teaching her children or otherwise leading the family or small groups in devotions. An argument can be made that Ylvisaker and his colleagues in essence were teaching the old custom of *noblesse oblige* to their students and community. For women there was always the complication of service meaning, among other tasks, menial labor, rather than service consistent with their station in life as ladies.

After the sermon and the rite of dedication at which Vilhelm Koren officiated, the group sang a hymn, followed by a speech in German by Pastor Pfotenhauer of the Missouri Synod with essentially the same message as Ylvisaker's. Then the pastor at the Missouri Synod congregation in Red Wing, Pastor Ernst John Franz Haertel, who had already been teaching German and religion at the school, gave the benediction.

The *Red Wing Republican* reported that, after the service of dedication, the crowd moved about, visiting, enjoying the prospects of the new school, and admiring what had been done.

> The crowd wandered about the grounds and the handsome building, enjoying the unrivaled scenes and inspecting the magnificent quarters of the school. Those who had never visited the place before naturally could scarce find words strong enough to express their pleasure at what they saw, while even to the others, the place presented new attractions that seemed more charming than ever.[514]

With that they repaired to the dining room for a lovely repast. The juniors had prepared a festive banquet for the seniors and the dining room was draped with festive buntings the colors of the class: orange, blue and lemon. It had been decorated to the nines, the paper said, with "flowers, greens and flags . . . a veritable beauty bower."[515]

After the dinner, commencement exercises were held. Several pastors made remarks, students displayed their newly acquired skills, either musical or literary. Marie Nordby, daughter of Rosina "Sina" Preus Nordby, gave a reading in Norwegian, *"Haakon Jarls Død" (Haakon Earl's Death)* by Oehlenschläger, others sang solos or played the piano, duets, or eight hands. Schubert's "Military March" was the selection chosen by the students who played for the celebration.

Valborg Stub sang a solo. Her sweet voice and manner "completely captivated all present," so she was prevailed upon to give an encore.[516] What she was thinking, we do not know, but we do know that she was not well. She did, however, enjoy such events and gladly performed at them. When Stub wrote about her to Larsen, in 1883, to tell him he was getting engaged, he remarked that not only was she very gifted, she was, contrary to many artists of her time, a devout Christian. In her writings, her warmth comes through, but she was becoming more and more ill and erratic in her letters to friends. She did not care for Minneapolis, especially Robbinsdale, which was some distance from the city and her studio. She may have expected the New World to be bigger than Minneapolis and more welcoming.

Valborg remained close friends with the novelist Drude Krogh Janson, Kristofer Janson's former wife, and Oline Muus. Mrs. Stub had

probably heard quite a bit on the subject of divorce and women's rights from them. Both she and her husband had seen up close what the women's movement looked like in Norway from their many travels, especially its strong rejection of both the Bible and the church. In the high echelons of society they inhabited when they were living in Christiania, the Stubs hobnobbed with people who knew Ibsen and Bjørnson. She even had sung several solos accompanied by Edvard Grieg. The Stubs both knew how anti-church the women's movement

Valborg Hovind Stub

at home had become, and he, at least, understood that without Christ it would wreak damage on their entire culture to say nothing of their lives.

Mrs. Stub had a fairly significant public career. Not only did she perform at such events, but she had a studio in downtown Minneapolis where she taught piano and vocal culture to many young people, and her recitals were followed with interest. She taught the young men at the seminary how to chant—*å messe*—and was so popular that the students protested loudly when the board recommended that she not be rehired for the job.[517] She had just finished editing a collection of Nordic lieder, *Songs from the North* (1895), featuring the best of these songs in an English translation by her friend from Madison, Aubert Forestier. Hardly any piano bench among Norwegian-Americans could be without it. Her devotion to her career was supported by Stub, when she left him and son Ingolf for a semester to study with Madame Marchesi in Paris in 1889, a common destination for ambitious young women singers at the time. Stub seemed to be fully supportive of her efforts, helping her by writing famous composers and poets in Scandinavia and requesting on her behalf permission to print their works in her book. However, about this time he also suffered a nervous condition, almost as though he caught her problems. On their last trip to Norway in 1894, from which they had just returned, he lost his voice and could not speak for nearly six months.[518]

Stub also made some remarks at the commencement ceremony in Norwegian. He was now professor of Old Testament at Luther Seminary and capable of eloquence in English, German, or Norwegian. His remarks met with hearty applause during and after the speech. The gist of his remarks was on the "uplifting power of education" and the responsibility of women to uplift "the level of their sex, and in that way elevate the moral and social level of the world."[519] This is not quite the same rhetoric as that which celebrated a woman's place in the home. Rather it celebrates her higher moral example. This is the same argument in a different voice and from a slightly different position. While Stub was not a feminist in our sense, he lived in a situation in which his wife expected that she be seen as more than just a homemaker and mother of his children. He seemed to have been devoted to her and the right of a woman to have a career outside her home.

Mrs. Stub

About this time *The North*, a Twin Cities' newspaper in English for Scandinavians, had solicited his opinion on the right of a married woman to have a career as a teacher outside the home, given her previous training and the blessings it could be to the marriage. The Minneapolis Board of Education had passed a resolution which read, "The employment of a married woman as teacher may be allowed in special cases. Marriage by a teacher during the term of her employment shall be reason for the cancellation of employment."[520] The resolution sparked a local controversy. Noteworthies, including the University of Minnesota president, Cyrus Northrup, were asked to comment on the ruling. Stub had written, "In my opinion, it would be a blessing to many

Cyrus Northrup

schools and communities to have married women as teachers instead of young unmarried women, yea, even girls."[521] For Stub it was unjust to keep fully qualified married women from teaching in the public schools. They would bring their added maturity to the education of students, more than the young girls who usually taught for a brief time before marriage. Most agreed with Stub.

After another solo by Mrs. Stub and another encore, President Allen gave a brief history of the school and his estimate of its bright future. The program concluded with the women's chorus singing J. L. Frank's "Blue Are the Heavens." Eight students then received their diplomas. A unique part of the ceremony, one that became traditional, involved the giving of a peace pipe from the Indian tribe in the area to recognize that the school was built near a traditional Indian burial grounds. This was given each year to the next class by the graduating class.

Accreditation

The Ladies' Seminary flourished for the next twenty-five years, mostly because of the dedication and hard work of President Hans Allen. From the school came many a genteel pastor's wife whose cultivated habits helped her husband's ministry wherever they went. The building and the beauty of its location and ambiance clearly attracted many to its doors. On October 14, 1908, the traditional founding day of Luther College, the school dedicated a new music building also designed by Architect Gauger. With an auditorium that could seat 332 and a balcony that could hold another 150, the school could schedule concerts of famous traveling musicians that the community would attend. The auditorium featured two grand pianos, a Kilgen pipe organ on the stage, and six beautiful stained glass windows which made the room an elegant venue for concerts and events of many kinds.

The Music Auditorium, Concert Hall

Now the school buildings, both beautiful structures with unrivaled opportunities for views of the river and the woodlands across it in Wisconsin, afforded the girls an elegant location during their schooling, a site as scenic as Luther College in Decorah. As Nellie Allen, daughter of President Hans Allen, wrote in a brief memoir,

> Summer or winter, we enjoyed the view of the river, the woods and the hills. In those days there was a great deal of activity on the river with the big side-wheelers making regular runs. At night their big searchlights lit up the front of our home and cast huge shadows of the men on deck. It was an interesting era.[522]

After the school was built, the Synod pastors' conference was held there yearly. It was more centrally located and easier to get to than Decorah, because of its location on the river, and it was every bit as fine a site as Luther College —maybe even better, with its dramatic views and upscale buildings.

The Conservatory of Music began in 1907, led by Dr. Bernard F. Laukandt, a pastor in the Missouri Synod and a well-regarded musician. His work, however, involved much more than teaching music. In addition to counterpoint, composition, orchestration, harmony, piano, and organ, he taught French, German, and English Bible. Music, however, was his first interest. He defended it in a pamphlet he wrote to explain the necessity of music in a good education, maintaining that music needed to be cultivated because it of "its refining influence on the mind." He did have another mission at the school:

B. F. Laukandt, Mus. Dr.

Director of the Conservatory of Music, Lutheran Ladies' Seminary, a College for Girls

Degree received from the Grand Conservatory of New York. He has held his present position for the past ten years as

TEACHER

and

PIANIST

During the year Prof. Laukandt will be available for a limited number of concerts.

For further particulars and engagements write

to encourage German Lutheran girls to attend the school. This helped to increase the enrollment. He also believed strongly in teaching the Lutheran faith: "The main purpose of the founding of the Seminary was also to build and maintain a school where Lutheran parents could entrust their daughters."[523] Laukandt became a leading force in attracting German Lutheran girls. By the time World War I began, over thirty percent of the students were German. Instruction could be in English, German, or Norwegian, depending on the students and subject.

While it had originally begun as a Ladies' Seminary, the requirements of the America educational system soon came to bear on how the school shaped its curriculum and faculty. In 1911, after considerable examination, the school received a notice of accreditation from Albert Rankin of the University of Minnesota: "Your school has been placed upon the accredited list of schools in the state for entrance in the departments of Science, Literature and the arts."[524] This meant that graduates of the school would receive credit for their work at the university as if it were a junior college, if they went to the university to study in the named departments. When President Allen announced it to the student body and faculty in January 1912, he declared a day of celebration, and the president of the university was invited to a festive convocation and dinner. Later Allen reflected on what the school had achieved

> We believe that a judicious and liberal education should imbue all students with a truly Christian spirit, and not merely the acquiring of knowledge, or accomplishments, which are to be used for the purpose of display. The education that our Seminary inculcates goes down to the depths of being, and seeks to lay the foundation right.[525]

Three months after the accreditation was announced, Minnesota Governor Adolph Olson Eberhart (1870-1944) came to Red Wing for the purpose of congratulating the school on its success. At a festive banquet the students, board, and faculty took pride in their accomplishments and their growing reputation in the region.

The Ending of the Ladies' Seminary

The story of the Lutheran Ladies' Seminary at Red Wing begins to unravel, unfortunately, while the world was in the throes of World War I—even before the United States declared war. Several forces had aligned to create something of a perfect storm. Prejudice against the Germans as the European war grew more and more intense and the United States appeared to be more and more on the side of the British against the Germans. The sinking of the *Lusitania* on May 7, 1915, turned American opinion against the Germans. Things became increasingly difficult for German-Americans as the war seemed inevitable. When war broke out, the feelings against Germans became fierce. Walsh says these sentiments had caused President Allen's resignation in 1916, that he had grown discouraged by the growing resentment of German involvement at the school, and that he resigned in exhaustion after twenty-three years as president. He had been the mainstay of the school for over two decades. Raising money and keeping the enrollment up and growing was hard work. His ability to raise money and increase enrollment had been fundamental to the survival and prospering of the school.

After America entered the war, in the summer of 1917, the enrollment declined by thirty percent. Almost all of those leaving were Germans. Dr Laukandt resigned and left to be president of the Bethany Ladies' College in Mankato, a school run for the "Marthas and Marys" of the Missouri and Wisconsin Synodical Conferences. (It was purchased by the Little Norwegian Synod and became Bethany Lutheran College in the 1930s.) With his resignation, the school no longer had to fight against the anti-German sentiment among the Norwegians, but the loss affected the bottom line of the school.

Allen's replacement, Ditlef H. Ristad (1863-1938), a capable and learned man, agreed fully with the mission of the school. Ristad had taught German, history, and Christian doctrine at Albion Academy. He was president of Park Region College in Fergus Falls, Minnesota, when he left to become president of Red Wing Lutheran Ladies' Seminary. In a letter printed in the Synod's paper not long after he assumed the office, he offered the reasons for a girl to get an education at the Ladies' Seminary. He knew that some graduates would need to earn their own livings as teachers, now that the prosperous (*vel staaende*) farmers did

Ditlef H. Ristad not want their daughters to become servants in other people's homes and would be glad if they could work as stenographers or clerks in stores.

That was not the main mission of the seminary, however. Most important to Ristad was that the girls receive an education for its own sake, "and for the vocation God has called them to in our homes." For Ristad, the girls needed to be prepared for both the work of their hands and the work of their spirits in the home (*Haand og Aand arbeid*). The mission of the Red Wing Ladies' Seminary was to find a way to teach both spiritual development and that of the hands "so they could be one."[526] The recognition by Ristad that women might need to work outside the home was consistent with Koren's from some twenty years earlier, but the prospect seemed a bit more likely now. Still he maintained with all the others that the main goal of the school was to prepare wives and mothers who could raise up a new and faithful generation.

Ristad, though a highly respected intellectual who cared about the curriculum at the school and worked to make the requirements and the courses more rigorous, had no stomach for the practical and administrative work it took to keep such a school running. He assumed it would sell itself. About this he was wrong. The school's enrollment and support plummeted. His failure to recruit new students with much vigor began to tell. He resigned in 1919, two years after the merger of 1917 that created the Norwegian Lutheran Church in America. Ristad's age was a factor in his retirement, but so was a growing and debilitating debt of $40,000, exactly what it had cost to build the first building twenty-five years earlier. He was replaced by Thoralf Anderson Hoff (1879-1947), an up and coming pastor in the new church, serving Trinity Lutheran Church in Red Wing. Hoff had just returned from the war in France where he had served as a chaplain.

The New Church—The NLCA (ELC)

Perhaps the most complicated reason for the decline was the much-heralded merger of most of the Norwegian-American Lutheran synods on June 9-10 of 1917. It created the Norwegian Lutheran Church in America (NLCA), which later became the Evangelical Lutheran Church (ELC), presided over by Hans G. Stub, scion of the Norwegian Synod. The merger agreement dissolved the three seminaries of the older synods—the Hauge Synod seminary in Red Wing, United Seminary in Como Park, and Luther Seminary in the Hamline neighborhood some miles east of the United campus—into one named Luther Seminary to be located on the United Seminary site on Como Avenue. Luther College and St. Olaf College were designated as the colleges of the church.

Red Wing Lutheran Ladies' Seminary was left out of the agreement, although, as the church got itself organized, it was on a list of schools to be considered for support. The strongest supporters of the school, besides the alumnae, were the ladies aids of the NLCA. Mrs. Langemo described an inspection of the school on April, 19, 1918, by a delegation of women from the new church body. It included President H. G. Stub's third wife, Anna, from St. Paul; Mrs. Caroline Koren Naeseth (daughter of Vilhelm and Elisabeth Koren); Mrs. Opsal (wife of the chair of the Red Wing Board); Mrs. Ristad, the former President's wife—all from Red Wing; and Mrs. T. H. Dahl of Minneapolis, whose husband had been president of the United Church. Langemo described their thorough investigation,

> Classrooms and classes were visited, students' rooms pried into, halls, stairway and corridors—Yes, even the broom closets were carefully examined. They reported that they didn't find much to criticize, though they did suggest that white iron beds should replace the wooden ones as soon as possible.[527]

The reason for the inspection was the resolution of the board of Trustees of the church that the property,

> valued at $200,000-$225,000 was to be turned over to the Norwegian Lutheran Church by the Red Wing Corporation as soon as the church body is ready to receive it. At the meeting of the Board of Directors officers were vested with the authority to make the necessary legal transfer of the property.[528]

This move showed the seriousness with which the women, at least, took the future of the school in the new church. Ristad had proposed that the Hauge Synod's Red Wing Seminary and the Ladies' Seminary cooperate, if not merge; the two schools could, by sharing their faculties, become a college. While this might have worked, the Board of Education of the church rejected it and chose rather to merge the college department of the Hauge's Synod school with St. Olaf and the theological seminary with Luther Seminary. This was the ending of the Hauge's Synod seminary, although Luther Seminary agreed always to keep professors of that tradition on its merged faculty. What was left in Red Wing of the Hauge

Hauge Synod's Red Wing Seminary, 1907

Synod was a "pro Seminary" for pre-sem students who received a call to ministry somewhat later in life. It did not survive the Depression.

The Lutheran Ladies' Seminary, while a much beloved institution of the Synod, did not receive official support from the new church. The school's finances and enrollment under Ristad's leadership had continued to decline. T. A. Hoff looked to be the kind of man who could get the school going again. He had good ideas and believed in the mission of the school.

> Education includes growth and religious character, growth in knowledge, growth in wisdom, growth in virtue, and in all that equips women with the largest possibilities for service as a home-maker and as a useful member of society; that it may fortify her for the struggles that are almost certain to come to her in life; and that her life may be adorned with truth, beauty, and goodness, learning and religion must go hand in hand.[529]

Hoff, like his predecessors, agreed with the mission statement of the school and the idea of preparing girls to become ladies who could run the home in a way that would continue to improve society. As the Roaring Twenties were about to explode over the country, he also recognized the trend away from such an education, admitting that many of the graduates would become "breadwinners in some other kind of work."[530]

Hoff praised the leadership of the Ladies' Seminary for maintaining the school with its "segregate education." While such schools became more and more difficult to maintain as the century wore on, it was not really until after the 1950s that co-education began at Harvard and other Ivy League institutions. Still the effort to keep a separate school to educate young women to be ladies did not appear to be a pressing concern for the new church, although Hoff's new administration and energy seemed to be staunching the decline. He made a proposal to the Board of Education of the new church to raise an endowment fund of $100,000. The Eastern District supported it and sent in a resolution to the national convention adding the stipulation that the

T. A. Hoff

fund when gathered would belong to the Synod.[531] The Board of Trustees approved it and gave the fund $500, ruling the collection could not begin until January 1, 1920. While these were not overwhelming statements of support, the school looked to be moving forward with hope and talented leadership. The future looked good for the school.

Fire at Red Wing Lutheran Ladies' Seminary, 1919

Fires

However, it was not to be. The Synod's curse of fire once again struck hard. On December 5, 1919, fire broke out on the third floor of the south wing. Despite the low water pressure on the hills, the fire was finally controlled, and the damage, which was major, mostly from water and smoke, was not enough to end the work of the school. Because of the fire damage, the school had to be closed for two weeks in December. The origin of the fire was never discovered, but it had destroyed the kitchen, dining room, and the entire Domestic Economy Department along with several dormitory rooms.[532] Hoff rallied the school's supporters and alums who now numbered in the thousands and, with insurance, was able to rebuild and be ready for the students to return after Christmas vacation. While there was suspicion of arson, it could not be proved.

By January 1920 the school was ready to open again for the second semester. The school, under the shrewd leadership of Hoff, had managed so well it had a surplus of over $12,000 despite the fire and the costs associated with repairing the damage. Graduation was to be held on June 8, at the conclusion of a couple of days of traditional commencement exercises. The institution looked eagerly toward the next year and a class larger than any—so many more, in fact, that they had to hire more teachers. However, on June 7, 1920, another fire broke out at 2:00 a.m., again in the main building in a bathroom, some thought because an unattended gas heater had been left burning. In an hour and a half the entire building lay in ruins. The 200 students living in the building and their many guests had to flee in order to save their lives. They lost almost all of their belongings—trunks, luggage, clothing, and books. Two pianos of the thirty-three the school owned were saved, but all of the others were destroyed, as was the pipe organ in the auditorium.

For a variety of reasons, when Hoff tried to notify the fire department, he could not reach the central station. Finally he ran to see what he could do on site. A riverboat on the Mississippi had seen the fire, and the fire department finally came, but it was too late. The entire building lay in ruins. Once again arson was suspected by the same disgruntled student, but it could never be proved. To replace the loss, figured to be at some $250,000, Hoff estimated, they would need over $500,000.[333] The insurance would cover barely one-fifth of that. The graduation ceremony on June 8 was held as scheduled on the grounds near the smoking ruins of the building.

To Rebuild or Not

The question of whether or not to rebuild the Lutheran Ladies Seminary occupied its supporters for a while. A major question had to do with its funding. It was about to be considered a school of the new NLCA, with all the support that would bring, but there had been no official decision at the time of the fire. The Board of Trustees wanted the entire church at its annual meeting to make the decision whether to rebuild. Some wanted to rebuild on the site, which would receive local Red Wing support. Others wondered about other sites. Granite Falls made a proposal to move the

Domestic Science students with Mrs. Gellerup

school to its city. Another more likely proposal was to convert the Luther Seminary campus in Hamline to a school for girls.

At a meeting in Red Wing about this time, church officials, Red Wing businessmen and pastors, and faculty met at the St. James Hotel to discuss the future of the school. C. J. Sargeant, president of the Red Wing Chamber of Commerce, spoke of the promises the city council had made to assure better fire protection, so that the school could be rebuilt on its beautiful grounds. President Stub then gave a talk that "made everybody think."[534] He believed the school, even though it had not been officially a school of the church, was regarded by the church as its own. He then reiterated the suggestion that the school be moved to Hamline, where the seminary building now stood nearly empty or at least not well used. At first there had been an attempt to have seminary classes and dorm rooms at both the Hamline and Como Avenue campuses, but this became less and less attractive as the two schools began working together as one school. While Stub personally had good memories and much sympathy for the lovely location of the school, very likely remembering his times there with Valborg twenty five years earlier, he thought that it was incumbent on the city of Red Wing to keep its promise of better fire protection and that the people of Red Wing guarantee ample financial support for the school to be rebuilt on its former site. He would see to it that the proposition be put before the church body, if these conditions were met. Schak Joakim Ylvisaker (1873-1948), leading youth pastor from Fergus Falls, made an impassioned speech on the need to rebuild the school and argued that

Schak Joakim Ylvisaker it was a perfect time to do it. At that point, several present at the meeting had to leave in order to catch the train to Minneapolis, and the meeting adjourned without hearing from O. O. Erling, chair of the NLCA's Board of Trustees, and Rev. Lauritz Andreas Vigness (1864-1947), the secretary of the Board of Education of the NLCA. [535] That the meeting broke up before any action could be taken seems almost planned. Stub, despite his sentimental attachment to the school, was probably also thinking of saving the building they already had at Hamline. This is not difficult to understand, given his fiduciary concern for the new church. A perfectly suitable building, standing open and essentially unused now that most of the seminary had relocated to the Como Avenue building, seemed to be a waste of resources.

Luther Seminary in Hamline

Very shortly thereafter, the NLCA Church Council recommended to the 1920 annual meeting of the NLCA that "The Luther Seminary building at Hamline shall be used as a school for young women."[536] As United Seminary—what is now Bockman Hall—on Como Avenue seemed to be the better building, the school at Hamline could be made available to the Ladies' Seminary. It had rooms for students and everything the Ladies' Seminary would need: chapel, dining rooms, class rooms, etc.[537] Despite Stub's warm recollections and sympathy for the school, his hand seems to be in these decisions. The building at Hamline was a much better solution to the problem. On the other hand, such a resolution meant that the Red Wing community would have little enthusiasm for the location in Hamline. For reasons that are never really stated, the new church chose neither to rebuild in Red Wing nor move to Hamline. The church voted at its annual convention not to sanction the move to Hamline.

> The Board of Education and the Board of Trustees were empowered to act in the matter of rebuilding and locating the Lutheran Ladies' Seminary in so far as the Norwegian Lutheran Church of America may be affected in its educational policies or may have the authority to act.[538]

This strange turnabout left the Ladies' Seminary without a home and the Hamline seminary building virtually unused. On December 21, 1920, the Ladies' Seminary board officially vacated the Red Wing seminary grounds after it determined that it would be impossible to rebuild.

Despite that resolution, attempts were made to rebuild. The October 21, 1921, issue of the *Lutheran Herald* announced that the schools would be rebuilt and "it is probable that work on the handsome new structure will begin this fall."[539] The secretary, H. L. Hjermstad, spoke confidently and gave detailed plans of the building as designed once again by Architect Gauger. Speaking with the Red *Wing Republican,* he spoke optimistically of the future, a school which would be built along broader lines and more attractive to more students because it would not be so elite. From this vantage point it seems disconnected with reality. The report made it seem as though things were going along nicely and in line with the ebullience of the Roaring Twenties.

In 1922, at its annual meeting, the NLCA declared "the Church does not favor rebuilding [the Lutheran Ladies' Seminary] at this time. Some other location than Red Wing should be decided upon, due to the fact that the Church already has one school in that city [the Pro-Seminary]."[540] One member of the group dissented from the recommendation. As the resolution was going forward to the convention, Pastor Knut Bjørgo announced to the gathering that the name of the school had been changed to Trinity School for Girls, probably an effort by Trinity Lutheran to keep such a school in town.[541] The deliberations which caused this change have all gone to the grave with these leaders. They did not put into writing the real reason, but the name change indicates that the supporters of the school understood that the name "ladies" seemed outdated as did "seminary," now no longer understood as appropriate for a school for girls. It may have been Trinity because Pastor Bjørgo and the Red Wing Trinity Lutheran congregation may well have proposed to rebuild and run the school on its own. The records are puzzling, as those who have tried to tell the story over time seem to indicate. The resolution prepared by the Board of Trustees and the Board of Education for some reason did not appear before the next meetings of the church in convention.

Todd Walsh, in his latest manuscript, makes the case that the real reason for the failure of the school to rebuild was a financial scandal that, typically, did not make the reports of the day. From his perspective it was the treasurer, Carl Frithjof Hjermstad (1865-1939), who made inappropriate investments with the seminary's funds and, as something of a compulsive gambler, made it impossible for the school to continue with the losses he incurred. The story is fairly convincing, but not necessary to relate in detail here. It does explain that curious silence of sources when there is a scandal.[542] The organization chose not to divulge the scandal to protect their own reputation, as much as the reputation of the organization. Everyone probably knew the real story. Thus the curious meeting in Red Wing, with the principals leaving before hearing from everyone and thus failing to make a decision, can probably be explained by their awareness of Hjermstad's fiduciary betrayal.

That was probably the proverbial straw that broke the camel's back and gave those uncomfortable about rebuilding such a school a good excuse. The new church—with St. Olaf, Augustana, Concordia, Pacific Lutheran, and Waldorf, the junior college—provided many more options for women. This lessened the need for a woman's school. Although Luther remained a men-only college, women who wanted an education in a church college had more choices than ever. Perhaps, the church did not consider it necessary to provide another place for women in the church to attend school. They had several good schools women could attend. For many reasons, not simply financial, the school decided not to rebuild.

On February 25, 1932, as the Depression deepened, the Red Wing Lutheran Ladies' Seminary was dissolved at the order of the Goodhue County District Court. It was put into receivership for final liquidation. On May 7, 1935, the beautiful site of the seminary, nothing more than ashes and ruins, was sold for $2,100. A genteel institution had gone up in smoke like many other buildings of the Synod. It was a unique and worthy attempt, but such an institution would never be again.

CHAPTER EIGHT

Getting Women the Vote in Church

It is the old Christ hatred that cries we will not have any dominion over us. Away with Christ and family life and marriage, school. Let everything be heathen and the golden ages will come again. . . . Surely we live in the latter days!

—Hermann Preus, 1870

At the end of the nineteenth century, it was clear to church leaders that the struggle for women's emancipation would be the issue of the next century. Until then the Norwegian Synod had not fully debated the question theologically, though it had expressed discomfort with the movement. The issue rose to prominence as congregations began to give women voting rights.

As noted above, the women of the church first got their voting rights in ladies aids organizations, not in secular society. Even at that stage, however, they knew they had to dissociate themselves from any hint of influence from Cady Stanton or even that of the milder, but more determined, Susan B. Anthony.

Even before the formation of the Norwegian Lutheran Church in America in 1917, one of its predecessor women's organizations made this clear. Hannah Rorem Rønning, in her 1901 opening speech as president of the Hauge Synod Mission Dove Society, reminded the members that their first responsibilities were in the home, but the Gospel also required them to meet the needs of their sisters across the sea. The traditional biblical view that women had to submit to their husbands made them careful about flaunting their independence.

Hannah and Halvor Rønning

Ladies Aid meeting at Ole Groven's

Despite these signs of dissociation from the radical feminism of the day, the movement to give women voting rights in congregations grew. The discussion of the issue in the church periodicals of the Norwegian-American Lutherans included familiar arguments. The pietist Haugean and Conference churches tended to argue from a sense of what seemed spiritual, with less concern for order and hierarchy. As pietists, they tended to value the gifts of women rather than rules. They also knew the Bible was contradictory on the issue. The more orthodox Synod men argued the biblicist position using the same hermeneutical method on the women's issue as they had on slavery. On the issue of women speaking in church, they preferred the verses in 1 Timothy 2:12 commanding women to be silent rather than the one in 1 Corinthians 11:5-6 suggesting women speak in the assembly but only with their heads covered.

In 1888 Norwegian-American Lutherans were watching closely other churches and their positions on women's right to vote. They discussed

the Methodists' consideration of women's right to vote at their General Conferences. *Lutheraneren* reported what it thought to be an odd question in that report: If women could vote in their home congregations, why not at the General Conference?[543] Both *Budbæreren* and *Evangelisk Luthersk Kirketidende* reported on the General Conference of Methodists in 1892 with special attention to the question of women's place in the church. These interested all the Norwegian-American churches because they were also considering the issue themselves. The press noticed it about the time of the twenty-fifth anniversary of the colorful Melchoir Falk Gjertsen's pastorate (1847-1913) at Trinity Congregation in Minneapolis. Gjertsen

Melchior Falk Gjertsen

campaigned to get Trinity Congregation to allow women to vote in congregational meetings.

The idea shocked many people, but Trinity was not the first to give women the vote. In August 1894 the *Evangelisk Luthersk Kirketidende* reported that the Kvams congregation in Ottertail County, Minnesota, had granted women the right to vote in its congregational meeting that year. The editor, Johannes Ylvisaker, criticized the report in a note written not long after his stirring speech at the dedication of the Red Wing Lutheran Ladies Seminary. Such a "reform means ruining everything. What God says in his Holy Word means nothing to these people."[544]

Ylvisaker proved to be a keen critic of women's suffrage in congregations and in civil society. Ironically, this rebuke in the *Evangelisk Luthersk Kirketidende* caused readers to respond proudly with the record of women's suffrage in their own congregations. Pastor Heiberg of the Hauge Synod wrote to say that the first Lutheran church in the world to give women the vote was in Barnes County, North Dakota, in 1893.[545] Pastor Knut Birkeland (1857-1925), a champion of temperance and thus a strong advocate of women's suffrage, expressed astonishment at Ylvisaker. He reported that he had organized many Lutheran churches, and in each of those congregations women were given the right to vote. He claimed the first church to grant women the right to vote was the St. Olaf Congregation in Fort Dodge, Iowa, in 1883. This provoked a comment from Ylvisaker. "These are the first Lutherans to overthrow God's Word!" Pastor Aaberg from North Dakota wrote an angry letter questioning whether such congregations read the Bible at all. He appealed to the traditional proof texts against women speaking in the churches.[546]

Pastor A. A. Aaberg

The discussion became even more heated as the bitter controversy concerning Augsburg and the Friends of Augsburg came to a head in 1893-1894, just when the Synod was building the Ladies' Seminary. At this time the Augsburg party began separating itself from the United Church; the Friends of Augsburg were joining together to prevent the defeat by the St. Olaf forces of the Augsburg proposal to be the school of the United Church. As these meetings went on, the church papers noted that, when the Friends of Augsburg tallied their numbers, women were included. That seemed unfair to the reporters, who regarded it as simply a technique to swell the numbers of voting members, or worse, as an absolute disregard of God's Word.

After the Friends of Augsburg broke away, the United Church took control of the *Lutheraneren,* which had been edited by Sverdrup. Its new editor, F. A. Schmidt (1837-1928), editorialized, "It can be reported as an oddity that at the Augsburg Friends' meetings, there were gathered together 35 from the Willmar congregation alone, not counting women and children."[547] In a column commenting on Sverdrup's theology of the laity, Schmidt reminded his readers of what Paul had to say about women speaking in the congregation. As he considered Sverdrup's position on women and men in the church, he conceded that both men and women should have access to God's gifts. Who can forbid God's spirit from working where it will? Still, Schmidt expressed reservations, asking, "What does Paul say? Be silent in church."[548]

F. A. Schmidt

The *Lutheraneren* of December 12, 1895, reported Cady Stanton's eightieth birthday and her speech on that occasion. Why the editor included it is difficult to tell. Most interesting is the editorial comment at the end of the report on her speech, remarking that some old women (*kjærringer*) are like that.[549] Whether that is a respectful comment is not clear. There was some grudging respect for the old woman, but certainly her thought was deplored and not to be taken seriously by any biblically conservative leader. However, it was gaining approval in the society and needed to be addressed, although even by 1896 the General Conference of Methodists had still not granted women the right to vote or participate as delegates.

The *Lutheraneren* reported a comment of Pastor Birkeland, editor of the temperance journal, *Afholds Basunen,* about the struggle: "One would think in these days that Christians would not be so old-fashioned (*gammeldags*) as to refuse women as preachers or delegates."[550] The strong relationship between forces for prohibition and women's rights is apparent in Birkeland's comment. It may be that the WCTU was the most common way for Scandinavian immigrant women to participate in the suffrage movement. It was a connection that *Evangelisk Luthersk Kirketidende* noted with alarm.

Church journals began to ridicule how the emerging Lutheran Free Church conducted its meetings. Schmidt remarked with disdain that the

Luther College Professor's Wives Circle, 1903. Lulla Preus is in the center, to the right of the woman in the white skirt.

new church body, if it could be called such, had an incredible kind of congregational freedom: lopsided numbers of delegates at the meeting. How could it claim to be representative of the entire body if forty-eight delegates were from Minneapolis, twelve from Willmar, ten from St. Paul? Worse, included among those numbers were a good many women. The latter, Schmidt added dryly, was presumably on the basis of a newly found apostolic word that lifted the proscription of women speaking in church.[551] Another writer in *Lutheraneren* noted that, with such a strange way of organizing, the Lutheran Free Church could hardly be called an organization (*samfund*). Anyone can come, he wrote, professors, laymen, and women.[552]

By 1897 Trinity Congregation decided to give women the vote. This was duly reported in both *Evangelisk Luthersk Kirketidende* and *Lutheraneren*. The report, in both journals, mentioned that, when it was passed, someone asked whether women could hold office in the church as trustees, treasurer, or deacon; the question was met with universal laughter.[553] Except for leadership positions in women's organizations or Sunday schools, women could not hold such offices at Trinity, making the victory a little less sweeping than it appeared.

Since the women question was more and more urgent, the editors of *Evangelisk Luthersk Kirketidende* wrote a series of editorials on the topic as the new century dawned. Ylvisaker had seen in a magazine, *Lutherske Missionær*, the forecast that the next big controversy would be women's suffrage in the congregation. It went on to say that a congregation in which women did not vote was only part of a congregation. Ylvisaker expressed horror at such a comment. "They do not see that it [Scripture] really says women should not vote!"[554]

In April 1900 Ylvisaker as editor of the Synod's paper, considered the comments of the *Lutherske Missionær* further. Ylvisaker pointed out, with some justice, that it was a travesty of democracy to have women vote, but not speak in the congregational meetings, a solution which some congregations had devised. That seemed to be no answer at all. After a long series of theses on the right of women to vote and be included in the deliberations of a meeting, Ylvisaker argued, if everyone who was part of a society (*samfund*) needed to vote, then children should be allowed to vote. He concluded his article by saying that women's place was in the home, making the same argument he had made at the dedication of the Ladies' Seminary—that the home is both state and church in microcosm, and it would be the ruination of both if women left the home for the public world. If they had rights, they should also have duties. He concluded,

> We sorrow deeply over each report we get that a congregation
> has given women the vote. We know what the consequences
> of that will be. Women's emancipation is the death of wom-
> anliness. We should help women to stay at home.[555]

By 1904 the *Evangelisk Luthersk Kirketidende* began to train its eye on the difficulties it had with the WCTU. It noted that it was a pity the organization, which did a lot of good, was so strong on women's suffrage. While doing good, Realfe Olaf Brandt, Didderikke and Nils Brandt's son, agreed, but "it is quite against God's Word to let women vote. It is too bad we cannot support the WCTU, but if you support the local group you also must support the goals of the national organization."[556] This argument appears now and then and shows that it was the position of an organization on the status of women that determined how it was to be regarded.

Two notes in the August 24, 1904, issue argued that God's Word forbade women to speak in congregations, but if they had the right to vote in the state, they would want it everywhere. To give the vote and not the right to speak was wrong. More to the theological point, giving women equal rights would ruin the natural order. The order of creation stands behind many of these positions, the notion that women must submit to their husbands, or men. What is at issue in this argument is not the vote quite so much as the command that women should keep silent in church and the headship of the husband in the home. In a report on a meeting in Norway where the question of women's right to vote in the Mission Society (*Mis-*

sionselskab) was debated, the journal commented, "They have gotten this idea from the free thinker J. Stuart Mill who has won over Paul."[557]

Theological Conference on Women's Rights

As the Synod was debating internally about the suffrage question, it held a special conference in 1904 on women's suffrage. The major paper, "Modern Emancipation of Women," was by Christian Naeseth (1849-1921), husband of Caroline Koren and professor of Greek at the college. The paper shows the writer, as Koren and Ylvisaker, to be keenly aware of the cultural milieu surrounding the question. Naeseth had studied at Concordia Seminary in St. Louis, the University of Christiania, Cornell University, and Johns Hopkins University. He presented a careful piece on various ideas in the women's movement. He spoke knowledgeably, having read the sources that are still read, especially Mary Wollstonecraft

John Stuart Mill

and John Stuart Mill. Mill's primary problem with the church was "the legal subordination of one sex to the other."

Naeseth began with a report on ladies' colleges and their beginnings in the United States. He named Oberlin, founded as a co-educational school in 1833, and Vassar, in 1861. He also included the Red Wing Lutheran Ladies' Seminary in that number, which put it in the larger context of education around the world. His paper gives us a snapshot of women's education and suffrage in his day for women's schools, co-education, and ways some men's colleges found to include women in their classes. For example, Oxford allowed women "by courtesy" to attend lectures. In Norway the university opened its doors to women in 1882. Sixteen out of the twenty-eight private high schools in Norway were only for women. Because of them, at the time of his writing, over 260 women had matriculated at university and sixteen had graduated from the school of medicine.

Christian Naeseth

After more statistics about the state of women's education around the world, he then gave a brief history of the effort to give women the vote. Women of property had the right to vote in local elections in a number of states and countries. He then described what was happening in the church in respect to women's vote in congregations and national annual meetings of denominations. He also reported there were, as of 1901, around a thousand women pastors. These facts were important for him to summarize before he proceeded to the biblical and theological issues at hand.

Turning to theology and the Bible, he noted Cady Stanton's "so-called" Woman's Bible.[558] This was a version of the Bible based on the work of historical critics which interpreted the biblical texts in such a way as to favor women. Stanton, who had been well schooled in Greek, was an able scholar of the New Testament. It was not pleasing to the orthodox Naeseth who examined it. What she had to say about women's emancipation, he noted, "was not in line with the Bible."[559] More troubling, however, was Stanton's position. He worked through each of the biblical texts on women (something the church has done almost from its beginning—even the Wife of Bath in Chaucer's *Canterbury Tales* takes these texts, especially Timothy, to task). He found Stanton's work easiest to deal with, especially in regard to submission, the big issue, especially if one subscribed to the orders of creation an old Lutheran doctrine promulgated by the Missouri Synod. He even quotes a scholar against his case, who said "there is not a single word previous to the fall indicating any inferiority other than official subordination."[560] As Naeseth works through all of the texts about women in the Bible, from their keeping silent in the church to their not prophesying without their heads covered, he comes out on the conservative side, as could be expected, even when he addresses the question of women's vote.

His arguments against it are typical and of a piece with the notion that the woman who rules the home, where her natural authority is, has more power than any man. "Do not tell me that the casting of a bit of paper in a box once a year can offset the daily influence of a mother, or that vote can be better gained from a political platform than at the home fireside," he quoted from a woman who opposed women's suffrage.[561] Women did not need to enter into the "turmoils of the masculine life" to have power. They had all they needed in the home.

To sum up, Naeseth concluded that if we wanted to keep the home and marriage undisturbed and assure that true womanliness was not threatened, we had to say no to women's emancipation. It was also necessary to say that women should not speak in church but remain silent. Their place to speak was at home and in the family where they had the power. Naeseth did note that the Bible was a bit mixed on the issue, in one case saying women were to be silent, in another that they should not prophesy with uncovered heads. He concluded, "We in the church first and last, should go, not the way the wind blows, or where the river flows, but—what does the word of God say?"[562] About that he had no doubt.

At that time in Norway, women with property could vote in local elections; universal suffrage came in 1913. It took seven more years in the United States—the Nineteenth Amendment, passed in 1919, came into effect for the 1920 national election. Soon Prohibition passed. The topic of the special conference of the Synod on women's suffrage indicates as nothing else the urgency of the question for this group of pastors. As in their passionate concern to make certain that they protected the Bible on the issue of slavery, so too they sought to be faithful to the Bible on the issue of women and the vote. All told, the word was clear to Naeseth and his colleagues. One has to admire their serious theological engagement with these issues, whether or not one approves of their conclusions.

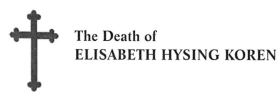

The Death of
ELISABETH HYSING KOREN

Elisabeth Hysing Koren (1832-1918) died in the Washington Prairie parsonage on June 6, 1918. She had lived on those grounds for sixty-five years, since 1853, when, on Christmas Eve, the young couple arrived to begin their ministry. As she wrote in *Fra Pioneertiden* (*From the Time of the Pioneers*), the Norwegian version of her diary published in 1914, she could hardly believe that she had lived such a long and rich life. She thought back to their first Christmas in Washington Prairie, when all they had from the old country and civilization was a small piece of chocolate. Their interest in life, their good humor, and their ability to work and dream gave them a long and fruitful life together.

Elisabeth Koren

She was born in Larvik, Norway, to a schoolmaster and politician who gave her the education appropriate to her class. Her mother died when she was eight years old. She lived a quiet life with her father after that, partly because of some difficulty hearing. In 1853, she married a distant cousin, Ulrik Vilhelm Koren, and they soon made their way to America, There he served as pastor of what was first known as the Little Iowa parish in Washington Prairie, not far from Decorah. Her life spanned the entire existence of the Norwegian Synod from its founding in 1853 to the merger with other Norwegian Lutheran groups that formed the Norwegian Evangelical Church in America in 1917. She was witness to its entire history, and her diary and letters are vivid primary sources of that history from a woman's point of view.

The obituary which appeared first in *Decorah Posten* was reprinted in *Lutheraneren* on July 3, 1918. Her funeral service began as the pallbearers carried her casket to the church from the parsonage grounds where she had spent her adult life. The church was packed with people who had come early in order to find places. "Her life was a life in beauty, like the summer day she was put to rest in the earth of Winneshiek County," the obituary read.

The service began with a favorite hymn, "With sorrow and complaint be moderate/Let God's Word give you comfort and counsel" (*Med sorgen og klagen hold måde*). Christian Keyser Preus, president of Luther College, preached. He must have remembered the many times his mother and Mrs. Koren had been together and the many letters they exchanged as he stood there preaching. He used the text on Mary and Martha, comparing Mrs. Koren to Mary, for "since her early childhood she had chosen the better part, which cannot be taken away." She had left Norway with her husband, not to find riches, praise, or honor, Preus remarked,

> No, she had left a fine and cultured home, family and friends in Norway to follow her husband to where he was called. She had lived a helpful and inspiring life among their people. Mrs. Koren did not belong to the people who advertised their calling or their Christianity. She had not taken part in the things that important contemporary women were known for; she believed that a woman's place was first and foremost in the home, and that their influence could never be stronger than it was through the raising of children in the home. The deceased had been a lady of few words, but her presence was stronger than others' words.[563]

After sharing some memories of Mrs. Koren, he noted that because of her diary, her life had been an open book to others.

Then the church choir sang the beloved hymn of Paul Gerhard, "Commit thy ways to God" (*Befiehl du deine Wege*), one that her husband had sung with her many times. After this, J. W. Preus, Linka's younger son, spoke in English. "Mrs. Koren had forsaken a cultured home for a pioneer's life of poverty and renunciation. She had, perhaps, more than others, much to give, and through the kingdom that was her home, her influence had formed both church and state."[564]

After his talk, the congregation sang a hymn, "The greatest gladness of my heart,/ is like a summer joy/ that God himself prepared me/ for all eternity" (*Min største Hjertens glæde*). In closing, her son Paul, now the pastor at Washington Prairie, standing beside the coffin, spoke of his mother's kindness and goodness. He began in English, but then changed over to Norwegian so the older people in the group would understand him. "The short and simple talk had a great impact," the paper commented. Then they sang the final hymn, "My death is all good for me/ for Jesus is my friend." (*Min død er mig til gode*) Then the hundreds of mourners passed  *J. W. Preus* by her casket to take their final glimpse of her. "While the church bell tolled and birds twittered the elderly lady was carried to her rest in the earth where so many others who knew her well in the olden days were also resting."[565]

While she was not raised in a parsonage, over time Mrs. Koren became the Mother Superior of the Norwegian Synod's pastors' wives,

The Egge cabin where the Korens lived their first three months in Washington Prairie

The Washington Prairie Church building

especially after Linka's death. Her diary, which ended with the birth of her first child, Henriette, is not all we have from her. Fortunately, her correspondents, especially Linka Preus, knew the value of her letters and saved them. Mrs. Koren's careful, good-humored descriptions of life as it developed in the Norwegian Synod, from its birth to its ending, in her parsonage and in the group of pastors and their families, are a treasure. Her eye caught details that sometimes even she did not understand. When she recorded the actions of the Egges, who must have wondered how they could bear the young couple's imperial ways for so long, she shows us how they regarded her as much as how she regarded them. Through life, as she grew and matured, the pioneer pastors' wives came to rely on her take on things, the people they met and were living with, their various character faults and virtues. When Linka died, Elisabeth's letters to her ended, so we miss nearly forty years of her sharp eye. What we do have is invaluable. Except for Nils Brandt, she outlived all of these pioneer pastors and their wives. It is somehow fitting that she was the last of the wives to go.

The Korens at their fiftieth wedding anniversary

I have included in full her accounts of the death and burial of Mrs. Larsen and Christiane Hjort because they give us a vivid picture of life and death over 150 years ago. Every summer since I first came upon these letters and Linka's diary in the Luther College archives, I have listened to her voice, her calm and careful prose. Her voice has been my constant companion over the years whenever I have returned to my work on this project. When another 150 of her letters to her father were discovered in the effects of Professor David Nelson in Decorah, Øyvind Gullixson, professor emeritus at Telemark High School in Bø, Norway, was asked to transcribe them for publication in Norway and perhaps in English translation. He shared a number of letters with me as I was finishing this book. When I sat down to read them, I heard once again that voice, Mrs. Koren at her best, her level gaze and even tone, describing to her father life in America and Washington Prairie.

We will not see her like again. Her life and effect on the culture that is Luther College is unique.

CHAPTER NINE

Co-Education at Luther College

After the fire and the decision not to rebuild the Red Wing Lutheran Ladies' Seminary, the question whether to admit women to Luther College, where the heirs of the Norwegian Synod still gathered, began to be asked again. The college had not addressed the admission of women for several generations. They had built the Red Wing school and were proud of their efforts to educate young women the way they had always been educated to be ladies. With the merger that formed the Norwegian Lutheran Church in America (NLCA) in 1917, under the presidency of Hans G. Stub, the church had several colleges that enrolled women including Red Wing. It was only after the fire that the Luther College community had to face, once again, the issue of how to educate its daughters.

Hans G. Stub

Co-education was a growing trend among many colleges that previously had only admitted men. Augsburg began as a seminary with a prep school to prepare men for the ministry, but invited women to enroll in 1921 for educational as well as financial reasons. Its curriculum was no longer exclusively theological, but it included a typical American college course with the usual requirements for a B.A. The Lutheran Free Church, like the Norwegian Synod, had also founded Oak Grove Ladies' Seminary in Fargo in 1906, which would go co-educational in 1926.

Luther College in the twenties, under the leadership of President Oscar Olson who favored the admission of women, avoided the issue of coeducation for a decade. After Olson was reelected president in 1931, he pressed harder, perhaps more confident of his power after his reelection. He told the faculty at its meeting of September 24, that he was going to advocate for co-education at the college. On September 29, the faculty passed a resolution endorsing his proposal. Nonetheless, at a special meeting of the faculty on October 12, he announced his resignation to the faculty.

This happened just before the celebrations of the seventieth anniversary of the college began on October 14, 1931. The event brought many alumni to the campus.

The question hung in the air during the entire celebration. Would the college, which for seventy years had advertised itself as a "college for men," change its very being in an effort to survive? The gathered alumni wanted to hear the argument for co-education and what it would mean and cost. Times were not good, as the Great Depression pressed deeper and deeper into the lives of people. While women would add to the enrollment and thus increase income from tuition, there were other expenses that could not be denied. This seemed to be a very real impediment to the change.

J. C. K. Preus, grandson of Hermann and Linka Preus, son of Christian Keyser Preus, president of the college from 1902 to 1921, and general secretary of the NLCA Board of Education—maintained to those gathered at the reunion, and later to the Board of Education, that even if one favored co-education, which he probably did not, the costs of the change would add to Luther's already crippling debt. If they had to refit a dorm for women students and hire women matrons, etc., the proposal was simply not feasible. The Board of Education tabled the discus-

J. C. K. Preus

sion, in essence vetoing it. In his letter of resignation Olson implied that, without the support of J. C. K Preus, he had no future as president.

Olson gave two reasons for his resignation, besides his knowledge that he had lost the support of the Board of Education of the NLCA and significant people in the Luther College community. The first was the decision of the faculty to try to increase enrollment by eliminating the general requirement of Greek and Latin, making them electives, something Olson felt greatly weakened the educational strength of the school. He had tried to walk a middle way on this, but worried that eliminating the requirement might "break the tradition that Luther College should give all its students a classical education."[566] He

President Oscar Olson

was willing to compromise, given that students were choosing not to come to Luther because of these stringent language requirements. Olson had preferred reducing the requirements rather than eliminating them. Though he did not like it, he understood that removing the classical language requirement was a matter of survival.[567]

Unmentioned in these deliberations is what it would mean for the boy's education. Dropping the requirement for Greek and Latin meant radically changing what had been understood for centuries in the West to be the heart of male education. Such schooling took the boy out of the home and sent him to a school where he would be, in some ways, hazed by Latin instruction. Walter Ong describes the process as something of a puberty rite in which young boys through intense male bonding moved from the family to the tribe. Latin toughened "the youngster for the extra-familial world in which he would have to live."[568]

Women may have learned both Latin and Greek, even Hebrew, from their fathers, but it was generally considered somewhat of a transgression. As the nineteenth century went on, young girls, like Cady Stanton who realized that they were not receiving the same education as their brothers, would find a way to learn these languages. (Stanton had the unusual chance to study at the co-educational school, Johnstown Academy, where in fact she did study Greek and Latin until she was sixteen.) On the whole, Latin was rarely part of the girls' curriculum until co-education became common.

Second, Olson believed that coeducation was a necessity. He was convinced that with the introduction of co-education, Luther College would attract such an attendance and would arouse so much goodwill, that her future, both financially and otherwise, would be assured.[569]

Luther's debt was serious enough that the future of the school seemed uncertain. That and the realities of the Depression posed such a threat to the survival of the college the argument for the admission of women seemed unavoidable. J. C. K. Preus, as general secretary of the Board of Education, met with the entire faculty in January 1932 to discuss the future of the college. The Board of Education had vetoed the proposal which both faculty and trustees had approved in the fall of 1931. Olson's resignation, which he had announced to the faculty in October, was made public by Johan Aasgaard, president of the church, on January 11, to be effective as of July 31, 1932.[570]

Olson wrote later that he realized that the Board of Education had taken an

> action that not only was unfavorable, but that left no prospect
> of securing favorable action as it appeared to me, I have fre-

quently balanced the pros and cons in my mind as to whether I should resign or not. . . . Then I learned that members of the Board of Education, including the president, with whom I have had a conversation about the matter, were of the opinion that it would be to the advantage of the College if I should resign. This caused me to decide to resign without hesitation. The fact that a number of the members of the College faculty also thought, as I was informed, that it would be to the advantage of the College if I should resign, made resignation easier for me than if they were all opposed to it.[571]

Olson felt blind-sided by the Board, and J. C. K. Preus especially. He felt the board had put him in an impossible situation, demanding that he balance the books without giving him the chance to do the one thing he felt could change the downward trend of enrollment and finances.[572]

The 1932 Convention of the NLCA, meeting in Minneapolis June 1-8, passed an emergency measure authorizing co-education at the college for credit, "provided it is approved by the president and the Board of Trustees of the College and by the General Board of Education of the NLCA."[573] The president of the NLCA, Aasgaard, and the Board of Trustees of the college quickly approved the measure.

The Luther College Corporation met on June 3, 1932, during the church convention. It affirmed, despite the emergency measure, that the school would continue as a "college for men" until such a change was made officially in Minneapolis by the church convention meeting at this time. During its meeting it received an addendum to the official report from the Decorah Chamber of Commerce urging the body to approve co-education at Luther.

> We know the people here would welcome the opportunity of sending their girls to Luther College. Decorah with its beautiful surroundings would make a most fitting place for coeducational students. And this community is heartily in favor of coeducation at Luther.[574]

It was signed by W. F. Baker, president of the Chamber, and E. L. Amundsen, secretary.[575]

The passing of the emergency measure was greeted warmly by area papers. The *Sumner Gazette* reported with approval "the action whereby women students will be permitted to matriculate and pursue courses of study." It went on to say, "We believe Luther College has taken a commendable step forward."[576] The expectations were that co-education would become a reality at Luther in the fall.

While these discussions were proceeding, the nomination and election of a president of Luther College were also underway. During the Luther College Corporation meeting the convention approved the election of Ove Jacob Hjort Preus, brother of J. C. K. Preus. As part of that approval the convention considered the following motion from the Board of Education:

> Whereas the entire background and tradition of Luther College for a period of seventy years is in question;
>
> Whereas a new president will take office this fall.
>
> Whereas it seems to be the consensus of opinion of the Board of Education and the Board of Trustees of Luther College that co-education will not solve the financial situation at Luther College as an emergency financial measure
>
> Be it resolved that this question of co-education at Luther College be referred to the two above mentioned boards for further consideration.

J. A. Nelson, a Decorah attorney, concerned for the survival of the college and for co-education, presented a substitute motion, keeping the first two clauses of the original but adding a completely different resolution:

> Whereas the entire background and tradition of Luther College for a period of seventy years is in question,
>
> Whereas a new president will take office this fall,
>
> Whereas there is urgent need of solving the financial problems of Luther College,
>
> Be it resolved that the matter of admitting a limited number of girl students at Luther College for credit be left to the best judgment of the newly elected president, subject to the consideration, approval and power to act on the part of the Board of Trustees of Luther College and the Board of Education.[577]

After some debate, the convention adopted the substitute motion. This gave the future President Preus both an opportunity and a problem. He knew full well the trustees of the college were for co-education while the Board of Education of the NLCA led by his brother opposed it. Notice of the resolution appeared briefly in neighboring papers. The *Ames Daily Tribune* reported that the church in its convention, after what it later would call an "altercation on the floor of the recent national church convention"[578] had "left decision of the co-educational proposal for Luther College at Decorah, Ia., up to the president of that institution. He will determine how many women are to be admitted."[579] The Board of Education had not yet spoken.

Contrary to expectations, the Board of Education of the church could not support the measure. On July 6, 1932, it met and, after much discussion, unanimously passed the following resolution:

> The Board is firmly convinced that the admission of girls will prove of but slight temporary advantage and will not permanently solve the financial problem of the institution; for this reason, and in the presence of the limitation placed upon us by the Articles of Incorporation and the By-Laws of Luther College, which were not altered by action of the convention, we find ourselves unable to concur in the resolution presented by the Board of Trustees of Luther College, calling for the establishment of co-education at Luther College.[580]

This was a blow to the supporters of co-education who thought their battle had been won.

In July 1932, J. C. K. Preus discussed the deliberations of the Board of Education in his report of the meeting in the *Lutheran Herald*. Among other objections the board had to co-education at Luther was that this temporary move to solve financial problems would become a thin-entering wedge that would make later objections to coeducation moot; the decision to enroll women would have been made. Another more effective argument against it was that it would incur heavy financial burdens to remodel the facilities for women. Neither church nor college could afford to do this. The board had even considered the suggestion that, with the inclusion of women, people would be more enthusiastic in their giving. To that J. C. K. Preus answered no. Even if that happened, additional revenue would be needed for the expense of making the campus ready for women. Furthermore, such an action would "precipitate a period of confusion as regards the future character of the school."[581]

Finally, J. C. K. Preus pleaded that it was in the best interests of the church to have a church-wide discussion of its educational institutions so that the decision of the Board of Education would be widely shared with the membership of the church. Preus then assured his readers that the board continued to work for the flourishing of Luther College as a "college for men."[582]

O. J. H. Preus Takes Charge

When O. J. H. Preus arrived in Decorah to assume his office as president of Luther College in August 1932, the financial situation of the college had grown worse. The convention had dropped the solution to the problem of co-education in his lap. Even though it was fairly clear that co-education could add to the student enrollment, there remained a significant and powerful group against the idea, notably the influential NLCA Board of Education; the board, as stated in Luther College's Articles of Incorporation, had to approve any change in the articles which at the moment said Luther was a college for men. In a sense, as Nelson argues in his history, Luther College was being run from Minneapolis more than any other college of the

O. J. H. Preus

church. The powers and actions of the Board of Education in the affairs of the college were greater than most knew. So President Preus had a difficult challenge: to get the college community and the Decorah community to convince the Board of Education that what he was doing was good for the college.

President Preus, given his challenge from the Luther College Corporation, addressed the problems of the college immediately, knowing that the survival of the college was at stake. The pressing issues were financial, which could be solved by a larger enrollment, the main argument for co-education. Even as he assumed the office, there was an active group in Decorah making plans for a college for women that would be closely connected with Luther. Whatever role he had in these conversations is not clear, but it was his good fortune that such work was being done. Many thought that co-education could solve the problem.

The *Decorah Public Opinion* regretted that the resolution for co-education had been vetoed by the Board of Education. Given the constitutional realities of the process, it recognized that there was no way the school could change by the fall semester. It would take another two years of careful and delicate negotiations to make the change, something it was confident would happen, since it was the way most colleges were going. It agreed that the college community may have experienced too rapid change in the past few years, especially with its curriculum revision. Though it regretted the delay, the editorial ended hopefully: "The advocates of co-education feel that Luther has a faculty and physical plant very well suited to the change; that the opportunity is here, so why not take advantage of it."[583] These sentiments were typical among the people of Northeast Iowa. Most accepted that the cost of the "additional buildings and equipment . . . would be prohibitive" but hoped the decision for coeducation would come soon.[584]

Decorah Junior College for Girls

The day Preus' term began, August 1, 1932, the efforts of the group planning a college for women came to fruition. Decorah Junior College for Girls was incorporated by a group of Decorah citizens, led by Thoralf A. Hoff, pastor of First Lutheran Church, formerly president of the Red Wing Lutheran Ladies' Seminary; the pastor of the Methodist church, O. Sandbach; J. P. Burling of the Congregational church; and several Luther faculty members. The group secured the use of the Weiser House in Decorah for its school. Ottar Tinglum, professor of sociology and Norwegian at Luther, was elected president. Decorah people, it was hoped, would find it more reasonable to send their daughters to school in town rather than away to college. President Preus hoped that the relationship between the two schools would be most friendly; he offered the girls use of Luther's library and scientific laboratories. The two schools had the same calendar, tuition, and fees.

In 1933, the worst year of the Depression, now the Decorah Junior College for Girls contracted with Luther faculty to offer instruction. It also made an agreement that it would turn over its assets to Luther if the two schools should merge, something Preus knew would be necessary in the future. He used the power of the emergency measure passed at the church convention to determine how many women to admit. By 1933 women were registering at the college, attending classes with the men, going to chapel, and participating in student activities such as the college newspaper, *College Chips*. Their course of study was the same as the men whose curriculum had just been changed to a general liberal arts degree with majors and requirements for graduation.

Over the course of the 1933-1934 school year, the proposal for the college to enroll women continued to be debated. President Ove Preus, in a speech to the Luther College Club, on May 15, 1934, fully expecting the decision for co-education would be made in June and argued the enrollment of women was part of a process of the "growth and development of the institution."[585] He pointed to the change in curriculum. Its removal of the classical language requirements was more fundamental to the character of the institution than the admittance of women would be.[586] About that he was right. To have gotten rid of these requirements was, in many ways, to prepare for women students to enroll at the college. That was never mentioned by Olson, who regretted the loss of Greek and Latin, even as he supported co-education. He had agreed to the reduction of the requirements to improve enrollment numbers. Had he also been thinking of women's enrollment at the time? He did not say, but Preus clearly saw the wisdom of the change and that it had made way for co-education.

Opposition became especially fierce after the *Lutheran Herald* reported that President Aasgaard, the Board of Trustees of the college, and the Board of Education of the church—which over the year had apparently changed its mind to favor co-education—would recommend to the 1934 Convention of the church that it pass the motion to amend Article II of the Articles of Incorporation, so that Luther could enroll women.

In answer to the negative reactions from those opposing co-education, members of the Luther College faculty sent a letter to the *Lutheran Herald* supporting co-education. Written by Professors Herman G. Talle, David Torrison Nelson, and Carl W. Strom, it noted the achievements of the old Synod which had built schools for both men and women. After the loss of the Ladies' Seminary, the Synod's heirs were left without a school for girls, which the faulty members admitted. They challenged Knut Stalland, an alumnus and strong supporter of Luther College. He had also suggested rebuilding the Red Wing Lutheran Ladies' Seminary. The professors responded:

David Torrison Nelson

> In the flush times when Lutheran Ladies' Seminary went down, it would have required only the will to maintain such a school for the Church to have kept it alive But no such support for the principle of segregation was forthcoming.

Now, they argued, the new church had schools all of which, except Luther College, enrolled women. Luther should get in line with the entire church and culture.

> It is becoming increasingly clear that it is extremely difficult to rally support for the principle of segregation in only one of our colleges. It is the view of the faculty that any attempt to force the maintenance of the principle of segregation at Luther College is contrary to the actual established policy of the Church and will lead to disastrous consequences to the College and the cause of education in the Church.[587]

The memory of the Ladies' Seminary still stuck in the craw of many people, and these faculty members remembered it well—even after twelve years—and knew that support to rebuild had not been there. The mysterious reasons for the demise of the Ladies' Seminary project were obviously known by these men, but remained secret.

George Torrison, an alumus, reacted especially against the faculty's argument that not much would change.

> These Luther traditions would be seriously affected if not wrecked. Luther College, at least to the many who are opposed to the change would no longer be the Luther College that it had been—the Luther College they had learned to love and for which they had given so much.[588]

Walter Ong helps us understand the ferocity of these objections and why they went so deep. He argued that Latin had been regarded by educators even into the twentieth century who

> felt that a boy's education was basically a puberty rite, a process preparing him for adult life by communicating to him the heritage of a past in a setting which toughened him and thus guaranteed his guarding the heritage for the future. . . . This association of Latin with a toughening marginal environment of a puberty-rite type was sufficient to keep Latin in its place as the basic discipline forming the prep school character, with its twin emphases on Latin and physical hardihood (modulated eventually into good sportsmanship).[589]

The defenders of maintaining Luther as a school for men believed this as much from their own experience as any theory. For them a loss of this kind of education meant that boys would not become men or leaders. It is of interest also to note the strong emphasis on sports of Luther College. Both Latin and the physical hardihood of Luther men were part of their identity.

This language can be found underneath the thought of the leaders in the Luther community. Johannes Ylvisaker in his sermon at the dedication of the Red Wing Lutheran Ladies' Seminary had briefly talked about not wanting feminized men or masculine women. J. C. K. Preus would also speak of "the

The Luther College baseball team

manly virtues" that Luther taught and which he thought would be gone with the advent of co-education. It helps us understand some of the deepest questions surrounding the move to co-education, not just at Luther but in many colleges at the time.

Girls of this tradition were to receive a different higher education, as we have seen. For them education was also a puberty rite. In this tradition, they left their mothers to study with their aunts. If they were sent away, it was to girls' schools like the Nissen School for Girls, Christiansfeld, or Red Wing Lutheran Ladies' Seminary. Ong argues that a young girl's reading of literature was also a puberty rite, and a break with her past, but it introduced her to "a pleasant, fanciful, romantic world."[590]

Despite these many strong objections from significant alumni, the Luther faculty once again approved the idea of co-education and appointed a committee to formulate a resolution to that effect. Their urgency was financial. Without that, the question would have come much later, even if many wanted co-education for the sake of their daughters. They adopted the resolution as a faculty on January 24, 1934, and presented the resolution on February 1, 1934, at a meeting of the Board of Education of the NLCA with the college trustees. It was to be presented at the church convention of 1934.

> Whereas, the president, board of trustees, and nearly [sic] the entire faculty of the College are of the unanimous opinion that this action is essential to the future welfare of the institution; and

> Whereas, it is the consensus of opinion of a large body of our church people in Iowa that the school as a co-educational institution would be enabled to serve adequately its natural constituency in that State, therefore,

Be it resolved by the Board of Trustees of Luther College of Decorah, Iowa, and the Board of Education of the Norwegian Lutheran Church of America: That Article II of the Articles of Incorporation of Luther College, of Decorah, Iowa, be amended to read as follows:

The purpose of this Corporation is to establish and maintain a Lutheran education institution of collegiate rank at Decorah, Iowa, that shall give young men and young women a good Christian college education, and, in particular, prepare young men for the study of theology with a view to subsequent service in the Christian ministry. . . ."[591]

President Preus' report to the convention provided statistics to demonstrate the critical financial situation of the college. The college had made drastic cuts. Faculty had not received raises. The church's annual appropriation to the college was only $23,000; interest on the endowment had come to only $4,437.33; income from the students was less than had been anticipated; finally, the interest on the debt of $140,000 used up funds with which they might have survived. The only bright spot was that income from Decorah Junior College for Girls was $5,638.75, which exceeded interest on the endowment by $2,302.42.

Preus had concluded his report by asserting that co-education had saved other schools and might help Luther. The proposed change in the Articles of Incorporation was to be presented to the convention the

The Weiser House, where the Decorah School for Girls was located

coming summer of 1934. At its meeting in February 1934, the Board of Education of the NLCA unanimously endorsed the idea that "co-education at Luther College . . . begin with the school year starting in September 1934."[592] Things seemed to be going smoothly toward co-education. The only caveat was that the change had to be ratified at the biennial meeting of the church and corporation in June.

The matter appeared to have been resolved, but suddenly, and abruptly, the Board of Education changed its mind and responded to the proposal for the summer convention. On April 11, 1934, the Board of Education, in a meeting with President Ove Preus and President Aasgaard, presented three possible solutions to the problem: 1) Luther College should remain a college exclusively for men; or 2) it should admit women; or 3) Luther Seminary should move to Decorah, and Luther College and St Olaf should merge into one institution on the St Olaf campus. Members of the faculty found

NLCA President Aasgaard

this strange reversal outrageous. They thought the resolution of February 1, 1934, had been equally supported by the Luther College board and the Board of Education. In explaining its reversal, the Board of Education said it had not "changed any of its fundamental convictions in the matter."[593] Once again, the faculty was outraged.

David Nelson's history of the college, *Luther College: 1861-1961*, indicates that the story of these deliberations has never been very clearly told. The minutes of the April 11, 1934, Board of Education meeting do not make it clear as to why the board had changed its mind. Nelson reports it from his own personal contacts and scrutiny of the minutes. According to Nelson, Aasgaard asked if a resolution was ready to present to the convention. A Board of Trustees representative from Luther said they had such a resolution before them from July 26, 1933. The chair, J. C. K. Preus, looked in the file and said "This will never do, gentlemen." Arguing that its language was unsatisfactory, they called in a lawyer, Carl F. Granrud, to draft a new one. What the Board wanted was a proposal that might restructure the church's entire educational system and make it more efficient.[594] It also may have been a last gasp attempt to stop co-education at Luther College. For certain, the board exerted far more control over Luther College than it did for St. Olaf. This grew to be more and more irksome to the Luther College community.

Two weeks later the *Lutheran Herald* reported on what had happened at the convention. It began its report with compliments to the convention for being calm and deliberate. The report from the special committee, which included the Board of Education, the Board of Trustees, and ten additional elected members, with the seminary and senior college presidents as advisory members, had prepared the report and questions. A statement preceded the report which was something of a confession, and rather odd. It confessed:

> our failure to seek and understand God's will and guidance at all times, our failure to view our problems in their true perspective and in relation to the whole program of the Church, and our unwillingness as individuals and as groups to submit to the will of God and to do our part in the full discharge of our God-given responsibility.

With that it asked God

> for forgiveness and the courage to proceed to make such decisions as shall lead us to a correct solution of our problems.[595]

What followed were two pages of questions. The first section had to do with the willingness of the church to raise an additional $74,000, added to its commitment of $183,000. Section II was the meat of the proposal and had been the cause of the uproar.

Its first question was that, if the church did not support the proposal to raise these funds, Concordia and Augustana should become junior colleges at a saving of $20,000, so Luther and St. Olaf could remain senior colleges. A second question asked whether Luther or St. Olaf should be eliminated by merging with each other. The third question was, if the answer to the second question was yes, where would the merged college be located? The fourth was whether Luther Seminary should be moved to whichever campus had been closed? The fifth was if they were not merged, should Luther become co-educational? The sixth and final question asked whether the church approved having both junior and senior colleges in the same area.

Noting the questions were difficult, the writers took umbrage at the implication they had not sought God's will. "In these business matters we cannot abdicate reason and submit to what someone may claim to be God's will."[596] The conversation about the several proposals began in the afternoon. The dismay on the convention floor was duly reported as was its length. Instead of a proposal to introduce co-education at Luther, the

NLCA convention in 1925, but the convention surely looked like this in 1932, 1934, and 1936 too.

convention had received a report on the church's educational institutions, their problems and possible solutions, including the merger of St. Olaf and Luther in some kind of "marriage." Both sides, especially the Luther side, erupted in protest. Henry O. Talle, faculty member, gave a speech at the convention foreseeing not an amicable marriage, but something more like a Civil War.[597]

The meeting lasted through the afternoon late into the evening. "The feeling on the question was growing quite tense and possibly many spent a sleepless night anxious about the outcome of this question." The next morning, to the great relief of the delegates, President Aasgaard, a trusted and beloved leader, took the floor and suggested that the question could not be solved, nor was there any good reason to lay blame on decisions of the past.[598] After a tense day of conflict, the convention was happy to refer the whole question of the church's educational system to the president of the church, the Board of Trustees of the church, and the Board of Education. Implicit in the resolution was the understanding that this group would resolve the question of co-education. The delegates returned home much relieved that the actions recommended had been delayed and provisions made to deal with the issues before the next convention.

Two months after this tense meeting on the future of the college, on August 13, 1934, about fifty alumni met at the college. After hearing reports from the administration as to the financial realities of the college, the group appointed a committee to plan a seventy-fifth anniversary in 1936 and establish a fund that would raise money for the college at its diamond jubilee. This in effect began the revival of Luther College from its lowest point. The proposal caused the Luther College community to spring into action. Melvin O. Grangaard, who had been central to the process of putting the college on a better financial grounding, essentially took over the fight. Within a few months Luther had paid off its debt and was able to leave the marriage proposal on the table.

In April 1935, the North Central Association of Colleges and Secondary Schools gave accreditation to the school, now the Decorah College for Women which offered a four-year program toward a B.A. Afterward Professor George A. Works of the University of Chicago, executive secretary of the association, remarked on the irony of accrediting a college "that has no plant, no campus, and no faculty."[599] In June 1935 two women graduated from the women's college, now essentially Luther College.

The *Lutheran Herald* printed several columns and letters from both sides. Ditlef Ristad, former president of the Red Wing Lutheran Ladies' Seminary wrote "Don't Give Up the Ship!" Ristad announced he was going to vote against the measure at the convention because there should be "one Lutheran senior college for men in the Middle West." Furthermore, he thought that passing the amendment would engage the other colleges in greater competition for women students, something they did not need at the time. He then brought up an issue which he, and many others, had likely been thinking about since the fire which destroyed Red Wing Lutheran Ladies' Seminary:

> I believe that when the time comes for the establishment of a senior college for girls exclusively, the church should through its official agencies build and direct it in a location most advantageous to the service for which it is created.[600]

He wanted a girls' school, not co-education. This was an old argument from before the rebuilding of the second Main Building in Decorah, when several in the Luther community had urged the school to become co-educational. That idea had been quashed by Laur. Larsen at the time of the fire, in 1889, just when the Ladies' Seminary was being planned. Building a school for women meant that Luther College could remain a college for men.

As of yet, the Board of Education had not yet spoken, but it did finally at the 1936 convention of the ELC. Led by Grangaard, who had worked on the legal language, it approved a resolution concerning all four of its colleges: "The Church supports four Senior Colleges. The four Senior Colleges shall be coeducational institutions." At the same time, the Luther College Board of Trustees declared the women who had graduated from the Decorah College for Women alumnae of Luther College. After the meeting of the Luther College Corporation the revised Articles of Incorporation of Luther College were adopted, establishing co-education, by a vote of 472 to 31. The conflict was over. Luther College was ready to begin its second seventy-five years, now as a co-educational institution. The decision gained the college many new supporters. As David Nelson concluded, "It was co-education 'which cut the cord of slow strangulation.'"[601] Luther College would survive.

In 1936 five women received their B.A. degrees from the women's college, among them Helen Hoff, daughter of T. A. Hoff, former president of Red Wing Lutheran Ladies' Seminary. She graduated summa cum laude. Later the Luther board made them alumna of Luther. This is a satisfying denouement to the struggle to admit women to the college, especially women from the Norwegian Synod tradition. Helen Hoff, soon to be married to Rolf Haatvedt, longtime professor and supporter of the college, stands for all of the women who had worked for the education of their daughters in the schools of the Synod. During the fiftieth anniversary of the Decorah College for Women, she told colorful stories of being in the first class of women at the college and how she had managed to excel in her studies, recounting her time in the classroom with older professors such as Billy Sihler, who did not like women in his class. Still, she excelled. By her testimony, she did not at all feel out of place, something another woman in her class thought was rather funny. Helen, she said, was well aware of her place in the college and was no shrinking violet. She remained a delightful force for good in Decorah and among the Luther faculty wives for many years.

Co-Education At Luther

Six years after Luther College admitted women, the Second World War broke out when Japan attacked Pearl Harbor on December 7, 1941, and America declared war on Japan and the other Axis powers. This left the college nearly bereft of men, when many left to serve in the military. Women students were suddenly in the majority, which made for a very different kind of community, especially at Luther. While women entered the labor force in the men's stead, as per Rosie the Riveter, there were enough women enrolled to keep the college going. The male students tended to be those heading to seminary with a 4-D draft classification. The year 1942 was also a year of another terrible fire, when the second Main Building burned to the ground. With the reduced student enrollment and the financial difficulties imposed by the war, it was not rebuilt until the 1950s.

When men returned from the war, women returned to the home—something of an oversimplification, but it was largely true, a fact Betty Friedan railed against in her *Feminine Mystique*. Women with a college degree still tended to marry and stay home as housewives. If something happened to their husbands, or they did not get married, their education was a safety net. It was not uncommon for girls as late as the 1950s to come to Lutheran colleges with hopes of marrying a minister. Several colleges offered classes to women students planning to marry pastors at a nearby seminary.[602]

Pre-seminary candidates at Luther and the other Lutheran colleges were plentiful enough that the Norwegian Lutheran colleges, especially Luther, continued to offer a rigorous pre-seminary course of languages—Latin, Greek, and often Hebrew—keeping faith with their founding traditions. In the 1950s over ten percent of the male students graduating from Luther College went on to Luther Seminary in St. Paul. The old model of the colleges as preparatory schools for the seminary continued to some degree as the colleges of the ELC sent their graduates to Luther Seminary in considerable numbers.

Women students still perceived that to be a pastor's wife was something of a public profession that gave them a chance to use their gifts to serve the Lord and the church. Many actually came to college with the stated intention to marry a future minister. In small towns the parsonage was still the center of the community, and the pastor's wife was hostess for the congregation in her home. In addition, she expected to be a leader in the ladies aid, lead the Bible study, run the Sunday school, direct the choir, teach piano, and even play the organ for church.

New Main at Luther College

To that end, deans of women at the various colleges taught their women students how to be ladies, good wives, and mothers, especially pastors' wives. They hosted many events which continued the tradition of hospitality with good manners and deportment, much like the girls had been taught at Red Wing Ladies' Seminary: how to lead a conversation at the dinner table, when and where to wear gloves, how to give teas, put on dinners, etc. This continued in a small way the education of girls to be cultured ladies.

The seminary continued to do its part in training men and their prospective wives in the finer things of life. Nora Preus Rogness, wife of President Alvin Rogness of Luther Seminary and great-granddaughter of Linka and Hermann Preus, gave a regular lecture to the Luther Seminary men on hospitality and manners, which became legendary. Faculty wives at seminaries put on fancy receptions

Alvin and Nora Preus Rogness

with white linen tablecloths, silverware, fine china, and crystal to demonstrate to future pastors' wives how it was done. Everyone still understood the basics of the vocation, up to the 60s. The 50s, however, proved to be increasingly difficult for the pastor's wife, as the role of women began to change. Pastor's wives were still thought to be part of the package by call committees, but increasingly they began to object, saying they had married the man, not the congregation.

Conclusion

The story of how the pastors of the Norwegian Synod worked to educate their daughters, from the kitchens in the frontier parsonages to Luther College, is a story that shows how a group of sophisticated and cultured pastors and professors and their wives lived through a time of great change and turmoil in relation to the role and education of women in society. They knew very well what was going on in society, both in Europe and in America. They understood the way in which many who favored equal rights for women attacked the church and felt that much of the feminism of their day was against Christianity. We hear that in C. K. Preus' eulogy to Mrs. Koren, who thought that a woman's place was in the home, which was her kingdom.

They based their views on the authority of Scripture and traditions they knew well. Their reading of Scripture, for example, in respect to the issue of slavery gave them problems. This question of the place of women was much more existential for them than the issue of slavery, and, biblically, more complicated, which Naeseth admitted. Not surprisingly, they used the same method reading of the Bible to find their answers to the question of what a woman was and how she should be educated. They wanted their daughters to become ladies, well educated and cultured.

Although high schools (academies) of the church provided training for women to become secretaries and teachers, pastors and professors associated with Luther College recognized their daughters wanted more than that. They had always believed, going back to the Renaissance, that a manly education involved training in the classical languages. They were continuing that tradition proudly. Not surprisingly it continued even into the 1960s, even after co-education. Greek and Latin at Luther College, taught by Pip Qualley, the venerable teacher, dean and advisor, was always thought of by grateful male students who survived his teaching, a cold morning shower that made men out of them.

It was unthinkable for the pastors and professors to imagine their daughters getting a male education, elite as it was. The speeches made at the laying of the cornerstone and the dedication services of Red Wing Lutheran Ladies' Seminary reveal the attempt of the founders to give their daughters a liberal education that still remained feminine and gracious. To accept the feminism of Cady Stanton and her sister suffragettes, with their desire to go to school with their brothers, would be to give their daughters a masculine education—as indeed Cady Stanton had gotten from her father when she asked to learn Latin from him.

As elites, the pastors and professors of the Norwegian Synod tried to find a way to continue that tradition even as the times were changing—and their classical departments and liberal arts education remained profoundly rich until most language requirements were dropped in the 1970s. Ultimately their tradition of single sex education could not be maintained as co-education became the norm in American education. More important financial exigency drove the decision as it had in many other colleges during the Depresssion. Co-education made it possible for many colleges like Luther to survive and grow into flourishing institutions today.

What changed more than anything as the college admitted women was men's education, exactly what the pastors and professors had feared.

It became more feminine as women were now given entry into the old masculine disciplines. While one can see this has been good for women, most educators today would say that boys are losing out in school now that education has been feminized. The question hangs fire even today, one that the proponents of co-education have never really answered: Do boys and girls need to be together or apart for their educations? Traditionalists and feminists have made arguments on both sides of that issue. It has still not been solved. The question of what courses are necessary is also still not settled, nor will it ever be, although thoughtful educators think some kind of core requirements from the old liberal arts curriculum of the West should still be part of a good education.

Linka's question about what good an education was for a woman hovers over all the speeches and language about how women were to think of their vocations. Her education had given her aspirations beyond domestic duties. Still, someone needs to keep house. She resented somewhat that her sex made these duties required of her. She did enjoy other parts of the pastor's wife vocation: teaching the faith to her children and others in her charge. She had learned through her schooling, especially music, literature, and wider reading much that her husband had learned in school, and she transmitted it to her children.

The lives of the early feminists almost always show a young girl envying her brother's education and place in her father's eye. Often they demanded they be taught the same curriculum at home by the fathers, or in some cases, as in Cady Stanton's, a school where they could learn the same as boys, and with them, in the classes. Economic necessity, in the case of many colleges like Luther, gave women students the chance to receive an education like the men they would eventually marry and with whom they would raise their children. This was what Rousseau and Nissen had suggested. They did not face the fact that, given such an education, women might want to do the same things as their brothers. Thus it is not surprising that such women as these began entering the professions, such as medicine, by the middle of the nineteenth century. It also is not surprising that as they did so, there seemed to be an almost hysterical attack on such transgressions. The medical advice by doctors such as Clarke on the girl needing to avoid study so her sexual organs can develop properly seemed to be along that line.

The thinking of these Luther College divines remained remarkably consistent and traditional. Koren sounded like Wergeland and many fathers of previous generations when he noted that daughters had a real vocation taking care of their parents, whether single or married. We can see them reaching back into their histories—to Martin Luther's life with Katie, to Christiansfeld or the Nissen Girls' School, then the *Comitia Dumriana* and the Lutheran Ladies' Seminary—to find models and examples for a way to educate their daughters in a respectable and appropriate manner. They educated their daughters very well, but the model of single sex schools was too expensive and not fashionable by the middle of the last century. Co-education became the better solution for their question on how to educate their daughters as well as their sons. In some ways, as the culture changed in its understanding of who could do what, the role of the pastor's wife as a desirable profession which had been around for centuries disappeared.

The Ending of the Profession of Pastor's Wife

The change in the understanding of women and their role in society was perhaps the most sweeping change for society in the 1960s and 1970s. Naturally, the self-understanding of the pastor's wife shifted and changed with the shifting and changing roles of women. Linka Preus knew exactly what the vocation required. When Diderikke Ottesen married Nils Brandt she knew she was signing up for a vocation for which she had trained in her own home as a pastor's daughter and at Christiansfeld. Being a pastor's wife was a vocation the ambitious woman might aspire to at her time. It was a profession that offered her freedom and the chance to use her considerable gifts in the congregation.

In many ways the pastor's family remained a unit of production, similar to the farm family. Everyone in the family was expected to understand the father's profession and how their place in the parsonage contributed to the flourishing of their family, congregation, and local community. The girls had been trained early on to manage the parsonage and its necessary production of food, clothes, and shelter. Nearly every waking moment for a woman in any home at the time had to be devoted to such elemental tasks, from raising the animals they would eat and use for clothes, preparing food to be stored and cooked, to preparing their clothes.

These skills were less and less necessary as the century progressed. After the Civil War, material and food could be purchased at stores in the city or a town nearby. This freed up the lives of all women to spend more time on other necessities. Still, as a housewife, the pastor's wife had to manage what were frequently limited resources for the feeding and clothing of the family. From Katie and Martin Luther's marriage on, it was frequently the wife who was practical and capable of managing the sparse resources of the parsonage. In many ways this became more and more wearing as the family moved from being self-sufficient on the farm to a parsonage in the town with fewer resources for producing food and clothes. In the New World this became even more trying, since the pastor was no longer supported by the state.

Along with the house, which the congregation thought of as its own, there was the problem of keeping it in proper repair and clean. Boards of trustees watched this closely and commented on the skill and character of the pastor's wife, if this were not done to their standards. It was a common theme. Few put the requirements as vividly as Koren did in his piece on the pastor's wife.[603] Cleanliness in the parsonage and in the personal attire of the pastor's family could be easily observed by the parish. Dwellers in the parsonage often found these judgments irritating, resenting their loss of privacy.

One finds references to the cleanliness of the pastor's wife in many books of advice to them. Arthur Hewitt wrote as late as the 1940s in *The Shepherdess* about an unkempt woman such as no pastor's wife should be:

> I am thinking of women of high culture and social pretentions and you may take it on the testimony of a nose-witness that many of them are the worst offender. Only yesterday I stood near one of them in conversation. She was as clean-looking a woman as I ever saw; her hair was perfectly cared for, her dress was fresh and neat, her skin was perfect—but her underclothes were broadcasting their, or her, need of the tub.[604]

He went on to observe that women faculty at a women's college were by far the worst in such offenses. Here are echoes of the nineteenth century notion that an educated woman favored her brain over her sex organs, something the pastor's wife should not do.

From the beginning—from Katie to Linka to very recently—pastors' wives attended to the spiritual lives of those in the family, especially since their husbands were frequently gone on visits to congregations far away from the parsonage. They had very little doubt about what they were to teach: Scripture, hymns, and Luther's Small Catechism. They also had devotional aids—books such as Luther's house postils and sermons—to read to their family for evening devotions or on Sundays when the family could not make it to church. It was not uncommon, even in the late twentieth century, for small congregations in remote locations to have church services only once or twice a month.[605]

Linka, Diderikke and other pastors' wives understood when they married that this was part of their vocation in the home, and most of them relished it. In fact, it could well have been why many of them aspired to be pastors' wives. It was a something of a public role of spiritual leadership. In the nineteenth century, as ladies aids were being established, pastors' wives became the natural leader of the aid, especially providing Bible studies and devotions. For a pastor's wife, helping the poor and finding the means to do so had always been part of her vocation.

As time went on, what gave Diderikke an opportunity for a vocation and freedom to exercise it began to feel like a straitjacket against which younger women chafed. The pastor's wife began to want to be an autonomous person, one who had not signed up for the family business. These implicit expectations began to cause friction between the congregation and the pastor's wife as she sought to establish her own identity. As feminists raised questions about the theology of marriage, that the two became one, or the notion that the pastor's wife was part of her husband's vocation began to erode. The idea that the two should be one, as Jesus said in Matthew 19, referring to Adam and Eve, did not mean one should be over the other. It was after the Fall that Eve first heard about submission. Later theologians would wonder if the coming of Christ returned husband and wife to mutuality, rather than the continued curse of headship from Genesis 3.[606] While Ephesians 5 seems to recommend submission, on deeper study, it says both should be submissive to each other. As notions changed, pastors' wives became conflicted about their roles.

Many books of advice for pastors' wives in the 1950s dealt with the fact that a pastor married a woman he loved for who she was, and she had married a man for who he was, not his job. As time went on, when call committees asked the prospective candidate about his wife and what she did and how she could fit into his ministry, many wives were offended. My mother's generation of pastor's wives heard in these protests a recipe for a troubled marriage, because neither the pastor nor his wife seemed to be realistic about the vocation they were entering. Still, having one's identity shaped by one's spouse came to be thought inappropriate for women in the late twentieth century. One former pastor's wife, after leaving him to become a pastor in a denomination other than her husband's, wrote,

"I am slowly digging out the anger and restructuring my identity."[607] For her becoming whole meant having an identity other than her husband's, something the women of Diderikke's and Sigrid Harrisville's generations would not have said, although they had strong and colorful personalities.

This also meant that the parsonage as a possession began to be an issue. While the record of these buildings, going back far into history, is not always good—congregations often failed to keep them in good condition—they did offer spacious housing to the families. By the 1970s, however, when pastors' wives increasingly declined to be part of the ministry team and wanted their own careers, pastors wanted to buy their own homes to build equity for retirement. Those who did so in the 1970s were fortunate, given the rise of property values, but, as the decades wore on, buying a house in a small town with a poor real estate market meant the pastor could be trapped in a home he could not easily leave. Today pastors in small towns may look at the former parsonage and think it could have been a fine place to live for its spaciousness and its place in the economy of the town.

Freud As an Issue

The dominance of Freud in the understanding of women raised another kind of issue regarding the typical pastor's wife. The notion of being a team in the parsonage, and the complimentary nature of the male and female, understood from either Christian theology or Rousseau, may have made the role easier to fill in the nineteenth century. However, Freud added to the theology of submission, a topic Koren and Ylvisaker had addressed biblically. As Freud's thought became the regnant way to think about women, the burden on both husband and wife was the wife's sexual fulfillment. This would assure her a happy adjustment to life as wife and mother in the home. One book on the subject, *The Shepherdess*, began with a somewhat frank chapter, given the time, on the wife as sexual partner. While in the past, the author argued, clergy wives may have thought sex was dirty and to be avoided, causing terrible frustrations to the husband and reasons for his straying, the new thinking was that sex should be enjoyed and the wife fulfilled.

> There must be sexual harmony, understanding, and communion if there is to be perfect spiritual love. To those who love perfectly, the sexual act is not carnal; it is the consecration of ultimate intimacy, the holy communion of married lovers. The physical gratification is there, more perfect of course

than in unadapted mates, but love and tenderness have so utterly transcended that which is physical as to make the experience a sacrament.[608]

This attitude, while consistent with Christian thought in the twentieth century, may have created an impossible ideal to reach. Not reaching it, according to the thought of the day, made the wife frustrated with her place in the home and the marriage. It may have added more stress to a clergy wife, if her husband and the marriage did not approach the ideal. This was especially the case if what the wife wanted was to be autonomous and, probably more important, get a job—to raise the family out of its poverty. In the 1950s the typical salary of a clergyman lagged far behind that of others.

Keeping the woman in the home after World War II fit with the 1950s longing for normalcy. Things changed radically over the next decades. At the same time the pastor's role in society was declining. The change in the understanding of women and their lives often placed the pastor's wife in a difficult position. As a frequent speaker at pastors' wives retreats, after I came to Luther Seminary in 1981, I was struck by the pain of these women as they tried to find their place now that the old model was disintegrating. The appointed counselor from the synod or church body was in high demand for counseling upset and distraught women who no longer knew what their roles were.[609]

In the summer of 1970, the American Lutheran Church (ALC) and the Lutheran Church in America (LCA) voted to permit the ordination of women. Now many of the wives who had married to enter a vocation they understood to be something of a spiritual leader saw their younger counterparts going to seminary. While many of the older pastors' wives favored the change, some could not escape feelings of jealousy. Not surprisingly, numbers of them began training for a second career as pastors themselves in the 1980s. While the scope of this book does not include a study of women becoming pastors, the decision to ordain women spelled the end of the vocation of pastor's wife as it had been understood over the 500 years of the Protestant parsonage.

All this said, the parsonage did serve important needs that still need to be addressed. As we have noted, the vocation of the pastor's wife was strongly connected with hospitality—a Christian virtue and congregational necessity. She saw to the entertainment of parish guests, the hosting of seasonal parties and gatherings, visiting church bureaucrats, etc. These needs still exist, and congregations have solved them in various ways, but perhaps not always so well. People long for authentic personal connections and community. The church might well consider how to meet these needs in creative and hospitable ways, ones that help a community flourish. It can no longer expect those in the parsonage to do so alone, but at the same time part of the vocation of pastors is to see that these things get done, whether or not they do them themselves. These are issues that need to be attended to in congregations everywhere. I hope that this history will help current pastors and their spouses to think about them.

Final Observations

In 1968, Sigrid Harrisville was the dorm mother in Brandt Hall at Luther College. She and her sister Martha Reishus Langemo lived there, dignified presences on the campus. The times, they were a changin', as the song had it. The old rules went the way of the Dodo bird after the birth control pill, the sexual revolution, and the burgeoning feminist movement of the 1960s and 1970s. Monitoring the student lounges to make sure couples had both feet on the floor became unpleasant. Not long after I arrived, Mrs. Harrisville left to join her son, Roy, Jr. who was teaching at Luther Seminary. There she remained a civilizing and elegant presence almost until her death in 1999. She represented to me the ending of a tradition that stretched far back to Red Wing Lutheran Ladies' Seminary and the beginning of the century, but even further back into the first parsonages built out on the prairies by fathers and mothers in the Norwegian Synod.

It is important to recall that the founders of Luther College, who opposed much of the thinking behind the suffragettes and the feminists of their day, sent their daughters and granddaughters to various colleges and graduate schools. Koren, whose speech showed him to be among the least friendly toward women's emancipation, had a daughter, Caroline, who served as preceptress at St. Olaf. She married Christian Naeseth, the author of the paper on women's emancipation in 1904, concluding women should be submissive. Their daughter, Henriette Christiane Koren Naeseth (1899-1987) graduated from Grinnell College and earned a Ph.D.

Henriette Naeseth

at the University of Chicago. She taught English at

Augustana College, Rock Island, Illinois, for many years. She nurtured generations of women scholars, among them Mary Hull Mohr, daughter of a Swedish Augustana Luther pastor, who devoted her entire teaching life to Luther College. Ruth Mostrom, also a pastor's daughter, began teaching at Luther College in the 1950s after graduating from St. Olaf, some years in public school teaching, and a time at Stevens College in Missouri. She came to teach Latin, now something women could teach, and ended up being a long-time registrar, a stable force for continuity over the next thirty-six years and a gracious mentor to many young women who came to teach at the college.

Laur. Larsen's daughters became equally distinguished in their professions. Hanna Astrup Larsen (1873-1945) had a distinguished career as editor in New York City. Her sister Karen Larsen (1879-1961), earned an M.A. in history at Columbia University (1919) and taught for many years at St. Olaf College in the history department. Mary Preus, great-granddaughter of Linka, served as student body president at Luther and went on to earn a Ph.D. in classics. She taught at Luther Seminary and later at the University of St. Thomas in St. Paul. Her life as pastor's daughter, a pastor's wife—married to Jonathan Preus, her first cousin once removed—and professor of classics embodied the yearnings of Linka for her own education and the education of her daughters as well as mastering the classical tradition, one of the deepest values of Luther College as a college for men.

Mary Preus

However one reads this story, attention must be paid to the tradition of the Lutheran parsonage in this country, as represented here by the Norwegian Synod, and how it adapted to the changing landscape and the changing times until the ordination of women in 1970. That changed parsonage life dramatically. This is a story of how they came into their own.

Parsonages down through history have provided Protestant countries with an astonishing number of leaders, women as well as men. Luther College fostered and benefited from the service of pastors' families. Its leadership often came from these accomplished families or the students they raised up. The pastors led a theological community that was learned, eloquent, and sharp. Their debates filled church history books for generations of American Lutheran theological history and deservedly so.

Those theological debates, which defined and gave identity to various Norwegian Lutheran colleges for decades, have faded into the specialized theological circles of American Lutheranism.

The history of the Luther College tradition, however, still lives on in vivid and lively ways because of the writings and sketches of Linka Preus and Elisabeth Koren. They are the ones who are read and appreciated today. Their accounts of the early settling of the land, the establishing of the parsonages, and their concern for the education of their daughters, still create a place and story around which the Luther College community gathers and how others come to know about Norwegian pioneer life in America. David Nelson, the historian of the college, saw it clearly in 1960.

> *Comitia Dumriana,* a female group of transitory existence with a certain fluttering daintiness and elusive fragrance of femininity veiling its hidden strength, which nevertheless hinted of future developments that neither the devotees of the classics nor the old Synod leaders, nor the shades of Walther and old Missouri, were able to stop.[610]

While there has been a proud recognition of the significance of Linka Preus and Elisabeth Koren, not enough has been said about the depth of their contributions to the tradition and their concern for the education of the daughters. More will, and should, be written. It is a worthy heritage and one that is not yet over. Indeed, Luther College's current president, Paula Carlson, grew up in a Lutheran parsonage and is now leading the school.

Endnotes

1   Elisabeth Koren to Linka Preus, February 6, 1859, Luther College Archives, 27:3-4.

2   Todd Walsh in his writings on the Red Wing Ladies' Lutheran Seminary called it a factory for pastors' wives.

3   See Walter Ong, "Latin Language Study as a Renaissance Puberty Rites," *Rhetoric, Romance, and Technology: Studies in the Interaction of Expression and Culture* (Ithaca and London: Cornell University Press, 1970), Loc. 2021.

4   Linka Preus, *Linka's Diary: On Land and Sea 1854-1864,* tr. Johan Carl Keyser Preus and Diderikke Margrethe Brandt (Minneapolis: Augsburg Publishing House, 1952), 62. This was in a letter to Linka from her future father-in-law, Paul Arctander Preus, on March 26, 1849. This translation includes letters to Linka, which are important, as this letter indicates.

5   Marvin G. Slind, editor, and Gracia Grindal, sketch editor, *Linka's Diary: A Norwegian Immigrant Story in Word and Sketches* (Minneapolis: Lutheran University Press, 2008), 239.

6   Ibid.

7   Ibid.

8   Erik Pontoppidan's *Collegia Pastorale Practicum* (1757), *Linka's Diary: On Land and Sea,* 121.

9   *Linka's Diary,* 292.

10 H. G. A. Jørgensen, *Sognepræst og Præstegaard: Dansk Præstegaards liv Gennem 1000 Aar* (København: G. E. C. Gads Forlag, 1937), 29.

11 Adam of Bremen, *History of the Archbishops of Hamburg-Bremen,* trans. Francis J. Tschan (New York: Columbia University Press, 1959), 212.

12 In the days of very low pastors' salaries, these offerings were crucial to the economic survival of the pastor and his family. My father braved every kind of bad Dakota weather to make these services as we needed every penny we could find. I remember one Christmas sitting at the front of the church as the people walked by and watching the dollar bills growing on the table. The boy next to me whispered, "Now your dad should be able to pay my dad for the car!"

13 Although there were no such tithes required in the New Land, the habit of supporting a pastor with gifts of food from the farm continued in my memory, and probably still does, in farm parishes of my childhood where people would leave a side of beef in the locker for us, bring chickens that were still alive for my parents

to prepare for our table, or cream, eggs, and many other such foods, meaning that my parents, both farm kids themselves, had to frequently butcher animals, make butter from cream, etc.

14 As late as the 1950s, my mother as pastor's wife knew that when people stopped by on a long trip they expected meals and places to sleep, and our parsonage, usually one of the larger homes in the town, had room for them.

15 Elisabeth Aasen, *"Billeder fra en dramatisktid: Norskerindringslitterature,"* in *Faderhuset: Nordisk Kvinde Litterature Historie* (Copenhagen: Rosinante, 1993), 140

16 Martin Luther, "The Estate of Marriage," Luther's Works (hereafter LW) 45 (Minneapolis: Augsburg Publishing House, 1962), 36.

17 Ibid., 39-40.

18 Ibid., 40.

19 See Linka's entries for October 1852, just before her son Christian Keyser Preus is born.

20 "Martin Luther to George Spalatin, November 30, 1524," LW 49 (Minneapolis: Augsburg Publishing House, 1963), 93.

21 Ibid.

22 Ibid.

23 Ernst Kroker, *Katharina von Bora: Martin Luther's Frau* (Leipzig: E Herberland, 1906).

24 "Martin Luther to John Rühel, May 4, 1525," LW 49 (Minneapolis: Augsburg Publishing House, 1963), 111.

25 "Martin Luther to Nicholas von Amsdorf, June 21, 1525," LW 49 (Minneapolis: Augsburg Publishing House, 1963), 117.

26 Martin Luther to Justus Jonas, September 4, 1535, LW 50, 94.

27 Martin Luther, "To my dearly beloved Katie, Mrs. Doctor Luther, etc., to the lady of the new pig market," LW 50, 208.

28 Martin Luther, "To the Councilmen of Germany," LW 45 (Minneapolis: Augsburg Publishing House, 1962), 366.

29 Martin Luther, "The German Mass, Liturgy and Hymns," LW 53 (Minneapolis: Augsburg Publishing House, 1965), 64.

30 Ibid.

31 Martin Luther, *Table Talk*, LW 54, (Minneapolis: Augsburg Publishing House, 1967), No. 396, 62.

32 Ibid. No. 847b, 174-175.

33 Ibid., No. 445. 72.

34 Ibid., No. 1237. 127.

35 Ibid., No. 3390b. 199-200.

36 Ibid., No. 5659. 470.

37 Ibid., 3178a. 191.

38 Slind, *Linka's Diary*, 269.

39 Jean-Jacques Rousseau, *Emile* (Classic Illustrated Edition, 2014), loc 7024.

40 Ibid.

41 Ibid., 7024.

42 Ibid., 7075.

43 Ibid., 7141.

44 See Ann Douglas, *The Feminization of American Culture* (New York: Avon Books, 1978).

45 Elisabeth Aasen, 140.

46 *Linka's Diary*, Slind, November 4, 1851. 259

47 *Linka's Diary: On Land and Sea: 1845-1864*, tr. and edited by Johan Carl Keyser Preus and Diderikke Margrethe Brandt Preus (Augsburg Publishing House: Minneapolis, 1952), 62. The Slind translation does not include the letters from others—and this quote of Linka's appeared in a letter to her from her future father-in-law, on March 26, 1849. In it he remembered her saying that several years before, wondering if she had had Hermann in mind at the time.

48 A light carriage with two or four low wheels and a collapsible top.

49 *Linka's Diary*, Slind, 30.

50 Ibid., February 15, 1845, 37.

51 Ibid., December 18, 19, 20, 1845, 57.

52 Ibid., April 1, 1850, 140.

53 Ibid., February 3, 1845, 37.

54 Ibid., December 22, 1845, 57-58.

55 Ibid., January 18, 1845, 31.

56 Ibid., February 6, 1845.

57 Ibid., March 6, 1845, 41.

58 Ibid.

59 Ibid., July 31, 1850, 154.

60 Ibid., December 12, 1850. 172.

61 Ibid.

62 Ibid., September 18, 1846, 68.

63 Ibid., Letter to Aunt Rosa, November 16, 1846, 72.

64 Ibid.

65 Ibid.

66 Ibid., April 10, 1850, 141.

67 Ibid.

68 Ibid., Letter to Aunt Rosa, January 7, 1847, 75.

69 Ibid., November 15, 1850, 130.

70 Ibid., February 2, 1845, 33.

71 Ibid., November 2, 1846, 71.

72 Hvoslef would later become bishop of Bergen and Halogoland.

73 Dietrichsen is credited with founding the Norwegian Synod in America. He was like many founders tough and difficult to get along with, but he had the foresight to build well. He was a Grundtvigian, and Hermann got into an argument with him which threatened his chance to get the call. It finally worked out, and Hermann led the Synod to revise its constitution to remove the offending Grundtvigian theology.

74 Slind, September 9, 1850, 158.

75 Gerhard Belgum in his doctoral thesis on the Norwegian Synod, "The Old Norwegian Synod in America, 1853-1890" (Yale, 1957), makes the claim that *Linka's Diary* is almost on a par with Augustine's Confessions in its spiritual wisdom and insight. Maybe a bit too much—but it does say this is a spiritual diary as much as a record of what happens during the days.

76 The Slind version of *Linka's Diary* mistakenly calls this *Hagl og List*, misreading *Makt* as *Hagl*, which means hail.

77 Christian Brinch, *"Familien Carlsen og Uranienborg," St. Halvard: Organ for Selskabet for Oslo Byes Vel* (Oslo: Aschehoug & Co., 1956), 106.

78 Ibid., 112.

79 Slind, January 9, 1845, 27.

80 Ibid., March 11, 1845, 42.

81 Ibid., March 12, 1845, 43.

82 *Linka's Diary: On Land and Sea*, 77.

83 Meeting with the A. C. Preuses and Dietrichsens.

84 *Linka's Diary: On Land and Sea*, 236.

85 Slind, May 1, 1848, 98.

86 Ibid., November 15, 1849, 132.

87 Ibid., June 19, 1850, 146.

88 Ibid., May 15, 1850, 209.

89 Elise Hovde to Bedstemoder, December 15, 1869, Luther College Archives 154:108-9. Luther College Archives hereafter LCA.

90 Lina Koren to Linka, February 13, 1870. LCA 154:108-16

91 Although Linka does not give his full name, the vicar is probably Jens Andreas Friis (1821-1896), a theological candidate at the time who went on to become professor of Samisk studies at the University of Christiania. He was also a student of Finnish and gathered folk tales from the Northern peoples in Scandinavian. He taught at the university until his death.

92 Slind, March 26 1845, 44.

93 Ibid., April 1, 1850, 140-141.

94 Ibid., January 18, 1845, 31.

95 Ibid., September 15, 1845, 52.

96 Ibid., October 1, 1845, 52.

97 Ibid., October 12, 52.

98 Ibid., October 24, 54.

99 *Linka's Diary: On Land and Sea*, 62.

100 Ibid.

101 Ibid., 64.

102 Slind, November 1, 1850, 126-127.

103 Ibid.

104 *Linka's Diary: On Land and Sea*, 78.

105 Slind, May 5, 1846, 60.

106 Ibid., May 26, 1850, 143.

107 It is not always that this was done. Linka records that her Aunt Rosa carried her own baby at its baptism on December 7, 1845. "The wee little girl was baptized here at home. Aunt Rosa held her, and the little ones and I were present as she received the name Agnes Louise," Slind, 32.

108 Slind, August 12, 157.

109 Ibid., August 26, 157.

110 *Linka's Diary: On Land and Sea*, 110.

111 Although the Norwegians did not have an historic episcopate, the bishops tightly controlled ordination; with the king and bishop in the state church it is not difficult to see the reluctance of bishops to ordain theological candidates going to America.

112 Arup was Bishop of Kristiania for some time and considered orthodox, but not polemical. He wanted the Conventicle Law done away with, among other things. He ordained several of the pastors who went to America.

113 Slind, September 24, 1850, 161.

114 Ibid., April 17, 1851, 191. Kierkegaard's *Works of Love* (1847) was just becoming well known in Norway, through the work of Gisle Johnson, the theological professor at the university. That Linka is reading these discourses just four years after their publication is a credit to her theological acumen.

115 Ibid., May 4, 1851, 205

116 Ibid., 129.

117 Ibid.

118 Ibid., May 15 1851, 209.

119 Ibid., May 21, 1851, 215.

120 Hilde Diesen, *Hanna Winsnes: Dagsverk og Nattetanker* (Aschehoug: Oslo, 2000), 248.

121 Slind, September 7, 1851, 256.

122 Ibid.

123 Ibid., 259.

124 Ibid.

125 Ibid., 260. Scott was one of the favorite novelists at the time for most Europeans and Americans who liked historical novels. Bernhard Severin Ingemann (1789-1862) was a Danish hymn writer whose works included historical novels about Danish history that were inspired by Scott.

126 Ibid., November 4, 1851, 260.

127 Ibid., November 24, 1851, 261.

128 Ibid., December 13, 1851, 264.

129 Letter from "Kalla" Keyser to Hermann, May 11, 1851. LCA 3:2:18.

130 Slind, December 13, 1851, 264.

131 Ibid.

132 Ibid., January 14, 1852, 267.

133 Ibid., January, 29, 1852, 268.

134 Ibid., February 1, 1852, 269.

135 Christian Keyser Preus, "Minder fra Spring Prairie prestegaard," *Symra: En Aarbog For Norske paa Begge Sider af Havet* (Decorah, Iowa: Decorah Posten Trykkeri, 1905), 15.

136 Hannah Winsnes, *Lærebog i de forskjellige Grene af Husholdningen,* 12th ed. (Christiania: J. W. Cappelens, 1888), 101.

137 Slind, October 5, 1852, 280.

138 Ibid., January 21, 1854, 296.

139 Ibid., November 5, 1855, 305.

140 Elisabeth Koren to Linka Preus, December 17, 1878.

141 Hanna Winsnes, 101.

142 Slind, November 4, 1851. 259

143 Ragna Nielsen, *Norske Kvinder i det 19de Aarhundrede* (Christiania: Det Norske Artie Forlag, 1904), 23.

144 "Thy Holy Wings" comes directly from this insight as does a phrase from "Day by Day" which early editors changed from like "a mother's" love to "father's" love.

145 Jewel A. Smith, *Music, Women, and Pianos in Antebellum Bethlehem, Pennsylvania: The Moravian Young Ladies' Seminary* (Bethlehem: Lehigh University Press, 2008), 161.

146 The Colletts were a large and influential family in Norway, Camilla being the most famous, but also Mrs. Anna Bors, who helped Elisabeth Fedde found the Deaconess hospital in Brooklyn, was a graduate. Jens Lauritz Arup was the bishop who ordained Hermann and several other immigrating pastors, Bugges were pastors and

professors, one Riddervold was a bishop, other pastors, and Blom also a well-known pastors' family. Taken from a list of students on the Christiansfeld rolls, 1838.

147 Camilla Collett, *I de lange Nætter* (Kristiania: Glydenhaug, 1906), 61.

148 Torill Steinfeld, Den *Unge Camilla Collett: Et Kvinnehjertes Historie* (Oslo: Gyldendal Forlag, 1996), 72.

149 *I de lange Naetter,* 61

150 Ibid., 74.

151 Ibid., 61.

152 Torill Steinfeld, 73.

153 Ellisiv Steen, *Camilla Collett om seg selv* (Oslo: Den Norske Bokklubben, 1985), 29-30.

154 Torill Steinfeld, 90.

155 See Caja Munch's comments on Mrs. Brandt. Caja Munch, "Letters from Wiota, 1855-1859," *The Strange American Way* (Carbondale, Missouri: Southern Illinois University Press, 1970), 83, 112.

156 See Addenda V, Lulla Hjort Preus "The Old Paint Creek Parsonage," from *Symra,* tr. J. C. K. Preus, and Addenda VI, "More about Paint Creek and the Hjorts," *Hermann Amberg Preus: A Family History,* published by J. C. K. Preus, 1966, 148, and154.

157 *Personalien der Mädchen Anstalte 1846* (Christiansfeld Archives).

158 See Gisle Bothne, *Den Norske Luther College 1861-1897* (Decorah, Iowa: Bothnes Forlag, 1897), 282. I have spent some time trying to confirm that she was presented to the king, but have only confirmed he visited Christiansfeld when Diderikke was there. Being presented to the king could have meant anything from a private audience to being greeted by him at some event where many others also were being greeted.

159 See Munch, 103.

160 Diderikke Brandt to Linka Preus, July 26, 1859, Rock River, Wisconsin, tr. Dikka Brandt Preus, LCA.

161 See footnote 157. Christiane once wished she could have had a *beruf,* like Diderikke at the college, and the many comments on Diderikke's inappropriate behavior by the other pastors' wives are my evidence here.

162 Which one is not mentioned, but Catharine Beecher's Ladies Seminary in Fox River, near Milwaukee, would not be a surprising choice. This history ended up at Lawrence College, that also includes the Downer School for Girls in Milwaukee.

163 Munch, 83.

164 Munch, 112.

165 Karen Larsen to Linka Preus, n. d., probably late 1860s.

166 Peer Strømme, *Halvor: The Story of a Pioneer Youth,* tr. David Nelson. (Decorah, Iowa: Luther College, 1960), 135.

167 Einar Boyesen, *Hartvig Nissen: 1815-1874 og Det Norske Skolevesens Reform,* Bind I (Oslo: Johan Grundt Tanum, 1947), 209.

168 The concept of *noblesse oblige* was a vital concept for the founders of Luther College and remained so when I arrived as a teacher there in 1968—and was a value, it was said, by notables like Pip Qualley in describing the Preus family and the kind of education Qualley was dedicated to during his many years at Luther.

169 Boyesen, 212.

170 James Hamre, *Georg Sverdrup: Educator, Theologian, Churchman* (Northfield, Minnesota: Norwegian-American Historical Association, 1986), 25-27. I used Hamre's language here and am grateful for his clear exposition of this for those who find some of these debates in Norway during the 1830s and 1840s too much inside baseball.

171 See Bothne who argued that the Latin schools in Norway became less Latin and Luther more so as time went on. Actually, Luther was more like the Nissen school. This explains why Luther students often went into Foreign Service; they knew how to learn languages. I will never forget an old veteran of the early Luther College curriculum explaining how many languages he took, adding that a teacher came to the school who could teach Sanskrit so they all had to learn that!

172 *Nissens Pigeskole og Privatseminar* (Christiania: Grøndahl & Søns Bogtrikkeri, 1900), 3.

173 Ibid.

174 Ibid.

175 Ibid.

176 Ibid.

177 VIlhelm Koren, "Nogle Erindringer fra min Ungdom og fra min første Tid i Amerika," *Symra: En Aarbog For Norske paa Begge Sider af Havet* (Decorah, Iowa: *Decorah Posten Trykkeri,* 1905), 44.

178 James Hamre does the best on this issue in his book on Georg Sverdrup and in several articles on the educational philosophies of several of the founders of Norwegian American schools.

179 *Livsbilleder fra Nordmændenes liv og historie i De forenede stater, D. 5: Norge i Amerika.*

180 Where Linka went to school, as she implies, is not easy to say. Primary education was a state requirement at her time, but she says nothing about where she went to school.

181 Slind, 259.

182 Kathryn Kish Sklar, *Catharine Beecher: A Study in American Domesticity* (New York: W. W. Norton Company, 1973), 17.

183 *National Tribune,* Washington, D. C., February 2, 1893.

184 Sklar, 175.

185 *Linka's Diary,* 198.

186 Elisabeth Koren, *The Diary of Elisabeth Koren 1853-1855* (Northfield, Minnesota: Norwegian-American Historical Association, 1955), 6.

187 Koren, 21.

188 Koren, 31.

189 Koren, 106.

190 Koren, 114.

191 Koren, 115.

192 Vilhelm Koren, "Til min Hustru paa vor Guldbryllupsdag," trans. Gracia Grindal, *Samlede Skrifter* IV, V. Koren ed. Paul Koren (Decorah: Lutheran Publishing House, 1912), 44.

193 Elisabeth Koren to Linka while they were in Norway, 1866-1867.

194 Vilhelm Koren, "Til min Hustru paa vor Guldbryllupsdag," 44.

195 Karen Larsen to Henriette Neuberg, January 8, 1866. LCA 154:102-106.

196 Mrs. Koren showed herself in her diary to be a shrewd observer of human foibles and the new world in which she found herself as a young women, but she seems not to realize how her sitting and reading and writing all day long may have irritated her hostess, Mrs. Egge, who had to work hard to raise her children, cook and clean for her husband.

197 Caroline Mathilde Koren Naeseth, tr. Henriette C. K. Naeseth, "Memories from Little Iowa Parsonage." *Norwegian-American Studies and Records* (Northfield, Minnesota: Norwegian-American Historical Association, 1943), 68.

198 Lulla Preus, "Minder fra den gamle Paint Creek Præstegaard," *Symra: En Aarbog for Norske paa Begge Sider af Havet* (Decorah: VII, 1911), 6.

199 Lulla Preus, 6.

200 W. A. Wexels, *Foredrag over Pastoraltheologien* (Christiania: Grondahls Forlag, 1853), 309.

201 Lulla Preus, 10.

202 Ibid., 12.

203 Strømme, 172.

204 Ibid.

205 Christiane Hjort to Linka Preus, October 1, 1869. LCA 154:108-13.

206 Lulla Preus, 8.

207 Karen Larsen and Laur Larsen, *Pioneer College President* (Northfield, Minnesota: Norwegian-American Historical Assocaition, 1936), 32.

208 Information provided for me by a great-grandson of Laur. Larsen, John Xavier.

209 Hermann spent some time looking for Hagbarth who had enlisted with the Illinois Volunteers and was in Company F. Hermann finally heard of his death and wrote Henriette to inform her he had been in the Danville prison where he died. Hermann Preus to Henriette Neuberg, March 17, 1864.

210 Karine Neuberg to Henriette Neuberg, May 6, 1862. 4:271:6.

211 Ibid.

212 *Decorah Republican*, October 20, 1862.

213 Karine Neuberg to Henrietta Neuberg, September 15, 1862. LCA 4:271:43

214 Karine Neuberg to Henriette Neuberg, September 21, 1862. LCA 4:271:41

215 Karine Neuberg to Henriette Neuberg, September 17, 1862. LCA 4:271:26.

216 Karine Neuberg to Henriette Neuberg, October 8, 1862. LCA 4:271:44.

217 Karine Neuberg to Henriette Neuberg, October 26, 1862. LCA 4:271;25.

218 Karine Neuberg to Henriette Neuberg, November 4, 1862. LCA 4:271:29.

219 Karine Neuberg to Henriette Neuberg, November 8, 1861. LCA 4:271:17.

220 Karine Neuberg to Henriette Neuberg, November 4, 1862. LCA 4:271:29

221 Ibid.

222 Karine Neuberg to Henriette Neuberg, November 12, 1862.

223 Karina Neuberg to Henriette Neuberg, December 2, 1862.

224 Ibid.

225 Karine Neuberg to Henriette Neuberg, December 18, 1862. LCA 4:271:28.

226 Karine Neuberg to Henriette Neuberg, December 26, 1862. LCA 4:271:38.

227 Karine Neuberg to Henriette Neuberg, January 4, 1863. LCA 4:271:12.

228 Karine Neuberg to Henriette Neuberg, January 9, 1863. LCA 4:271.

229 Report from the Nissen School. Email from Statsarkivet.

230 Laur. Larsen to Hjort, September 7, 1864.

231 Elisabeth Koren to Linka Preus, September 14, 1864.

232 Karine Neuberg to Henriette Neuberg, September 23, 1864. LCA 154:104:19

233 Karine Neuberg to Karen Olsen, October 15, 1864.

234 Karine Neuberg to Henriette Neuberg, October 19, 1864. LCA 154:101-25.

235 Karine Neuberg to Henriette Neuberg, October 19, 1864. LCA 154:101:-25

236 Karine Neuberg to Henriette Neuberg, October 31, 1864. LCA 154:103-15

237 Elisabeth Koren to Linka Preus, November 6, 1864.

238 Karine Neuberg to Henriette Neuberg, November 21, 1864.

239 Karine Neuberg to Henriette Neuberg, December 2, 1864.

240 Karine Neuberg to Henriette Neuberg, February 6, 1865. LCA 154:100-10.

241 Karine Neuberg to Henriette Neuberg, February 8, 1865. LCA154:104-18.

242 Karine Neuberg to Henriette Neuberg, February 9, 1865. LCA 154:103-19.

243 Karine Neuberg to Henriette Neuberg, March 1, 1865. LCA 154:103-18.

244 Karine Neuberg to Henriette Neuberg, March 3, 1865. LCA 154:104-1.

245 Ibid.

246 Elisabeth Koren to Linka Preus, April 11, 1865.

247 Karine Neuberg to Henriette Neuberg, 1866. LCA 154:104-5.

248 Karine Neuberg to Henriette Neuberg, August 23, 1865. LCA 154:104-2.

249 Laur. Larsen to Ove Hjort, 1866?

250 Karen Larsen to Henriette Neuberg, January 8, 1866. LCA 154:102-6.

251 Karine Neuberg to Henriette Neuberg, January 17, 1866? LCA 154:103-23.

252 Karine Neuberg to Henriette Neuberg, 1866? LCA 154:104-5.

253 The LCA has a collection of his carefully kept medical records, his financial credits and debits, along with the diagnoses he made and the medicines he prescribed for them.

254 Karine Neuberg to Henriette Neuberg, February 1, 1866. LCA 154:104-14. Peer Strømme in his *Erindringer* also records the good humor of Magelssen and his sorrows in losing both of his wives.

255 Karen Larsen to Henriette Neuberg, February 2, 1866. LCA 154:105-15.

256 Karine Neuberg to Henriette Neuberg, March 5, 1866. LCA 154:104-27.

257 Ibid.

258 Lulla Hjort Preus, "Minder fra Paint Creek Prestegaard," *Symra: En Aarbog for Norske paa Begge Sider af Havet* (Decorah: VII, 1911), 6.

259 Karen Larsen to Henriette Neuberg, March 22, 1866.

260 Karine Neuberg to Henriette Neuberg, March 25, 1866. LCA 154:104-21.

261 Elisabeth Koren to Linka Preus, April 12, 1866.

262 Linka Preus to Henriette Neuberg, April 1, 1866. LCA 271:13.

263 Karine Neuberg to Henriette Neuberg, May 9, 1866.

264 Elisabeth Koren to Linka Preus, June 5, 1866.

265 Hermann Preus, *"Syv Foredrag om de kirkelige forholde blandt de norske i Amerika."* See Todd Nichol's translation and essay on the seven lectures: *Vivacious Daughter* (Northfield, Minnesota: Norwegian-American Historical Association, 1990).

266 Hermann Preus to Laur. Larsen, November 28, 1866, The English Channel. LCA 96:25:33.

267 Hermann Preus to Laur. Larsen, May 8, 1867.

268 Henriette Neuberg to Linka Preus, August 25, 1867. LCA 154:106-12.

269 Elisabeth Koren to Linka Preus, November 3, 1867.

270 Elisabeth Koren to Linka Preus, February 1, 1870.

271 Henriette Landmark, probably Barbra Henriette Landmark (1840-1924), was the second wife of Professor Landmark. They were married in 1871; her maiden name was Landmark as well, and the 1870 Census of the U.S.A. lists her as a housekeeper in the Landmark household. Landmark, Luther's first librarian, returned to Norway in 1876 to lead the school in Kristiansund, Norway. Later he moved to Aalesund with his family.

272 Mrs. Koren goes out of her way to explain that Landmark had said she was his cousin, almost as if there were some suspicion of her origins and prior relationship to Landmark at the time in the small community.

273 Elisabeth Koren to Linka Preus, March 1, 1870.

274 Ibid.

275 Vilhelm Koren to Laur. Larsen, 1850s.

276 Elisabeth Koren to Linka Preus, February 21, 1864.

277 W. A. Wexels, 309.

278 C. F. W. Walther, "Materielen zur Pastoraltheologien," *Lehre and Wehre: Theologisches und Kirchlich-zeitgeschichtliches Monatsblat* (St. Louis: Deutschen ev. Luth. Synode von Missouri, Ohio, u.a. St. Louis, 1865-1871). After Mrs. Koren wrote this letter, an exhaustive series of articles by Walther on the vocation of pastor appeared, that ran over the next six years.

279 Vilhelm Koren, "Prestenes Hustru," *Samlede Skrifter* IV, 159.

280 Hermann Preus, "Tidens Tegn," *Kirkelig Maanedstidende* 15 (May 1, 1870), 139.

281 *Decorah Republican*, March 25, 1870.

282 *Kirkelig Maanedstidende* 16 (April 1, 1871), 238-239.

283 Ibid.

284 Ibid.

285 *Kirkelig Maanedstidende* 16 (August 1, 1871), 239.

286 Elisabeth Koren to Linka Preus, May 26, 1871.

287 Engel Brun Preus, wife of Adolph, died in 1860, before most of these families moved to Decorah and built the college. Adolph Preus returned to Norway in 1872.

288 The nicknames of the daughters, Minken and Lulla are elusive. Thora was thirteen when her mother died; Marie, eight; and Henriette Elisabeth, the youngest of the daughters, five. From the context, Lulla appears to be Thora. That could mean Minken was Marie. Herman, the only son, was four. Larsen had eight children with his second wife, Ingeborg Astrup.

289 E. Koren to Linka Preus. LCA 154:109-22

290 Karen Larsen, *Pioneer College President* (Northfield, Minnesota: Norwegian-American Historical Association, 1936), 198.

291 Ibid. 199.

292 *Linka's Diary*, Slind, November 4, 1851, 259.

293 Alexis de Tocqueville, *Democracy in America*, II, 209.

294 Harriett Martineau. *Society in America*, II, 257. Others have argued her list is not as long as it could have been.

295 www.answers.com/topic/common-school-movement#ixzz1DxsbPMqE

296 J. Magnus Rohne, *Norwegian American Lutheranism up to 1871* (New York: The MacMillan Company, 1926), 131.

297 Theodore C. Blegen, *Norwegian Emigration to America: The American Transition* (Northfield, Minnesota: Norwegian-American Historical Association, 1940), 247.

298 Ibid., 248

299 This system lasted maybe until the mid-1950s. In my father's congregation in Rugby, North Dakota, during the 1950s the congregation rented the public school building for a couple of weeks after the regular school was out.

300 Olaus Fredrik Duus, *Frontier Parsonage: The Letters of Olaus Fredrik Duus, Norwegian Pastor in Wisconsin, 1855-1858*, tr. Theodore Blegen (Northfield, Minnesota: Norwegian-American Historical Association, 1947), 59.

301 "A School and Language Controversy in 1858: A Documentary Study," trans. and edited by Arthur C. Paulson and Kenneth Bjørk, *Records and Studies* (Northfield, Minnesota: Norwegian-American Historical Association), 76.

302 Blegen, 252-253.

303 Hermann Preus, tr. Todd W. Nichol, "Lecture II," 63.

304 Ibid.

304 Blegen, 265.

306 Ibid.

307 Any student of Professor Paul G. Sonnack at Augsburg College and Seminary and later Luther Seminary would recognize Muus' statement as consistent with the civil religion Sonnack described in his America religion courses.

308 That Preus did this, I have no doubt, but I cannot prove he did; the scholarship repeats the date and Preus' proposal over and over again, but I cannot find the original source. It first appears, as far as I can tell, in an article in the June 22, 1895 in "Redwing Lutheran Ladies' Seminary's Indvielse," XXII *Evangelisk Luthersk Kirkeligtidende*: 386. Preus was ill. He was not able to attend the Red Wing meeting, which he noted in his 1875 report to the Synod's annual meeting.

309 William C. Benson, *High on Manitou: A History of St. Olaf College 1874-1949* (Northfield, Minnesota: The St. Olaf College Press, 1949), 14.

310 Benson, 58.

311 Ibid.

312 Ibid., 44.

313 Georg Sverdrup, *"Commonskolen," Professor Georg Sverdrups Samlede Skrifter i Udvalg*, Volume I, *Bibelske og kirkehistoriske Skisser og Afhandlinger* (Minneapolis: Frikirkens Boghandels Forlag, 1907), 376.

314 See Kristin Norseth's thesis, *La Oss bryte med vor stumhet! Kvinners vei til myndigehet i de kristelige organisationene i 1842-1912* (De teologiske Menighetsfakultet, 2007), 253.

315 J. A. Bergh, *Folkebladet*, 1920

316 August Weenaas, "Et Ord om Kvindeforeninger," *Lutheraneren* 5 (April 1871): 57.

317 Andreas Helland, *Augsburg Seminar Gjennem Femti Aar 1869-1919* (Minneapolis: Folkebladet Forlag, 1920), 47.

318 Ibid.

319 "Missions Beretning," *Budbæreren: organ for den Evangelisk-lutherske Kirke I Amerika*, ed Østen Hanson and Ole A Bergh, 2 (March 1871): 158.

320 *Budbæreren* 3 (October 1871): 77.

321 Einar Molland, *Norges Kirkehistorie i Det 19. Århundre, Bind I* (Oslo: Gyldendal Norsk Forlag, 1979), 167. Molland corrects the year which Kielland in her memoirs had remembered as 1842. That date persists in many retellings—including mine—of Kielland's achievement.

322 Those claims were also made by the daughters of the Synod pastors. One of the really moving stories of women in mission is the story of how Laur. Larsen and his wife finally relented in 1893 to let their daughter Marie go to Zululand to work with the Astrups among the Hottentots, as they were called then. When she died several years later, her parents were terribly grieved and must have spent some time in personal self-recrimination for having allowed her to respond to that higher call.

323 "Kirkekronike," *Kirkelig Maanedstidende*, 17 (March 15, 1872): 86-88.

324 Ibid., 144.

325 Ibid.

326 Ibid.

327 *Budbæreren* 6 (June 1874): 15.

328 Rosina Preus to Linka Preus, Luther College, Decorah, 28 February 1873, LCA.

329 Karen Larsen and Laur. Larsen, *Pioneer College President* (Northfield, Minnesota: Norwegian-American Historical Association, 1936), 31. Unfortunately for us, Larsen does not give us the source where we could look at that curriculum, nor can we discover where he taught in Christiania at the time. It would be easy to say the Nissen *Pigeskole*, but that would be pure conjecture as he is not listed in the faculty there for either boys or girls.

330 Karen Larsen, 45.

331 Karen Larsen, 31. The more I have read Larsen's admirable biography of her father—a difficult task for a daughter to do as professionally as she did—the more I have come to view with some suspicion her constant assurances that Larsen was fond of women and treated them well, implying he was something of a feminist. While I have no doubt he did like women and treat them well, his editorial comments on women's rights which he watched closely as editor of the church paper give me a sense she did not want those editorial comments to paint his character as anti-feminist which they could well be read to show. He was a courteous gentleman in the traditional sense and enjoyed his time with cultivated women like Mrs. Koren who shared his convictions about these things. While he would have treated Elizabeth Cady Stanton courteously, he would not have agreed with her.

332 Karen Larsen, 31.

333 Karen Larsen, 273.

334 Knut Fleisher to Hermann and Linka Preus, April 6, 1853. Just after *Uncle Tom's Cabin* was published, Linka was asking their friend Fleisher to send them a copy of it.

335 David Nelson, *Luther College 1861-1961* (Decorah: Luther College Press, 1961), 104.

336 Charles West, M. D., Lectures *on the Diseases of Women*, American edition, in Edward Hammond Clarke's *Sex in Education, or, a Fair Chance for Girls* (Boston: Rand and Avery, 1873), 19.

337 Karen Larsen, 274.

338 Karen Larsen, 284.

339 Mrs. Koren to Linka, Trinity Sunday, ca. 1868. LCA 154:110.3

340 Karen Larsen, 284.

341 Christiane Hjort to Mrs. Koren, May 1868. LCA 154:107-23.

342 Ibid.

343 At this time Wulfsberg was pastor in Albert Lea, but also the head of the publishing house of the Synod.

344 The loss of early letters and other manuscripts in this fire has never really been commented on, but I miss what was surely an archive of letters and drawings from Linka among other things.

345 Karen Larsen, 274.

346 Lina Koren to Linka Preus, November 24, 1872

347 Elise Hovde to Linka Preus, December 17, 1872.

348 Miss Gylling to Linka Preus, December 26, n.d., but probably 1872.

349 C.H. to Linka Preus, January 7, 1873.

350 Nelson, 127-128.

351 Laurence M. Larson, "Skandinaven, Professor Anderson, and the Yankee School," *The Changing West and Other Essays* (Northfield, Minnesota: Norwegian-American Historical Association, 1937), 135.

352 "Red Wing Lutheran Ladies' Seminary's Indvielse," *Evangelisk Luthersk Kirketidende* 22 (June, 22, 1895), 386.

353 The letters indicate that there were two Reque girls in the group, but who their fathers were, I cannot tell.

354 Stromme, *Halvor*, 167.

355 Rosina Preus (1854-1918) would marry Pastor Jørgen Nordby (1852-1926) in 1877; Caroline Koren (1856-1945) married Professor Christen Andreas Naeseth (1849-1921) in 1886; Edel Margarethe Brandt (b. 1857) married Reque (1864-1947); Lulla Hjort (1856-1931) married Christian K. Preus (1852-1922) in 1877; Mathilda Stub (1857-1900) married Pastor Hans Baggøe Thorgrimson (1853-1942) in 1884; Anna Marie Reque married Pastor Halvor Hustvedt

(1852-1932) in 1878; Thora Larsen married Dr. J. W. Magelssen after the death of her aunt, Magelssen's first wife Karine Neuberg; Emma Larsen married Nils Helle. Henriette Koren (1855-1938) did not marry. She lived out her days with her sister Marie (1874-1968) and her brother Paul (1863-1944) in the Washington Prairie parsonage where they had been born. Since Paul Koren followed his father in the Washington Prairie congregation, they continued to live on the old parsonage land until 1940 when he retired. After his death, Marie moved to LaCrosse, where she died in 1968.

356 Rosina to Linka Preus, December 17, 1872.

357 Ibid.

358 Elisabeth Koren to Linka Preus, September 3, 1871.

359 Lulla Hjort Preus, "Minder fra Painted Creek," *Symra*, 1911, 7.

360 Almost from time immemorial until the 1950s it was the custom for the congregation in the Norwegian tradition to give the pastor, *klokker*, and/or musician an offering. The congregation would stand up, walk to the altar with their money, and leave behind a gift of cash. The pastor's call letter would include a certain sum for the salary, the parsonage, and the offerings.

361 Christiane Hjort to Linka Preus, December 27, 1872.

362 Elisabeth Koren to Linka Preus, March 15, 1873.

363 Ibid.

364 Karen Larsen, 197.

365 Christiane Hjort to Elisabeth Koren, January 7, 1873.

366 Christiane Hjort to Linka Preus, October 1, 1869.

367 Rosina Preus to Linka Preus, January 14, 1873.

368 Elisabeth Koren to Linka Preus, March 15, 1873.

369 *Aftenposten*, May 26, 1882.

370 Rosina Preus to Linka Preus, January 19 or 12, 1873.

371 Rosina Preus to Linka Preus, January 20, 1873.

372 Ibid.

373 Elisabeth Koren to Linka Preus, February 9, 1873,

374 Norwegian Synod Church Council Minutes of 1873, 150.

375 Elisabeth Koren to Linka Preus, March 15, 1873.

376 From Mrs. Jacobsen to Linka Preus, March 10, 1873.

377 The meeting was in Holden, where Preus spoke in some detail about the kind of schooling young women should receive.

378 Christiane Hjort to Elisabeth Koren, February 14, 1873.

379 Nelson, 117. Nelson says it was Reque, but the older history of the college says it was N. J. Ellestad.

380 "Music at Luther College," *Luther's Semi-Centennial 1861-1911,* n.p.

381 C. K. to Linka Preus,

382 Elisabeth Koren to Linka Preus, May 6, 1873.

383 It is impossible to ascertain whether he wrote it for the dedication of the first wing, but this letter tends to confirm that it was written for the dedication of the second wing.

384 Elisabeth Koren to Linka Preus, May 6, 1873.

385 Ibid.

386 Paul Arctander Preus (1867-1883) the youngest of the Preus children, was born when the family was in Norway in 1867. Not strong at birth, his health was always poor. Linka's health, especially after his birth, was frail as well. Paul died when he was thrown from a buggy while at the college.

387 The Hjort family included eight siblings: Louise Augustus (1856), Otto Christian (1858), Diderikke (1860), Johanna (1862) Jakob (1864), Maren Pauline Ovidia [Linka] (1866), and Cathinka (1868).

388 Otto was studying in Norway, and Hjort had gone to Norway to visit him as well as attend a Mission Conference in Stavanger.

389 Elisabeth Koren to Linka Preus, July 22, 1873.

390 Elisabeth Koren to Linka Preus, July 29, 1873.

391 Elisabeth Koren to Linka Preus, August 25, 1873.

392 Elisabeth Koren to Linka Preus, August 31, 1873.

393 Elisabeth Koren to Linka Preus, July 22, 1873.

394 Elisabeth Koren to Linka Preus, September 2, 1873.

395 Elisabeth Koren to Linka Preus, October 10, 1873.

396 Elisabeth Koren to Linka Preus, October 22, 1873.

397 Although the records say Gudjohnson, they differ—Norlie says Gudthjohnsen, Icelandic usage would have said Gudjohnsdatter.

398 Bjarnason, a fiery redheaded Icelander who taught Latin, would found the Icelandic Lutheran Synod in 1885 and serve as its president until 1905.

399 Elisabeth Koren to Linka Preus, November 19, 1873.

400 Elisabeth Koren to Linka Preus, August 31, 1873.

401 Elisabeth Koren to Linka Preus, March 15, 1874.

402 Rosina Preus to Linka Preus, April 10, 1874.

403 Elisabeth Koren to Linka Preus, April 21, 1874.

404 Elisabeth Koren to Linka Preus, Bededag 1874 (second letter).

405 Rosina to Linka Preus, May 23, 1874.

406 Bilious fever is one of those diagnoses that were a kind of catch all for diseases we name differently. This was probably some kind of influenza that involved vomiting and diarrhea with a fever.

407 Lulla Hjort to Linka Preus, July 28, 1874.

408 Ibid.

409 Linka Preus to Lulla Hjort, November 21, 1874.

410 Ove J. Hjort to Laur. Larsen, December 14, 1874.

411 Ibid.

412 From Theodore Jorgenson, "Men and Attitudes in the Early History of St. Olaf College," *The Banner*, No. 7, June 1943: 14.

413 Henriette to Linka Preus, December 14, 1874.

414 Lulla Hjort to Linka Preus, March 9, 1875.

415 Thora Larsen to Laur. Larsen, July 4, 1876.

416 Thora Larsen to Laur. Larsen, February 24, 1877.

417 Laur. Larsen to Hjort, September 7, 1877.

418 Karen Larsen, 209.

419 Laur. Larsen to Hjort, September 28, 1879.

420 "Caroline Dorothea Margrethe Preus," *Evangelisk Luthersk Kirketidende* 8 (October 1, 1880), 631-632.

421 Ibid.

422 Ibid.

423 *Budbæreren* 13 (December 1881): 191.

424 *Folkebladet*, 1 (October 7, 1880).

425 Nina Draxton, *Kristofer Janson* (Northfield, Minnesota: Norwegian-American Historical Association), 37.

426 "Letter from Thora Magelssen to her father Laur. Larsen," March 29, 1880.

427 *Aftenposten*, January 5, 1882; *Adressecontoirs Efterretninger* I Bergen, January 13, 1882.

428 Muus v. Muus. Hennepin County District Court, 1883. File no. 13571, Hennepin County Government Center, Minneapolis as found in Kathy Ericson "Triple Jeopardy: The Muus vs. Muus Case in Three Forums," Minnesota History (Winter 1987), 306.

429 "Redegjørelse fra Holden Menighed," *Evangelisk Luthersk Kirketidende* 8 (November 1880): 771-776.

430 Joseph Shaw, *Bernt Julius Muus: Pioneer of St. Olaf College* (Northfield, Minnesota: Norwegian-American Historical Association, 1999), 265. Readers of Shaw will recognize how closely I follow his report on this tragic story. He has untangled many of the distorted accounts and made them much easier to follow.

431 Ibid. 266.

432 Ibid.

433 Ibid.

434 Ibid., 268.

435 Ueland, *Recollections*, 42.

436 The three pastors were Biørn, Bøckman, and Hanson. Muus chose Langemo, Severeide, and Finseth. Mrs. Muus chose O. Vig, Rygh, and Anderson. The congregations chose O. Solberg, N. Finn, and B. Lee, A Simonsen, O. Huset, and O. Eagen.

437 Shaw, 270.

438 "Redegjørelse," 776.

439 *Folkebladet* 1 (December 16, 1880).

440 Georg Sverdrup "Pastor B. J. Muus's Sag," XIV, *Lutheraneren og Missionsbladet*, ed. Georg Sverdrup December 1880 (Minneapolis: Augsburg Seminary), 412.

441 Ibid., 413.

442 *Evangelisk Luthersk Kirketidende* 8 (December 15, 1880): 196.

443 Andreas Ueland, *Recollections of an Immigrant* (New York: Minton, Balch & Company, 1929), 42.

444 Shaw, 272.

445 Shaw, 273.

446 Bjørnstjerne Bjørnson, *Land of the Free: Bjørnstjerne Bjørnson's America Letters, 1880-1881*, edited and translated by Eva Lund Haugen and Einar Haugen (Northfield, Minnesota: Norwegian-American Historical Association, 1978), 228.

447 Shaw, 296.

448 Einar and Eva Lund Haugen, *Land of the Free: American Letters 1880-1881* (Northfield, Minnesota: Norwegian-American Historical Association, 1976), 68.

449 Carl Christlock, *From Fjord to Freeway: 100 Years Augsburg College* (St. Paul: North Central Publishing Company, 1969), 43.

450 Draxton, 130.

451 Kristofer Janson, *Hvad jeg har oplevet* (Kristiania: Gyldendal, 1913), 236.

452 *Budbæreren*, 17 (April 1, 1885), 109.

453 Draxton, 146.

454 Shaw, *Bernt Julius Muus: Pioneer of St. Olaf College*. 296.

455 The other men were O. K. Simmons, C. H. Boxrud, R. H. Boxrud, A. H. Boxrud, N. K. Simmons, Dr. C. L. Opsal, C. F. Hjermstad, H. L. Hjermstad, Judge Albert Johnson, I. Nelson, and Christian Peterson.

456 This is a confusing bit of history for those who do not inhabit these histories every day. This would merge with the school of the Augustana Synod in the merger which created the NLCA (ELC) in 1917.

457 Festskrift: *Den Norske Synodes Jubilæum 1853-1903* (Decorah, Iowa, Den Norske Synodes Forlag, 1903), 160.

458 *Evangelisk Luthersk Kirketidende*, 9 (May 26,1882): 332

459 Gisle Bothne, *Det Norske Luther College 1861-1897* (Decorah, Iowa: Bothne, 1897), 282

460 Ibid.

461 Ibid., 282-289.

462 H. G. Stub quoted in Gisle Bothne, *Det Norske Luther College, 1861-1897* (Decorah, Iowa: Bothne, 1897), 287.

463 A. K. Sagen, "Address," *Evangelisk Luthersk Kirketidende,* 22 (June 15, 1895):389-390.

464 Christian Hvistendahl, "Beretning om et Møde," *Kirkelig Maanedstidende* 14 (April 1, 1869), 123-124.

465 Martha Reishus Langemo, A *History of The Lutheran Ladies Seminary, Red Wing, Minnesota* (St. Paul: Luther Seminary Archives, 1967), 2.

466 The Augsburg tradition, my tradition, although publicly always expressing appropriate condolences, never missed a chance to wonder whether God had something against the Synod as so many of its building burned down. The first two main buildings in Decorah, in 1889 and 1941. The Robbinsdale Seminary in 1895 and The Red Wing Lutheran Ladies' Seminary in 1920, not to mention several of the academies and then in 1961, the Preus Gymnasium.

467 Karen Larsen, 294.

468 See the *Decorah Republican,* June 27, 1889, for an extended and lively account of the deliberations of the committee from the Decorah perspective.

469 Karen Larsen, 294.

470 *National Tribune,* Washington, D. C., February 2, 1893.

471 Ibid.

472 Once again, I cannot find this. In his report to the 1875 Synod meeting, Preus apologizes for not being able to be in Red Wing in the fall of 1874 for the pastoral conference when he supposedly said that the Synod needed a *pigeskole* in Red Wing. *Synodalberetning,* 1875, 22.

473 Todd M. Walsh, *The Lutheran Ladies' Seminary of Red Wing, Minnesota, 1894 -1920.* (St. Paul: Macalester College, History Department, 1982), 26.

474 J. A Ottesen, *Kort Uddrag af Den norske Synodes Historie* (Udgivet og fremlaget ved Verdens Udstillingen i Chicago 1893 af en i den Anledning nedsat Komite, Decorah Forlag, 1893), 38.

475 Koren's sermon, "Tale ved Grundstenlaegningen af Lutheran Ladies' Seminary i Red Wing, Minn., *Samlede Skrifter* II, V. Koren, ed. Paul Koren (Decorah, Iowa: Lutheran Publishing House, 1912), 367.

476 Ibid.

477 Hans Baggøe Thorgrimsen, "From Rev. H. B. Thorgrimsen's Memoirs," *The Lutheran Church Herald,* XVIII (February 19, 1935): 187.

478 Even when I came to Decorah in 1968, the story was told with amusement and resentment that once Koren was driving his buggy along the road forced a farmer in his wagon off the road, as he commented to his companion that every once in a while one had to remind the farmers of their place. Because it fits the stereotype too well, I am a bit skeptical, but I have no way of disproving or proving the anecdote except to say it was Pip Qualley who told me.

479 Elizabeth Cady Stanton. "Address Delivered at Seneca Falls and Rochester," *Elizabeth Cady Stanton & Susan B. Anthony: Correspondence, Writings, Speeches*, ed. Ellen Carol DuBois (New York: Shocken Books, 1981), 34.

480 Koren's speech. 369.

481 Ibid., 370.

482 Ibid.

483 Ibid., 371

484 Ibid., 373-374. "The girl of the future" was a speech given by Ruth C. D. Havens in Washington, D. C., at the National American Suffrage Association in January 1893. She gave it many times and it was reported on in many papers of the day. Koren may have read about it in *The Evening Star*, Washington, D.C., printed on April 13, 1893, so it was newly on his mind.

485 Carl Christlock, my teacher at Augsburg, ridiculed this speech for precisely this reason—Koren, according to Chrislock, seemed not to have the foggiest notion of why they were building the school.

486 Marie Koren, "*Forbemerkninger,*" *Rhytmisk Koralbog, Udgiven efter den norsk synods foranstaltning, ved en Komite* (Decorah, Iowa: Lutheran Publishing House, 1904), n.p. Her work with this committee also places her in the ranks, maybe, of Harriet Reynolds Krauth Spaeth who edited *Church Book with Music*, 1893.

487 See footnote 279.

488 *Evangelisk Luthersk Kirketidende*, 1893.

489 Hans Allen, "Lutheran Ladies' Seminary," *Festskrift: Den norske Synodes Jubilaeum, 1853-1903* (Decorah, Iowa: Den Norske Synodes Forlag, 1904), 179.

490 See all the catalogues of the seminary.

491 Red Wing Lutheran Ladies Seminary, *Tenth Annual Catalogue*, 1905, 13.

492 Letter to Goodhue Historical Society, sent by Alice Hinnenthal who found her mother's Alma's letter in her personal effects, and sent it to the society on January 14, 1987. Few primary documents from the school give as vivid a picture of life at the school from a student's point of view at the time, not after years of nostalgia.

493 Ibid., 30.

494 Until the 1960s girls at most of the Lutheran colleges were required to wear dresses or skirts in the dining room and in classes, something the deans of women would watch for.

495 Langemo has a different set of numbers that say "it opened its doors for forty eager women who were joined by seventeen more as the school year progressed."

496 Todd Walsh has written a brief article on this topic.

497 The list of men signing as Incorporators, according to Langemo, grew to include a number of Luther College and Seminary pastors and professors: Dorotheus Johnsen Growe (1824-1904), Hans Allen, Ernest John Franz Haertel (b. 1870), J. Seebach, Ed Johnson, Professor Johannes Bjerk Frich (1835-1908), Pastors Andreas Kittelsen Sagen (1851-1907), Ole Pedersen Vangsnes (b. 1855), Marcus Thorsen (b. 1840), Michael Olsen Borge (b. 1846), Lars Jensen Jerdee

(b. 1859), Nils Paul Xavier (b. 1839), Johan Linnevold (b. 1868), The Honorable A. K. Finseth, A. C. Erstad, and Hans Johnson. Bjørgo served as President of the Corporation.

498 The faculty of the first year included a variety of men and women who have long since disappeared into the mists: Mrs. Ingerid Egge Markhus (1848-1918), Miss Anna Odjord, Pastor E. F. Haertel (b. 1870), Miss Hanna Borresen, Miss Maren Michelet, Pastor Bjørgo, Miss Hanna Mord, Miss Harriet W. Deuel, Miss Doris Nilsen, Miss Ingeborg Halvorsen, Miss Hanna Forton, and Mrs. Marie Gellerup, the housekeeper.

499 Walsh, 26.

500 Red Wing Lutheran Ladies Seminary, *Tenth Annual Catalogue*, 1905, 13.

501 Langemo, 13.

502 *Catalogue*, 13.

503 Langemo, 10.

504 "Indvielsen af Redwing Luth. Ladies' Seminary," *Evangelisk Luthersk Kirketidende* 22 (June 1, 1895), 377-378.

505 A. K. Sagen, "Address," *Evangelisk Luthersk Kirketidende*, 22 (June 15, 1895), 389-390.

506 Johannes Ylvisaker, "Tale ved Indvielsen af Redwing Luth. Ladies' Seminary," *Evangelisk Luthersk Kirketidende* 22 (June 15, 1895), 405.

507 Ibid.

508 Ibid., 407.

509 Ibid., 408

510 Lydia Bredesen Sundby, Reunion of Students of Lutheran Ladies' Seminary held at Hotel Blakes by the Lakes, Alexandria, Minnesota, June 25-26, 1955. 2.

511 Ylvisaker, 408.

512 Ibid., 409.

513 Tora L. (1878), married to Nicolai Astrup Larsen, Olaf S. (1880), treasurer at St. Paul Hospital; Nils M. (1882), who became Executive Secretary of the ELC's Young People's Luther League; Sigurd C. (1884), who earned a Ph. D. at Leipzig University where his father had studied and who later became Professor at Bethany Seminary in Mankato; Inga Marie (1886), married C. S. Thorpe; Lauritz (1890), medical doctor at St. Paul; Gudrun, who did not marry (1892), was organist at Christ Church in St. Paul; Carl B. (1896), Professor at Concordia College, for whom the library is named; Ragnvald (1898), who became a doctor; J. Wilhelm (1900), who was president of Luther College. All of the girls either married pastors or went into church work.

514 *Red Wing Republican*, June 9, 1895.

515 Ibid.

516 Ibid.

517 See *Evangelisk Luthersk Kirketidende*, 14 September 1895. The Church Council discussed this thoroughly and three of the four districts agreed with the proposal to hire Mrs. Stub, but the Minnesota District did not. While the issue seemed to

be the money, there was some other reason for the refusal, but I cannot find what it was.

518 See *Evangelisk Luthersk Kirketidende,* 1894.

519 Ibid.

520 H. G. Stub, *The North,* September 16, 1891.

521 Ibid.

522 Nellie Allen, "My Memories of Early Days at the L.L.S. "(Goodhue County Historical Society).

523 Laukandt, *"Katalog des Lutherischen Mädchenseminars und Konservatoriums der Music,"* 14. As translated in Walsh's paper.

524 Langemo, 14.

525 Allen, 2.

526 D. G. Ristad, "Vore skoler: Lutheran Ladies' Seminary, Red Wing, Minn." *Evangelisk Luthersk Kirketidende:* 1916.

527 Mrs. T. H. Dahl, *The Lutheran Church Herald* I (April 18, 1917).

528 *The Lutheran Church Herald,* 2 (April 19, 1918): 252.

529 T. A. Hoff, *Cresset,* 1920. n.p.

530 Ibid.

531 ELC Annual Report, 1919, 236.

532 Walsh, 57.

533 "Lutheran Ladies' Seminary Destroyed by Fire," *The Lutheran Church Herald* 4 (June 15, 1920): 369-370.

534 *Lutheran Herald* 4 (July 13, 1920): 457.

535 Ibid.

536 Ibid., 369-370.

537 *The Lutheran Church Herald,* 4 (July 6, 1920): 419.

538 Ibid.

539 *The Lutheran Church Herald* 5 (October 11, 1921): 1035.

540 Report of the Norwegian Lutheran Church in America, 1922, 170.

541 Ibid.

542 Walsh, 57.

543 *Lutheraneren* (May 12, 1888): 151.

544 *Evangelisk Luthersk Kirketidende,* 21 (August 18, 1894): 521.

545 Ibid.

546 *Evangelisk Luthersk Kirketidende* 21 (October 20, 1894): 657.

547 *Lutheraneren,* (September 1895): 1.

548 *Lutheraneren,* (October 31,1895): 137.

549 *Lutheraneren,* (December 12, 1895): 225.

550 *Lutheraneren,* (May 21, 1896): 321.

551 *Lutheraneren,* (August 11, 1897), 528.

552 *Lutheraneren,* (July 7, 1897), 425.

553 *Evangelisk Luthersk Kirketidende,* 24 (February 13, 1897): 116.

554 *Evangelisk Luthersk Kirketidende,* 28 (February 1900): 183.

555 *Evangelisk Luthersk Kirketidende,* 28 (April 4, 1900): 322.

556 *Evangelisk Luthersk Kirketidende,* 32 (June 1, 1904): 611.

557 *Evangelisk Luthersk Kirketidende,* 32 (August 24, 1904): 923.

558 Christian Andreas Naeseth, "Den moderne kvindeemancipation," *Theologisk Tidskrift* 1904): 231.

559 Ibid., 232.

560 Ibid., 237. The English scholar is a Rev. Hays.

561 Ibid., 250.

562 Ibid., 251.

563 *Lutheraneren* (July 3, 1918): 852.

564 Ibid.

565 *Lutheraneren* (July 3, 1918): 852. Although this is not the entire obituary, I have translated or paraphrased much of it since it gives such a fine vivid picture of Mrs. Koren's funeral and the high esteem in which she was held.

566 Oscar Olson, "Change in the Curriculum," *Annual Report to the Church, Department II: Education,* 225. 1932.

567 Ibid.

568 See Walter Ong, "Latin Language Study as a Renaissance Puberty Rites," *Rhetoric, Romance, and Technology: Studies in the Interaction of Expression and Culture* (Ithaca and London: Cornell University Press, 1970), Loc. 2021.

569 Oscar Olson, *College Chips,* as found in the *Lutheran Church Herald* 16 (June 21, 1932): 785.

570 The records here are somewhat confusing. David Nelson's history, which is usually unimpeachable, tells the story with different dates, but the records in the newspapers are what I am reporting, even if Nelson was among those who joined with several other faculty in support of the move and had lived through the experience.

571 Oscar Olson, *College Chips* (January 26, 1932) in *The Lutheran Church Herald* 16 (June 1932): 785.

572 Oscar Olson, Autobiographical Sketch, n. d. LCA.

573 *The Lutheran Church Herald,* 16, (June 1932), 785.

574 Corporation Journal: Minutes Luther College Corporation, Department II, Education, Report of The Tenth General Convention of the Norwegian Lutheran Church of America (Minneapolis: Augsburg Publishing House, 1932), 245.

575 Corporation Journal: Minutes Luther College Corporation, Department II, Education, Report of The Tenth General Convention of the Norwegian Lutheran Church of America. (Minneapolis: Augsburg Publishing House, 1932), 245.

576 "Co-education at Luther," *The Sumner Gazette*, (June 30, 1932): 2.

577 "Consideration of Report, 3 B., Department II: Education, 241.

578 *Ames Daily Tribune* (July 9, 1932): 1.

579 "Luther President to Decide Number of Coed Students," *Ames Daily Tribune* (June 9, 1932): 9.

580 J. C. K. Preus, Secretary, Board of Education, "No Co-education at Luther College," The *Lutheran Church Herald* 16 (July 19, 1932): 873.

581 Ibid.

583 Ibid.

583 "A Day of Reckoning," *Public Opinion*, Decorah, quoted in *Lutheran Church Herald*: 42.

584 "No Co-education at Luther College, Church Board Votes, *The Sumner Gazette* (August 4, 1932): 6. See also the *Lime Spring Herald*, (July 21, 1932): 1. It printed the same press release as *The Sumner Gazette*.

585 "Coeducation at Luther Sought," *The Mason City Globe-Gazette* (May 15, 1934): 5.

586 Ibid.

587 Faculty at Luther, "Coeducation at Luther, *Lutheran Herald*, 18 (March 13, 1934): 248.

588 George Torrison, "Coeducation at Luther, *Lutheran Church Herald* 18 (April 24, 1934): 394-395.

589 See Walter Ong, "Latin Language Study as a Renaissance Puberty Rites," *Rhetoric, Romance, and Technology: Studies in the Interaction of Expression and Culture* (Ithaca and London: Cornell University Press, 1970), Loc. 2021.

590 Ibid.

591 "Change of Articles of Incorporation of Luther College," *Lutheran Church Herald* (February 13, 1934): 143.

592 "From our Exchanges," *Postville Herald* (February 15, 1934): 2.

593 Report 36, quoted in Nelson, 261.

594 Nelson, 261.

595 "Educational Problems," The Eleventh General Convention. XVIII, *Lutheran Herald* (June 26, 1934): 579-583. The special committee members were: Attorney Dosland, Moorhead, Minnesota; Dr. O. A. Tingelstad, Parkland, Washington; Dr. N. Astrup Larsen, Sioux City, Iowa; Rev. Molberg, Hudson, South Dakota; Mr. B. K. Sauvre, Glenwood, Minnesota; Rev. K. B. Vaaler, Colton, South Dakota; Mr. H. O. Talle, Decorah, Iowa; Rev. T. A. Hoff, Decorah, Iowa; Re. Z. J. Ordal, River Falls Wisconsin; Rev. S. C. Simonson, Madison Wisconsin.

596 Ibid. 580.

597 Nelson, 269.

598 The subtext in these discussions is baffling. Clearly there was talk of blame for bad decisions made by someone or some group. Could it have been the scandal behind the demise of Red Wing Lutheran Ladies' Seminary or the deep indebtedness of the college? Nothing in the records that I have seen clears this up.

599 Nelson, 264-267.

600 Ditlef Ristad, "Don't Give Up the Ship!" The *Lutheran Church Herald* 20 (May 1936): 435.

601 Nelson, 264-267.

602 When I was speaking about this to a group of retired clergy and Lutheran college graduates, they reported such classes in the late 1940s and 1950s—which I suspect were not on the list of courses offered, but were rather like evening meetings taught by professors' wives and others.

603 See page 163.

604 Arthur Wentworth Hewitt, *The Shepherdess* (Willett, Clark and Company: Chicago, New York, 1943), 11.

605 Lloyd Svendsbye, president of Luther Seminary, told me once how difficult it was for him to adjust to services every Sunday morning. Growing up as he did in western North Dakota during the Depression, he said they simply did not have the means to support a pastor in their small town, nor were there pastors available to serve. Thus it was common for pious parents to read Luther's postils to their families on a regular basis where there was no church.

606 Roy Harrisville argued this at a Luther Seminary faculty meeting, saying that the death and resurrection of Jesus should make at least some difference to the understanding of the "curse of Eve" in the garden. Her seed, Christ, did bruise the head of Satan and mutuality was restored, always, of course, with the danger of sin overcoming both man and woman.

607 Roy Oswald, Carolyn Taylor Gutierez, Liz Spellman Dean, "On Liberating the Clergywife," *Married to the Minister: Dilemmas, conflicts and joys in the role of the clergy wife* (Durham, North Carolina: Alban Institute, 1980), 4.

608 Hewitt, 5.

609 I cannot forget the several pastors' wives retreats I attended in the 1980s when Dr. Lee Griffith, the psychological counselor of the ALC, would meet with troubled pastors' wives. One day he stood up and said, "It is so wonderful being with you all and I want to talk to as many as I can, so I have opened up a couple hours after midnight so we can meet." I found it troubling that there was so much pain and so little understanding of the tectonic shifts in the role and understanding of the parsonage.

610 Nelson, 127.

Index

214, 215, 216, 217, 219, 220, 222, 224, 226, 228, 229, 230, 231, 233, 239, 304, 375, 376, 377, 378
Northrup, Cyrus 306
Northwest Ordinance 176
Norway 5, 9, 12, 14, 15, 17, 18, 19, 22, 23, 24, 45, 46, 47, 48, 50, 56, 59, 63, 66, 75, 76, 77, 79, 81, 82, 83, 84, 85, 86, 89, 90, 91, 94, 98, 99, 100, 101, 103, 104, 105, 108, 111, 113, 114, 115, 118, 119, 120, 121, 123, 127, 129, 130, 131, 134, 137, 140, 143, 145, 147, 149, 151, 153, 154, 155, 156, 157, 158, 168, 169, 170, 172, 175, 179, 182, 184, 186, 187, 188, 190, 192, 193, 194, 196, 197, 198, 199, 202, 203, 204, 205, 207, 210, 219, 223, 225, 226, 228, 230, 232, 233, 234, 237, 238, 240, 241, 242, 243, 244, 251, 253, 257, 261, 262, 264, 272, 276, 282, 283, 294, 300, 301, 305, 325, 326, 328, 329, 332, 366, 367, 369, 370, 372, 373, 378
Norwegian Constitution Day 222
Norwegian-Danish Augustana Synod 255, 380
Norwegian-Danish Conference 290, 254
Norwegian Synod 2, 7, 8, 9, 12, 13, 15, 16, 18, 19, 44, 75, 82, 84, 105, 107, 108, 109, 120, 135, 144, 145, 150, 157, 158, 163, 164, 167, 172, 176, 177, 178, 179, 180, 181, 182, 183, 184, 185, 186, 189, 188, 190, 192, 196, 197, 199, 201, 202, 204, 209, 222, 223, 227, 232, 233, 234, 241, 244, 249, 251, 252, 254, 255, 256, 257, 263, 264, 265, 266, 268, 271, 272, 274, 275, 276, 282, 298, 310, 311, 312, 319, 320, 322, 326, 328, 329, 330, 331, 333, 341, 349, 351, 352, 359, 360, 365, 377
Nynorsk (New Norwegian) 108, 109

O

Oak Grove Ladies' Seminary 333
Oberlin College 326
Oconomowoc, Wisconsin 106
Oehlenschläger (poet) 109, 128, 304
Oftedal, Sven 186, 241, 242, 247, 248, 251, 252, 253
Olson, Oscar 16, 333, 334, 385
Ong, Walter 335, 342, 343, 362, 385, 386
Ordination 22, 73, 74, 132, 252, 358, 360, 366
Ordination of women 252, 358, 360
Otteson, Christiane see Christiane Otteson Hjort
Otteson, Diderrike Aall see Diderrike Otteson Brandt
Ottesen, Jacob Aall 63, 105, 130
Ottesen, Otto Christian 203

P

Pacific Lutheran College 274, 319
Page Academy 149
Panic of 1893 270
Park Region College 310
Parochial schools 179, 181, 184, 185, 237, 255
Parsonage 2, 10, 12, 13, 16, 17, 18, 19, 20, 21, 22, 23, 24, 25, 26, 27, 31, 32, 36, 38, 39, 42, 43, 44, 46, 48, 49, 50, 53, 57, 60, 62, 64, 66, 72, 78, 79, 82, 83, 84, 85, 88, 89, 90, 91, 105, 106, 117, 121, 123, 124, 125, 129, 130, 132, 133, 134, 147, 155, 156, 162, 163, 169, 182, 191, 200, 202, 204, 206, 212, 216, 217, 218, 220, 221, 226, 227, 228, 232, 235, 237, 240, 258, 259, 262, 270, 289, 291, 292, 298, 328, 329, 330, 331, 350, 354, 355, 357, 358, 359, 360, 361, 363, 377, 387
Peer Gynt 201, 235
Piano 58, 61, 62, 63, 85, 102, 130, 134, 149, 150, 155, 156, 158, 160, 199, 206, 210, 214, 218, 222, 228, 229, 230, 231, 253, 286, 293, 298, 304, 305, 308, 350
Plymouth Church, Brooklyn 194